QAA
Chief Executive's Office

RESHAPING THE UNIVERSITY

QAA
Chief Executive's Office

Reshaping the University

The Rise of the Regulated Market in Higher Education

DAVID PALFREYMAN

and

TED TAPPER

OXFORD
UNIVERSITY PRESS

OXFORD
UNIVERSITY PRESS

Great Clarendon Street, Oxford, OX2 6DP,
United Kingdom

Oxford University Press is a department of the University of Oxford.
It furthers the University's objective of excellence in research, scholarship,
and education by publishing worldwide. Oxford is a registered trade mark of
Oxford University Press in the UK and in certain other countries

First Edition published in 2014

Impression: 1

Published in the United States of America by Oxford University Press
198 Madison Avenue, New York, NY 10016, United States of America

British Library Cataloguing in Publication Data

Data available

Library of Congress Control Number: 2013957857

ISBN 978–0–19–965982–1

Printed and bound by
CPI Group (UK) Ltd, Croydon, CR0 4YY

Preface

The central thesis of this book is that there is no longer a UK system of higher education. A system that has had so much written about it since the publication of the Robbins Report in 1963 no longer exists. It cannot be viewed as a UK system since devolution has led to different political values shaping developments in the nations of the British Isles, with higher education in Scotland and Wales subject to more state steering than was true of the pre-devolutionary years. The label higher education is increasingly inappropriate since the mix of institutions offers very varied programmes and caters for students with widely contrasting motivations for furthering their education. A better term would be tertiary education (TE), combining all post-18 education whether delivered in further education colleges or within universities—local, regional, national, or global in reach, and that are increasingly engaged in collaborative ventures. Most of these universities still remain technically not-for-profit institutions while behaving competitively and entrepreneurially, but in England now some are profit-making, shareholder-owned, commercial enterprises.

The purpose of the book is to explore, with particular reference to England, the development of this emerging TE model. How is the emergence of these dominant characteristics to be explained? At the heart of our explanation is the steady move from public funding and institutional autonomy to the flourishing of a state-regulated market. Increasingly, the role of the state is to regulate the higher education market as it does for the delivery of so many other social goods and, indeed, for services that were once controlled by public corporate bodies (for example, post, telecommunications, and the energy/water utilities): the provider-state becomes the regulatory state. Hence the subtitle of the book, 'The Rise of the Regulated Market', which raises the interesting issue of exactly what the role of the state will be by, say, 2020, which we turn to in our final chapter.

In the course of pursuing our task we will make extensive reference to developments in US higher education. This is because the US provides a relatively advanced model of the marketization of higher education, one that acts as a possible road map for the English model to follow. However, although we are sympathetic to government attempts to diversify the English system of higher education (including offering encouragement to private, even for-profit, providers) we remain convinced that the best way forward is to promote change through the operation of a state-regulated market. Perhaps in this respect, US higher education has much to learn from the English strategy for promoting change.

Politics is at the heart of our explanatory framework of how English higher education has developed in recent years, both the impact of political ideas and the machinations of the political process. However, politics does not operate in a vacuum; it has to take cognizance of both economic and social trends. What is the value in the public funding of higher education in comparison with, for example, healthcare or welfare benefits? What should be the impact of a sustained economic crisis upon the public support of different social goods? Can a mass system of higher education expect to be funded in the same way as an elite system? How significant an impact upon policy decisions is the portrayal of higher education as a private, as opposed to a public, good?

Pressure to change higher education also has to take into account the fact that the existing model has a prevailing structure which is not necessarily very malleable, and will incorporate values and practices that are deeply rooted, historically and culturally, within the academic community itself and may not be easily influenced by external pressure. The road, therefore, to the state-regulated market has been far from smooth and diverts along different ways dependent upon the particular policy focus. The year 1965, for instance, saw the start of a binary model in which the universities were complemented by a public sector of higher education consisting mainly of the polytechnics. Henceforth, it was increasingly meaningful to think in terms of the British system of higher education of which the universities were but a component part. However, the 1992 Further and Higher Education Act, by amalgamating responsibility for both the funding and policy steering of the universities and the public sector, unified the binary model while at the same time creating funding councils with national identities.

A unitary model of higher education was rapidly established in which the former public sector institutions were entitled to award their own degrees and acquire the university title. Thereafter, the same rights were granted to other higher education colleges and institutes, which offered mainly advanced technical and professional programmes. As if there were no end to the expansion of higher education, many colleges of further education started to offer higher education programmes and to award foundation degrees (two years in length). Moreover, the growth of the public sector provision of higher education has been augmented by a parallel, albeit so far more limited, expansion of privately funded programmes in newly created institutions, both charitable and for-profit. Therefore, the right to award degrees and bear the university title has expanded considerably in the past two decades and currently shows no signs of abating as the criteria for gaining degree-awarding powers and being allowed to use the title are continually adjusted.

Critically, the 1992 Further and Higher Education Act reaffirmed the central thrust of the 1988 Education Reform Act that had abolished the University Grants Committee, replacing that august body with the funding councils which in turn inaugurated the new public management (NPM) model of governance. Policy control of higher education development was placed under the auspices of the government while policy implementation was ceded to the quasi-state with the funding councils at its core. The 1988 Education Reform Act explicitly brought into the open the formal policy relationship of the state and the funding council, with ultimate control resting in the hands of the incumbent government. Developments initiated by the 1992 Act brought to the fore the issue of institutional diversity within higher education. Are there no limits to the idea of the university? Is it possible to expand that concept to incorporate for-profit institutions that may offer at best a limited number of degree programmes, transmit knowledge mainly through distance learning, lack research missions (and indeed also libraries)?

The intention of this book is, therefore, to place the emergence of the state-regulated market within the context of these transitions. Why was it felt necessary to create a binary model and then to transform it—at least formally—into a unitary model? The contention is that, except in a limited sense, a unitary model has failed to develop; and indeed it is problematic whether serious attention has ever been paid to what such a model would entail. Today the unitary model is not so much a system of higher education but rather composed of fluctuating sectors that, while sharing certain characteristics, are increasingly differentiated from one another in terms of their purposes, how they function, and also indeed their brand values in terms of attracting students or signalling the employability of their graduates.

Although the development of higher education is driven by the policy directions established by successive governments, this is not simply politically imposed but emerges through a process that involves the interaction of an increasing range of interests. It is not so much an open and pluralist struggle amongst organized groups but rather that the political parties and governments suck in those who share their values in order to explore how policy goals can be instigated. Moreover, policy implementation (as opposed to policy formation) is influenced to an increasing degree by the operation of a state-regulated market whose *modus operandi* is the responsibility of quasi-state organizations of which the funding councils are the most significant. As with policy formation, the policy implementation strategies draw in the organized interests, although this is not to deny that there is also government pressure to ensure that politically acceptable decisions are made.

The idea of institutional autonomy remains firm, however, and higher education institutions can respond to the external pressures through their own initiatives: that said, their ability to act is constrained by the dictates of the regulated market. For example, and to give but two examples, there are restrictions (albeit soon to be lifted) on the recruitment of home-based and EU undergraduates (both in terms of how many students can be recruited and their broad disciplinary distribution), and core public funding to support research is subject to a regulatory process organized by the funding councils.

While it is possible for a university to restructure the academic programmes that it offers and also to concentrate research in a limited number of fields (and perhaps even find private income to finance it), it is impossible to ignore entirely the hand of the state when planning institutional change. Nonetheless, it is important to examine how institutions respond to the constraints of the state-regulated market and how they can exercise their autonomy to plan their futures. There may be state and quasi-state steering, but both remain negotiated, rather than imposed, forms of control.

General texts on the development of British higher education are sometimes justified by the perception of their authors of a contemporary crisis, even if they shy away from using the term. For Bruce Truscot (*Redbrick University*, 1943; *Redbrick and These Vital Days*, 1945) and Walter Moberly (*Crisis in the University*, 1949), the crisis was about threats to the university system's established underlying values, while for Peter Scott (*Crisis of the University*, 1984), the crisis was his claim that the university was failing to respond to the challenge of transforming Britain into a modern society. And very recently, for some the crisis stems specifically from the marketization of higher education, which the incumbent Coalition Government is seen as intent on intensifying (Roger Brown and Helen Carasso, *Everything for Sale: The Marketisation of UK Higher Education*, 2013; Stefan Collini, *What are Universities For?*, 2012; but for a recent, reflective overview of marketization see, Claire Callender and Peter Scott (eds.), *Browne and Beyond: Modernizing English Higher Education*, 2013). For the proponents of this assertion, the crisis is a consequence of the assumed negative impact marketization will have upon the English model of higher education—its values, structure, and practices, or rather upon their perception of what the ideal model of English higher education should be.

The authors of this book are more persuaded by the argument that the British model of higher education is—almost as always in recent decades—in a state of steady change rather than experiencing a crisis. The funding council model of governance, taking different national paths, has now been in operation for some two decades; and the long march (still ongoing) towards permitting institutions to set their own fees and determine for themselves how many students they will admit has been unfolding for almost as long. It is undoubtedly true that a different model of higher education is emerging: one that in broad policy terms is more explicitly steered by the state, with greater internal differentiation as institutions respond to the established policy parameters in the light of their own market positions, and also one that is more reliant on private funding even though the upfront payment of student fees may be underwritten by public support. It is always possible to contrast a crisis-ridden present with an idyllic past or an imagined promised land, but it is more fruitful to plot what is happening and explain why.

In 1995 the revised and expanded edition of A. H. Halsey's *Decline of Donnish Dominion: The British Academic Professions in the Twentieth Century* was published, to be followed in 2000 by Maurice Kogan and Stephen Hanney's *Reforming Higher Education*, and then in 2009 by Malcolm Tight's *The Development of Higher Education in the United Kingdom since 1945*, and now the recent appearance of Michael Shattock's *Making Policy in British Higher Education 1945–2011* (2012). Our volume, in the sense that it also attempts to plot the process of change in British higher education, has affinities with all four books. With a stronger political approach than the essentially sociological Halsey volume, it outlines what has replaced donnish dominion in the shaping of British higher education—that is the emergence of the state-regulated market; so distinguishing it from the Kogan and Hanney, Tight, and Shattock volumes that purposely avoid taking a clear theoretical position. Our focus is upon understanding the process of change and how it functions at both the system and institutional levels. In other words, the book analyses not only the development of British higher education, but also presents an interpretation of why and how change has occurred. It also carries a message: the state-regulated market as the system steering mechanism is with us for the foreseeable future, and there is no turning back to an essentially publicly funded and almost exclusively public model whose development is internally driven.

David Palfreyman
and Ted Tapper

Oxford
January 2014

Contents

**Part IV. Towards the Free Market:
English Higher Education 2020**

Abbreviations

ABRC	Advisory Board for the Research Councils
AHELO	Assessment of Higher Education Learning Outcomes
AHRC	Arts and Humanities Research Council
APR	Age Participation Rate
ARWU	Academic Rankings of World Universities
ATTI	Association of Teachers in Technical Institutions
BBSRC	Biotechnology and Biological Sciences Research Council
BIS	Department for Business, Innovation, and Skills
CC	Competitive Commission
CDBU	Campaign for the Defence of British Universities
CDP	Committee of the Directors of Polytechnics
CEO	Chief Executive Officer
CMA	Competition and Markets Authority
CNAA	Council for National Academic Awards
CPI	Consumer Price Index
CSR	Comprehensive Spending Review
CU	Coventry University
CUA	Conference of University Administrators
CUC	Coventry University College
CUC	Committee of University Chairmen (Chairs)
CVCP	Committee of Vice-Chancellors and Principals
DAP	Degree-awarding powers
DES	Department of Education and Science
EGM	Emerging Global Model
EHEA	European Higher Education Area
EPSRC	Engineering and Physical Sciences Research Council
ERA, 1988	Education Reform Act, 1988
ESRC	Economics and Social Research Council
FE	Further education
FEC	Further Education Colleges
FHEA, 1992	Further and Higher Education Act, 1992
GCSE	General Certificate of Secondary Education
GPA	Grade Point Averages
GPO	General Post Office
HE	Higher education
HEC	Higher Education Commission
HEFCE	Higher Education Funding Council for England
HEIs	Higher education institutions

HEPI	Higher Education Policy Institute
HESA	Higher Education Statistics Agency
HMRC	Her Majesty's Revenue and Customs
HNC	Higher National Certificate
HND	Higher National Diploma
IB	International Baccalaureate
ICL	Imperial College London
IMF	International Monetary Fund
IPPR	Institute for Public Policy Research
JCR	Junior Common Room
KCL	King's College London
KIS	Key Information Set
LMU	London Metropolitan University
MBA	Masters of Business Administration
ML	Modern Languages
MOOCs	Massive Open Online Courses
MRC	Medical Research Council
NAB	National Advisory Body for Public Sector Higher Education
NCIHE	National Committee of Inquiry into Higher Education
NERC	Natural Environment Research Council
NHS	National Health Service
NSP	National Scholarship Programme
NSS	National Student Survey
NUS	National Union of Students
OECD	Organisation for Economic Co-operation and Development
OFFA	Office for Fair Access
OFGEM	Office of Gas and Electricity Market
OFSTED	Office for Standards in Education
OFT	Office for Fair Trading
OFTEL	Office of Telecommunications
OFWAT	Water Service Regulation Authority
ORR	Office of Rail Regulation
PCFC	Polytechnics and Colleges Funding Council
PGT	Postgraduate taught courses
PISA	Programme for International Student Assessment
PNL	Polytechnic of North London
QAA	Quality Assurance Agency
RAEs	Research Assessment Exercises
RCUK	Research Councils United Kingdom
REF	Research Excellence Framework
RI	Royal Institution
RSA	Royal Society for the encouragement of Arts, Manufactures, and Commerce

SEFC	Science and Engineering Facilities Council
SLC	Student Loans Company
SRU	Super Research Universities
SSR	Staff to student ratio
STEM	Science, Technology, Engineering, and Mathematics
TE	Tertiary education
UCU	Universities and Colleges Union
UCL	University College London
UFC	Universities Funding Council
UGC	University Grants Committee
UUK	Universities UK
UWE	University of West of England
VC	Vice-Chancellor

Part I

British Higher Education as a System: Shifting Perceptions, Changing Realities

1

The Governance of British Higher Education: State, Market, and Institutional Decision-Making

Abstract: This chapter explores first the emergence of the contemporary model of governance in English higher education. The key transition was the shift instigated by the 1988 Education Reform Act from the University Grants Committee to the funding council model of governance. Post-1988, the overall development of the higher education system would be controlled politically with the quasi-state apparatus assuming responsibility mainly for policy implementation and regulation. The chapter then examines the impact of the Coalition Government's 2011 White Paper *Higher Education: Students at the Heart of the System*. Will the state-regulated market that has come to control the development of English higher education move closer to a free-market model? Although there has been the virtual withdrawal of public funding for the payment of undergraduate fees, steps to augment the information that prospective students receive, and the expansion of a privately funded sector higher education, the argument is that it is here to stay—a claim which the book will repeatedly embellish.

SETTING THE AGENDA

This chapter presents our interpretation of how the delivery of higher education in Britain is currently governed. The focus is mainly upon England because it is the largest component within the British model, and because the arrival of devolution in 1992 has undermined much of the administrative and political coherence of the British system of higher education. Although the intention is to concentrate upon the contemporary model of governance with some prognosis on unfolding developments, the chapter commences by looking back to the latter years of the University Grants Committee (UGC) when it was a key player, perhaps *the* player, in the governance of the universities, and certainly the body most responsible for steering their development. Secondly, it will trace the emerging role of the state in the governance of higher education and how the 1988 Education Reform Act firmly placed control of higher education policy for both the universities and the so-called public sector of higher education in the hands of central government. Henceforth, the development of higher education would be shaped by a mode of governance that conformed to the so-called new public management (NPM) model in which central government controlled policy making while the funding councils were responsible for a combination of the distribution of public funding, the formulation of proposals to implement government policy, and the oversight of how effectively the system was functioning.

Periodically, governments present their plans for the future development of higher education, which take the form of issuing a White Paper and inviting consultation. In June 2011, the current Coalition Government published its own White Paper, *Higher Education: Students at the Heart of the System*. The third section of this chapter examines whether this document is but a stepping stone to the emergence of a new model of governance for English higher education. The 1988 Education Reform Act had ushered in the funding councils (the Universities Funding Council—UFC, and the Polytechnics and Colleges Funding Council—PCFC) to replace respectively the UGC and, for the public sector of higher education, the National Advisory Body (NAB). Henceforth, it would be clear as to where responsibility for the formal overall development of the system would reside. What the 2011 White Paper suggests is a partial relinquishing of state control; one which would allow individual higher education institutions to respond more directly to their market positions and control more effectively their own patterns of development. Also, for institutions deemed to be in good academic standing, there is the promise of a light touch regulatory regime. Moreover, these changes to the publicly funded sectors could occur within the context of a system that is more diverse in character, incorporating universities with a limited range of degree programmes run by for-profit companies.

The placing of the analysis of the contemporary governance of English higher education in an historical framework is partly a result of its intrinsic interest—to understand why the polity felt obliged to change the relationship between the universities, state, and society; how those changes occurred; the form they took; and what their consequences were. Equally important is the need to show how radical the change in the governance of English higher education has been, and, although there are ingrained values, the structures and procedures of governance have evolved considerably over time. Thus, the chapter presents a picture of change, rather than continuity, in the governance of English higher education.

In addition to the mechanisms of the formal structure of governance, the policy-making process in higher education is also entrapped in a political context that shapes outcomes. Governance is about how the process of decision-making works politically. Therefore, the fourth part of the chapter offers an overview of the changing politics of decision-making, as the model of governance has moved from the paramount role played by the UGC, through the state-regulated market operated by the funding council but underwritten by policy goals that are determined by government priorities, and onto the current intrusion of the idea that institutional and system development should be shaped by responses to the input of informed customers in the form of both students and the government. To put it succinctly, the move has been from the politics of internal self-regulation and development to a world character-ized by pluralist conflict orchestrated within the framework of government policy preferences moulded by its dominant values. A brief conclusion draws the arguments together.

THE UGC IN ACTION: STEERING THE SYSTEM?

In his history of the Committee, Moodie (1983) saw the UGC as oscillating between the roles of 'buffer, coupling, and broker' as it negotiated the relation-ship between the universities and the state. However, it was not until July 1946 that its terms of reference were modified to give it a planning role:

> ...to assist, in consultation with the universities and other bodies concerned, the preparation and execution of such plans for the development of the universities as may from time to time be required in order that they are fully adequate to national needs.

> (As quoted in Owen, 1980: 263)

Therefore, until 1946 the UGC brokered a relationship between the universi-ties and the state that was essentially dependent upon its negotiation of the financial obligation of the Treasury to underwrite an increasing amount of university expenditure. Prior to 1946, the pattern of university development had been driven from below, that is by the universities themselves and not by the UGC, which adhered painstakingly to the principle of university autonomy.

After 1946, the coupling function could take on a political dimension with the possibility that the UGC could either broker a policy strategy that was acceptable to both government and the universities or act as a buffer as it attempted to protect the universities from political intrusion. However, it would be a perverse interpretation of the post-1945 history of the UGC to see it as actively bent on preparing and executing plans for the development of the universities along lines that it felt were consistent with national needs, which begs the question of why—even after consultation 'with other bodies concerned'—it should be the arbiter of what those national needs were that the universities should fulfil.

However, it would be parsimonious with the evidence to suggest that post-1945 the UGC failed completely in its remit to formulate plans for the development of higher education in Britain. There are a number of initiatives that are worthy of consideration, of which four will be briefly analysed: the founding of the new universities of the 1960s, the attempts to rationalize the disciplinary profile of the overall system, the move to the selective allocation of core research funding through the research assessment exercises (RAEs), and the decision to take on the responsibility for implementing through a process of selective cuts the government's decision to reduce its overall funding of higher education in the early 1980s. The issue in each case is how effective was the UGC at controlling the development of British higher education?

In the initial post-war years, the UGC felt that the existing universities could meet not only 'the demands of the returning ex-serviceman' but also fulfil 'the recommendations of the report of the Committee on Scientific Manpower' (UGC, 1962: 91), but by the mid-1950s the stance had changed and 'the possibility that new institutions might be needed began to emerge when the situation that was likely to occur in the later sixties and seventies was being considered' (UGC, 1962: 92). As commentators note, the main pressure for the founding of the new universities was an increase in the size of the most relevant age cohort coupled with an expansion in the numbers of those acquiring the requisite qualifications for university entry (Shattock, 1994: 75–78). The pressure was reinforced by the apparent unwillingness of the existing universities to increase their undergraduate numbers (Briggs, 1991: 313).

At a later date, John Carswell (the UGC's Secretary from 1974–77) was to comment that this expansion was, 'a slow and expensive form of provision' (Carswell, 1985: 61). However, for the UGC it was not simply about how the system could cope with increased demand but also how it could encourage innovation: '…there is need for constant experimentation in the organization of university teaching and the design of university curricula. New institutions, starting without traditions with which the innovator must come to terms, might well be more favourably situated for such experimentation than established universities' (UGC, 1962: 93). Indeed, it is precisely because of innovations in their organization of knowledge that the seven 1960s English foundations (East Anglia, Essex, Kent, Lancaster, Sussex, Warwick, and York) acquired the label of 'new universities'.

Given, therefore, that the process of founding the new universities was under the guidance of the UGC, it is entirely unsurprising that—albeit in somewhat differing forms—they instigated new maps of learning. In view of the fact that this expansion incorporated seven universities (to which can be added Stirling University and the New University of Ulster) this can be seen as a reasonably significant development in the overall character of the system of higher education. However, there was no guarantee that it would be more than a change that affected the margins of the current structure rather than bringing about a major reconstitution of its pedagogical character and, as Perkin (1969) has argued, in other respects (the social backgrounds of their undergraduate students, and their governance and administrative structures), the new universities were not especially innovative. This was the effective management of an important initiative rather than an attempt to reshape the overall direction of English higher education. While other universities might have learnt from the new models, this could not be interpreted as planned system development.

Thanks to its subject sub-committees, which had been an integral part of the UGC since 1921, the Committee had the means to shape directly the development of the academic disciplines. However, in an unflattering review of their performance, Shattock claims that at least until the 1960s '...none of the many subject committees were anything but standing committees meeting now and again when required' (Shattock, 1994: 60). As the economic crisis of the 1970s unfolded, to be followed by the cuts in the Treasury's support for higher education, the UGC turned to its subject sub-committees to assist it in the attempt to rationalize the provision of certain disciplines, or—as the critics would argue—to enable it to meet the impending cuts in public funding. Its *Report on Russian and Russian Studies in British Universities* (UGC, 1979) not only made the general case for larger disciplinary units, but also appeared to be saying that the Committee has to accept responsibility for protecting disciplinary standards and development even at the expense of the welfare of institutions and their staff (Shattock, 1994: 61). However, while there may have been widespread agreement about the need to avoid the proliferation of too many small academic departments, inevitably there was enormous controversy about where the axe should fall. Moreover, it was possible that a more general rationalization of academic provision could undermine the very stability of some universities, and certainly run counter to the ideas of institutional autonomy and system diversity.

The limitations, therefore, on employing the subject sub-committees as an instrument of planning were considerable and there was no serious attempt to use them in this manner outside the context of financial crisis. It seemed as if the primary aim was not so much the protection of disciplinary standards and development, but rather how best to meet government-imposed financial constraints. Secondly, there was a clear clash of principles when the UGC's long acceptance of institutional autonomy ran up against its planning role, and it was the more deeply ingrained former that appeared generally to carry the day. Similarly, while in the face of government-imposed financial constraints the UGC may have advocated its responsibility for securing disciplinary standards, there was also a powerful ingrained instinct to protect the institutions on its grants list; after all, several of the weaker universities on its list would not have been granted the university title without strong UGC support. Finally, there was the enormity of the trauma generated by the attempt to impose rationalization as the affected departments and their universities fought back. Could the UGC have complete faith in the judgements of its subject committees?

The UGC's role in the founding of the new universities of the 1960s was an undoubted success, albeit one with but a limited impact upon the wider model of British higher education, whereas its attempts to reshape the structure of the academic map of the universities through its subject committees undoubtedly could have had a broad impact upon the system, but the outcomes can only be described as disappointing. In contrast to both of these initiatives is the Committee's instigation of the research assessment exercises, which has had a more profound influence upon British higher education. The first RAE took place in 1986 and, although Kogan and Hanney (2000: 97–98) maintain that the major credit should be given to the UGC's then Chairman, Peter Swinnerton-Dyer, the instigation was a long time in the making with considerable pressure coming from the Advisory Board for the Research Councils (ABRC). The argument was that funding needed to be concentrated upon centres of excellence if the quality of research output was to be maintained. In the context of declining government support for core research funding it was critical, therefore, to ensure that resources went disproportionately to those who had the best track records in producing high-quality research. The solution was to establish the RAEs, which have taken place periodically since 1986. The next exercise, to be known as the Research Excellence Framework (REF), is scheduled to occur in 2014.

In spite of considerable hostile complaining within the academic community, the RAEs constitute a resource distribution model that has had considerable political support. They meet the broad demand for the selective and competitive distribution of resource funding. Although the assessment process is very much under the control of the funding councils, they are not immune to government intrusion as seen in the early demand that the Higher Education Funding Council for England (HEFCE) should impose a more selective distribution of funding for the English universities, and the current need for those panels that will undertake the 2014 REF to evaluate the real world impact of research. Moreover, within the academic community there have always been those who believe, particularly in the sciences, that the best way to ensure quality research is to concentrate funding; that excellence is more likely to emerge from the creation of a critical mass rather than from the dispersal of expertise. However, academic sentiment at large is undoubtedly placated by the fact that the bulk of the evaluative process remains subject to a considerable degree of peer review. Essentially, quality is evaluated by the academic judgement of individual inputs rather than measured solely on the basis of metrics.

The possible broader implications of research assessment: research as in opposition to (rather than in harmony with) teaching, the formation of national and international university league tables based mainly on research outputs, and the increasing importance of research for generating an institutional financial input as well as prestige—are very much dependent upon the values that you want a system of higher education to represent. Regardless, it is impossible to deny the success of the RAEs as an effective instrument of governance: enduring over time, maintaining a broad base of support, and being very influential in shaping institutional and individual behaviour. It was a harbinger of a model of governance that was beginning to emerge in Britain: the channelling of higher education development through the operation of a state-regulated market that has developed more fully since the demise of the UGC.

Probably the most controversial and painful decision in the history of the UGC was its decision to take responsibility for distributing the 17% cut to its annual grant spread over a three-year period, commencing in 1981. The selectivity of cuts was very sharp, ranging from 44% to 6% for individual universities, and the criteria that determined them was never published (Salter and Tapper, 1994: 127). Evidently, the Committee had decided to become the conduit of government policy and it would have been inappropriate for it to have attempted to assume the role of a buffer. The obvious line of defence for the UGC's stance is that the government would have imposed the cuts regardless of how the Committee decided to act. It saw its intervention as securing the best long-term interests of the university system and believed that if the cuts had been imposed by, say, the Department of Education and Science, the consequences would have been disastrous. However, its decisions on how the funding cuts were to be distributed were clearly driven by its own interpretation of what constituted desirable development and it would have been enlightening to have had those underlying principles in the public domain.

Unsurprisingly, particularly in the most adversely affected universities, academic reaction was exceedingly negative. It was perceived as *The Attack on Higher Education* (Kogan and Kogan, 1983) and some argued that the members of the Committee should have resigned rather than acted on the government's behalf. However, it has been claimed, in spite of growing hostility in the academic community, that conversely in the 1980s the UGC increased its authority vis-à-vis the universities and regained its respect in government circles (Shattock and Berdahl, 1984; Shattock, 1994: 20–26). Perhaps the question should be asked that if this restoration of fortunes did in fact occur, how is the demise of the UGC and its replacement by the funding council model of governance to be explained?

The answer to the question is to be found in a combination of the far-reaching changes that had overcome British higher education since the UGC's inception in 1919 combined with the radically different political context in which it was located by the 1980s. By the 1980s there was a system of higher education rather than simply the universities and much of its development had little to do with the UGC, and certainly was far from under its control. It made increasing sense to think of the universities as but one sector in a system of higher education which, if it were to be planned, could be done most coherently as a collective entity. Although the UGC's formal remit may have been changed in 1946 to give it a planning role, it was almost impossible for it to achieve this in any effective sense in view of its core values and operating procedures. The universities were seen as autonomous decision-making bodies that in particular determined their own academic development, which would inevitably restrict the role of the Committee's subject committees, and especially one that embraced either the closure or amalgamation of departments. Furthermore, the Treasury-sanctioned recurrent grant was allocated as a block grant, which the universities used to meet their needs as they defined them. While there was an expectation that the UGC would steer the universities towards fulfilling national needs, there was no detailed understanding of what this meant in precise terms, how it was to be accomplished, or the time period in which change could be expected to occur. In the context of a small, and in comparative terms relatively inexpensive policy commitment, perhaps this situation could be tolerated but it became increasingly politically intolerable as in the late 1980s the system became larger (mass rather than elite), more diversified in character, and more of a burden on the public purse. The least that could be expected to emerge, even if the UGC were to survive, was a funding body placed on a statutory basis (the UGC had materialized in 1919 out of a Treasury Minute) with a formal obligation—buttressed by its membership, structures, and procedures—to plan the development of higher education in Britain.

THE FUNDING COUNCIL MODEL OF GOVERNANCE: FROM THE 1988 EDUCATION REFORM ACT TO THE 2010 BROWNE REVIEW

The dominant political sentiment, however, was not to reformulate the UGC but rather to create a new model of governance for higher education. The 1988 Education Reform Act (ERA) not only brought the era of the UGC to a close with the creation of the Universities Funding Council (UFC) but also removed the public sector of higher education out of the hands of local authority control by replacing the National Advisory Body for Public Sector Higher Education (NAB) with the Polytechnics and Colleges Funding Council (PCFC); the membership of both the UFC and the PCFC to be appointed by central government. The 1992 Further and Higher Education Act (FHEA) took the process of change one step further by amalgamating the two funding councils while, under the impulse of devolution, creating separate funding councils with national remits, which in the case of Scotland and Wales were placed under local political control.

There was little political will to create a renovated UGC which would have the formal authority and the means to govern the development of higher education in Britain. Although it may have been part of the equation, it was not so much a question of disenchantment with the UGC, but rather a manifestation of the fact that the government itself believed that this should be its responsibility and not left to unelected bodies that had been dominated either by the academic community or the local authorities. Over a period of time, governments of different political persuasions had come to the conclusion that higher education should be more closely concerned with meeting national economic and social needs as they themselves defined them (Salter and Tapper, 1994: 117–130). While post-1945 the UGC's remit incorporated a planning role, which required it to pursue the development of the universities in a manner that was consistent with their promotion of national needs, the Committee's overall performance would scarcely support the case that it encompassed a clear utilitarian view of what those national needs were.

What was required was a model of governance that placed responsibility for the formulation of higher education policy in the hands of the government in order that it could steer the development of the system in a politically acceptable direction. But at the same time, the policy implementation process needed to be politically negotiated through the interaction of the government, funding councils, and the higher education institutions. This would at least mitigate the appearance of central state control and, depending on the policy enforcement mechanisms, could give some credence to the idea that institutional autonomy retained some of its viability. Following Lord Croham's *Review of the University Grants Committee* (Department of Education and Science, 1987) the solution was to be found in the funding council model of governance which was realized in very similar terms in both the 1988 and 1992 Acts.

The 1988 ERA stated that:

> The Council [UFC] shall consist of fifteen members appointed by the Secretary of State, of whom one should be appointed as chairman. (ERA 1988, clause 131.2, as quoted in Tapper, 2007: 33) Between six and nine of these members were to be drawn from the higher education community

[and]

> …in appointing the remaining members the Secretary of State shall have regard to the desirability of including persons who appear to him to have experience of, and to have shown capacity in industrial, commercial, or financial matters, or the practice of any profession.
>
> (ERA 1988, clause 131.3, as quoted in Tapper, 2007: 33)

Although over time the UGC itself had come to incorporate lay members, the diverse composition of the funding councils and the appointment of their members by the Secretary of State were placed on a statutory basis.

More significantly, the legislation laid out the responsibilities of the various parties and their relationship to each other. Under the terms of the 1988 legislation, the central responsibility of the funding councils was to administer 'funds made available to the Council by the Secretary of State for the purpose of providing support for activities eligible for funding under this section', and this funding could be made 'subject to such terms and conditions as they [that is the funding councils] think fit' (ERA 1988, clauses 131.4 and 131.6 respectively, as quoted in Tapper, 2007: 33–34). With respect to information flows, the funding councils would act as the conduit between the institutions in receipt of grants and the government. The institutions were required to make available the information that the funding councils needed to perform their functions, while the funding councils could provide the Secretary of State 'with such information and advice relating to activities eligible for funding under this section as they see fit' (ERA 1988, clause 131.8b, as quoted in Tapper, 2007: 34).

The 1988 legislation spelt out the policy supremacy of the Secretary of State in terms that are both clear and straightforward. The Secretary of State could make grants 'to each of the Funding Councils of such amounts *and subject to such conditions as he may determine*', and 'confer or impose on either of the Funding Councils such supplementary functions he thinks fit', and 'in exercising their functions...each of the Funding Councils *shall comply with any directions given to them by the Secretary of State*' (ERA, 1988, clauses 134.6, 134.1, and 134.8 respectively, as quoted in Tapper, 2007: 35, emphasis added).

However, the difference between the operation of the funding councils and the UGC, at least in its latter years, should not be over-exaggerated. From 1964 onwards, when overall departmental responsibility for the UGC was removed from the Treasury and placed under the auspices of the Department of Education and Science (DES), it had grown accustomed to receiving periodic government reports, as well as requests for information, on the universities. Moreover, by the 1980s the Committee was in regular receipt of statements outlining ministerial priorities (Booth, 1987: 87).

The critical difference is that post-1988 the power relations had been formally spelt out and the dominance of the state is there for all to see. However, if the funding councils were to retain any credibility then it was critical that this dominance should not be exercised too explicitly on too many occasions. There needed to be a measure of trust between the government and the funding councils, that the latter would find the means to implement government policy effectively, and, moreover, that government would at least take into consideration any advice that the funding councils transmitted as it formulated its policy options.

Although the UGC was always formally committed to the idea of institutional autonomy in the sense that the universities determined their own development, as we have noted it became more of a planning body in the

1980s as financial stringency descended and it started to assume responsibility for rectifying some of what it clearly saw as unwise developments that had arisen out of autonomous institutional decision making. What role would the higher education institutions have to play within the framework of the funding council model of governance? If the Thatcher Government had wanted a centrally planned system of higher education then it would have simply abolished the UGC and placed responsibility for the management and development of higher education within one of the central departments of state, or established one that would perform those functions. But, while there was a desire for centralized policy control, there was no appetite for centralized planning. It would have been ideological anathema for a Thatcher Government to go down that route.

What the funding council model of governance has required of the higher education institutions is decisions on how they intend to respond to the demands imposed by a state-regulated market. Until very recently—and as we write the constraints are being eased—the recruitment of undergraduates, excepting those with overseas (that is non-EU) residence, has been strictly regulated. There are agreements for individual institutions on both the total number of students who can be admitted and their disciplinary allegiances. To break the agreement incurs financial sanctions. By way of direct contrast, participation in the RAEs is at the discretion of institutions and they can decide what units of assessment as well as what faculty they want to be included in the evaluative process.

One of the policy objectives of successive governments has been to broaden the social base of undergraduate recruitment, and consequently there has been a long-standing 'widening participation' agenda. There is an expectation that all universities will broaden the social base of their student recruitment over time, with published targets and the monitoring of progress through the publication of performance indicators (on which see, HEFCE's *Guide to Performance Indicators,* 2003). The message was reinforced by the creation of the Office for Fair Access (OFFA), which was established by the 2004 Higher Education Act. It has been the task of OFFA to reach 'access agreements' with the universities that intended to charge variable fees after the passage of the legislation. The universities have to devote some of their fee income to encouraging access by running events such as summer schools for would-be applicants and awarding grants to undergraduate students from poorer families. To date, all the universities have negotiated agreements with OFFA. Moreover, it is important to note that there is no legislative basis for requiring universities to meet targets on broadening the social range of their student intake, and certainly no means of punishing financially those that fail to do so. This is a regulatory mechanism that relies on political exhortation, bureaucratic pressures, and financial incentives (there was a teaching premium for recruiting applicants from poorer families) rather than enforceable target-setting. Even in the age of state-regulation it is still accepted that ultimately it is the higher education institutions that decide whom they admit.

Furthermore, it should not be thought that the higher education institutions have no option but to conform to the dictates of the state-regulated market. Historically, quality control in higher education was heavily dependent upon academic self-regulation—a combination of academic control (expressed most notably in the role of external examiners) and the judgements of professional associations. Following the 1988 ERA there was a steady emergence of quality control mechanisms that eventually led to the formation of the Quality Assurance Agency (QAA). Although the QAA grew out of a process of negotiation amongst the higher education interests and state agencies, there was never—especially within elite university circles—much sympathy for it. Indeed, from its very inception in 1997, many individual academics and some of the higher education institutions expressed their displeasure at its activities. The particular target was departmental inspections that evaluated six performance categories resulting in a possible overall maximum score of 24 points. The pressure applied by the universities—Brown (2004: 131) points particularly to the good connections of influential members of the Russell Group to the Prime Minister's Office—which resulted in the emergence of a 'light touch' regime in which the quality review of individual departments was essentially abandoned in favour of institutional audits.

The relationship between government, funding councils, and higher education institutions is not, therefore, immutable and also varies according to the policy issue under observation. The very tight control on student numbers was shaped by the financial support that the Treasury provides to meet teaching costs—for a long time in direct payment to the universities of student fees and now in the underwriting of income-contingent student loans. The Treasury has an understandable vested interest in controlling its expenditure and being fully aware of its commitments. The more indirect (lax, some would argue) promotion of the 'widening participation' agenda not only reflects the traditional concern for institutional autonomy but also is a recognition of the problems that are likely to emerge if targets are enforced. Undoubtedly such enforcement would have a negative impact upon the morale (not to mention the finances) of the targeted institutions and almost certainly generate a major political row. The modifications to the quality assurance regime have more to do with changing political priorities than any recognition of the undue bureaucratic burden it placed upon the universities. The Blair Government was moving towards the policy of variable student fees (secured in the 2004 Higher Education Act) and the promise to mitigate this bureaucratic burden was one possible way of securing some support from the academic community for this critical policy initiative. The White Paper, *The Future of Higher Education* (Department for Education and Skills, 2003), discusses both the plan to introduce variable fees and the need to lessen the bureaucratic constraints with which the universities had to comply.

Although it is clear that the 1988 Education Reform Act instigated the dominant control of central government over the higher education policy-making process, there is still some equivocation as to precisely where in government this power actually resides. The legislation refers to the responsibilities that could be assumed by the Secretary of State. Currently the higher education portfolio is located in the Department for Business, Innovation, and Skills and the Secretary of State is Vince Cable. However, the Department has a Minister of State for Universities and Science (David Willetts) who, significantly, is also responsible for the research councils as well as higher education, which means that the two major streams of public support for higher education are the responsibility of the same department.

In the context, however, of a squeeze on public expenditure there is always the possibility of Treasury intervention. In view of the fact that the liabilities of the Student Loans Company are underwritten by the Treasury, it is inevitable that its mandarins would take a close interest in what fees the universities are charging and the number of students they are admitting. But this is the kind of intervention that any government department is likely to experience from the Treasury, and while these are very important policy issues, there are numerous other developments in higher education in which the Treasury will not have the slightest interest. Indeed, that was one of the strongest arguments in favour of transferring government oversight of the UGC from the Treasury to the then Department of Education and Science (DES). Understandably, other than controlling expenditure and making sure that resources were used appropriately, the Treasury had no policy stance on the universities, whereas some looked to the DES to provide coordinated direction for the whole system of education, including the universities. Moreover, as the later section of this chapter 'Beyond the Funding Council Model of Governance? From the Browne Review to the 2011 White Paper' will demonstrate, the current Minister for Universities and Science has been exceedingly active in promoting new directions in higher education policy, and there is little doubt that is where responsibility for government-initiated developments in higher education now resides.

A more interesting question to ponder is why policy responsibility for higher education and the research councils should be located in a department which does not have 'university' in its title but does include 'business' and 'skills'. It is difficult not to draw the conclusion that at least in part this must reflect a value-laden premise—that central to the purpose of the universities is the enhancement of business and the promotion of skills. The notion of higher education as a vital economic resource now lays claim to the title of the very department in which policy responsibility for the universities and research councils is based.

The funding council model of governance has not only changed the relationship of the universities to the state but also has acted very significantly upon how universities are governed. Most observers (Shattock, 1994: 114; Kogan and Hanney, 2000: 185–187; Deem et al., 2007) argue that the new managerial ethos in higher education was greatly stimulated by the publication in 1985 of the Jarratt Report (Committee of Vice-Chancellors and Principals, *Report of the Steering Committee for Efficiency Studies in Universities*). Kogan and Hanney have written:

> But it was Jarratt (1985), the government-inspired report, which promoted the statement of objectives, the creation of new management structures, with chief executives in place of the *primus inter pares* roles of vice-chancellors, the introduction of management terminology, and performance indicators.
>
> (Kogan and Hanney, 2000: 186)

But undoubtedly the process of change has been speeded up by the introduction of the funding council model of governance. The state-regulated market requires prompt and effective responses from the higher education institutions on a whole range of broad concerns—student access, research performance, quality control, and even governance and management structures. Consequently, the administrative apparatuses have expanded and power has gravitated to councils and senior management teams and away from senates and front-line academics (although perhaps less so in Oxford and Cambridge, Tapper and Palfreyman, 2010 and 2011).

BEYOND THE FUNDING COUNCIL MODEL OF GOVERNANCE? FROM THE BROWNE REVIEW TO THE 2011 WHITE PAPER

It was inconceivable that the severe global economic crisis that broke in 2008 would not have profound repercussions for the funding of British higher education. Underwritten by the argument that there were private economic returns for those who had completed higher education degrees, variable fees to be paid for through income-contingent loans (Barr, 2001; Barr and Crawford, 2005) had already been introduced in England. In November 2009, *An Independent Review of Higher Education Funding and Finance* was set up by the then Labour Government under the auspices of Lord Browne for the professed purpose of *securing a sustainable future for higher education*, which everyone suspected would recommend a sharp increase in variable fees.

Browne's Review was published in October 2010, and the Coalition Government, which was now in power, swiftly secured parliamentary approval (December 2010) to permit higher education institutions to raise variable tuition fees by up to £9,000 per annum from the academic year commencing in 2012. And unsurprisingly (at least to all seemingly bar the Coalition Government), many universities announced that they would either be charging the maximum permitted fee or a figure close to it (the Browne Review had not specified a ceiling on fees). The latest stage in the saga is the publication in June 2011 of the White Paper, *Higher Education: Students at the Heart of the System* (Department for Business, Innovation, and Skills, 2011). Although consultation has taken place, as yet no draft legislation has appeared but the White Paper does propose changes for which no parliamentary sanction is required and contains suggestions, that if acted upon, would further modify the state-regulated market. Moreover, there are proposals that could result in the steering of higher education development more by institutional responses to market pressures than by state regulation. There is greater encouragement for the expansion of a private sector that would also incorporate for-profit institutions.

The strict control exercised over the institutional recruitment of undergraduate students has been relaxed, and is soon to be removed entirely. For the 2012–13 entry, universities have been allowed to admit as many students they felt they could adequately cater for who achieved A-level grades of at least AAB (or equivalent qualifications and grades). Moreover, 20,000 places were reserved to be distributed amongst institutions charging an annual fee of no more than £7,500. These were moves clearly designed to persuade some universities to moderate their proposed fee increases. Those institutions, not obviously the most prestigious but nonetheless intending to charge fees of £9,000 per annum could find themselves shunned by the highly qualified applicants if more prestigious universities were prepared to increase their undergraduate numbers. For those institutions lower down the hierarchy it made sense to keep their fees below £7,500 per annum in order to ensure an almost guaranteed student intake. However, the long-term operation of this refined regulated market in the distribution of student numbers depends on the impact of variable fees on the pattern of student recruitment as well as the Treasury's estimate of the future financial burden of student loans upon the public purse. Weak demand for places may well require some universities to lower their fees, while the Treasury may became more relaxed about the potential demands upon the public purse either because the economy improves and/or the repayment of student loans is proceeding smoothly. Thus, a scenario has been created that is currently only just being played out and there may yet be issues concerning the efficient operation of the new market in UK/EU undergraduates.

The Browne Review (October 2010: 4) claimed that 'many prospective students do not get adequate advice or information to help them choose a course of study'. This was followed up by the White Paper: 'Wider availability and better use of information for potential students is fundamental to the new system...Better informed students will take their custom to the places offering good value for money'. And the claimed result would be that, 'excellent teaching will be placed back at the heart of every student's experience' (Department for Business, Innovation, and Skills, 2011: Paragraph 2.24). The providers of higher education are now required to place on their websites a *Key Information Set* that serves the purpose of enabling students to make comparisons on courses, costs, and the employment records—including starting salaries—of their graduates. However, whether it will have the desired effect upon teaching quality remains to be seen.

Underlying these changes is the perception of higher education providers (rather than universities) as offering a service (teaching and learning) that leads to the acquisition of a valuable product (mainly degree programmes) in the context of a regulated market. It is important, therefore, that their prospective customers (those intending to become students) are highly informed about how the product is to be acquired, and are provided with measures of its potential value. Moreover, this is meant to be a competitive market and one of the ways in which the providers differentiate themselves is in terms of the prices they charge for the delivery of their products (teaching) and the acquisition of those products (learning). In this context the success of the higher education provider is dependent upon both the effective provision of a valued product and the ability to evolve in ways that demonstrate sensitivity to changing market conditions, which could mean either establishing a market niche or abandoning established programmes with declining appeal. Rather than being entitled *Higher Education: Students at the Heart of the System*, perhaps it would have been more appropriate for the White Paper to have carried the title *Providing Higher Education in a More Competitive Market-Place*?

However, the changes are not only about manoeuvres to drive down the financial burden on the Treasury as well as to require higher education institutions to make more information available to their prospective students, but they could impact directly upon—if the necessary legislation is forthcoming—the regulatory state apparatus. The White Paper was followed by the publication in August 2011 of a 'Technical Consultation' document, *A New Fit-for-Purpose Regulatory Framework for the Higher Education Sector* (Department for Business, Innovation, and Skills, 2011). The framework document suggests that there could be a risk-based approach to regulation with, under the auspices of HEFCE, only a light-touch accountability regime for 'high performing providers'. The outcome could be more infrequent institutional audits which are currently undertaken by the QAA, while presumably high performers could be identified by admissions and graduation data, supplemented by information gleaned from the National Student Surveys, and reinforced by the records of past institutional audits. It appears as if the intention is not to terminate the role of the regulatory state but to make its focus more discerning.

HEFCE, as the lead regulator, could also be made responsible for deciding whether degree-awarding powers and the university title should be granted to institutions. In part, this possible move is closely related to the Coalition Government's desire to diversify the provision of higher education, which is intended to stimulate by encouraging the entry of privately funded, including for-profit, universities. Moreover, there is no bar on non-teaching bodies entering the field. As reported in *Times Higher Education*, Pearson Education has '…launched Pearson College, which will from this autumn offer a BSc honours degree in business and enterprise, validated by Royal Holloway College, University of London' (Morgan, 16 August 2012: 12). Pearson College joins the market-place alongside other for-profit providers, such as notably, BPP University College, which acquired this title in 2010 but has had degree-awarding powers since 2007 (BPP, 1 November 2011), and more recently has acquired the university title.

Like Pearson Education, BPP offers a small number of professional pro-grammes (accountancy/finance, business/management, and law) and employs a distance-learning pedagogy with an emphasis on online learning. In this model of the university higher education is a commodity that can be packaged and sold as if were a commercial product. It can be argued that, although the entry of private providers will undoubtedly help to diversify the English model of higher education, the price to be paid is a radical reformulation of the very idea of the university to the point that its definition is essentially politically controlled by the government of the day. Is it appropriate to apply the university label to an institutional provider that offers a very limited range of degree programmes with for the most part a clear vocational focus, concentrates overwhelmingly upon teaching, with a pedagogy centred basically around distance learning, and has as a major driving force the need to make a profit? The answer may well be that the idea of the university has been in constant flux and over time has assumed many different forms; that it is more important to create a diverse higher education system rather than sustain a pristine idea of the university.

Although carrying the university title and having the right to award degrees may give private providers both status and a possibly enhanced appeal in the market-place, they do not come without obligations. The issue is what information needs to be provided before the university title and the right to award degrees can be granted and, moreover, to what regulatory requirements do the universities have to submit in order to sustain these rights? The problem is compounded by the fact that some of those who are choosing to study at private higher education bodies are applying for loans from the Student Loans Company to finance their studies. What is occurring is a blurring of the distinction between the privately and publicly funded segments. The private sector institutions require government support if they are going to be a higher education provider, especially if they aspire to acquire the university title and award their own degrees. At the same time, the public sector institutions across the board are increasingly dependent upon private funding and also, like competent privately funded institutions, they need to control tightly their proposed future developments in order to ensure long-term viability.

It is possible that the blurring of the two sectors could be intensified were the government to split the funding contract it makes with the universities into two separate contracts, one for teaching and the other for research (Baker, 22 December 2011: 6–7). Egan, HEFCE's deputy chief executive, is reported to have said at a recently held conference:

> The key issue is, can you take research funding and not teaching funding with all the obligations that go around that? I know people are raising that point. It is a very important policy choice and not one HEFCE would make.
>
> (as reported by Baker, 22 December 2011: 6)

The issue is whether the government would be prepared to lighten the regulatory framework for higher education providers whose students were not reliant upon the Student Loans Company to finance their studies. Undoubtedly, the current publicly funded universities would have to find alternative providers of financial support for their prospective students. Moreover, there is the point that much of the regulation acts as a form of quality control which goes with the right to be called a university and award degrees, and is not dependent solely upon public funding. In view of the emphasis in the White Paper upon the need to enhance the quality of teaching in higher education, it seems unlikely that the days of the regulatory state are numbered. The answer is likely to be a considerable easing of the burdens of regulation with less frequent evaluation of institutions with good track records (a so-called light-touch regime), coupled with greater reliance upon the pressure that better informed prospective students will supposedly exert upon improving teaching quality. Moreover, these are developments that are explicitly incorporated in the White Paper as opposed to being possible outcomes. But not until the legislation appears will we know how institutions will jump, and indeed just how tightly regulated the HE market will become.

CONTINUITY AND CHANGE

The governance of British higher education has moved through different stages, each of which each reflects a changing model of higher education, different societal values, and an evolving political context. Until the 1960s, higher education meant university education; it was an elite system dominated by values moulded in the world of the universities and essentially hidden from the mainstream political gaze. The universities served a public good and determined how that public good was to be defined. As such, and especially because they did not bear heavily upon the public purse, universities could be seen as autonomous institutions that determined their own development while the system was gently steered by the inbred UGC, whose primary function was to distribute the public funding that increasingly underwrote university expenditure.

Although higher education in Britain has evolved steadily over time, from the 1960s onwards it has become a very different model. Undoubtedly the most significant change has been the creation of the public sector of higher education, which was a key part of the move from elite universities to a mass system. Inevitably, expansion meant that higher education required more public expenditure and, almost as if in return, policy direction fell into political hands. While formally higher education institutions may have remained autonomous bodies, increasingly their development occurred within a context defined by politically determined goals. The creation of the funding councils marked the introduction of a new model of governance—one adapted to a mass, diverse, publicly funded, and politically directed model. Although in its latter years the UGC struggled to hold the middle ground, there was no way that it could have continued to survive and still retained anything approaching its traditional identity.

Many of the factors that brought about the funding council model of governance still persist, but there are new ideas and pressures that at the very least are forcing a rethink on how it should function. There is strong government interest in seeing a further diversification of the system of higher education and small, specialized private providers are acquiring the right to award degrees along with bearing the university title. The provision of higher education can now be delivered as a commercial activity and is designed to yield a profit. Moreover, the public funding of higher education teaching has all but ceased, although the government underwrites the costs of income-contingent student loans. With the general move towards the diversification of income streams, the distinction between publicly and privately financed segments has blurred. At present, the implications of these developments for the model of governance have yet to be finalized. The regulatory state will survive, but in what form is as yet unclear, and to say that it will be a light-touch regime begs more questions than answers—questions to which we will return.

2

Exploring the Unitary Model:
A Diversity of Definitions

Abstract: Much of the political intervention in English higher education
has been directed at attempts to shape its overall structure. This chapter
explores the shift from the university model to a system of higher
education, thanks to the creation in the 1960s of the binary model
composed essentially of the universities and the polytechnics. Why,
with the passage of the 1992 Further and Higher Education Act, was the
binary model subsequently abandoned? Would a unitary model mean the
creation of a system of higher education in which universities increasingly
shared common purposes and came to possess similar identities? This
chapter notes the steady official exhortation of the need for a diversified
model of higher education, albeit with little clarity as to precisely what this
would mean for either the identity of individual institutions or the overall
coherence of the system as a whole. It argues that the English model of
higher education has steadily become more internally differentiated and
stratified over time, countering the earlier developments of the initial
post-binary years in which developments were suggestive of a two-way
academic drift—that is, from the polytechnic model to the traditional
idea of a university and vice versa.

UNIVERSITIES OR HIGHER EDUCATION
INSTITUTIONS?

Writing in 1992, Halsey argued that, 'Britain is the most extreme case of
expansion of universities in terms of a particular idea of what a university is
and should be' (Halsey, 1992: 11). Although cross-national comparisons may
confirm the accuracy of this claim, in the very same volume Halsey presents
a broad historical overview of the '*ideas* of the university' with particular reference to the Anglo-American tradition (1992: 23–57). Whereas there may
be a measure of convergence about the purposes of a university (to express
it broadly—and notwithstanding the legacy of John Henry Newman—the

transmission of established knowledge interacting with the pursuit of new knowledge), ever since the rise of the nineteenth-century civic universities, two broad traditions have embraced the delivery of those purposes in England. On the one hand there is the collegial model, which has been shaped overwhelmingly by the Universities of Oxford and Cambridge. On the other hand, there is the civic model emerging out of both the University of London as well as those universities that sprung up throughout the nineteenth century in the cities of the Midlands and the North of England, embellished by the University of London and its colleges (Anderson 2006; Baatz 2013).

The framing of the expansion of English higher education within the parameters of these two models was reinforced by two important pressures. Firstly, new universities often emerged after spending a period of time under the tutelage of an established university. In a move that parallels the contemporary validation of private-sector degree programmes by an established university, several future universities would offer their students external degrees as structured and examined by the University of London. Not surprisingly, therefore, when they acquired the university title they had a ready-made model to follow. However, perhaps more important in the shaping of twentieth-century developments was the centralizing influence of the University Grants Committee (UGC). To acquire the university title and to be placed on the list of institutions to which the Committee awarded grants, it was essential to have the support of the UGC. As our analysis of the foundation of the 1960s new universities revealed, the UGC did have a clear idea of what it believed was desirable system development, and it was in a position to make its opinions felt when the acquisition of the university title was being pursued. Perhaps ironically, this was even more so once the university title had been acquired because by then it was more a question for the UGC of how to steer system change rather than impose institutional development.

This chapter considers five interrelated themes. Firstly, it analyses the foundation of the binary model in which a so-called public sector of higher education emerged to complement the existing university system. Why was the decision not taken in 1965 to widen the character of the prevailing university system by incorporating within it a different stratum of institutions, each of which would bear the university title? Secondly, what was the thinking behind the abolition of the binary model in the 1992 Further and Higher Education Act, to be replaced by a unitary model which entitled the former public sector institutions to acquire the university title and award their own degrees? Thirdly, examines the attempts to diversify over time the unitary model, which includes an interpretation of the significance of the emerging private sector, including for-profit institutional providers. The fourth part of the chapter analyses the interpretations of diversity that have emerged in attempts to restructure the unitary model. The intention is to provide a more rounded understanding of the concept of diversity. The conclusion then provides a broad perspective on the consequences for the structure of English higher education of the drive for diversity.

THE BINARY MODEL

Almost as an introduction to the Robbins Report we find the words:

> However well the country may have been served by the largely uncoordinated activities and initiatives of the past, we are clear that from now on these are not good enough. In what follows, therefore, we proceed throughout on the assumption that the needs of the present and still more of the future demand that there should be a system.

(Committee on Higher Education, 1963: 5)

Moreover, the UGC was aware of the fact that any such system would need to define both 'a general conception of its objectives' and the 'coordinating principles' that bound together its constituent members. However, the analysis of what these should be is conspicuous by its absence in the Report. In his *The Polytechnic Experiment, 1965–1992*, Pratt has argued that in effect the Robbins Report wanted to see an expansion of higher education in Britain through the continuation of the past experience of academic drift, which had seen an extension of the university system through the steady incorporation of 'a long tradition of higher education' that had expanded in those colleges run by public authorities 'outside the university or autonomous sector' (Pratt, 1997: 11). In other words, if the Robbins route had been followed, although the university system would have expanded, the intention was to ensure that its essential character would remain virtually intact.

Ultimately, the development of the system, based on the traditional university model as envisaged by the Robbins Report, was thwarted by the political acceptance of the binary model. In April 1965, the recently elected Labour Government belatedly committed itself to the binary cause in a speech made at the then Woolwich Polytechnic by Anthony Crosland, its Secretary of State for Education. To some extent the commitment was the consequence of the influence exerted by Toby Weaver (described as 'the catalyst' for the binary policy by Sharp, 1987: 39), who since 1962 had been the Department's deputy secretary 'responsible for higher education policy', while recognition is also given by Pratt to the political lobbying of the Association of Teachers in Technical Institutions (ATTI), and in particular a policy document produced by one of its leading members, Eric Robinson (Pratt, 1997: 8). In effect the expansionist thrust as envisaged in the Robbins Report is redirected by a counter-ideological drive dependent upon an alternative vision of higher education underwritten by powerful political interests (including those local authorities who wanted to retain their stake in the delivery of higher education) promising that the polytechnics would be 'the people's universities' (Robinson, 1968).

Although by 1965 there may have been more than one tradition of higher education in Britain, the implication is that it took the creation of the binary model for this to be fully appreciated. However, the need to establish the binary model also appears to be an acceptance of the claim, that if the expansion of higher education were to be achieved through the established university sector, then it could not be reshaped in ways that some argued would best serve the national interests. In other words it was a claim that universities were inherently conservative institutions, and that the purposes of the university system were almost beyond political redirection. Thus, while the binary model may have helped to enhance the variety of British higher education, it can also be seen as a convenient political manoeuvre that enabled the government to avoid tackling head-on the relationship between the universities, the state, and society.

A further problem is that the binary model was composed of two unequal sectors. While both the universities and polytechnics designed their own degree programmes (which, where appropriate, were ratified by professional associations), the universities awarded their own degrees whereas the polytechnics did not. The degree-awarding body for the polytechnics was the Council for National Academic Awards (CNAA), which also had the authority to ratify (or not) proposals for new degree programmes. In addition, and more significantly, the polytechnics were funded by the local authorities that exercised both formal administrative and policy control, although the polytechnics drew up their own development plans. The universities were autonomous decision-making bodies receiving an annual block grant within a quinquennial planning cycle from the Treasury via the UGC. Although with the passage of time critical changes were to occur, in 1965 the polytechnics were essentially managed institutions whereas in the universities 'donnish dominion' (Halsey, 1992) was probably close to its zenith.

But for the critics of university expansion through that process of absorbing the other providers of higher education, it was the fear of losing the social character and established traditions of knowledge that were built into this alternative model which most concerned them. The non-university sector of higher education was more likely to draw upon a local working-class clientele, with students studying part-time, pursuing sandwich degrees, or following non-degree higher education programmes—many of which would embrace technical courses often with a clear vocational orientation, which sometimes had an established relationship to the local manufacturing base. However, while the creation of the polytechnics may have helped to sustain these traditions, it can also be argued that it shielded the universities from pressures to which they should have been exposed. Arguably, therefore, as the university system is expanded (thanks in part to the impetus provided by the Robbins

Report), while at the same time being incorporated into a binary model of higher education, so that very 'particular idea of what the university is and should be' to which Halsey refers is reinforced.

Regardless of how much the tradition of higher education associated with the polytechnics may have been valued in the eyes of its proponents, in status terms it could not compete with the model that was perceived to prevail in the university sector. The perceptions may have been misguided, or were a consequence of differences in funding and control of policy development rather than intrinsic academic qualities, but, nonetheless, they were real. The pressures for change came from above and below. Over time, central government became less concerned with preserving a role for the local authorities in the polytechnic and colleges sector and more persuaded by the need to exercise tight control over public expenditure (Pratt, 1997: 250–260) coupled with a desire to provide a direction for higher education policy across the board (Salter and Tapper, 1994: 133–147). The pressures from below came from within the public sector institutions themselves. They centred upon the differences between the university and public sectors in terms of funding mechanisms and the control of institutional development. However, they also embraced academic developments, and Pratt has argued that the academic boundaries between the two sectors became increasingly blurred, essentially because of movements within the university sector.

> The universities…began to acquire characteristics hitherto the prerogative of the polytechnics (and which they had previously eschewed). They increasingly emphasized the vocational relevance and content of their courses. They opened access to non-traditional students. They began to welcome and rapidly increased the recruitment of part-time students. They turned increasingly to applied research.
>
> (Pratt, 1997: 309)

Nonetheless, the movement was not all in one direction as the relative academic weight within the polytechnics shifted away from the applied sciences to the social sciences, from part-time to full-time students; accompanied by the development of institutional research agendas and an increasing emphasis upon research profiles in the appointment and promotion of faculty. It was possible, therefore, for academic drift to occur in both directions within the binary model.

Although the advocates of the binary model of higher education may have had a reasonably clear idea of the values and practices they wished to preserve, the model could not be described as a system with defined objectives and coordinating principles as the Robbins Report had advocated. While established practices would inevitably constrain the pattern of institutional development, there were no prescribed constraints on how the universities and polytechnics should evolve. The bars were financial and political rather than statutory and ideological prescriptions. The consequence was inevitably a mixed pattern of change with institutional development responding to the internal distribution of power as this interacted with the funding and wider decision-making bodies. While there may have been both an idea of the university and of the polytechnic, these were not rigidly defined concepts, and certainly had no statutory basis, which would prohibit particular evolutionary paths.

THE MAKING OF THE UNITARY MODEL

The unitary model was created in two stages. The 1988 Education Reform Act (ERA) not only replaced the UGC with the UFC but also established the PCFC as the successor to the NAB. The Act stated that 'A local education authority shall no longer be under a duty to secure the provision for their area of facilities for higher education...(ERA 1988: clause 120.1), and higher education corporations were to be established that would assume the responsibility for managing the affairs of institutions that were identified by the Secretary of State (ERA 1988: Clause 121).

In a formal sense, therefore, the binary model survived the 1988 Education Reform Act, although the legislation achieved the objective of centralizing control over both the funding and policy direction of the system of higher education as a whole. But the stage was set for the emergence of the unitary model:

> The Universities Funding Council and the Polytechnics and Colleges Funding Council...shall be dissolved, and...all property, rights, and liabilities to which either of the existing councils were entitled or subject immediately before that date shall become by virtue of this section the property, rights, and liabilities of the Higher Education Funding Council for England.
>
> (Further and Higher Education Act 1992: clause 63.1)

The 1992 Further and Higher Education (Scotland) Act made parallel provisions for Scotland with authority transferred to the Scottish Higher Education Funding Council. The potential fusion of the hitherto separate sectors was completed by requiring the Privy Council to permit any institution which provided higher education to award degrees (which resulted in the dissolution of the Council for National Academic Awards), and, moreover, the ex-polytechnics and colleges could, with the consent of the Privy Council, change their names with most of them acquiring the university title in a comparatively short period of time, although Anglia Polytechnic University (now Anglia Ruskin University) demonstrated that it was hard for some to let go of the past.

While it is plausible to see the 1988 Education Reform Act as driven by economic and political considerations (essentially the desire for central government to control the funding and policy direction of higher education), it is more difficult to interpret the 1992 Further and Higher Education Act in the same terms. Obviously the coordination of funding and policy direction would be easier from the perspective of central government if there was but one funding council to deal with rather than two as had been the case between 1988 and 1992, and there is always an incentive for governments to tidy up administrative loose ends. Moreover, with the centralization of financial and political control, the government—at least in theory—was in a position to steer the development of higher education along the path that it felt was most appropriate to meeting the national interests. In other words, if there were particular traditions it wanted to sustain it could take the necesary action. If the polytechnics had represented a desirable form of higher education in terms of fulfilling national needs, then governments could have acted to ensure their preservation and the binary model would no longer have been needed to act as a protective shield, but government did not act and polytechnics became history.

There are, however, two major problems with this line of argument. Firstly, there is no uncontested understanding of what those national needs are that higher education should attempt to fulfil or, even if those needs can be defined, how a system of higher education can be structured to achieve them. As we have argued, the binary model was in part the manifestation of a conflict about the traditions of higher education. It represented the outcome of an ideological struggle to create a structure that would best maintain two different understandings of higher education. Secondly, permitting the public sector institutions to acquire the university title meant that they were now embraced by the historical ties that had enveloped the relationship between the state and the universities. The universities were seen as autonomous institutions that controlled their own development and, although Chapter 1 documented the steady encroachment of the state upon that autonomy, it was more a question of policy steering through a regulated market rather than being constrained by the imposition of a straitjacket. Thus, although the 1992 Further and Higher Education Act created a unitary model of higher education in England, it failed to establish a system in the sense of establishing coordinating principles amongst its constituent parts, the universities. While in government circles there may have been a growing sense of what the purposes of higher education were, there was little understanding of how the system could be structured to achieve those desired ends.

It can be argued, therefore, that the 1988 legislation gave a statutory basis to the key policy decisions but in political terms the 1992 act was essentially about the devolution of responsibility for British higher education while creating a more streamlined administrative structure to underpin its governance. Furthermore, it can be claimed that by 1992 the two sectors within the binary model had converged to such an extent that in practice it had become a unitary system. In other words, different traditions of higher education had been amalgamated to form if not a new then a revised idea of the university. The question is whether this revised idea would be embraced by all the constituent elements, the individual institutions, and their representative bodies, within the system? Alternatively, if there was to be a diversity of institutional missions, could there be equal respect for all the varying contributions? For those inclined to reflect normatively about higher education policy, it is the latter possibility that held most promise (Pratt, 1997: 305–329; Watson, 1998: 65–81; Scott, 2001: 186–204). While the years of the binary model may have witnessed a convergence between the two sectors of English higher education, it would be naïve to say that by 1992 they were of equal status and held each other in equal regard. Could the extension of the university title to the polytechnics and permitting them to award their own degrees provide a significant further impetus to convergence?

FROM A 'PYRAMID OF PRESTIGE' TO THE DIVERSIFIED MODEL

It is important to remember, however, that, although the former public sector institutions were acquiring the university title, they were joining a system already composed of different parts and with its own internal status hierarchy. Besides the broad distinction between the Oxbridge collegiate model and the nineteenth-century civic universities (including London), which we have already noted, by 1992 the twentieth century had seen the emergence of the smaller civic universities (for example, Southampton), the incorporation of the colleges of advanced technology (for example, Bath and Loughborough), and the foundation of the new universities of the 1960s (for an overview of the system's evolution see Tight, 2009). While the twentieth-century universities tended to follow the civic model in terms of academic organization and institutional governance, there was genuflection to a watered-down collegiality in both their halls of student residence as well as in the colleges of the new universities of Kent, Lancaster, and York, and indeed in those colleges of the much older University of Durham.

Although these sectors broadly adhered to the same idea of the university (the transmission and expansion of knowledge as worthwhile ends in their own right, a commitment to honours degree programmes organized around areas of knowledge defined by disciplinary boundaries, the admission under university control of well-qualified students who would then study full-time, follow a structured degree course, and graduate—at least in England—in three years, all coupled with the belief in the autonomous development of the university), nonetheless there was an internal 'pyramid of prestige' (Halsey, 1961). Later,

Halsey was to write, 'The history of British higher education from Victorian times to the present is one of evolving hierarchy' (Halsey, 1992: 59). This was a perspective underwritten by his surveys of the views of British academic faculty, which were undertaken in 1964, 1976, and 1989. Although there was some differentiation between universities by subject rankings, the 1989 survey revealed that academic opinion believed Oxford and Cambridge had a huge lead over the rest of the British university system (Halsey, 1992: 192–199).

It is self-evident, therefore, that the mere extension of the university title would not within itself undermine the 'pyramid of prestige' within the unitary model. Indeed, at least initially, it could be expected to be a broader pyramid as it now incorporated a sector of institutions that historically had been regarded as the second tier within British higher education. However, there is a certain irony in the fact that, although since 1992 there has been a unitary model of higher education in England, there has also been growing official support for institutional diversification. In recent years the unitary model, therefore, has not been seen as a means of encouraging the apparent convergence of sectors that had occurred between 1965 and 1992 but rather as a system composed of different institutions that should be committed to performing contrasting roles. Indeed, the National Committee of Inquiry into Higher Education (NCIHE, the Dearing Report) recommended that, '...diversity of institutional mission, consistent with high quality delivery and the responsible exercise of institutional autonomy, should continue to be an important element of the United Kingdom's higher education, and that this should be reflected in the funding arrangements for institutions' (NCIHE, 1997, recommendation 61).

Post-Dearing there then followed a long period in which official support for a diverse system of higher education was periodically reiterated, although concrete policy action to secure it was far less forthcoming. In August 2000, HEFCE issued for discussion a policy statement entitled, 'Diversity in Higher Education', which made the following claim:

> A diverse higher education sector is one with the capacity to meet the varying needs and aspirations of those it serves: students, employers, purchasers of HE services, and the wider community.
>
> (HEFCE, 2000: 4)

And, having made the point that these 'needs and aspirations' were becoming more varied, diversity could also assist:

> ...in the understanding of how higher education can contribute to the economic, social, and cultural development of the nation. In this sense diversity of HE provision is not an end in itself. It is a means of securing the best fit with the needs and wishes of stakeholders, both current and future.
>
> (HEFCE, 2000:4)

The support for diversity was also reinforced in very broad terms by the 2003 White Paper, *The Future of Higher Education*, which stated the then government's intention: 'To recognize and encourage diversity of role, with universities and colleges proud to be different and to play to their individual strengths' (Department for Education and Skills, 2003: 92). However, the White Paper also put forward some specific suggestions with implied policy proposals that have a very contemporary resonance:

> We propose to change the system, so that the University title is awarded on the basis of taught degree awarding powers, student numbers, and the range of subjects offered. This will send an important signal about the importance of teaching, and about the benefits for some institutions of focusing their efforts on teaching well.
>
> (Department for Education and Skills, 2003: 55, 4.33)

> At the same time, we will examine and modernize the criteria for degree-awarding powers to reflect the increasing diversity of higher education. The current system does not sufficiently reflect factors such as new virtual learning models, or the legitimate roles of those outside the university sector in providing high quality higher education learning.... .
>
> (Department for Education and Skills, 2003: 55, 4.34)

Significantly, these proposals follow immediately on from a comment on the California State Universities, which are a component part of a differentiated system of higher education defined by state legislation. It is almost as if the New Labour Government was raising the possibility of moving in the same formally structured direction as higher education in the state of California.

The White Paper was followed by the HEFCE strategic plan for 2003–8, which unsurprisingly reiterated the themes of the White Paper ('Our vision is for an HE sector in which institutions are at once more diverse and increasingly interconnected'—HEFCE, 2003a: 35) but shied away from providing any concrete means of how this was to be achieved. In fact, while New Labour's extended period in office (1997–2010) was marked by significant changes in English higher education, of which the most important was the introduction of variable fees in the 2004 Higher Education Act, there was not a great deal of new policy specifically designed to encourage institutional diversity. The one exception was the introduction of two-year foundation degrees in September 2001, which led to the expansion of higher education in colleges of further education as well as cooperation between the colleges and universities to ensure their delivery, although there has been some debate as to how distinctively different they are from the already established Higher National Diploma/Certificate (for a claim that they are indeed distinctive see Wagner, 2004).

More telling than direct government policy in promoting diversity has been action at the grass roots. Firstly, there has been the emergence of private providers who have started to offer higher education programmes—often working in con-junction with publicly funded universities—as a marketable product. Secondly, there has been the reshaping of institutional missions responding to changing market conditions and the nuancing in the provision of public funding. The first serious British manifestation in the twentieth century of privately funded higher education was the foundation of University College, Buckingham, in 1976, which received its university charter in 1983. The emergence of Buckingham was in part driven by the belief that the provision of higher education should be privately funded and most certainly not subjected to political direction. Undoubtedly, it was growing antipathy to state intervention, manifested in the form of the UGC's increasingly intrusive action (in part in reaction to funding cuts), which really stimulated the wider debate about the future control of the development of higher education. Change was more a consequence of growing anxiety at the course of government policy rather than a new-found faith in the market, although Buckingham's founders did have that belief.

For quite some time, Buckingham remained the United Kingdom's only privately funded university but over time, in direct response to public funding cuts, all universities have become increasingly dependent upon their ability to secure private revenue. In effect, the public funding of the university was steadily eroded, thus blurring the distinction between the private and public providers of higher education. Another significant step in this direction has been the Coalition Government's recent decision, following the publication of the Browne Review (*Securing a Sustainable Future for Higher Education: An Independent Review of Higher Education Funding and Student Finance*, October 2010), to withdraw most of the public funding that supported higher education teaching and to allow universities to charge undergraduate fees up to a maximum of £9,000 per annum. In effect, the funding of higher education teaching has been privatized with the costs met by income-contingent student loans underwritten by the Treasury.

Underlying these changes is the perception of universities as offering a service (teaching and learning) that leads to the acquisition of a valuable product (mainly degree programmes) in the context of a regulated market. It is impor-tant, therefore, that their prospective customers (those intending to become students) are well-informed about how the product is to be acquired, and are provided with measures that demonstrate its potential value. Moreover, this is meant to be a competitive market in which the providers differentiate themselves in terms of the prices they charge for both the delivery of their products (teaching) and how they are acquired (learning). Higher education, therefore, is promoted as a commodity that is delivered by a number of differ-ent providers, both publicly and privately funded bodies, some being for-profit institutions.

This approach does not preclude privately funded institutions acquiring, like the University of Buckingham, the university title, but the stress is upon the entry of new providers into the higher education market-place rather than the attempt to redefine the idea of the university. However, the 2011 White Paper, *Students at the Heart of the System* (Department for Business, Innovation, and Skills, 2011), like the 2003 White Paper of the New Labour Government before it, also raises the question as to whether a provider needs to embrace a range of disciplines and have a student population of a certain size before it merits the university title. In both cases the overall tone of the documents is such that it directs us to a response driven by the assumed need to create a more diverse system of higher education. Consequently, we are led to think more of the idea of a university system rather than the idea of a university.

INTERPRETING DIVERSITY

Although there has been an explicit commitment to introducing a more diverse model of English higher education at least since the Dearing Report, our overview of what constitutes official thinking on the topic demonstrates little in-depth understanding of what this means in practice. Firstly, there is a tendency to imply that the enhancement of diversity is a self-evident good for English higher education. It is, therefore, more important to advocate the cause rather than justify it. Interestingly, even the evident sceptics seem to find it difficult to come off the fence and offer a critique. For example, the report of Universities UK (UUK), *The Growth of Private and For-Profit Higher Education Providers in the United Kingdom* (March 2010), focused on the boundaries between, as well as the interaction of, the public and private sectors and reached the following anodyne conclusion: '... that the private sector is here to stay and will grow, but that it offers both opportunities and threats which will depend on where individual universities stand in the marketplace and how government policy responds' (UUK, March 2010: 6). Obviously, in view of the range of its internal interests, it would have been difficult for UUK to have joined either the advocacy or opposition camps, but it would have been helpful to have some analysis of what 'opportunities and threats' were likely to be incurred by enhancing diversity through an expansion of the private sector of higher education. Is the potential negative impact of expanding the private provision of higher education greater than its possible contribution to making the system more diverse?

The persistent government line is that greater diversity is required in order to establish a better fit between higher education and the needs of society. Moreover, the issue is clearly raised in both the White Papers of 2003 and 2011 as to whether the university title and the right to award degrees should be extended to a wider range of higher education providers. The possibility was raised, to some extent now fulfilled, that the university title would be granted to essentially teaching-only institutions with relatively small student numbers, covering a very limited range of academic disciplines, and which could be privately funded, possibly for-profit, bodies. The assumption was that to move down this path would not only increase the diversity of higher education, but would also enable it to meet more fully the needs of society. In part this would mean greater responsiveness to its stakeholders, including the fee-paying students whom it is assumed will demand a quality product for their expenditure.

In a recent overview of the private sector, Morgan has written: 'A picture emerges of a diverse sector, made up of not-for-profit institutions with charitable status and for-profits . . . a sphere with both small institutions and large providers operating from more than 20 locations across the UK' (Morgan, 1 March 2012: 37). However, although some of the institutions may support research (Cooper, 8 March 2012: 34), they are overwhelmingly committed to delivering teaching programmes. Moreover, while there are exceptions (for example, the New College of the Humanities), the dominant focus of the courses they offer is in the fields of business, management, finance, accountancy, law, computer sciences, the performing arts, and media studies. Conspicuous by its absence is the provision of the laboratory-based disciplines in the applied and natural sciences. It is difficult not to draw the conclusion that the disciplinary biases are driven by a combination of market and cost considerations. The private sector needs to offer courses with market appeal that, at least in relative terms, are not costly to sustain. Thus, while there may be institutional variety in the private sector (Middlehurst, 2013) rather than adding diversity to the overall academic map of the system it tends to reinforce the presence of an explicitly vocationally oriented element within higher education. The emphasis is on the marketable commodity rather than the promotion of new forms of knowledge. It is diversity in terms of size (small), range of disciplines covered (narrow), funding (mainly private), and academic orientation (teaching rather than research). However, it is for the most part intellectually conservative, presenting tried and tested forms of knowledge rather than offering anything approaching what could be termed 'new maps of knowledge'.

Diversity, therefore, does not necessarily mean the provision of new knowledge or organizing existing knowledge differently, but is more about making some of the forms that already exist more widely available. This is particularly true with respect to pedagogy; not so much what is taught but rather how it is taught. The University of Buckingham has persistently emphasized its commitment to tutorial teaching, which has been strongly reinforced by the New College of the Humanities (Furedi, 16 June 2011; New College of the Humanities, 22 September 2012). Both cases can be seen as a reaffirmation of a traditional pedagogy rather than the promotion of diversity. Nonetheless, they represent commitments to sustaining a mode of learning that they believe is under threat in British higher education. In that sense, they are helping to maintain pedagogical variety while, presumably, adding to their market appeal.

The University of Buckingham also established degree programmes that can be completed in two years, rather than the more usual three. Recent pedagogical developments have in fact placed a strong emphasis on distance learning built around a core of online programmes with considerable flexibility in the length of time it takes to complete a course. They are basically following the model that is most notably associated with the Open University, in which the structure of the degree programmes is shaped by the needs of the student. Over time, other publicly funded higher education institutions have moved in a parallel direction incorporating more part-time students and greater pedagogical flexibility including shorter (in terms of length but not necessarily academic demands) degree programmes. As the squeeze on their finances has forced the publicly funded higher education institutions to seek private resources so, in order to sustain their student base, many have found it necessary to adapt their pedagogies. An excellent example is the decision of the University of Coventry to establish as a subsidiary Coventry University College that will construct degree programmes designed to be completed in just over 18 months (Coventry University College, 22 September 2012).

Diversity, therefore, has been interpreted in two different ways. Firstly, the supposed need for higher education providers with different goals and contrasting institutional characteristics. Thus, there is an assumed need for universities that will focus primarily upon teaching, which could offer only a very limited range of degree programmes, could be comparatively small in size, could be privately funded, and even managed by for-profit corporations whose primary business might be non-educational. Secondly, there has been an emphasis on the need to restructure the organization and transmission of knowledge. Thus, the construction of either intensified degree courses with a two-year graduation target or part-time programmes, with the possibility that both are coupled with more distance learning (new virtual-learning models, in the words of the 2003 White Paper). Whereas the first interpretation of diversity would bring about a new idea of the university while almost certainly confirming the established understandings of what is knowledge, the second would extend practices already embedded in English higher education, although arguably not to the degree that they should be.

Although the arguments for a more diverse system of higher education are almost ritualistic (the desire for a closer fit between higher education and the needs of society), and there is a lack of clarity about what in concrete terms diversity actually means (providing different forms of knowledge or providing it in different ways), nonetheless it is reasonably clear what the change strategy has been. On the one hand, there has been the emergence of the private providers encouraged by at least the tacit support of successive governments in the expectation that their primary focus will be upon high quality teaching. On the other hand there has been greater selectivity in the distribution of public funding to support research. In listing the distribution of HEFCE research income for 2010–11, *Times Higher Education* noted that,

> The biggest recipient of research income from HEFCE, the University of Oxford, will benefit from a 2.4% rise; its £129 million allocation is more than that of the Million+, GuildHE and University Alliance groups combined.
>
> (*Times Higher Education*, 17 March 2011: 7)

Although governments have at best only partially succeeded in creating a differentiated market with respect to student fees, the research assessment exercises have sent a clear message about the need to concentrate public funding for research. The implications of which, as we will argue, have been very significant for the restructuring of English higher education.

CONCLUSION: THE EMERGING FUTURE

Recent developments in English higher education, in spite of official support for the diversity agenda, do not flow in one direction. Integral to the traditional idea of the English university is the commitment to autonomous institutional development underwritten by academic collegiality. And yet we have seen an almost universal movement towards university governance under the control of vice-chancellors who, in their capacity as chief executives, lead senior management teams. As academic senates have declined in significance so the power of university councils, invariably composed of a majority of lay persons, has increased. Universities have become more tightly managed institutions with senior posts frequently occupied by former academic faculty who have changed their career lines. It is as if there is a model of the efficiently managed university to which all institutions should conform (Tapper and Palfreyman, 2010: 93–110). Moreover, this development has received a considerable amount of support, with a key early step being the publication of the Jarratt Report (CVCP, 1985), to be followed by the Dearing Report, which proposed 'a code of practice on governance and, as part of that, we think that, as a general rule in the interests of effectiveness, membership of a governing body should not exceed 25' (NCIHE, 1997: 25). Then there is the Lambert Review, which argued there should be 'a significantly lighter touch regulatory and accountability regime to well-run universities' (Treasury, 2003: Recommendation 7.5). Whilst in general the approach has been to offer recommendations and to argue that universities need to decide for themselves their structures of governance, the wind has been blowing steadily in one direction carrying with it the message that reform is long overdue.

The long-term squeeze on public financial support for higher education teaching resulted in many universities seeking out market funding. There were several sources of non-public funding: the charging of full-cost fees for non-EU overseas students, undertaking research with private sector resources, the commercial use of the university's plant, drives to augment the size of endowment income, and the launching of appeals. With the introduction of variable fees of £3,000 per annum in the 2004 Higher Education Act, and even more so the raising of the ceiling up to £9,000 for 2012 entrants, home-based and EU students now represent a sizeable base for enhancing private income even though fees may be paid from income-contingent loans underwritten by the Treasury. In terms of funding, therefore, the general trend is one of convergence between the private and public sectors. While for some public sector institutions over 50% of income still comes via the funding council route, for others it is less than 25% (Baker, 7 April 2011: 35–42). There are, therefore, public sector universities that in terms of their income sources are moving close to the privately funded institutions.

Interestingly, some students in the private sector are in receipt of financial aid from the student loans scheme, which puts their institutions in danger of being entrapped by the tentacles of the regulatory state. The argument is that the state needs to be assured of the quality of the education offered to these students in receipt of publicly financed loans, and should such institutions receive the right to award their own degrees these pressures will simply intensify. Thus the private sector institutions may well be embraced by the state-regulated market alongside their publicly funded counterparts. Unsurprisingly, the current Coalition Government has opened up the discussion on what the regulatory framework for higher education should be, with the evident intention of ensuring that it is not so demanding as to deter would-be private providers or prove unduly burdensome for HEIs with good track records (Department for Business, Innovation, and Skills, August 2011).

In view of the fact that core to the identity of higher education institutions is their academic missions, if diversity is to have a substantive meaning then it should be defined in these terms. There have been moves by the Coalition Government intended to enhance high quality teaching and some public funding remains in place to support the teaching of STEM subjects (science, technology, engineering, and mathematics). The intention is to ensure that high quality teaching is central to the agenda of all universities, and there is no university that would admit to not having this as one of its goals. While the continued public funding, along with the political support, of the STEM subjects may help to sustain a measure of diversity by making it difficult for universities to close departments in these disciplines, the overall academic direction of the new providers—as we have noted—is to gravitate towards the marketable knowledge areas rather than to promote new knowledge areas. This is reinforced by the fact that the academic restructuring that has occurred in the publicly funded universities inevitably has also been influenced by market considerations—closing down courses with declining student demand while expanding those that have market appeal.

The distribution of student numbers shows that for the academic year 2009–10, the three largest subject areas were: 'business and administrative studies' (14.2%), 'subjects allied to medicine' (12.2%), and 'education' (9.1%). While between 2003–4 and 2009–10, most expansion took place in: 'architecture, building, and planning' (40.4%), 'veterinary sciences' (36.1%), and 'mathematical sciences' (30.1%), although in each case their representation in the total student population remains comparatively small. In the same time period, the declines in student numbers have been in 'computer science' (25.5%), 'combined degree programmes' (9.1%), and 'historical and philosophical studies' (2.8%) (Universities UK, 2011: 9, Table 1.9). In view of an overall expansion of 13.3% in student numbers between 2003–4 and 2009–10, those subject areas with declining numbers or which failed to expand by 13.3% (notably 'languages') really do appear to be under threat, although perhaps the relative decline in computer studies can be credited with an unsustainable earlier boom. What the general pattern of subject area distributions shows is a model that changes slowly, and in which there is a steady drift towards the vocationally oriented disciplines and against the humanities. However, although the New College of the Humanities may be swimming against the tide, there is always likely to be a niche market for quality providers.

It can, therefore, be argued that in terms of certain critical variables, the structural trend within English higher education is towards convergence rather than divergence. However, it would be difficult to claim that this has led to the emergence of a more homogeneous model with shared institutional identities and enhanced mutual respect. The move has not been so much towards diversity but rather towards fragmentation and stratification. This is a model composed of sectors, consisting of different higher education providers that project contrasting missions. While the university title may provide a common label, increasingly the future is seen in terms of the need for effective institutional action, part of which will be the presentation of a particular identity reinforced by association with those whom you consider to be your peers, meaning those proclaiming the same identity. The most striking example of this is the emergence of the organized groups of universities which form a status hierarchy with the 24 members of the Russell Group universities at the top. And like the erstwhile 'pyramid of prestige' the status hierarchy is not completely rigid, as illustrated by the recent expansion of the Russell Group to incorporate the Universities of Durham, Exeter, and York along with Queen Mary College, University of London (see Chapter 9 for an analysis of this development).

While the hierarchy is in part a reflection of historically entrenched differences (for example, the wealth of some of the Oxbridge colleges, their well-established social and political links, and their international reputations), it is also underwritten by the shift in the academic agenda from teaching to research, coupled with the rise of the international league tables, and reinforced by the direction of contemporary public policy. In those tables purporting to measure international excellence, the same British universities appear over time: the Universities of Cambridge and Oxford are at the top end of the scale, followed closely by Imperial College and University College London, with a smattering of Russell Group institutions following on behind. Much the same can be said of that most crucial of national ranking lists, that is the distribution of financial resources determined by the research assessment exercises. Moreover, there has been direct government intervention, in opposition to the wishes of HEFCE, to make the outcome of the exercises more selective in the distribution of funding (Tapper, 2007: 187–205). The 2003 White Paper remarked:

> ...we will also make sure that the very best individual departments are are not neglected, by making a clearer distinction between the strong and the strongest....
>
> (Department for Education and Skills, 2003: 23)

Subsequently, negotiations took place to identify a numbers of departments that were then awarded a 6* grade and given extra funding. In view of the fact that ranking in the international league tables and membership of the national mission groups is so dependent upon university research output (the Russell Group claims that it 'represents the 24 major research-intensive universities of the UK'—Russell Group, 29 October, 2012), then it is evident that government policy is one of the pressures that is responsible for a stratified model of English higher education.

However, this evolution of the unitary model into a stratified, if not rigidly so, system has emerged out of the piecemeal development of government policy interacting mainly with decision-making at the level of the individual institutions. There has been no attempt to construct a master plan that defines its overall goals and the principles governing the relationship between its constituent elements. Underlying it is a much broader definition of the university, one that embraces a range of models including the provision of higher education in colleges of further education. It is realistic to think of it as containing different sectors, which have varying purposes and modes of functioning. Nonetheless, while the established idea of the university persists—more especially the stress on establishing a research tradition, continuing a commitment to high quality teaching, and an emphasis on broad sociocultural, as well as academic, goals—it is inevitable that the model will have a structural hierarchy. Currently, for an institution to be awarded the university title suggests the acquisition of a status symbol which provides greater prestige and possibly improves market position but within itself tells us little about the goals, values, or the practices of the institution, but it is these, rather than the title, which will define the overall structure of the system.

3

The Dearing Report: Sustaining British Higher Education as a System

Abstract: The chapter identifies the reasons for the creation of the Inquiry under the auspices of Dearing, outlines its main recommendations, and discusses its impact upon the development of higher education in England. Along with all commentators on the Inquiry, it identifies the main reason for its creation as essentially financial in nature—the sharp decline in per-student funding coupled with the threat of some universities to contemplate the imposition of fees. Its recommendations on fees were its most significant input, and eventually led to the levying of variable undergraduate fees to be paid for through income-contingent loans. In other respects, the Inquiry was a relative failure. It put forward a twenty-year plan for higher education that would be steered by a compact between government and the dominant higher education interests. A diverse, albeit not too internally diverse, higher education system would be steered by a compact embracing funding, regulation of teaching and learning, the pursuit of research, modes of institutional governance, and the need to embrace a local/regional role. In fact, what has developed is the steering of higher education through a state-regulated market rather than a grandiose compact, and the higher education system has become increasingly differentiated into different segments.

WHY DEARING?

Although the 1992 Further and Higher Education Act led to the emergence of a unitary model of higher education in Britain, its primary focus was upon the governance of the system: the respective responsibilities of the state apparatus, the quasi-state bodies, and the higher education institutions, and in relation to these issues it built on the 1988 Education Reform Act. There was no attempt to define either the overall goals of the new model or how they should be met. The fact that the National Committee of Inquiry into Higher Education (NCIHE—the Dearing Inquiry) was set up five years later to make recommendations on these matters is strongly suggestive of the argument that British higher education has evolved in a piecemeal rather than in a purposeful manner and is driven by pragmatic considerations rather than by any notion that its development should be planned (Shattock, 2012). However, the Inquiry's broad terms of reference would suggest that at long last an agreed model was about to emerge and henceforth higher education in Britain could be described as an explicitly constructed system:

> To make recommendations on how the purposes, shape, structure, size and funding of higher education, including support for students, should develop to meet the needs of the United Kingdom over the next 20 years, recognizing that higher education embraces teaching, learning, scholarship, and research.
>
> (NCIHE, 1997: 5)

However, as the failure to expand the higher education system on the basis of the recommendations of the Robbins Report (perceived, at least in university circles, as more illustrious than the Dearing Inquiry) had demonstrated, it is far easier to make recommendations than to ensure their implementation.

Moreover, it is difficult to give these grandiose terms of reference a lot of credence if one accepts the widely held view that the Dearing Inquiry was established essentially to resolve the question of how in the future higher education should be funded (Barr and Crawford, 1998; Wagner, 1998). Indeed, given present-day realities, its central purpose could be interpreted as very limited: to make recommendations that would enable government to shift some of the responsibility for the funding of teaching and learning onto students and their families. In other words, it would help to legitimatize a policy shift that governments had been attracted to but had failed to implement. For example, although in the mid-1980s as Secretary of State for Education Keith Joseph had addressed the possibility of requiring students to pay tuition fees, he was deterred from proceeding by the opposition of backbench Conservative MPs, and since then it had been seen as 'a step too far' to be embraced as party policy (Stevens, 2003). Obviously if the Inquiry did assist the instigation of this policy shift, then it could be interpreted as a considerable triumph regardless of how the merits of the policy itself were evaluated. However, this may give too much weight to the Inquiry's impact, for even with respect to the funding recommendations, they could be seen essentially as a convenient instrumental step forward. Faced with the sharp decline in the unit of resource for teaching and learning, the universities were threatening (perhaps without real intention of carrying through their threat) to impose, their own fees. The setting up of the Inquiry was, therefore, to forestall this possibility, to allow the government time to determine its own course of action. It should be remembered that the Inquiry had been agreed to by both the then Conservative Government and the Labour Opposition, which consequentially also took higher education policy out of the impending 1997 General Election campaign (Watson and Bowden, 2007: 8).

While this chapter has drawn attention to these Machiavellian interpretations of the Inquiry, its central purpose is to present and analyse the Committee's perspective on how the English system of higher education should evolve. The central claim is that rather than proposing new courses of action it reinforced emerging developments, which were to shape how higher education in England has functioned until at least the 2011 White Paper. The chapter concludes by considering what remains of the Dearing legacy as well as presenting those pressures which have undermined its conception of how the English system of higher education should be structured and function in the future.

THE COMPACT DESIGNED TO MAKE ENGLISH HIGHER EDUCATION A SYSTEM

In Chapter 2, we noted that the 1963 Committee on Higher Education (the Robbins Report) had argued that Britain needed its higher education institutions to function as a system that had both 'a general conception of its objectives' and 'coordinating principles'. Although it failed to define explicitly what these should be, it was clearly implied that would-be new universities should be incorporated into the established model and embrace its dominant values, structures, and purposes. Thus, the system would continue much as before but be augmented in size with more universities and more students. But this was not to be, and a binary model emerged—each part of which incorporated its own tradition of higher education and broadly speaking followed separate paths. It is not too far-fetched to argue that the mission of the Dearing Inquiry was to rectify this situation by creating a coherent system out of the two traditions. In decidedly overblown language, the Report argued that its title—*Higher Education in the Learning Society*—represented a vision that the United Kingdom should attempt to create.

> It should, therefore, be a national political objective to be world class both in learning at all levels and in a range of research of different kinds.

And how is this to be achieved?

> In higher education this aspiration should be realized through a new compact involving institutions and their staff, students, governments, and society in general.

(NCIHE, 1997: 8)

In effect, the Dearing Report called for a compact to be established that would draw together government, society, and the higher education institutions to ensure the provision of world-class teaching and the pursuit of cutting-edge research.

This presented a visionary perspective of higher education with which it is impossible to disagree. However, we need to know what the precise areas are that the compact should embrace and what the concrete obligations that each of the parties had to sign up to in order to make it a success. This is critically important because in the section of the Report entitled 'Next Steps' we read: 'Our recommendations add up to a coherent package for the future of higher education. We do not intend that those to whom they are addressed should choose to implement only some of them. The new compact requires commitment from all sides' (NCIHE, 1997: 38). Ironically, although the Inquiry supported the continuation of institutional autonomy ('We see great value in maintaining the long-standing practice of the Government remaining at arms' length from individual institutions and therefore in retaining the intermediary Funding Bodies'—NCIHE, 1997: 36), the implication is that autonomy has to be exercised within the framework of an agreed, presumably through negotiation, compact amongst the involved interests. At best, therefore, autonomy would be constrained by the compact and, although it can be rightly argued that this has always been the case (like all publicly funded institutions universities had to function within the constraints of a budget), the Inquiry clearly wanted a more embracing package of commitments. Interestingly, if a compact was to have any substance then it would also constrain government behaviour and perhaps deny it the policy flexibility that, for example, economic circumstances frequently require. Whereas constraints on university autonomy are a reality, it is impossible to imagine governments, compact or not, making binding commitments to higher education regardless of their wider policy obligations.

The Inquiry's terms of reference were exceedingly broad and the result was a massive output: consisting of three main reports (the National Committee's Report, the Scottish Committee's Report, and a Summary Report to which should be added five appendices detailing the work the Inquiry itself undertook, and fourteen additional reports on specialist topics prepared by commissioned scholars). Lord Dearing himself informs us that there are over 1,700 pages of text in the paper version. The compact was to embrace a range of concerns on which the dominant higher education interests would attempt to reach an accord that would be steered by the Inquiry's recommendations. There were proposals to initiate a fundamental change in the relationship between the universities, state, and society in four areas:

1. Devising an appropriate funding strategy
2. Constructing the framework for ensuring high quality teaching and an effective learning process
3. Supporting scholarship and research
4. Establishing a code of practice for the good governance of higher education institutions

It was imperative that in reaching an agreement there should be a commitment on the part of the higher education institutions to achieve certain concrete policy goals. This chapter focuses on those two goals which would impact upon the relationship between higher education institutions and the wider society with potential repercussions for the Inquiry's proposed compact:

1. To embrace an enlarged and more socially diverse participation rate
2. To develop local and regional roles

To add to the difficulties of securing an accord, the Report argued that not only would institutional autonomy be respected, but also the compact would require only a parsimonious extension of the university title, and much of the expansion of higher education would take place in colleges of further education, which would not entail the growth of degree-level courses but rather of non-degree programmes. Furthermore, there was a repeated commitment in the Dearing Report to the need for sustaining a diverse system of higher education. Although some have argued (Trow, 1998) that this was essentially a token gesture rather than a goal underwritten with substantive funding recommendations, it does raise the question of whether it would have been preferable to think of a system composed of differing sectors underwritten by more than one compact, rather than the construction of a supposedly unified model based on a compact composed of all the varying interests that embrace further and higher education. The issue is how much institutional diversity a compact can absorb.

STRUCTURAL CHANGES

Funding Higher Education

There are good reasons for addressing first the Dearing Report's recommendations on the funding of higher education. At the time of the Inquiry's formation there was a real funding crisis. In the words of the Report:

> The present public spending plans for higher education assume a reduction in real terms of expenditure per student of 6.5% over the two years 1998–9 and 1999–2000. This is in addition to the more than 40% reduction achieved since 1976.
>
> (NCIHE, 1997: 27)

Furthermore, 'capital funding for equipment and the refurbishment of institutions' estates' was also being substantially reduced (see Greenaway and Haynes, 2000; Tapper, 2007: 153–155). Moreover it is the analysis of the funding crisis to which the Report gives most of its attention and which is considered by critics to be its most convincing work. As Wagner writes:

The Funding Working Group was the largest of those it established and had the most committee members on it. The research commissioned was the most thorough in depth and breadth... The five chapters and 83 pages devoted to the subject in its main report are the most carefully written, with a level of systematic argument backed up by data not found elsewhere in the report.

(Wagner, 1998: 64–65)

Most importantly, it is the recommendations on funding that are universally considered to be the most significant contribution to the debate on the future development of higher education policy, and not only for the British system.

There are several important dimensions to the funding recommendations of the Inquiry. The costs of funding teaching and learning should be shared by the state and those who benefit from it, and 'those with higher education qualifications are the main beneficiaries, through improved employment prospects and pay' and so consequently 'we suggest that graduates in work should make a greater contribution to the costs of higher education in the future' (NCIHE, 1997: 28–29). The recommendation was that students should be required to pay a flat-rate fee of £1,000 per annum (to cover approximately a quarter of the annual costs of educating the undergraduate student population). Students would be eligible for income-contingent loans to pay their tuition fees whereas living costs would be underwritten by a combination of means-tested grants and income-contingent loans. The assumption was that requiring students to make a contribution to paying fees would not deflate the desire to participate in higher education because repayment would be determined by the level of the individuals' future salaries rather than by their present economic circumstances, although this does assume a universal cultural reaction in terms of being comfortable with such debt.

Barr and Crawford (1998: 74–75) have argued that the Dearing Report's recommendations on the funding of higher education may well have been very different if in the auditing of the student loans scheme if its accounts were not classified as public expenditure. Although there is nothing that directly confirms the suspicions of Barr and Crawford, the Report does argue strongly that student loans should be treated differently by the Treasury from student grants. The point is straightforward: if the underwriting of loans is counted as public expenditure then this would augment higher education's public expenditure borrowing requirement at a time when the Treasury was keen to curtail it.

Not surprisingly, the responses to the Inquiry's funding recommendations were mixed. Most of the opposition came from the camp claiming that the provision of higher education was overwhelmingly a public good and thus should be publicly funded, whereas the supporters of the Dearing proposals accepted its argument that graduates as beneficiaries should underwrite some of the costs. However, there was overwhelming support for the argument that, if students were to be required to meet some of the costs of higher education (either a contribution to tuition fees and/or their living costs), then this was best done by means of an income-contingent loans scheme. The then government (the first 'New Labour' Government under the leadership of Blair with Blunkett as Secretary of State for Education) immediately accepted that the current loans scheme (to underwrite student living costs) should be moved from a mortgage-style to an income-contingent repayment model.

However, the Dearing funding proposals were barely off the press before the Secretary of State, although accepting the principle of income-contingent loans, stated that the government would impose a means-tested fee of £1,000 per annum, which would be paid upfront. As Wagner wryly notes:

> The government obviously has clear political objectives in the introduction of any student contribution scheme. These are that neither students nor their parents or partners should have to pay more *now* than they would have had to under existing arrangements.
>
> (Wagner, 1998: 75)

The circle could be squared because means testing meant that students from poorer families would not have to pay the tuition fee, while increasing the minimum means-tested loan by £1,000 to cover living costs meant that wealthier parents could simply transfer some of the support for their children's living costs to paying their tuition fees. Until reintroduced there would be no means-test grants to cover living costs, although the Dearing Report had argued for their retention because they were concentrated upon students from the poorest families.

Although there had been bi-partisan political support for the creation of the Dearing Inquiry, no party could pledge itself to accept all of its recommendations, and the response of the Labour Government was bound to be selective and driven at least in part by political considerations. It also needs to be remembered that the imposition of tuition fees was a very controversial political issue for all the major political parties and there is no doubt that it would alienate a section of the electorate. Within the Labour Party there was undoubtedly a strong body of opinion that, regardless of what scheme was adopted, would see the imposition of fees as a strong deterrent to expanding participation in higher education and especially for those social groups that were already under-represented.

Shattock judges Blunkett's response to be a consequence of more prosaic political reasons: '...Blunkett had given a private commitment to the NUS in the run up to the General Election in respect to low income students that maintenance grants would be means-tested but that fees would be remitted in the new arrangements post Dearing' (Shattock, 2012: 162). As we have noted, although the amount that could be borrowed to cover living costs was means tested, in fact maintenance grants were replaced by income-contingent loans and it was the flat-rate fee that was means tested. But the important point is that the Inquiry's funding strategy underlying its proposed compact inevitably was going to be politically redefined regardless of which party won the 1997 General Election.

In terms, therefore, of the funding dimension of the proposed compact, the Dearing Inquiry was unsurprisingly only partially successful in shaping government policy. However, the principle that students should make a contribution to paying fees was established with the agreement that student loans should be repaid through an income-contingent mechanism. The hotly debated 2004 Higher Education Act subsequently enacted the principle of variable fees (up to a maximum of £3,000 per annum) to be repaid by all students through income-contingent loans, although it also reintroduced means-tested maintenance grants. However, following the publication of the Browne Report (*Securing a Sustainable Future for Higher Education*) in 2010, the current Coalition Government has removed all public support of teaching, except for STEM subjects, and increased tuition fees (still to be repaid by income-contingent loans) up to a maximum of £9,000 per annum. If the Dearing Inquiry can be said to have established a compact embracing the higher education interests, it is clear that its terms of reference have changed. The government appears to be saying that there should be public funding to support the teaching and learning process in higher education only for those subjects that are deemed critical to fulfilling national needs, otherwise funding should be provided by student tuition fees. It would seem that the perception of higher education as an essentially private good has gained considerable ground in government circles from the time when the Dearing Inquiry estimated that its proposed £1,000 per annum fees would cover approximately 25% of the total costs of teaching and learning. The thinking appears to be that, if higher education is a private good, why subsidize its acquisition with public funding, especially when in the context of a global economic crisis there are more pressing demands upon the public purse?

Even if it is argued that successive governments have been driven overwhelmingly by economic considerations in determining their higher education funding strategies, there is little doubt that they have tried to legitimize their policy decisions on the basis of value preferences. Thus the opposition to requiring students to pay fees was countered by two countervailing themes: higher education gave its recipients the potential to earn additional income (supported by considerable evidence) over those who had not received it, and its beneficiaries came disproportionately from the more economically privileged sector of society. For student fees to be paid for out of the public purse meant that the poorer members of society were providing a subsidy to its richer members. Likewise, it could be argued that it was critical to provide some public funding to underwrite the costs of teaching and learning because exposure to higher education allegedly helped to turn the individual into a more publicly responsible citizen: more economically secure and thus likely to pay more taxes, more knowledgeable and thus more likely to enhance the nation's economic performance, both more socially responsible and politically aware, and even embracing a broader cultural horizon. Certainly the decision to continue with some public funding to underwrite the teaching of the STEM subjects has been legitimized in terms of the potential national economic returns that supposedly follow from securing a large pool of graduates in these disciplines.

Nonetheless, it is clear that the ideological policy drivers are invariably employed to justify political decisions that are economically driven. Thus the Dearing Inquiry's support for student tuition fees was part of a long-term movement towards lessening public responsibility for underwriting the costs of teaching and learning in higher education with the process moving forward with the arrival of variable fees, and further still thanks to the recent almost complete removal of public funding. Any idea of a meaningful compact between the dominant interests with respect to the funding of higher education is virtually impossible. The government's responsibility for managing public expenditure, coupled with the range of its policy obligations, makes a compact that has real substance highly unrealistic. The best that the National Committee could have hoped for was a range of broad promises without any substantive commitments; and that is precisely what it got.

In a generally hostile overview of the proposals of the Dearing Inquiry, Robertson has written:

> It mattered less that the technical criteria of the funding question were understood...but it was crucial that Government could introduce the principle of tuition payment into the public domain without political cost. Indeed, the historic paradox of the Dearing Inquiry is that its one major success, getting the technical criteria on funding right, is matched by its greatest failure, getting the political criteria on funding wrong....
>
> (Robertson, 1999: 131–2)

While Robertson's judgement is correct it is, nonetheless, important to raise the question of whether it would have been really possible to have fixed the political criteria before the publication of the Inquiry's Report and, moreover, to make the point that subsequent events appear to demonstrate the long-term viability of the funding proposals as well as their broad political acceptability. Perhaps the failure was Blunkett's rather than Dearing's?

The Teaching and Learning Process

The Dearing Inquiry states boldly that 'Our vision puts students at the centre of the process of learning and teaching' (NCIHE, 1997: 15). In fact, although the Committee calls for more information to be provided to students by the universities and there is an expectation that as fee-payers students will be more demanding as to the quality of the education they are receiving, it is its own interpretation of how the teaching and learning process should be managed that is central to this claim. There are four ingredients to its proposals:

1. The funding councils 'should immediately establish a professional Institute for Learning and Teaching in Higher Education'

2. All universities should offer a 'programme specification' for each programme it offers which identifies the knowledge/understanding as well as the skills to be acquired

3. There should be a framework of qualifications with 'recognized standards at each level'

4. Degree-awarding institutions needed to create 'a UK-wide pool of academic staff recognized by the Quality Assurance Agency, from which institutions must select external examiners'

(NCIHE, 1997: 16–21 and 45)

The Dearing recommendations, if not imposing an agenda upon the Quality Assurance Agency (QAA), were at the very least presenting that recently formed body with a range of proposals that it should consider taking forward.

What these recommendations of the Dearing Report, along with the wider evolution of the quality assurance agenda culminating in the agreement that led to the creation of the QAA in 1997, point to is the emergence of a very different relationship between the universities (at least for those universities founded before 1992), the state, and society. The National Inquiry was advocating a standardization of the teaching and learning process, which would be imposed through a process of academic corporatism (Tapper and Salter, 1998) and monitored by the QAA, with degree standards protected by the QAA-approved panel of external examiners. Clearly, this was a threat to both institutional autonomy and an attack on diversity. However, it went with the grain of the recent historical experience of higher education, including the long-held right of professional bodies to accredit academic programmes which, if successfully completed, permitted entry into professional practice. Moreover, it was also a response to the fears, often expressed in political quarters, that academic standards in the age of mass higher education were indeed in decline.

The Dearing Inquiry's proposals for the restructuring and monitoring of the teaching and learning process in higher education are but another manifestation of the rise of the regulatory state, but they represent a marked extension of its tentacles. However, there was a clear recognition that matters such as programme specification, the definition of benchmark standards, the examining of degrees, the training of academics, and the assessment of institutional quality should be defined by procedures which are determined and managed in large part by the academic profession. It is the quasi-state rather than the state in action, although the intention was that this action should be officially sanctioned, even underwritten by legislation.

If the Dearing recommendations on this front had been fully implemented, then the regulatory state would have been integral to the Inquiry's proposed compact on higher education. In fact the actual demands of policy in this field have oscillated and they remain far from being settled (for an overview of the relevant political struggles see Tapper, 2007: 167–186, and to bring the picture up to date, Shattock, 2012: 187–212). However, although in this policy field government remains the dominant factor, the fact that the regulatory process requires the active participation of academic interests means that there is a less unequal distribution of power than is the case in relation to the public funding of higher education. While the quality agenda has encroached severely upon institutional autonomy, there was nothing in the regulatory apparatus proposed by the Dearing Report to suggest that it could function without the cooperation of the universities. Moreover, governments have been prepared to adopt a flexible approach to the enforcement of quality assurance mechanisms in order to curry favour with the universities. Thus, in early 2003 the Department reported:

> We have introduced a new quality assurance system for Higher Education...I look to the Council to monitor closely the implementation of the new arrangements to ensure that our objectives for the new systems are met.
>
> In particular, the new arrangements should remove unnecessary burdens from institutions....

> (Department for Education and Skills, 2003a: 4–5)

The essence of the change was a move from departmental inspections, with an assessment of quality judged on a 24-point scale, to institutional audit, which was frequently referred to as a lighter-touch quality regime.

Interestingly, the current Coalition Government, in spite of removing nearly all the public funding that supported teaching and learning in higher education, encouraging the development of a private sector, and opening up consultation on the implementation of a less intrusive regulatory regime (Department for BIS, August 2011) is still retaining its faith in the regulatory state. For example, the QAA continues to issue a *Quality Code for Higher Education* (periodically updated and retitled), which makes the following comments on subject benchmarks:

> They provide general guidance for articulating the learning outcomes associated with the programme but are not a specification of a detailed curriculum in the subject.
>
> Subject benchmark statements also provide support to HEIs in pursuit of internal quality assurance. They enable the learning outcomes specified for a particular programme to be reviewed and evaluated against agreed expectations about standards.
>
> Subject benchmark statements allow for flexibility and innovation in programme design...Their use in supporting programme design, delivery, and

review within HEIs is supportive of moves towards an emphasis on institutional responsibility for standards and quality.

(QAA, 2012)

With its emphasis on 'agreed standards' and 'expectations', the non-specification of 'detailed curricula', the acceptance of 'flexibility and innovation', and the stress on the need for institutions 'to take responsibility for standards and quality', this is almost 'pure Dearing'. The regulatory state is still very much alive, but there is a clear attempt to convey the message that it permits flexible interpretation of programme specifications and wants the initial responsibility for monitoring quality to be in the hands of the universities, although it is the regulator which controls the framework within which they will operate.

Supporting Research and Scholarship

The Inquiry's recommendations on the future of research in higher education were far less radical than those aimed at restructuring the teaching and learning process. A call for a general increase in the public funding of research in higher education is accompanied by very specific recommendations: the establishment of an Arts and Humanities Research Council, the requirement that the Research Councils meet the full indirect costs of the programmes and projects they fund, and a proposal to set up an Industrial Partnership Development Fund to encourage the joint funding of research in higher education (NCIHE, 1997: 21–22).

The really critical change in the funding of research in higher education was the decision made by the UGC, at the time headed by Peter Swinnerton-Dyer, to distribute selectively the core public funding of research. Consequently, in 1986 the first Research Assessment Exercise took place. The Dearing Inquiry remarked: 'We endorse the policy of targeting funding on high quality departments'; but followed this with the statement, 'but there is also a need for funding to support the research and scholarship which underpin teaching in those departments which do not aspire to be at the cutting edge of research'. It then recommended to the Funding Bodies that,

> ...the next Research Assessment Exercise is amended to encourage institutions to make strategic decisions about whether to enter departments for the Exercise or whether to seek a lower level of non-competitive funding to support research and scholarship which underpins teaching.

(NCIHE, 1997: 22)

In fact this parallels one of the recommendations of the Roberts Review (Joint Funding Councils, *Review of Research Assessment*, 2003), which followed RAE2001. However, rather than persuading universities to opt out of the research assessment exercise, and perhaps receive some research income through an alternative mechanism, it has proven a more viable option simply to distribute core research funding more selectively. This is the policy that has been pursued in England (with the Scottish and Welsh governments refraining from imposing such a tough line upon their funding councils), although it was not a policy with which HEFCE concurred (Tapper, 2007: 194–201). The consequences for English higher education have been dramatic. In 2010–11 it meant that:

> The biggest recipient of research income from HEFCE, the University of Oxford, will benefit from a 2.4% rise; its £129 million allocation is more than that of the Million+, GuildHE and University Alliance groups combined.
>
> (*Times Higher Education*, 17 March 2011: 7)

In effect, English higher education has been restructured to create a system composed of different sectors, with the level of public funding for research as the key differentiating financial variable. Inevitably, such a wide variation in the distribution of public funding to support research would make it difficult to sustain the compact that Dearing was advocating.

While the Dearing Committee's recommendations on the public support for research and scholarship in higher education are limited, they do reveal a good understanding of the nature of the compact it was attempting to establish amongst the dominant interests. The Report reiterates its support for a diversified model of higher education, which in part will be seen in the presence of a number of research-intensive universities. However, there was no discussion of the possibility that some universities would not have a research mission, and, moreover, all institutions were to be embedded in a common framework that determined how they received their public funding, the regulation of their teaching and learning commitments, and the organization of their governance. It appears that diversity would be limited in its scope and driven from below rather than imposed from above. Indeed the role of the state, besides providing funding for higher education, was to impose order, which was perceived as a necessary precondition for ensuring that the universities fulfilled their societal obligations.

The Good Governance of Higher Education Institutions

In conjunction with the recommendations on the creation of quality assurance mechanisms for teaching and learning, the Inquiry's proposals for the good governance of higher education are embraced by similar Reports: the Jarratt Report (CVCP, 1985) that preceded it and the Lambert Review (Treasury, 2003) that followed it. Moreover, the Committee of University Chairmen (CUC), which had emerged after the Jarratt Report, published in 1995 its

Guide for Members of University Councils and Governing Bodies (Shattock, 1998: 46). Although the Dearing Inquiry recognized that many higher education institutions had made 'impressive improvements in efficiency in the face of a dramatic fall in public funding per student over the past 20 years…', there was sufficient evidence of institutional failure to justify the assertion that some fell 'far short of the performance of the best' (NCIHE, 1997: 25). The Inquiry felt that in order to improve the situation there needed to be 'a code of practice on governance, and, as part of that, we think that, as a general rule in the interests of effectiveness, membership of a governing body should not exceed 25', and where it did exceed 25 members it should be demonstrated why this was a prerequisite to achieving effectiveness. Furthermore, the governing body should review at least once every five years, with 'appropriate external assistance and benchmarks' its own arrangements for undertaking its role and how effectively the institution for which it was responsible had performed (NCIHE, 1997: 26).

Shattock claims that these proposals 'were very much influenced by Dearing's own preferences for the post-1992 universities' more business-like model' (Shattock, 2012: 223). This may well be so, but it could also reflect the Inquiry's pronounced business representation, approximately one-third of the Committee's membership, although it does beg the question as to why a university council should be seen as performing a parallel function to a board of company directors. The reference to 'appropriate external assistance and benchmarks' is directly parallel to the Committee's recommendations on how to ensure the quality of teaching and learning in as much as in both cases there appears to be a suspicion of internally based professional judgement and a desire to use agreed 'objective' criteria to evaluate performance. Again there is a parallel intention to restrict, although not deny, institutional variation: differentiation can be permitted but it needs to justify itself in terms that indicate its effectiveness in securing agreed goals. However, while the criteria used to evaluate the quality of the teaching and learning process could be determined through the mechanisms of academic corporatism, it is more difficult to discern precisely how a definition of good governance was to be agreed. The right of at least the pre-1992 universities to determine how they governed themselves was a key ingredient of institutional autonomy and, while it was one thing for the CUC to issue guidelines, it was quite another matter for the Dearing Inquiry to suggest the imposition of a Code of Practice. Furthermore, it would have required the passage of legislation to have imposed it (Shattock, 1998: 47), which would have grossly undermined any notion of institutional autonomy.

However, what has to be recognized is that there have been significant changes in the governance of English higher education institutions since at least the 1985 Jarratt Report (Deem, Hillyard, and Rees, 2007; Tapper and Palfreyman, 2010: 93–110; Shattock, 2012: 213–214). Moreover, it is reasonable to argue that these changes have generally speaking been in a direction that is at least consistent with the values implicit in the recommendations of the Dearing Inquiry. At one level Jarratt, Dearing, and Lambert espoused recommendations, reinforced for the most part by government support if not actual legislation, that it was claimed would result in the implementation of good practice. But persistent exhortation was nothing compared to the expanding external pressures for accountability and the financial constraints that the universities had to face. As universities struggled to meet these pressures, the consequence was a marked decline in the authority of most academic senates, an increase in the powers of councils, which did become somewhat slimmer in size and on which lay representation was increased, and, as we have noted, this was coupled with the emergence of senior management teams under the leadership of vice-chancellors who often assumed the title of chief executive. For the universities the changes were not simply a question of the need to incorporate good governance practices but rather how best to organize their affairs so they could survive and, in some cases, possibly thrive.

CONCRETE POLICY GOALS

Expanding and Widening Participation

Since the Second World War, the size of the undergraduate population in British higher education had expanded leading to a shift from an elite to a mass system (Trow, 1973). But that growth had been far from even, and post-1994 it was deemed by the then Conservative Government that there was a need for a period of what was termed 'consolidation' following the rapid expansion of the late 1980s and early 1990s. Much of the funding crisis that the Dearing Inquiry was set up to resolve had been caused by the increase in student numbers, which was matched by a rapid decline in the per-capita funding of the enlarged student population. It was deemed by many to be 'expansion on the cheap' in spite of the fact that in the 20 years prior to the Dearing Inquiry public funding for higher education had increased in real terms by 45% (NCIHE, 1997: 11).

For the Committee, one of the purposes of resolving the funding crisis was to bring about further expansion:

> The UK must plan to match the participation rates of other advanced nations: not to do so would weaken the basis of our national competitiveness. Our first conclusion is, therefore, that higher education should resume its growth.

> (NCIHE, 1997: 13–14)

And a rise in the full-time participation rate by young people 'must be envisaged from the present 32% to a national average of 45%, or more'. Accompanying this support for expansion was a commitment to the widening participation agenda:

> Despite the welcome increase in overall participation, there remain groups in the population who are under-represented in higher education, notably those those from socio-economic groups IV to V, people with disabilities and specific ethnic minority groups.
>
> (NCIHE, 1997: 14)

To work towards a resolution of the problem, the Inquiry advocated the policy of providing financial incentives to universities 'which can demonstrate a commitment to widening participation, and have in place a participation strategy, a mechanism for monitoring progress, and provision for review by the governing body of achievement' (NCIHE, 1997: 14).

Both increasing access to, and broadening the social basis of, higher education had been widely supported as a desirable objective long before the Dearing Inquiry reported. What the Committee did was reaffirm a well-established formal commitment that was subsequently underwritten by the reintroduction of means-tested maintenance grants in the 2004 Higher Education Act as an additional public contribution to those under-represented groups who gained university admission. Furthermore, in 2004 the Office for Fair Access (OFFA) was established to ensure that those universities charging variable fees (in fact all of them) devoted a percentage of this income to encouraging a broader social profile in their pattern of applications. The policy drivers have been the promotion of social mobility, the enhancement of social inclusion, and the assumed need of the economy for a more educated workforce. As always, there are questions about the levels of political and economic support and whether all universities are making sufficient progress. However, intrinsic to the understanding of institutional autonomy is that universities have the right to control their own admissions procedures, and along with all other inquiries, the Dearing Report reaffirmed this need to sustain institutional autonomy. If there were to be a compact, therefore, within which higher education evolved it would need to reconcile pressures that pushed in different directions.

Somewhat ironically, although there is no need to doubt the Dearing Committee's commitment to the widening participation agenda, it did suggest that much of the expansion should take place in the colleges of further education and should be below the level of the first degree. Although there is no concrete evidence that the Committee advocated this because it would be both a cheaper form of higher education and help to broaden the social basis of access, it does seem peculiar that it chose to ignore the fact that the big expansion of higher education that had already occurred pointed to the attractions of the undergraduate degree programmes for most of those who wanted to participate in higher education. Indeed, as Parry argues, the overwhelming bulk of the expansion of higher education in England has occurred in the universities rather than the colleges of further education in which recruitment to higher education courses remained static between 1997 and 2010 (Parry, 4 November 2012).

Local and Regional Roles

The historical record would reveal that many English universities were founded as a result of local initiatives. The nineteenth-century redbrick universities were the embodiment of civic pride and even the foundation of the so-called new universities of the 1960s, although their genesis was orchestrated by the UGC, was in each case enabled by a significant local input. Moreover, most of the post-1992 universities were at one time local authority institutions with a student catchment area drawn from nearby neighbourhoods, and often providing courses designed to secure employment in the local labour market. Over time, higher education institutions across the board transcended their local roots and came to badge themselves as national, sometimes even international, institutions.

The Dearing Inquiry wanted higher education institutions to at least replenish their local identities:

> As part of the compact we envisage between higher education and society, each institution should be clear about its mission in relation to local communities and regions.
>
> (NCIHE, 1997: 23)

Again the Inquiry was furthering a cause that was already taking root. Universities were being urged to develop, in addition to undertaking teaching and research, a third mission of providing services for their local communities. The linkage could involve cooperation with local businesses or performing tasks in the local community which aided positive social projects. Resources were provided by the funding council under the auspices of the Higher Education Reach-Out to Business and Community (HEROBC) programme, which was subsequently incorporated into the Higher Education Innovation Fund—HEIF (Tapper, 2007: 156). Higher education institutions were under pressure to demonstrate their direct social and economic benefit to the wider society, which would bolster the case that they provided a public as well as a private good.

CONCLUSION: THE DEARING MODEL OF A HIGHER EDUCATION SYSTEM

Writing in 1998, Robertson evaluated the model of the English system of higher education that would flow from Dearing's Inquiry in the following terms:

By emphasizing the importance of regulation and control over system diversity, the Inquiry has vested greater authority in the hands of a regulatory state and eschewed market-based alliances of providers, service users, and other stakeholders as a means of driving the system.

(Robertson, 1998: 15)

And he went on to conclude that:

The tension between steerage by government action or through the market will not lessen. It is an inescapable fact that diverse systems of any kind work best in the context of markets.... it is the case that negotiated transactions between students and providers invariably lie at the heart of university systems and the introduction of private contributions intensifies this relationship.

(Robertson, 1998: 22–23)

Although the Dearing Inquiry's terms of reference record that its goal was to make recommendations that would guide the 'purposes, shape, structure, size, and funding' of British higher education for the next 20 years, the evidence is that it was entrapped in a contemporary time warp. Rather than attempting to envisage the context which would be shaping higher education over the next 20 years, its thinking was underpinned by the then prevailing image of higher education as a publicly funded system bounded by a relatively narrow interpretation of the idea of the university. It was less a genuflection to the elite stratum of the prevailing university system (as Robertson claims) and more a question of entrapment in a particular interpretation of what should count as higher education. Certainly there could be diversity but it had to be constrained with the individual members of the system having, at least in some measure, shared identities.

Moreover, if the widely held view that the Inquiry's primary purpose was to solve the funding problem, then why would anyone expect it to come up with a wide radical panacea? British higher education had a positive international reputation and the provision of public funding had, by and large, been seen as enhancing its virtues. Moreover, it was part of mainstream political thinking, with strong support in the wider society, that in return for public funding higher education needed to be publicly accountable. As the chapter has argued, the Inquiry's embracing of the regulatory state was but part of a wider development in English higher education that both preceded and followed it. What the Dearing Inquiry did was to reinforce an already present regulatory control model dependent upon government action, the quasi-state, and academic corporatism, while attempting to sustain the impossible idea of British higher education as a system composed of institutions of roughly equal status pursuing broadly similar goals.

Perhaps the most telling criticism of the Dearing Inquiry is that it was too idealistic (or perhaps, naïve) in imagining that a meaningful compact consisting of the government, the universities, and the involved societal interests could be formed to shape the future development of English higher education. At best it could be a compact of unequal partners bound together by very broadly defined commitments, which either had little substantive content or—especially with respect to public funding—could be readily evaded. Subsequently, many of the Dearing recommendations came to fruition, and indeed still impact upon how English higher education functions, but this is not the result of any compact, rather because they have garnered political support which has resulted in government action.

Given that the Inquiry was meant to plan for a model of higher education that was going to emerge over the next 20 years, what pressures should it have identified that would shape the model? Robertson is right to stress the importance of market forces, although it can be argued that the Dearing Report itself helped to augment that pressure by legitimizing the principle that students should make a contribution to underwriting at least some of the costs of their tuition, and, furthermore, by its strong support for an income-contingent loans scheme to enable students to meet those costs. It is obvious that the need for institutions to secure a viable base of fee-paying students will steadily reshape the programmes they offer to prospective students. However, market forces are not only about the pattern of demand generated by fee-paying students but also incorporate institutional entrepreneurialism. Or rather it is perhaps the interaction of the two pressures.

The private sector was taking root at the time the Dearing Inquiry was established and its subsequent expansion has been more than matched by the increased profile of specialist, both privately and publicly funded sector institutions that have been encouraged to seek the university title by the current Coalition Government. The university system has become much more diversified since the Dearing Inquiry reported and, moreover, higher education has also expanded into the colleges of further education, including foundation degree programmes. While the Dearing Committee may be criticized for not foreseeing such developments, it was one of the Inquiry's working principles to constrain too much diversity, and thus it wanted only a parsimonious extension of the university title and for the expansion of higher education in the colleges of further education to be confined to non-degree level courses. The Report may not have given due weight to an expanding pressure upon the prevailing model of higher education, but this may be explained not so much by its failure to predict the future but rather because it wanted to forge the prevailing model into what it believed would be a more coherent and sustainable system.

Besides almost ignoring the rising pressure of market forces, the Inquiry also overestimated the strength of government support for the long-term funding of higher education. For proponents of Dearing's idea of a compact the decision of the Coalition Government to withdraw nearly all the public funding that underwrote the costs of teaching and learning in higher education must come as a bitter blow. Students become customers and degree programmes are commodities to be purchased as a private good. The compact may exist in the sense that government support enables a viable student loans scheme to function, but it is the hallmark of a pragmatic and politically driven relationship between the parties and not one in which government accepts the idea that higher education is a public good that is perhaps worth pursuing as an end in itself. Rather than a compact, what appears to have emerged post-Dearing is a system that functions through the operation of a government-regulated market in which institutions compete for both public funding (most notably in the research assessment exercises) and student fee income (within the context of a government-imposed maximum variable fee, the manipulation of the distribution of student numbers to influence the level at which fees are set, and controls over how such income is to be used).

What market forces—often stimulated by, and acting in conjunction with, government policy—have done since the Dearing Inquiry is to encourage greater diversity within the system of higher education. This has resulted in a range of developments that make it impossible to envisage English higher education as a coherent system, the development of which can be steered by a compact. The Dearing Inquiry wanted higher education institutions to reaffirm their local/regional identities and, while this has occurred, there are some universities that think it is much more important for them to secure a prominent position in the so-called world class league tables. While very few universities would label themselves as 'teaching only' organizations, there are many higher education institutions for which this would be an appropriate label. The question for the future is whether this diversity, to which the Dearing Inquiry paid little more than lip-service, and which has now belatedly arrived, will be matched by a decline in the state regulation and academic corporatism to which It gave such a boost? Or is the English model post-Dearing destined to follow ever more closely its continental counterparts with respect to quasi-government regulation (Neave, 1998), while in terms of funding both England, and perhaps even eventually the continent, follow the path set by the United States?

Part II

The Pressures for Change: Internal and External

4

Universities and Markets: (I) Historical Background and Contemporary Context

Abstract: Much of the contemporary opposition to the politically driven introduction of market forces as a driver of change in higher education seems to assume that this is a very recent development. This chapter argues to the contrary. It illustrates how both the ancient collegiate universities as well as the nineteenth-century civics were heavily dependent upon student fees, private benefactors, and endowment income. Moreover, both models embraced highly vocational ends: Oxbridge serving the interests of the Anglican Church and the civics educating lawyers and medics, as well as many courses being linked to local commercial interests. The period in which the universities basked in the benevolence of public funding was relatively short—between 1945 and 1976 at the longest; and thereafter parsimony has been the rule thanks to periodic economic crises and the funding pressures generated by mass higher education. The apparent recent lurch towards private funding, a shift towards vocationally oriented degree programmes and the decline of academic authority vis-à-vis lay-dominated councils all need to be evaluated in relation to this wider historical context rather than the so-called 'halcyon days' of the post-war years.

INTRODUCTION TO CHAPTERS 4 AND 5

In Chapters 4 and 5 we explore the interaction between universities and the market-place, first historically and then from the perspective of economic theory. And we use the word 'universities' advisedly—rather than, say, 'higher education system'—since the central thesis of this book is that 'the British HE system' no longer exists (indeed, a system we have written about in so many books and articles during the past three decades!). It is not 'British' since devolution has created very different (and still evolving) political attitudes towards how universities should be funded to serve both society and the economy, with HE in Scotland and Wales seemingly on the way to becoming in effect nationalized and being subject to greater state control than ever before. It is not really 'HE' since the mix of institutions and the range of student abilities suggest a better term would be tertiary education (TE), combining all post-18 or post-secondary education whether delivered within further education colleges or within universities. The range of institutions is varied (and even widening)—local, regional, national, and global; yet also they are increasingly collaborating and networked. Most will still remain technically not-for-profit institutions while behaving competitively and entrepreneurially—but, in England, there are also now new profit-making shareholder-owned commercial enterprises. Indeed, an evolution of HE and of universities much as so presciently proposed by Robinson (1968) in talking of the need for a 'comprehensive' vocational post-school TE system focused on the then new polytechnics. This book, however, concentrates on England rather than Britain or the UK and here we find a major shift in the opposite direction to that currently being taken by Scotland and Wales.

As discussed throughout the book, a British and indeed UK HE system emerged in the 1960s as part of the post-war welfare state, notably via the Anderson Report (1960) on student funding offering up the concept of free HE as a public good and then the Robbins Report (1963) on university expansion delivering more of that free HE through institutions located firmly in the public sphere in terms of being publicly funded and being seen as providing a public good. Less than 2% of the age cohort attended university in 1938, 4% by the early 1960s, 9% by 1970, 14% by 1985, and around 45% by 2010. And this remained so through to the 2000s as indeed a 'system' by way of the delivery within theoretically and legally autonomous private charitable chartered or statutory corporations of a quasi-public sector/service. That system is now fading away into history. What was essentially a state-driven or state-steered system is becoming a market-driven series of (possibly overlapping) HE sectors or segments which form an implicitly hierarchical and highly stratified pyramid of over 150 HEIs, operating within an HE market that is state-regulated (but in ways still evolving). The role of the state is being reduced to regulating the HE market as it does for so many other aspects of economic activity which were once state-provided and then fell foul of the neo-liberal agenda (for example, telecommunications, the railways, the energy/water utilities, and most recently the postal service). The early twenty-first-century Zeitgeist is, ideologically, the search for a Smaller and Smarter State—a process also driven by the need to curtail the growth in, and indeed preferably reduce, public spending in the Age of Austerity. Hence the subtitle of the book as 'The Rise of the Regulated Market' and also the interesting issue of exactly what the residual role of the state in HE will be by, say, 2020—perhaps only the funding of whatever is deemed to be strategically important scientific and technical research of supposed benefit to the economy along with the provision of consumer protection for students buying university education from a diverse range of suppliers? And all to be managed by an 'OFTE' (Office for Tertiary Education) in the way that telecommunications, the utilities, and financial services have their regulatory bodies created by government? After all, the use of the word 'Funding' in HEFCE's title is increasingly redundant as it ceases to provide teaching grants to the many HEIs where there is little STEM activity, nor research grant to the very many where the RAE/REF scores are low.

In this first of these two linked chapters, we will briefly explore the early history of the university and then focus more on its twentieth-century evolution, arguing that its enjoyably comfortable years as the recipient of generous state funding during the 1960s and on into the 1970s was just a golden interlude rather than a golden age. This period of donnish dominion within an expanded-elite university system has, however, powerfully conditioned how the university is viewed as an ivory tower preferably to be located firmly on the lofty acropolis rather than, as it usually has been historically and now will again so be, down in the grubby agora. This is a process of change begun by the financial crisis of the mid-1970s and accelerated by the Thatcher Government cuts of 1981 in university funding, as well as one influenced by the trend towards corporatism and managerialism along with marketization and commodification at the expense of collegiality within universities pretty well worldwide. It is one acutely painful to the academic profession which had benefited hugely from a process of producer-capture during the middle decades of the twentieth century of the civic university model once firmly and proudly controlled by its lay-dominated council. We argue that it is important to have some appreciation of this historical background when discussing the state of the university today and speculating on its immediate future, and in terms of assessing whence the various stakeholders are coming as they comment on (and often lament) the current state of the university. In the second of the two chapters exploring 'Universities and Markets' we will consider the conceptual analysis of the government delivery of services as opposed to their provision by the market, along with such ideas as market failure and the residual role of government in correcting for such market failure. Again, we assert that it is helpful when discussing what is happening so acutely in English HE—and indeed not happening to nearly the same degree in, say, Scotland's universities— to have some awareness of the economic theory of market provision as against government delivery of essential services.

In writing this chapter along with the next (indeed the book generally) and thinking about the size, shape, and structure of English HE/TE by 2020, we are well aware that there will be a general election in 2015 and possibly a change of government. Short of an economic miracle, we would be surprised to see England—in the context both of continuing 'austerity' and the need to fund an ageing population as well as also of the steady demise of the Welfare

State—shifting back to low-fee (let alone free) university education in the way that Scotland and Wales (for the moment) are trying to stave off the introduction of higher tuition fees. It is arguable that British HE policy over the past thirty years has been driven mainly by the fortunes of the economy and that governments of various political colours have been forced to respond in much the same way, usually by attempting to reduce or at least slow the growth of public spending on HE.

There has also been the development of mass HE as the Robbins expanded-elite system massified from the mid-1980s (somewhat belatedly by OECD norms), moving from some 15% of 18–21 year-olds being in HE post-Robbins to now around 45%; a process of massification partly the result of a policy stance (or hope) that more HE productively enhanced the nation's stock of human capital and partly a response to the pressure of increased demand for HE as the number of young people staying on at school post-16 expanded (as well as the expectations of the 1960s expanded first generation of graduates being that their children would semi-automatically also benefit from going into HE, a ratchet effect that helps propel OECD nations steadily towards a near-universal and very costly HE participation of approaching 70%). This meant that the cost to the taxpayer, but for successive years of cuts from 1981 (aka 'efficiency savings' during the 1990s), would have become unsustainable even sooner in the context of economic fluctuations, of other competing demands upon public spending, and of a drift towards lower levels of taxation. In fact, very few OECD countries can afford to finance mass HE (no matter how committed they are to it politically) at the unit of resource levels enjoyed by UK HE during its golden interlude that peaked in the late 1960s—perhaps the Nordic nations come nearest.

The introduction in England and Wales from 1999 of £1,000 tuition fees for UK/EU undergraduates and their subsequent ratcheting up to £3,000 and now (for England) £9,000 has been a recognition that squeezing the taxpayer-funded unit of resource was becoming counter-productive if British HE was to remain viable as a global brand, and if the super-elite of world-class universities was not to be tempted to break away from being quasi-public (and as discussed in Chapter 3 concerning the politics of the Dearing Report). It was time for cost-sharing to run alongside taxpayer-retreat, as in an increasing number of other countries (Heller and Callender, 2013), which from 2012–13 has become a cost-shift, with the degree of taxpayer-retreat being almost total in terms of direct funding of undergraduate teaching in English universities by 2015–16 (and also there is the 40% or so reduction in HEFCE funding for capital projects as another element of taxpayer-retreat). There is, therefore, indeed a compelling long-term logic to how English universities have ended up where they are, although the final 2012–13 twist of the almost trebling of tuition fees as a clear policy decision does take English HE into unchartered territory (even if some US state universities are also charging at a similar level as a result of successive seemingly random annual hikes since 2008 rather than an express policy stance on cost-sharing between taxpayer and student: Heller, 2011).

It is unlikely that the political parties will have issued their manifestos for the 2015 general election by the time this book is published, but, in so far as their stances on HE and especially on tuition fees are clear, we hope to be able to indicate in the Conclusion whether the result of that election, which-ever party (or parties) end up forming a government, might mean any radi-cal reversal of the current high tuition fees policy aimed at creating 'an even more diverse sector that is highly responsive to student choice and sensitive to changing demand' (David Willetts, Minister for Universities and Science, in *Times Higher Education*, 22 June 2013: 22). And, whatever may be happening on fees over the next few years, there are real worries that the science budget will be hit as the austerity policy bites deeper, such funding having been fairly well protected so far. An overall cut might, however, be eased for a few uni-versities if it also forces increased selectivity in the allocation of the shrinking cake, a process of concentration which, of course, has already taken place over successive RAE iterations since the late 1980s: this might be the only way the country can compete internationally as other nations enhance the financing of their elite institutions (Palfreyman and Tapper, 2009).

That said, in relation to the likely permanence of high fees, it could be that, potentially, too much and too dramatic market failure as the full impact of England's high-fees experiment becomes clear will mean some reversal of the 2012–13 introduction of tuition fees at up to £9,000 (or at least their freezing at that capped level well beyond 2015–16 as the earliest point at which they may otherwise be allowed—belatedly—to increase in terms of keeping pace with costs-inflation within universities). We are also aware of the much-discussed and even hyped potential for disruptive innovation in the shape of digital learning generally and of Massive Open Online Courses (MOOCs) specifically to impact significantly upon how universities function, some seeing major change ahead while others see just another scare-story about the end of the traditional university operating its annual timetable of three terms with very long summer vacations and with chalk and talk lectures as operational arrangements dating from the beginning of universities in the Middle Ages. Yet MOOCs just might bring salvation in that, combined with the competition of the for-profits, the cost (and price) of HE could perhaps be driven down to sustainable levels (the issue of understanding the cost structure of HE and of cost containment, let alone cost reduction, is discussed in Chapter 5; and that of the possible dramatic impact of MOOCs in Chapter 8; while we address the growth and role of the for-profits in Chapter 11).

At present it seems that any government post-2015, of whatever political persuasion, will have to face up to the escalating cost of the student loans system and the likely high level of non-repayment (estimates have been steadily revised towards 40% or even beyond from an initial 32%—Heller and Callender,

2013; HEPI, May 2012; McGettigan, 2013—and see also the November 2013 NAO Report on 'Student Loan Repayments' (HC818/2013–2014 at www.nao. org.uk) criticizing the BIS over a weak debt collection strategy relating to what will by the early 2040s be a student loan book of some £200m compared to just under £50m in 2013). And the HEPI Report No. 64 on 'The Cost of the Government's Reforms of the Financing of Higher Education – An Update' (December 2013 at www.hepi.ac.uk) pulls no punches in seeing the proposed removal of the cap on UK/EU undergraduate student numbers (announced in the Chancellor's Autumn Statement of 5 December 2013) as posing a real risk to the public finances if HEIs then simply expand unchecked (on top of the already escalating cost of the student loans arrangements to meet the £9,000 fees as in itself creating a future fiscal black hole), unless subsequently either taxpayer funding of HE is increased or 'a cheaper package' emerges for funding HE—instead of relying, as seems to be present policy, on the 'not sustainable' idea that the sale of the student loans book will finance any such limitless expansion (especially limitless if HEIs suck in countless EU applicants), a concept that 'has many of the characteristics of a Ponzi scheme'.

Thus, it may become necessary, in order to get to such 'a cheaper package', in some way, to limit the open-endedness of the student loan arrangements, especially if, in the absence of effective price competition, almost all universities continue to levy fees at the capped maximum. The terms of the borrowing could be adjusted: say, an increased interest rate for some/all graduates and/ or repayments beginning at a lower salary threshold. The amount available per student could be capped at lower than £9,000 for tuition fees per annum, with fees then being reduced or universities having to provide private loans for some and waiving fees for others in the name of needs-blind admission—or universities curtailing their costs to match the loan availability, its maximum being in effect a government/taxpayer voucher towards the annual cost. The overall number of student places eligible for public loans could be rationed, perhaps by setting a minimum A-level or UCAS points score for eligibility for the fees loan regardless of whatever lower points score may suffice for entry to some HEIs (but who decides on what grades in which subjects?). Government financing of research and/or of the teaching subsidy for STEM subjects might have to be reallocated, as might widening-partcipation grants. All such options present major policy dilemmas and risk upsetting the student-graduate/family or the universities, or both (see Barr and Crawford, 2005, for the theory of and history of student loans, and for affirmation of the essential equity and overall fairness of variable fees funded by income-contingent loans as the progressive means of financing HE rather than it being a totally free public good—in addition, see Barr, 2001, chs 12 and 13; along with Barr, 2012, ch. 12). Some of the options also perhaps risk damaging national economic prospects if there really is a direct causal link between the expansion of HE and improved economic growth (as explored in Chapter 5), or if in fact some universities are using the extra income from the £9,000 fees to further cross-subsidize research activity which is perhaps the real driver of HE's contribution to economic development (again, see Chapters 5 and 6 on just what the student is paying for and getting or not getting for his/her—£9,000 tuition fee).

While the government so keenly expected that the charging of the full capped £9,000 tuition fee from 2012–13 would be 'exceptional', as discussed in Chapter 10 almost all HEIs will now be charging this maximum for 2013–14. Thus we are still some way from a real market in HE, or at least one differentiated by price—although perhaps no government would anyway ever permit uncapped UK/EU undergraduate fees, given the potential cost of financing student loans and given also the risk of expensive market failure. Moreover, much as it may irk the government to see the £9,000 as now in practice commonplace (if not almost universal) rather than theoretically exceptional, at least it can perhaps take some solace in that, for some of these HEIs, the £9,000 provides the opportunity for even greater cross-subsidy from teaching income to research expenditure and so, if the research activity of HE is indeed what really matters by way of contribution to the economy (rather than HE simply churning out yet more graduates as a contribution to human capital), there may still be some advantage for the taxpayer and nation in providing the extra loan capital for higher tuition fees—even if a third or more of such loan debt will never be repaid. In addition, at all £9,000 HEIs a proportion—in some cases exceeding £1,000—will find its way, as in effect a tax on the students, into funding the access and widening-participation social equity agenda dear to the hearts of many politicians.

There is, of course, nothing puzzling about why HEIs want to charge £9,000 if they can get away with it within an imperfect market rigged to their advantage, and every reason to do so also because, in the absence of any other reliable mechanism for the student-consumer to detect teaching quality, the high price becomes the proxy for high quality: HE as a Veblen good (Chapter 11 considers the potential for increased regulation of the HE market using competition law). The only puzzle is what happens to the £9,000 (even after allowing for some leakage in support of the HEI's OFFA agreement regarding the financing of widening-participation initiatives) if so little at almost all HEIs is actually spent on the direct provision of undergraduate teaching. This puzzle is all the more perplexing for those many HEIs where the teaching fee income is not cross-subsidizing academics' time on demonstrably high quality research activity, that at least for their graduates thereby enhances the brand-value of the HEI's degrees in terms of such brand-value signalling their greater employability; while (as mentioned above) also hopefully contributing to GDP as well as more widely to the greater good, where such research output actually has any such non-monetary value. In terms of public policy-making—and perhaps even more so than in the funding of schools, hospitals, transport, and so on—there is an impenetrable black-box within HE by way of the actual processes whereby its inputs of student fees are converted into academic and other labour plus infrastructure costs, so as to provide the outputs of employable graduates, applied or pure research, intellectual property exploitation, consultancy, and other community engagement aspects of an HEI's overall activity.

HISTORICAL LESSONS: THE MEDIEVAL AND CIVIC LEGACY; THE GOLDEN INTERLUDE; AND CONTEMPORARY REALITIES

In Anderson (2006: 4) we get a neat history of British universities: the medieval Oxford (emerging in the 1190s) and Cambridge (1210s) were 'essentially vocational and utilitarian'; they both slept through a very long eighteenth century (as indeed did many other institutions, such as London's livery companies and the Inns of Court—Palfreyman, 2010 and 2011) from the Restoration to the Victorian reforms by way of Royal Commissions in the 1850s and 1870s (the device also used to wake up the army, local government, the public schools, the livery companies, the Inns of Court, the civil service—on the relative oddity of Oxford and Cambridge in the development of the European university, see Brock and Curthoys, 1997, ch. 2)—while the Scottish universities did rather better intellectually during the Scottish Enlightenment. In the nineteenth century, University College London (UCL) appeared in 1828 and King's College London (KCL) in 1831; then the civics came along in the 1890s and 1900s as 'the work of local elites with their roots in industry and commerce' (Brock and Curthoys, 1997: 73) and as 'an expression of civic pride' in the great industrial and trading cities of Birmingham, Leeds, Liverpool, Manchester, and Sheffield. They were focused on mining, brewing, metallurgy, textiles, industrial chemistry; and offered part-time degrees from the start to local students (75% of the student body in the 1900s and still 60% by 1950). On the comparable evolution of the US land-grant universities after the 1862 Morrill Land Grant Act (aka the 'A and M' universities that focused on agriculture, mechanics, and mining), see Thelin (2011), Lucas (1994), and Rudolph (1990); noting also the critique of their low-grade technical vocationalism in Flexner (1930) who in contrast praised the English universities, and even more so those of Germany, for being more concerned with higher education. The lay members of the University Council were very much in charge of the English civic universities (compared to the medieval guild of masters as the inmates in charge of the asylums at Oxford and Cambridge)—initially the redbricks' professors were 'simple employees' with limited constitutional authority (Brock and Curthoys, 1997: 79; Moodie and Eustace, 1974: Chapter II). Student fees provided about half their income, with local and central government grants the rest.

Nothing much happened between the wars in the 1920s and 1930s, other than the development of halls of residence as the civics developed Oxbridge airs and graces by way of a 'greater emphasis on the university as a community' (Brock and Curthoys, 1997: 121). Indeed, the limited academic and research ambitions of the redbricks were criticized by Truscot (1943 and 1945). In chapter 4 (entitled 'The Leisured Professor at Bay') of his 1943 volume, Truscot wrote of 'a large number of idle professors' holding 'life appointments for the lazy' and doing nothing once tenure had been secured and they were safely occupying 'one of the softest jobs to be found on the earth's surface' (no wonder, as a Professor of Spanish at Liverpool, he wisely used a pseudonym!). Taxpayer-funded HE expansion was blessed by the 1963 Robbins Report, building on the 1960 Anderson Committee's introduction of student grants: thus 'universities came to be seen as a public service with a strong element of autonomy' (Brock and Curthoys, 1997: 135). The UGC annual block-grant reached 80% of university income by the mid-1960s as fee income fell away to less than 10%. The 1960s plate-glass 'new universities' were dominated managerially by their academics—even if, as with the civics or redbricks, the lay-members were constitutionally and theoretically sovereign. They were national in aspiration rather than local; they were glamorous compared to the gloomy civics of Coketown; they were heavily residential, reflecting a national recruitment of the student body via UCAS (established 1961 as UCCA)—and they were resented by some such as Kingsley Amis as 'more will mean worse'. Across the binary line, the polytechnics also expanded as vocational truly public sector local institutions, owned and controlled by their LEAs. These two parts of the UK HE system were unified in 1992 as the latter became universities, and their directors rapidly morphed into vice-chancellors with suitable ceremonial gowns (and many shiny new maces were commissioned for degree days): the polytechnics keenly ascended from the grubby agora to the ivory tower upon the acropolis (just as the civics had moved away from their routes in vocational and part-time degrees during the 1930s–1950s).

Massification from an expanded-elite system began in the mid-1980s (belatedly by OECD norms: UK full-time undergraduate numbers doubling by the late 1990s from some 400,000 in the mid-1980s and then more than trebling by 2011 as 1.25m was reached), but that brought additional funding problems over and above the 1981 cuts of some 20% overall in UGC funds. At the same time there were pressures from the 1985 Jarratt Report's demands for greater efficiency and from the introduction of the RAE in 1986; there followed the abolition of tenure from 1988, as well as that year's disappearance of the cosy academics-dominated UGC and its replacement by a harsher businessmen-dominated funding council (as discussed in Chapter 1). Anderson (2006: 163) in reaching the 1990s thus sees it as 'State or Market?' with 'the breakup of the post-war consensus on social reform and the role of the state'. When we add in 'consumerist demands' and increased pressure for 'economic functionality' arising from neoliberal ideology (as well as politi-cians' desperation to be thought of as doing something and thereby having at least some means of influencing the economy), it is not surprising that British academics ended up as managed employees as well as becoming an increasingly casualized and depressed 'profession' (Halsey, 1992) as the unit of resource halved and the staff-student ratio doubled, as they became account-able and monitored. And then the 1997 Dearing Report ushered in £1,000 top-up tuition fees for UK/EU undergraduates, which were nudged up to £3,000 as variable fees from 2006 (and that cap duly became £9,000 from 2012). HE had become a private benefit, as an investment good (perhaps also a consumption and consumer good, as well as a positional good) through which students 'improve their earning power rather than their minds' (Anderson, 2006: 184) and hence was now to be paid for by the individual, rather than by society as once it used to be in the belief that there were massive social benefits to HE as a public good (see also Stevens, 2003).

By the 2000s, Anderson sees the universities as firmly located within the market-place: 'That market is partly a real one, in which change will be driven by student demand, and partly a proxy market in which the state pushes the universities in the directions thought desirable by a variety of financial sticks and carrots, backed by audits, targets, and performance indicators' (Anderson, 2006: 185). As Anderson also perceptively comments—and in doing so is, of course, writing prior to the 2011 White Paper with its focus on the student-as-consumer and the resulting 2012 £9,000 fees: 'Whatever the attractions of returning higher education to the marketplace [as in the medi-eval origins of Oxford and Cambridge and as for the origins of the Victorian civics], it is unlikely that any government in an advanced, democratic state will surrender the power to regulate a social institution which is so central not only to economic performance and scientific research, but to the quality of the nation's leadership, the standards and effectiveness of its professions, and its citizens' perceptions of social justice. Such public concern is more rather than less likely as higher education becomes a matter affecting the majority of families' (Anderson, 2006: 188–189). We endorse what Anderson states: HE's undergraduate teaching may no longer be directly funded by the taxpayer as a public service, but its scientific and technological research is still very much state-financed as a hoped-for instrument of economic growth through intellectual property invention, dissemination, and exploitation; and also political reality and caution requires the state to maintain some sort of consumer protection role for the students now to be paying so much for HE (as discussed in Chapter 6). Hence it indeed seems probable that, just as government readily shifts HE from the public sphere to the market-place, it will not abandon HE entirely to the free-market nor rely on the market to be totally self-regulating: too much is at stake, while welcoming the rise of the market, not to also ensure it is a regulated market (albeit not necessarily a manipulated market rigged in favour of the student-consumer or of the university-producer).

The increasing role of government in sponsoring science and technology within HE for fear of national economic decline and/or in the hope of stimulating economic growth goes back to the 1880s (Searle, 2004: 626–635; and in fact such concerns stretched back even into the 1850s—Hoppen, 1998: 304–315), culminating in the 1919 creation of the UGC as a buffer between the Treasury and the universities as taxpayer money flowed into HE, but without the universities being in effect nationalized (Shinn, 1986). The state's granting of money to the universities from 1889 (£15,000) came with strings attached by way of expectations and accountability (Vernon, 2004). It was, however, only as the UGC ended the cosy and benign funding regime of quinquennial stability in the mid-1970s, and then implemented the 1981 cuts selectively across universities before becoming the UFC and later the HEFCE, did institutions begin to feel directly managed by what seemed steadily to be turning into an intrusive agent of government stressing accountability, efficiency, and HE's expected contribution to economic progress (Shattock, 1994). Thus, Belloc's nineteenth-century quaint 'Remote and ineffectual don' (albeit a canny operator in university politics—Cornford, 1908) had by the 1960s at the peak of 'the golden age of the don' (1945–75 as Annan (1990: 509; 1999: 137) sees it) become Munby's respected, needed, and valued 'Don in office, don in power' (serving on Royal Commissions and as the sought-after advisor of government in the meritocracy of the planned economy). And this 1960s dynamic don duly gave way to the modern frazzled 'tenureless' academic, moaning about the worsening staff-student ratio, endless budget cuts, marketization, quality-audit, form-filling, performance indicators, students-as-consumers, and being badly managed by petty incompetents over-promoted away from the lecture room: the dons faced 'rustication from Whitehall' as government had less need of the 'Great and the good' (Paxman, 1990: 183).

The era of donnish dominion had indeed faded into the age of New Public Management (Halsey, 1992; Annan, 1990, ch. 23, 'The Dons Learn Bitter Realities'; and also Annan, 1999, ch. 14, 'Down with Dons'): 'The golden age of the dons vanished into the past. Their buoyancy and self-confidence dwindled…the dons' Pompeii disappeared under the ashes of their hopes' (Annan, 1990: 522). Except, arguably, in the Oxbridge collegial bubble where it was and indeed is still *c*.1965 in terms of resourcing the fiction-portrayed, oak-panelled, and port-soaked academic lifestyle and SCR commensality as duly encountered by readers (and indeed viewers) of *Porterhouse Blue* (Sharpe, 1976) along with the 'Inspector Morse' of Dexter's many crime novels (and now Morse's TV successor in 'Inspector Lewis' as well as the younger Morse shown in *Endeavour*—Carter, 1990; Dougill, 1998). That said, even in Oxbridge the relative purchasing power of the don's salary has sharply declined, despite a deepening interest in fund-raising from the alumni (even for the Fellows of

Porterhouse as they grapple with the real world—Sharpe, 1996). But at least the dons now have the bonus of central heating within the tutors' 'rooms' embedded in the ashlar quadrangles and courts, as well as the benefits of rather better chefs (Tapper and Palfreyman, 2010 and 2011). Yet, amidst this all-too-easily satirized lifestyle, there functions a competitive world-class research university to match the US elite such as Harvard, Stanford, MIT, or Berkeley, while also being an institution that still takes seriously a mission to deploy adequate resources to teach undergraduates properly and hence compete with such US liberal arts colleges as Dartmouth (Palfreyman, 2008).

Perkin chronicles the rise of 'a corporate society' within which there was 'the triumph of the professional ideal'—including for academics the golden age of donnish dominion—followed by 'the backlash against professional society' as the economy faltered and as free-market ideology came to vilify 'the state-supported professions' as 'occupations parasitic upon the wealth-creating private sector' (Perkin, 1989: 472)—the universities and dondom were under attack (Annan, 1990: 516–518). In fact, Jenkins (1995: 154–155) speculates that, in 'taming shrews' as the 'turbulent priests' of academe, Mrs Thatcher may later have felt her government had gone too far in restricting university autonomy through over-centralization. Bogdanor, in assessing Margaret Thatcher's impact upon and legacy to UK HE after her death in April 2013 ('The revolution that wasn't', *Times Higher Education*, 25 April 2013: 44–45), comments that she had appreciated society was changing, producer-oriented corporatism was yielding to consumerism; but there was still a 'disconnect between rhetoric and reality in her approach to higher education' in that she did not take positive steps to encourage for-profit HE provision and market-based tuition fees, and hence her HE policy was 'paradoxical' in speaking of freedom while 'in practice it legitimized a massive centralization of power'.

Certainly, Lady Thatcher in her autobiography (Thatcher, 1993: 598–599) comments that 'by exerting financial pressure' the government 'increased administrative efficiency and provoked overdue rationalization', and so, were the 1981 cuts more triggered by the simple practical need to reduce public expenditure or by an ideological wish to jolt the universities out of their post-prandial slumber having gorged on taxpayer funding for too long? And as she says it indeed led to universities 'developing closer links with business and becoming more entrepreneurial' (Palfreyman, 1989; Clark, 1998, 2004); while the introduction of student loans as a move away from grants, combined with the stress on international student fees as a shift from dependence on UGC grant, led to 'greater sensitivity to the market'. It is acknowledged that all this 'encountered strong political opposition from within universities' (but Oxford's denial of an Honorary Degree is not deemed worthy of mention by Lady Thatcher as merely the dons shaking their puny fists!), while 'other critics' were 'genuinely concerned about the future autonomy and academic integrity of universities'—and she adds: 'I have to concede that these critics had a stronger case than I would have liked'. It had not been intended that there should be 'a philistine subordination of scholarship to the immediate requirements of vocational training': 'That was certainly no part of my kind of Thatcherism'. Hence before leaving office, she started work 'on a scheme to give the leading universities much more independence' as 'a radical decentralization of the whole system'. The Iron Lady was, in fact, rather more of a pragmatist than the usual view of her presiding over an 'ism' would suggest. Moore (2013) asserts that 'Thatcherism' was less a cogent philosophy and instead a mere 'disposition of mind and character'; HE simply got caught up in the political turmoil of the 1980s.

Some would say that these 'leading universities' have suffered from weak leadership and have failed to grasp the opportunity of the freedom hinted at by Lady Thatcher above, and as also much mooted under Blair in the mid-2000s. They have instead unwisely clung on to the apron strings of Nanny State. The Vice-Chancellor of Oxford in his 2012 Oration at Congregation lamented the further retreat of government funding for HE as 'a trend that has caused a great deal of anger, sorrow, and soul-searching'—while also launching plans to up the University's fundraising target from £1.25bn to £3bn and hence conceding that such increased self-sufficiency must be the answer in the context of a broken state. Indeed, the danger of over-dependency on state grants was noted way back in the 1920s when the Asquith Commission on Oxford University saw private benefaction as 'the real hope of prosperity and development for the universities' and when the Canadian academic, Stephen Leacock, warned Oxford that 'the place will not last another two centuries' if it did not 'capture a few millionaires' by giving them 'honorary degrees at a million pounds sterling apiece' (quotations from Harrison, 1994: 644). New College, like several colleges, now offers a special category of 'Wykeham Fellowship' for such generous donors (and still at an entry level of 'only' £1m!). Similarly, back in the 1900s an early text on university management fully appreciated, at least for US universities, the role of such benefactors (Eliot, 1909). However, by the time of the mid-1960s Franks Commission on Oxford, the consensus was that dependency 'on large grants from public funds' was acceptable, and even if it 'inevitably involved' the concomitant degree of 'control' by the (admittedly benign, then academics-dominated) UGC (quotations from Harrison, 1994: 651). This dependency is shown (Harrison, 1994: 679–681) by the fact that of the total income for the university in 1925–26 grants provided 15%, fees 22.5%, and endowment 60%; by 1953–54 the grants percentage had trebled; by 1963–64 fees were down to 12.5% (only climbing back to some 25% by 1980–81 as Oxford belatedly and reluctantly began to charge higher fees to international students, as encouraged by government since the late 1960s: and full-cost fees for such students appeared from the early 1980s).

Yet, while there certainly was direct government pressure for change impacting upon universities, there were also quasi-external pressures operating upon them via their own representative bodies. There was the landmark 1985 Jarratt Report (CVCP, 1985) on the university needing to be managed strategically and with efficiency, and later detailed guidance on the role of the lay governors as they reasserted their historic dominance in university finances and the resourcing of activity (CUC, 1998 and subsequent revisions). A US text (Morris and Hjort, 2012: 2–3) dates the infection of HE globally with the virus of 'the corporate model and the language of new managerialism' back to the Jarratt Report (citing Strathern, 2000). In fact, Green had presciently noted that not only had the much-increased financial dependence upon government funding by the 1960s 'necessarily raised the question of accountability which could in turn have important implications for the universities' cherished autonomy and freedom' (1969: 317)—with 'hints of more rigid supervision and control to come' (1969: 342), but also 'administration' within universities had begun to suffer from 'over-bureaucratization and impersonal relations' as 'a serious threat to academic self-government' (1969: 165)—just as 'lay interference in the universities' since 1945 had 'markedly declined' and 'scholars' control over their own affairs has increased' (1969: 165). Perhaps the golden age of dondom was indeed mere golden interlude, and one not running from 1945 to as late as 1975 or so, but one crumbling at the edges even by the late 1960s (Moodie and Eustace, 1974: Chapter VIII). We discuss in Chapter 5 what the policy drivers were within UK HE from the 1980s that ended donnish dominion and sent the universities cascading down from the acropolis into the agora: mainly the government's varied responses to the many crises within the national economy, but also an element of political neoliberal ideology (although some commentators detect little, in fact, by way of any underlying themes or trends or driving forces, just pragmatic random (even panicky) policy-making on the hoof: Kogan and Hanney, 2000—and, given what we know about the human mind in decision-making mode, this should not perhaps surprise us—see Kahneman, 2011). Moreover, at the end of Chapter 5 we explain just why HE had such weak lobbying capacity against both the Tory cuts of the 1980s and the subsequent 'efficiency-gains', as cuts came to be known in the 1990s and beyond, let alone now in the Era of Austerity as they compete for taxpayer funding with, for example, schools, hospitals, and the police.

In considering where universities are now positioned in relation to the market-place, however, we must note that, until universities drifted into the cosy, benign, and well-funded embrace of the public sphere from the 1950s/1960s, they were always to some degree or other market-oriented and subject to external forces. In, for instance, Rashdall's 1895 magnum opus on the medieval university, it is seen as being distinctly vocation oriented. His timely publication influenced the emergence of the Victorian civic university-colleges as fully-fledged, independent chartered universities in the 1900s (including Imperial) in that 'the whole idea of the vocational university as being in the main-stream of medieval tradition' (Sanderson, 1975: 208) was validated and gave self-confidence to this first wave of new universities. Sanderson adds: 'Indeed "vocationalism" became, like "efficiency", one of the new cult words of this period.' (1975: 209). Thus, Chamberlain in championing the University of Birmingham wrote in 1899: 'we desire to systematize and develop the special training which is required by men in business ... to conduct the great industrial undertakings in the midst of which our work will be done' (Sanderson, 1975: 216). And by 1913–14 of the 3,750 or so students at Birmingham (867), Leeds (663), Liverpool (861), Manchester (1014), and Sheffield (349), some 475 were in 'Pure Science', about 890 in 'Medicine', around 410 in 'Engineering', and *c.*210 in 'Technology'—a little over 50% in all studying what we would today label as 'STEM' subjects; the same was true at UCL, while at KCL the figure was *c.*80% (Sanderson, 1975: 242–243). Whatever they later became by the 1960s, these institutions in the 1900s were not ivory towers. Like the medieval university, they were serving their regional and local economies— just as much as the polytechnics once also did with pride until, after their 1988 release from the LEAs and then becoming universities in 1992, they became private corporations like the chartered universities and so technically and formally left the public sector. But, paradoxically, and like the old universities, most academics employed within them probably wanted to remain within the cosy public sphere and lamented the 1990s (renewed) marketization of HE.

So, a few words about Rashdall (1895, 1936) and what we know about medieval universities thanks mainly to him and more recently Cobban (1988 and 1999), and then onto a brief exploration of the some of the histories of more modern institutions (Chapman, 1955, on Sheffield; Clarkson, 2004, on Queen's Belfast; Ives et al, 2000, on Birmingham; Kelly, 1981, on Liverpool— along with Harrop, 1994; Pullan, 2004, on Manchester; Sanderson, 2002, on UEA), as well as a consideration of how Halsey (1992) portrayed the end of the twentieth century's flirtation with 'donnish dominion'. Hastings Rashdall was an undergraduate member of, and then for some years a tutor at, New College, Oxford, where he will have appreciated William of Wykeham's intention, as the founder in 1379, of creating a vocational institution to produce graduates able to serve church and state. Storey, in Buxton and Williams (1979), writes: 'Wykeham was seemingly less interested in pure scholarship than in the utility of university education as a professional training' (see also Davis, 2007: 4)—although he also wanted a chantry to sing for his soul in perpetuity, as New College does to this day some 635 years later as a choral college. In his text he is clear that, then as now, only a minority of students were there for sheer intellectual endeavour (despite academics, as ever, liking to think of and hope for 'swarms of enthusiastic students eagerly drinking in the wisdom that fell from the lips of famous masters' (Rashdall, 1936, III: 444).

For 'the great mass' university was 'the door to professional life' via the church as 'a synonym for the professions' (Rashdall, 1936, III: 445–446)— men were 'taught to think and to work rather than to enjoy' (Rashdall, 1936, lll: 456); practicality trumped culture and especially via 'the creation, or at least the enormously increased power and importance of the lawyer-class' despite 'the evils which society still owes [as then] to lawyers' (Rashdall, 1936, lll: 457). In fact, the significance of law as a subject was greater in the continental medieval universities than in Oxford and Cambridge, given that the teaching of the common law was concentrated in the London Inns of Court as 'a virtual [third] university' (Rashdall, 1936, lll: 458; see also Palfreyman, 2011). And Rashdall also notes that the medieval university was not a model to be glibly invoked in support of the then current idea and ideal that necessarily 'a university must embrace all faculties' and that 'the great business of a university [should] be liberal as distinct from professional education' (1936, lll: 461). That said, Rashdall makes some very pertinent and prescient comments in relation to our age of digital learning and what that may mean for the traditional university being replaced by the virtual university of MOOCs: a true university will have to bring together 'face to face in living intercourse, teacher and teacher, teacher and student, student and student' given the need for 'personal contact' and 'personal intercommunication' to engender 'life' and 'enthusiasm' in effective teaching (1936, lll: 463).

The vocational nature of the medieval university is also stressed in Cobban (1988): 'The roots of the medieval university phenomenon were formed in utilitarian soil... [as universities aimed at meeting] the careerist ambitions of the age [and adopted] vocational priorities... [while seeing themselves as] service agencies... [since] medieval European society had at its disposal only limited finances for the purposes of higher education... [and expected] returns of a concrete nature... [from these] vocational institutions responding to vocational needs' ('Scare resources were not available for the subsistence of ivory towers'). Thus, at medieval Oxford, the teaching of the 'dictamen' as 'a training in practical subjects that would assist in non-academic areas of employment' met 'the concerns of the business world' (just as does the Saïd Business School today selling its MBA at a fee of £45,000 or so)—and 'an intensive training in business studies could perhaps be compressed into six months or so' (Cobban, 1999: 146–147—the Oxford MBA is now a one-year course). Realists from time to time, and with respect to the modern university, similarly recognize how the vocational often trumps the liberal arts: for example, Bell and Grant, writing when the halcyon days of the university safely located within the public sphere had barely begun to end, dismiss as myth the idea of universities 'as places of pure learning' as opposed to delivering 'vocational preparation' (Bell and Grant, 1973: 52) and as supposedly having 'always concerned themselves with the pursuit of knowledge for its own sake' (Bell and Grant, 1973: 140). They also tellingly comment upon 'how rarely the universities are prepared to use the techniques, of disinterested searching enquiry, often claimed as peculiarly their own, on themselves' (Bell and Grant, 1973: 142).

The university world prior to the era of taxpayer subsidy is described in Chapman where we learn that, astonishingly, at Sheffield in the 1900s a donation of £5,000 gave an individual a seat for life on the lay-dominated council of thirty members—and £10,000 (c £1m in 2013 terms) bought the same for corporate donors (Chapman, 1955: 128). From the history of the University of Birmingham (Ives et al., 2000)—as 'the archetypal campus university' with the civics' iconic clock-tower as found on similar Victorian buildings such as town halls, workhouses, and lunatic asylums—we note illustrations of the general themes and trends discussed above: that the Victorian lay-members were firmly in charge (initially the Council's boardroom was not made available for meetings of the humble professors on the lowly Academic Board, later the Senate!); that its vocationalism meant at the time it was disparagingly labelled by critics as a 'Bread and Butter University' offering 'Graduates in the School of Tariff and Values' (Oxford students came up with the ditty: 'He gets a degree in making jam/At Liverpool and Birmingham'); that in the pre-war History Finals papers 'not more' than nine questions were to be answered within the three hours; that the first budget cuts of 5% came in 1975–76 and those of the early 1980s amounted to a further 17%; that the state provided 39% of university income in 1918–19 and after a surge by the 1960s this had fallen to below that figure by 2000 (33%); that by then Birmingham University was on the way to turning full circle back to being 'a utilitarian knowledge factory' (Ives et al., 2000: 424) once again recognizable to its early founder Josiah Mason and his 1880s 'College for the Study of the Practical Sciences'; that the university recruited almost 55% of its students from maintained schools by the late 1930s compared to only 25% at Oxbridge.

Prior to the emergence in the latter decades of the nineteenth century of such vocational educational institutions as Birmingham's Mason's College or Manchester's Owens College, there was a kind of tertiary or adult education delivered in the Literary and Philosophical Society and later in the Mechanics Institute to be found in most major towns. Here the likes of Davy (Bristol), Dalton (Manchester), and Stephenson (Newcastle) gained and spread utilitarian scientific and technical knowledge to be deployed in furtherance of the industrial revolution gathering pace from the 1780s (Hilton, 2006: 168–174). Similarly, the Royal Institution (RI) began in London in 1799, employing both Davy and Faraday; while the Birmingham Lunar Society flourished in the 1780s with members such as Priestley and Watt. The Royal Society for Encouragement of Arts, Manufactures, and Commerce (RSA) developed from the 1750s with a mission to 'embolden enterprise, enlarge science, refine art, improve our manufacturers, and extend our commerce' and its early members included Adam Smith and Benjamin Franklin. Yet, interestingly, in terms of the ongoing debate over the contribution of higher education to economic development there is barely any mention of this historical expansion of vocational higher education and then specifically of the creation of utilitarian

universities in the later decades of the nineteenth century and the early decades of the twentieth century. A generation of the well-read and well-educated
could be forgiven for thinking that English universities have always occupied
only the acropolis; that Warwick's dangerous liaison with the West Midlands
car industry was just an aberration (as indeed duly portrayed by Thompson,
1971) and all in all that universities have never had any connection with the
market-place or with vocational education.

Incidentally, at what level were tuition fees pitched over the decades of the
last century compared to the current variable fees capped at £9,000? The fee
charged to UK/EU students is now standard for any and all undergraduate
courses at a university, varying between around £6,000 and the full £9,000
charged by a small majority of universities in 2012–13 and by a large majority
for entry in 2014–15 (the average across the range being some £8,250 and hence
rather above the *c.*£7,500 that government hoped would result from market
competition, and with the maximum £9,000—it erroneously predicted—being
levied only by a few institutions...). In the past, tuition fees were varied according to the type of course, presumably reflecting the higher cost of offering science and technology compared to the humanities—and even according to the
year of study (year one being cheaper than for subsequent years). For example,
at the University of Birmingham the fees for 1925–26 were as follows (the
figure in square brackets is the value expressed in 2013 terms): £25 per annum
[*c.*£1,300] for Arts and Science undergraduates, with a few pounds extra for
examinations; but with significantly higher fees for courses costing more to
teach (£32 for Chemistry, £35 for Engineering year one and £62 [*c.*£3,200] in
subsequent years, £37 and £46 for Metallurgy, £42 and £52 for Mining, and
with Medicine at £106 per annum [*c.*£5,500]) and also much lower fees for
Law at under £9 for year one and just over £10 [*c.*£500] in subsequent years.
For 1935–36 the fees were: still at £25 per annum [*c.*£1,500] for Arts and Pure
Science, with Law also unchanged; but those for Applied Science had been
standardized at £40 and £50 (except the 'BSc in Industrial Fermentation' was
cheaper, as was the Diploma in 'Malting and Brewing'). And for 1955–56 they
were: £40 [*c.*£1,000] for Arts or Pure Science, with Applied Science reaching
£52/£61 (Medicine at £60 and Law at only £19).

Thus, the fees structure clearly reflected not only the varying costs of teaching but also across the decades the variable levels of government subsidy, growing by the mid-1950s and hence reducing the burden upon students by way of
fees. By the 1960s, of course, undergraduate education was effectively free for
UK citizens as the state picked up the tab in almost all cases, and began to provide generous grants for living costs; this remained the case until the £1,000
flat-fee 'contribution' was introduced in 1998–99, rising to a capped variable
fee of £3,000 by 2006–07, and then £9,000 from 2012–13. Fees at Sheffield
were not wildly different from those at Birmingham: in 1925–26, the core fee
being £24 compared to £25 per annum, and with a higher fee for certain more

costly subjects; by 1935–36 it was nudging £27 compared to Birmingham still at £25 (and with 'non-British subjects' as 'students from outside the British Empire' paying 'an additional 20%'), and the fee for Engineering, Mining, or Metallurgy at £41; and by the mid-1950s the Arts fee was still just under £27 (much lower than for Birmingham by then at £40) but Pure Science was £35, while Law was a mere £16 and Applied Science £41—but Sheffield's headline figures hid extras by way of a wide range of 'Laboratory Fees' for 'loan of apparatus', 'hire of a microscope', 'maps' (in Geography), 'dissecting instruments', 'cost of breakages', 'locker rent'. And it can probably be assumed that fees were broadly the same at other major redbricks such as Manchester and Liverpool.

In fact, concerning the 'affordability' of these fees at the civics during the decades of the last century, compared to the £1,000/3,000/9,000 in this century so far, the comparison with standard inflation (for instance, £25 in 1935 equals *c.*£1,500 today) is probably not a proper one: there are factors such as overall family wealth and disposable income which mean that £25 perhaps felt to the student/family rather more like the £3,000 of the 2000s, while the Applied Science fees would have been a greater burden than experienced by contemporary students (prior to the £9,000 of 2012–13)—and, of course, all such fees would have been faced without the benefit of a modern universal income-contingent loans scheme to cover tuition fees (let alone also much of the living costs: hence students in the 1920s and 1930s mostly lived at home and commuted into university). It would seem that the civics were indeed conscious of operating within a competitive market for undergraduates: at the University of Birmingham in the 1920s, for instance, the Annual Reports refer to the need to attract more students by offering appropriately high academic standards but not financing better teaching by falling into the trap of ever-increasing academic fees lest that might mean losing applicants to competitors; while over at Sheffield by the mid-1950s the over-complexity of its fees structure was recognized, implying that such opaqueness was unhelpful in recruiting students.

Oxford snobbery concerning the vocationalism of the new civics—all that mining and brewing—was not confined to its independent school undergraduates conjuring up ditties: in 1913, a proposal for a Diploma in Commerce and Economics was killed off since the dons 'did not think it their role to help in keeping Britain ahead of its competitors' (Brock and Curthoys, 2000: 854). The prevailing attitude was as summed up by Dr Spooner, Warden of New College, in the Congregation debate who worried that 'too much of the brains and vigour of the country' might be drawn towards the 'wealth-amassing career of commerce or business' at the expense of 'the more ennobling careers of the clergyman, the student [academic], the man of science, the teacher, the lawyer, the doctor, and even the public servant' (Brock and Curthoys, 2000: 854). In fact, Oxford's PPE degree emerged fairly soon after (from 1920) and, of course, has since become rather popular, eclipsing even Modern History for applications (although now in turn the Engineering, Economics, and Management course, dating from the 1960s, attracts its high numbers). And for a discussion of an even more general academic snobbery prevailing against technological education post-war, see Barnett (2001, ch. 22, 'Education for Industrial Defeat') as well as Wolf (2002); over an even longer timescale for the UK's depressing dysfunctional dichotomy between academic and vocational education, see Hammond, 2013. Wolf makes the telling comment that 'vocational education is for other people's children'—unless, of course, it takes the form of medicine, dentistry, or law at an elite university, when such instrumental degrees, as posh vocationalism, lead to genteel middle-class professions rather than rough working-class trades!

Thus, even by the last decades of the nineteenth century, the vocational institutions such as Owens College from which the civics soon developed were making their mark, and just as even Oxford was experimenting with organizational reforms and new disciplines useful to the Victorian economy's utilitarian needs (albeit not in jam-making), the critics of HE's commercialization and commodification soon appeared. William Morris in 'The Aims of Art' (1886) lamented the perversion of the noble concept and purpose of the university as its leaders, 'the guardians of this beauty and romance so fertile of education, though professedly engaged in "the higher education" (as the futile system of compromises which they follow is nick-named), have ignored it utterly, have made its preservation give way to the presence of commercial exigencies, and are now determined apparently to destroy it altogether' (May Morris, editor, 'The Collected Works of William Morris', London: Longmans Green and Co, 1910–15, Volume XXIII: 85–86). Morris would, of course, be seeking broad liberal education, but in his case with added elements of arts and crafts (perhaps 'Greats with Furniture Making' or 'Natural Sciences with Wallpaper Design').

The rise of the civics as a response to the market forces generated within the new centres of nineteenth-century industrialization is described generally in Sanderson (1972: chs. 3 and 4): 'The vitality of the English civic universities movement thus owed much to its intimate connections and interrelations with industry.' (1972: 120). And it can also be seen specifically from the history of Liverpool University (Kelly, 1981): Liverpool's University College setting up home in a redundant lunatic asylum in 1881 and then occupying its 'redbrick' Victoria building (with clock-tower) from 1892. The University of Liverpool was chartered in 1903, with the lay-members refusing to grant democratic and sovereign decision-making to the academics—one lay-member commenting that 'in order to give confidence to men of business it will be necessary to give power to those who hold the purse' (Kelly, 1981: 130). In 1921–22 some 1,500 of the *c.*2,600 students were drawn from what we would now label Merseyside, and about 65% were studying vocational/professional subjects. The first purpose-built hall of residence (Derby Hall) was funded mainly from donations in the early 1930s. Expansion came in the 1950s/1960s but with adequate funding, so that by the mid-1970s the staff-student ratio was a generous 1:8, with 190 [*sic*] members of the academic staff constituting the sort of unwieldy Senate duly targeted in the Jarratt Report of 1985. Harrop (1994) picks up the story as the university faced 'ten turbulent years' in coping with 'the new policies and demands of a hostile government'—starting with the July 1981 UGC cuts letter taking the complacent HE sector by surprise. In fact, the arrogant universities had ignored the plea from Shirley Williams in her mid-1970s letter as Education Minister for them to consider 'thirteen points' of potential economies and certainly there had been some budget reductions since the mid-1970s: Palfreyman's first task as a new administrator at Liverpool in 1976 was to plan a 5% cut in the funding of the Centre for Latin American Studies; while at Warwick during the 1980s it was rather more fun at 'the entrepreneurial university' where making money eliminated the need for dreary economies (Palfreyman, 1989). By the mid-1980s the University of Liverpool was seen, relative to the 1960s new universities, to be one of the sleeping-giant civics, smugly drifting in a time warp: 'fundamental change' and 'a wholly new world' beckoned as the recommendations of the influential Jarratt Report (1985) had indeed 'fallen on fertile ground' with the new VC embracing the Jarratt CEO role very successfully—and, as the economies bit deeper, even the Senior Common Room was closed as an economy in 1986, amidst academics complaining that without such an informal meeting place 'social fragmentation' was 'positively and rapidly worsening our power to withstand the current challenges [and] external attack' (Harrop, 1994: 75–76). The university 'had become a fragmented collection of scholars rather than a community' (Harrop, 1994: 77), and a pre-1980s collegial process of working to a consensus ('which could be stultifying' where 'selfish' and 'largely autonomous' members 'rarely took a university view') became the managed university of the 1990s; a change not lamented by all, for some at Liverpool welcomed innovation and a reawakening.

Meanwhile, a few miles away over in Manchester, another of the great sleeping-giant civics was also being transformed in the 1980s, having lived off its 1920s/1930s intellectual reputation for rather too long even if Manchester did pretty well in the first RAE of the mid-1980s. Pullan tells the story: 'endless talk of income generation and savings targets' began with the 1981 cuts (2004: 187) and were reinforced by the strictures of the 1985 Jarratt Report that (quoted in its words) 'universities are first and foremost corporate enterprises to which subsidiary units and individual academics are responsible and accountable' (Pullan, 2004: 218)—it being left to the newly created senior management teams led by the CEO-VC to tell the Howard Kirks of academe (Bradbury, 1975) that things had moved on. Taxpayer subsidy fell from almost 80% of university income in the mid-1970s to 50% by the late 1990s (Pullan, 2004: 322) and the SSR of 1:8 became 1:20 'or even, in some parts of the university, 1:30' (Pullan, 2004: 295)—this worsening SSR, combined with the pursuit of the cash and kudos of research, meant undergraduate teaching was neglected. Yet the pessimistic view of such changes was not shared by a younger generation of academics who were 'inclined to despise their elders for complaining so loudly and refusing, like a species destined for extinction, to adapt to change' (Pullan, 2004: 298). For another civic, across the Irish Sea from Liverpool, see Clarkson (2004) on Queen's University Belfast (QUB) where a similar story of fluctuating state largesse between 1945 and 2000 unfolds in ch. 4, entitled 'Who pays?'—government grants providing some two-thirds of total income just after the war, peaking at eight-tenths by the early 1970s, and falling off to less than half by the mid-1990s; and the UGC operating 'with the lightest of touches' giving way to the interference of the UFC and 'a trek through a trail of bureaucracy with no assurance of a pot of gold at the end' (Clarkson, 2004: 51). Clarkson also notes that 'at the beginning of the 1950s more than 60% of [QUB] students had no financial support beyond what their families gave them'—only after the Anderson Report of 1960 did UK HE become a free public good.

So, were the 1980s less traumatic at the 1960s new universities compared to the 1900s civics? Certainly Warwick University personified a different entrepreneurial and zesty style, but others like Sussex slipped off the pedestal of being 'Balliol-by-the-Sea' as competition increased, while UEA (Sanderson, 2002) 'showed a resilient and sustained morale' as it dealt with a 12% cut in the early 1980s and its SSR of 1:13 slid to *c.*1:20 by the 1990s. And Sanderson is realistic in noting that UK HE was high-cost compared to other nations and also to the resourcing of schools ('some rebalancing could be justified')—as well as there being 'little evidence' that HE expansion had done much for the economy and the ideological factor of attacking what were seen by many as 'under-employed, self-seeking, inefficient academics' (Sanderson, 2002: 303–304). In fact, Sanderson calls for what is now coming to pass some ten years after he wrote: 'freedom to charge fees' and 'set up a genuine market', removing 'the humbug that all universities are supposed to be excellent in every way, and the even greater humbug that an expensive state bureaucracy can enforce it so' (Sanderson, 2002: 414). Thus, says Sanderson, 'free market arguments are not as outlandish as one may suppose' (he also perceptively asks whether, anyway, the traditional bricks and mortar university is not threatened by digital learning). Yet, as Shattock (2012: 168) comments, the state has difficulty in allowing a free market within HE: while British universities have had a theoretical legal freedom as autonomous private corporations to charge tuition fees (and have indeed profitably, indeed enthusiastically, exercised that right in relation to postgraduate courses and international students as two lucrative markets since the early 1980s), in relation to their main chunk of business activity in teaching UK (and later EU) undergraduate students 'between 1945 and 2004 fees were controlled and manipulated by the state and, since 2004, when the costs of the higher education system in effect outweighed the ability of the state to cover them, they were hedged around with maxima and moderating provisions which severely limited managerial autonomy'—'In no area of policy has the state more consistently abrogated to itself key decision-making powers...'.

The case studies of individual English universities, therefore, neatly illustrate the themes and trends discussed earlier. As do some bald statistics (Carpentier, 2012: 368): in the early 1920s, UK universities' income was 35% student tuition fees and 45% public funding (UGC and local government grants)—the remaining 20% was endowment income; the former fell away to a low of 5% by the early 1970s when the latter reached almost 90%; grant-funding by the mid-2000s had fallen back to 45% with fees then at 30% (cf fees at 30% and grant at 40% in the USA; and 10%–85% in France). The 2012–13 new fees regime will by 2015 see fee income in English universities increased dramatically and the grant subsidy of UK/EU undergraduates largely phased out, so that an HEI with little by way of teaching in the STEM subjects and a weak RAE/REF performance will receive almost no public funding (while the fees–grant balance will also shift even more towards fees in the USA, and—who knows—one day even the French may have to introduce serious levels of tuition fees as they deal with their public sector deficits: across Europe generally the average income from student fees and charges is less than 10% at present...).

And, of course, the numbers vary widely at institutional level: in 2010–11 the London School of Economics (LSE) had only 15% of public taxpayer funding via HEFCE grant plus UK research councils, since its income from fees was over £100m (with that from its international student fees at some £70m) in a turnover of £234m; at Cambridge the figure was 25%, where research income from non-government sources is very high (as well as having substantial endowment income); Oxford, Manchester, KCL, and UCL all hover around the 40% mark while Imperial College London and Bristol reach *c.*45% (*Times Higher Education*, 18 October 2012: 9—based on the HEFCE recurrent grant data). Shattock (2012: 12) shows fee income as 32.5% for universities in 1935–38 and falling to 17.7% by 1949–50 as UGC grant surged from 34.3% to 63.9% (the redbricks had more than doubled their student numbers between 1945 and 1950, following calls for the number of scientists to be doubled—Harrison, 1994: 187); UGC grant reached 75% in 1960–61 as fees dipped below 10%; and then the unit of resource (public funding per student per annum) drops from a base of 100 in 1976 to under 60 by 1995 as the public spending cuts hit HE and the golden age ended (Harrison, 1994: 131). UK HE financial data for 2011–12 shows funding councils provide 30% (and falling as fees increase) of total income at £28bn, UK/EU fees 25% (and growing), international students 10%, research grants/contracts 15%, and miscellaneous (including endowment income at a few HEIs) 20%. HEIs spend some £27bn, 30% on academic staff and 25% on other staff. The 24 Russell Group universities bag about 45% of all income, including 75% of research income—and just five HEIs (Oxford, ICL, Cambridge, UCL, and Manchester in that order) secure some £1.5bn of the £4.5bn for research grants/contracts.

There have not so far within this chapter been many references to Halsey's 'Decline of Donnish Dominion: The British Academic Professions in the Twentieth Century' (1992) and it is important to now say a little more about this seminal text. The post-war HE expansion (albeit limited by OECD norms) was just too costly in terms of the hyper-generous staff-student ratio (SSR) to be sustainable and especially as the economy faltered, let alone whether or not the idea of ever-more HE became challengeable in the public mind and whether there were neoliberal ideological concerns over HE having in effect become an inefficient nationalized industry. The SSR is, of course, a crude measure, since the quantum of undergraduate teaching depends also on just how much teaching is done as opposed to time spent on research (probably only around 25% of academic time on the former at the research-focused HEIs while more than double that at others): it was around 1:10–11 in the 1920s/1930s, perhaps 1:7–8 by the 1950s/1960s, and 1:18.5 or so now. Along the way, the academic profession 'may have dug its own grave': as it expanded and ended up with 'a trend towards proletarianization'; as 'donnish power' gave way to 'a loss of status and the deterioration of working conditions' in the context of the state trying to cope with economic decline while also growing HE numbers; as 'managerialism' squeezed out 'collegiate cooperation'; as 'explicit vocationalism' displaced 'implicit vocational preparation'; as an enhanced and steeper stratification or hierarchy of the institutions emerged within the HE system, along with a developing segmentation within the HE pyramid; as the academic enterprise fragmented. Thus, Halsey sees the outlook (in the early 1990s) as 'bleak' for HE, admittedly 'expensive', in the face of a 'conspicuously aggressive' attack 'on the basis of dogmatic preference for market solutions' and to which HE responds only with 'bewilderment' tinged with 'deep bitterness'. In fact, some twenty years on from Halsey writing in the early 1990s, little has really changed for Oxford and Cambridge since the halcyon days, at least in terms of resourcing the privileged Oxbridge bubble as already noted; and indeed the latest fees increase to the new cap of £9,000 pumps more money into the elite universities which also benefit strongly from the increased selectivity of research funding. The key issue remains, however, in terms of the financing of mass HE delivered largely within what amounts to the many teaching-only universities how that cost is to be shared between taxpayer and student/family; and also whether in the process there is a noble academic profession or merely a casualized academic labour force (indeed proletariat).

Just as Halsey tracks the rise (post-1945) and fall (post-1975) of donnish dominion, so Rothblatt (in Collini et al., 2000: ch. 10: 'State and Market in British University History') warns against thinking that the 1980s, by introducing the concept of market forces into HE 'rudely shattered' a 'largely benign' long-term historic relationship between the state and universities. In fact, the very benign era of government intervention since 1945 until *c*.1975 had 'effectively postponed critical discussion of the role which markets played' in HE. We have seen how the medieval university was vocational and responsive to its market; Rothblatt argues that English HE development in the nineteenth century also involved market forces, and indeed that even the unreformed Oxbridge colleges had a range of 'market factors' operating upon and within them. Thus, the issue of 'market-related higher education' surrounded the emergence of the University of London in the earlier part of the century, when there was in addition an extensive 'educational consumer culture'; and the pattern was repeated for the civics from the 1880s as well as Scotland long having a 'market-related university system'. The reformed Oxford and Cambridge, along with the growing University of London (UCL, then KCL), served a market demand 'for quality education' from the Victorian middle-classes—and later the civics supplied science and technology higher education as vocational and professional credentialism. The post-war welfare settlement and consensus, interventionist and collectivist, left the state as 'the sole buyer of university services' until, to the inconvenience of the producer-oriented academic profession, the neoliberal ideologues and the economic realities of the 1980s unveiled a new state–universities–markets relationship (one which may be now settling down as the state's role within a regulated HE market becomes clearer in the 2010s).

And, while the decline of donnish dominion may still be firmly lodged within the folk memory of older academics, times have moved on: in the press coverage of Lady Thatcher's death and political legacy, for instance, during the week of 8 April 2013 there was almost no mention of the Thatcherite impact upon the universities and the brief item on the 'Thatcher legacy' in *Times Higher Education* (11 April, 2013: 7) contained only the usual superficial and trite comments along the lines of 'an unmitigated disaster for universities' leaving behind 'a disillusioned workforce as staff morale collapsed' (a more considered assessment from Bogdanor appeared a week later, as already referred to previously). In the more general extensive coverage on the Thatcher legacy and years we were, however, reminded that Marquand had wisely pointed out that for Mrs Thatcher and her interpretation of the neoliberal ideology: 'It was the disciplines of the marketplace that attracted her, not its freedoms.' For UK HE, the 1980s were about an inevitable and painful adjustment from being generously (and perhaps over-) funded during the golden interlude of 1945–75; while the 1990s/2000s were about dealing with massification.

The current phase in the 2010s is about determining whether politicians really mean to move towards a free market (and, if so, exactly how universities will respond) or in practice are still using the market to impose discipline upon a quasi-public sector and on a collective of supposedly autonomous entities behaving like nationalized utilities. The former seems too bold a sce-nario and, involving (as it should for markets to work properly) the occasional market failure in the form of insolvent HEIs and their distraught students/employees, would probably give rise anyway to government intervention; the latter scenario propels English HE towards the rise of the regulated market. Arguably, towards greater institutional autonomy, albeit to be exercised within the context of a regulated market-place (especially as UK/EU undergraduate numbers are soon to be uncapped, and perhaps even the tuition fees they are charged). Does this represent a possible shift back to markets exercising control over universities rather than governments? Acting through the channels of the provider-state, governments were increasingly benign after the Second World War until the Welfare State consensus became unaffordable in the face of 1970s economic decline, and was then further challenged by the rise of the neolib-eral political agenda. Baatz (2013) analyses the history of English universities from 1852–2012 in terms of 'From Freedom to Control' but for us the shifts are more complex: from market freedom to steadily more benign public provision but accompanied by intensifying government steering, and now onto a possible return to market freedom by 2020? We turn in Chapter 5 from the history of markets in HE to the theory of markets in HE.

5

Universities and Markets:
(II) Theory and Critical Debate

Abstract: While accepting the fact that the main reason for the move towards charging students at English universities full-cost fees was economic (that is the decision of different governments to lessen the reliance of English higher education upon the public purse), this chapter also explores the neoliberal thinking behind the policy. There are two particularly important themes: higher education is a private, as well as a public, good and thus it is only fair that its advantaged recipients should bear at least some of the costs of its provision, and universities will take their teaching responsibilities more seriously if they find themselves in a market context in which students start to act like rational consumers. In the process of exploring the issues, the chapter draws upon comparative national examples of requiring students to pay fees. While there has been a widespread global move in this direction, there is no evidence to demonstrate what (if any) the ideal balance for higher education should be in terms of public or private funding. This is a matter resolved by a combination of political struggle and economic necessity. While broadly conceding that mass higher education systems are likely to be at least in part privately funded, the chapter points to the possibility of market failures and thus the need for state regulation to guard against the potential negative outcomes of marketization.

In this second of two linked chapters, we consider the economic theory of the relationship between universities and the market-place. Capitalism has largely eclipsed the other options of communism, socialism, and fascism over the past half-century to become the globally dominant form of economic organization, and it mainly operates alongside democracy as well as a commitment to individual freedom within the rule of law. The difficult tension is in balancing such individual freedom and also the appropriate degree of market freedom against a desirable and appropriate element of collective action and of regulation so as to achieve social justice where unrestricted capitalist competition would prove unpalatable within a democratic society; the problem is that such political, bureaucratic, and legal regulatory intervention 'creates incentives for circumvention and corruption' (Meltzer, 2012: ch. 2). Over-regulation dampens market dynamism and depresses economic growth: in the more stridently capitalist USA, the annual growth rate exceeded 3% in the 1980s and 1990s, compared to the UK at *c.*2.5% as it deregulated and denationalized so as to move on from 1960s/1970s Welfare State corporatism, and as compared to France or Italy at, respectively, 1.9% and 1.4% in the 1990s, as they 'made the political choice of more welfare spending, less work, and higher unemployment' (Meltzer, 2012: 50–51). But ill-considered and excessive deregulation can, of course, exacerbate market failure, as with investment banking during the 2000s in the US and UK (Posner, 2009; Davies, 2010; Palfreyman, 2010: 74–88).

While 'The Market System' (Lindblom, 2001) may be ascendant, it will always have its persistent inefficiencies, its inevitable failures, and its occasional crises: it is imperfect, but the least imperfect of the available options (Kay, 2003). There may once have been utopian expectations of the ability of government to manage the economy which have been shattered with the collapse of communism (Brown, 2009), but equally there have been, and still are, many economists and politicians with utopian perspectives on the power and efficacy of markets (Cassidy, 2009). If Brown traces the rise and fall of communism, Cassidy does the same for the extreme evangelical faith in free market ideology and excessive deregulation as 'the Greenspan Bubble Era' popped in 2007. Thus, we are left, as ever, with having to decide what the market can realistically be relied upon to provide (with some risk of market failure which might be limited by an element of government regulation) as opposed to what government has to provide (with some risk of government inefficiency in doing so) because the market cannot or will not supply such goods and services. It may be that over the past three decades or so there has been too great a shift—or a drift—from 'a market economy' to 'a market society' so that 'the moral and civic goods that markets do not honour and money cannot buy' have been neglected in the context of an over-emphasis on 'market values'; and that 'the era of market triumphalism' may in fact be ending as society asks 'whether there are some things money should not buy' because 'some of the good things in life are corrupted or degraded if turned into commodities' (Sandel, 2012; see also Brown and Jacobs, 2008, on the need to achieve 'the best balance' between market and government delivery of healthcare, education, and transport). Moreover, moving from the general to the particular, the entity usually charged with delivering goods and service via the market—the firm, company, or corporation—is alleged to be increasingly failing in its duty to society because of faults within its governance structure (Mayer, 2013).

Stiglitz is, like Sandel (2012), critical of markets as neither efficient nor stable if left entirely free and totally unregulated; he laments 'flawed economic policies' that are 'based on flawed economic theories and ideology' and that 'exacerbate inequality' (especially in the USA and, now increasingly also in the UK): 'markets must once again be tamed and tempered' (Stiglitz, 2013: xlii) and government must correct market failures along with egregious rent-seeking behaviour. The US student loans policy is, argues Stiglitz, an instance of such market failure in that because such loans are non-dischargeable in bankruptcy this has 'meant that lenders had little incentive to see to it that the schools [HEIs] for which the students were borrowing money were actually providing them with an education that would enhance their income' (Stiglitz, 2013: 118, and see also: 244–246). This implies, of course, that within US HE there is also market failure in the supply of for-profit HE as well as government failure in allowing the provision of poor quality public HE. In addition, it seems odd that the task of quality control for the HE industry should be pinned on these third-party lenders rather than on the HEIs themselves, along with their HE collective 'trade' bodies and/or on government agencies with a consumer protection duty. Gingrich (2011: 49–50) explains 'this puzzling rise of markets' since the 1980s as a way for politicians 'to challenge incumbent producers' in the context of economic constraints.

So, where does this leave universities and the provision of higher education? It leaves HE where hospitals and healthcare, schools, and local government services are—that is, caught up in the continuing political battle between the neoliberal ideology and the survival of the Keynesian Welfare State. The Welfare State was rooted in the nineteenth-century ideas of the British Fabians and Bismarck's Prussia, developed via Lloyd George's Liberal Party introducing health insurance and pensions in the 1900s, and then notably through the all-party consensus on the social security recommendations of the Beveridge Report of the mid-1940s (Ryan 2012: 900–905, and Timmins, 2001; on the economics of the Welfare State see Barr, 2001 and 2012—and on why the Welfare State never took root in the USA compared to Europe see Prasad, 2012). The Welfare State was (is) certainly not socialism, but it was a clear step within a capitalist economy beyond the liberal night-watchman state and its emphasis on market relations and individual self-reliance; and it needed (needs) 'not only generalized benevolence to sustain it but an expanded sense of social justice' (Ryan, 2012: 900–905). There has indeed to be a political consensus about the state being the only and/or the best way to provide certain key aspects of a citizen's legitimate needs. But our concern is narrower: what is the possibility of such a consensus as to the role of the state or of the market, or of the balance of each, in the early decades of the twenty-first century, in the provision of HE within England in terms of doing so with economic efficiency, at an affordable cost to taxpayer and/or student, and paying due attention to social justice by way of access and widening participation?

The neoliberal agenda sees privatization, competition, deregulation, liberalization, commercialization, corporatization, and marketization as a way of pepping up sleepy monopolistic public services suffering from producer-capture through the rent-seeking behaviour of academics, doctors, teachers—if not in fact replacing them with cheaper and more innovative private sector provision, as a means of engendering entrepreneurialism and accountability (Steger and Roy, 2010; Ward, 2012). The neoliberal agenda, however, has had and still has (perhaps increasingly has) its trenchant critics in terms of its limitations (Crouch, 2011; Mirowski, 2013). If neoliberalism became the dominant global economic paradigm by the 1990s, the financial crisis of 2008 onwards might, arguably, have seen off any unquestioned faith in free market economics and reliance on the supposedly self-regulating market. Yet this has not really happened—much as Crouch hopes that the neoliberalism model 'is wearing out' and calls for a renewed stress on the need 'to embrace collective and public goods' (2011: 180), expecting salvation in the same way that the gigantic market failure of the 1930s Great Depression led to the post-war Beveridge Welfare State and Keynesian economic consensus over government intervention, so ushering in the 1945–1975 golden age of controlled capitalism and of 'big government'. Indeed, the 1980s alleged ideological undermining of the Welfare State might have been more a fuzzy combination of a simple and desperate search for savings in public spending (as now again underway with 'austerity') and a political attack on post-war corporatism as a clunky process that put too much faith in the efficacy of large-scale state planning and government intervention, encouraging the monopolistic nationalized industry and cartel over the interests of the citizen-consumer.

Thus, despite clear market failure of recent years in banking and financial services, we still have the market reforms of HE that are the theme of this book and also there is, for instance, the 2012 Health and Social Care Act which is engendering greater private sector competition and marketization within the National Health Service (NHS). Even activity not within the public sector can be liberalized and deregulated by similar legislation (as with the now-emerging results of the Legal Services Act 2007—Palfreyman, 2011: ch. 7)—although, so far, the radical revamping of English HE by way of the 2010 Browne Report and the 2011 White Paper, leading to the 2012–13 £9,000 fees cap, has not needed a new Higher Education Act (see Callender and Scott, 2013, on the historical context, political responses, and future impact relating to the Browne Report; and Chapter 11 for discussion of competition law in terms of HE regulation, along with Chapter 6 regarding the impact of consumer law upon HE). The beginning of the trend to place the idea of the market at the forefront of the debate on the provision of education dates from Friedman (1962), but there has long been recognition that it is often an imperfect choice between the risk of market failure and the dangers of government intervention (Wolf, 1993)—as well as being a long and crude 'search for alternative ways to pay for higher education', culminating in the 2011 White Paper and the 2012–13 £9,000 fees cap as in effect 'the denationalization of higher education in England' (Shattock, as ch. 2 of Callender and Scott, 2013). The issue then becomes whether HE is a service better provided by government, even if with bureaucratic inefficiencies; or by the market, even if with the risk of market failure—and, if by the market, what to do about social equity in terms of access and widening participation (Tapper and Palfreyman, 2005). At one extreme, some would simply terminate the taxpayer's '£14.3 billion annual subsidy' of HE, and also end the 'suppressing, distorting and capping of tuition fees' as having 'perverse and unintended consequences' by interfering with price signals within the HE market (Stanfield, 2009). At the other extreme, some would return to free (or at worst low-fee) HE as an adequately funded vital public service (see, for instance, McGettigan, 2013—and for 'an economic critique of marketization of higher education' and of 'the idea of profit-making by universities' as being simply 'a step too far', see Williams as ch. 4 in Callender and Scott, 2013); while Watson (2013) provides an interesting 'take' on what HE is all about, in terms of both its historical evolution and also the current wide-ranging social, political, cultural, and economic expectations of it.

The contest, then, is between HE as a public sphere activity (Pusser et al., 2012) and one where HE is commodified, commercialized, and corporatized; with managerialism replacing collegiality as its governance style (Tapper and Palfreyman, 2010 and 2011) and also the student becoming a consumer or customer in terms of just what is to be 'the student experience' (Kandiko and Weyers, 2013), as well as what it all may mean for the academic profession and others employed in HE (Watson, 2009; Gordon and Whitchurch, 2010; Trowler et al, 2012; Barcan, 2013; Whitchurch, 2013). The focus of (and probably the only matter of real concern to) government is then on the contribution of HE to 'the knowledge economy' (Temple, 2012), notably through intellectual property creation and its exploitation—sometimes via international collaboration and partnerships (Anderson and Steneck, 2011; Sakamoto and Chapman, 2011), along with global organizations (Bassett and Maldonado-Maldonado, 2009). Government will also be interested in the links of universities to the local region or community (Pinheiro et al., 2012; Watson, 2007; Watson et al., 2011). Thus, the stress will be on the economic contribution of the university in relation to all the other possible futures for the university in the twenty-first century (Barnett, 2012), and in contrast to the (really fairly recent) traditional concept of the university as an ivory tower focused on the disinterested creation and transmission of knowledge.

Just three of many examples lamenting the halcyon days of the ivory tower and of Donnish Dominion within it are: Hussey and Smith, 2010; Docherty, 2011; and Collini, 2012. Collini (2012) stresses the 'intellectual, educational, scientific, and cultural' value of the university as 'a public good' in contrast to the way 'successive governments, of whichever party, have attempted to impose an increasingly economistic agenda on universities over the past two decades'. Docherty (2011) views the ratcheting up of tuition fees and the present, almost total withdrawal of direct taxpayer grants to universities for undergraduate teaching as 'an attack on the fundamental principle that the university exists as a key constituent in the public sphere'. Hussey and Smith (2010), rather more realistically, note 'the debased educational experience that many students now suffer' and its 'often doubtful quality', regretting that liberal education (Ryan, 1998—and way back to Turnbull (1742) and Baldwin and Palfreyman (1547) as discussed in Palfreyman, 2008: 13–20) as the purest form of higher education is simply not affordable for all in the context of a mass tertiary and vocational education system. They also note 'a mycelium of managers' as indeed an entirely legitimate comment on administrative bloat within British HE, as also in US HE (Ginsberg, 2011). Neild (2012), for example, notes that 'the growth of bureaucracy' at Cambridge has almost doubled its cost to 7% of turnover compared to two decades ago.

And thus government also becomes fixated about the accountability of the HE system (Stensaker and Harvey, 2011) and with quality control inside HE (Land and Gordon, 2013), as well as with the financing of students through HE (Heller and Callender, 2013). It is enmeshed in the detail of the governance, management, and accountability of individual universities (Shattock, 2006; Huisman, 2009; Farrington and Palfreyman, 2012: chs 4, 5, 6). Not that British universities have generated much by way of crises through sloppy management (Warner and Palfreyman, 2003). Governments may even be keen to create global, world-class, elite institutions or at least to hang on to the ones already within the national system (Palfreyman and Tapper, 2009). The attentive reader will note that the themes and trends of neoliberalism and economic *laissez-faire*, of managerialism and accountability are pretty well global issues affecting to some degree or other HE within most countries and thereby demonstrating the globalization of HE. They are not merely a matter of something going on within English HE (see, for instance, Amaral et al. (2009) and Gornitzka et al. (2005) on HE reform and change elsewhere in the EU and within the Bologna Process nations, and also King et al. (2011) for a truly global range of case-studies). What is unique about England is that the level of tuition fees charged from 2012–13 for undergraduate education in almost all of its universities does stand it apart in terms of the cost to the student from all but some US flagship public institutions, and the US private not-for-profit universities and colleges.

Similarly, the reader encountering material regretting the university being reduced to an engine (as successive governments have hoped) of economic growth and lamenting the commodification of HE will perhaps wonder why it has taken until very recently for such protests to emerge (notably the 2012 launch of the Council for the Defence of British Universities, CDBU) when, in fact, the impact of the declining unit of resource has been felt since at least the 1990s, having been halved by 2000 compared to 1980 and the staff-student ratio almost doubling. It is as if such critics have been insulated within

Oxbridge bubbles (where indeed the unit of resource and the staff-student ratio has remained untouched since the golden interlude of the 1960s, thanks to the availability of endowment assets and, it has to be said, the energy and entrepreneurship of colleges in marketing themselves as conference venues and even as tourist attractions). These elitist Rip Van Winkel dons (especially in the Humanities as a subject area feeling particularly beleaguered at present, even within Oxbridge) have seemingly woken up and discovered just how far standards have slipped as massification has occurred within the HE system and so much of HE has been reduced to vocational training; they now seek presumably, and somewhat belatedly, to wind the clock back by thirty years or so.

They call, in vain, for what?—for enhanced public funding of teaching, for higher standards in degree examining, for a return to donnish dominion, for all the UK's 150 or so universities to be funded as if their academics were really research-active? The CDBU manifesto is vague when it comes to actions as opposed to lamentations. They are, sadly perhaps, not to be taken seriously in terms of HE (or indeed TE) policy-making for 2020 and beyond. They cannot possibly expect a mass HE system to be funded at the same level of unit of resource as an expanded elite system of 40 years ago that educated only a privileged few—perhaps only Norway, with oil money and a small population, could afford to do so. They are confusing the research-oriented elite institutions concerned with perpetuating the academic clerisy (and, as a by-product, producing well-paid bankers and lawyers) with the real-world HE undertaken in what are in all-but-name teaching-only universities (as analysed in the RAE data discussed in Chapter 7). There is a need to move on and recognize the now highly stratified nature of these 150 or so HEIs and the arrival of the new kids on the block in the shape of the unashamedly teaching-only, for-profit suppliers of HE (see Chapter 11).

In fact, Robbins appreciated way back in 1980, in reviewing the expansion arising from his report of some two decades before: that expanding HE may have to mean a shift away from unsuitable 'highly specialized first degree courses'; that endless expansion should not be a given since the admission of 'just anybody' and 'regardless of enough evidence of ability to profit by the teaching provided' would be 'a recipe for complete chaos'; that income-contingent loans 'rather than subsidies' were really the way to fund mass HE (and it was 'a matter of regret' that the Robbins Report (1963) had not stressed the loans option as already raised in the Anderson Report (1960)—and indeed as also proposed by the Institute of Economic Affairs as early as 1960; and as now almost to be achieved by *c*.2015); and that an undue emphasis on research was 'bad enough to be disturbing' in that it 'wasted' a lot of academic time and left students and teaching 'neglected' as 'a fantastically perverse state of affairs' (Robbins, 1980). Such concerns over the faculty's failure to take its undergraduate teaching duty seriously will be further explored in the second part of Chapter 6, but suffice to note here that it is also a long-standing issue in higher education in the US (see Barzun, 1991). It is not a matter of worse HE, but very different HE, in effect TE. And each wave of HE expansion comes, of course, with its critics along the lines of 'more means worse', and from the same era as Robbins note the concern that students 'drift', as they have 'in every age', into HE so as to get a degree that 'will enable them to get a job' and where they do 'a modicum of work without any real involvement or enthusiasm' (Green, 1969: 329—citing also Ogilvie (1962) and Butterfield (1962) on 'The Problem of the Modern University'). Similarly, there were fears of lowered academic standards in the expanded civics of the 1900s given 'the multiplication of universities', creating 'a great evil' and also thereby 'making degrees too cheap' (note the concept of the student paying fees; correspondence written 'by knowledgeable and influential persons' quoted in Sanderson, 1975: 222–223).

Compared to the CDBU at least Bailey and Freedman (2011) offer a clear manifesto, albeit as a set of utterly unrealistic 'demands' upon government and on universities—for example, 'Restoration of maintenance grants and abolition of fees...'. The praising of the 2010 student protests against the £9,000 fee, and rather silly comparisons with Hungary in 1956 ('Students against Stalin') and with 'The 1968 Student Movement' now look dated, given that those 2010–11 HEI occupations have largely petered out, the fees are being collected, and the 'struggle' has dismally failed to spark 'a social crisis into which workers, organized and unorganized, are drawn' (Bailey and Freedman, 2011: 122). It has been the CDBU, however, that has attracted media interest, being labelled as a creation of the 'great and good' (its 65 initial members, drawn from 'the UK's most esteemed thinkers'). They call for universities to be freed from excessive and wasteful audit and accountability, as well as regretting 'students being encouraged to behave like consumers' (*Times Higher Education*, 8 November 2012: 5 and 7; similarly, *Financial Times*, 14 November 2012: 2, under the headline, 'Academics oppose university reform').

The CDBU asserts: that 'the very purpose of the university is grossly distorted by the attempt to create a market in higher education'; that universities' leadership has been 'remarkably supine' in the face of 'this onslaught' upon 'the central values of the university' as a result of 'misconceived government policies'; that 'the authoritarian managerial structure and the expanding bureaucracies' need to revert to 'a more collegial and democratic way of doing things' as 'academic self-government' reasserts itself over 'the business-corporation model'; and that 'a more appropriate relationship between universities and government' is required (*Times Higher Education*, 8 November 2012: 35–39, Sir Keith Thomas writing on behalf of the CDBU). In short, the CDBU demands that universities should be given the taxpayer's money and left alone—and indeed that the faculty lunatics should be left firmly in charge of the academic asylum! That said, the CDBU does have flashes of realism when it acknowledges that 'universities must put their own houses in order, most obviously by paying more attention to students' whose teaching has suffered 'disparagement' because of 'the emphasis on research' (they neglect one—as it happens a captive—market while chasing another). Another 'manifesto' for the CDBU appeared in the *Oxford Magazine* (Simon Head, Michaelmas Term, 2012): the fear is that universities are being made 'subordinate in so many ways to the private sector', are having to 'compete with one another as businesses do', and are suffering under the yoke of 'the university-as-corporation'; the demands are for the end of the RAE/REF, for 'strengthened academic self-government', for the abolition of the 'deeply destructive and retrogressive' and 'ever higher' tuition fees paid by the student and hence thereby removal of 'his or her power to exercise sovereign consumer rights in determining academic priorities and values' ('Students are not consumers...They are more like apprentices attached to teachers as master craftsmen...the profoundly misconceived notion of students as consumers...').

It is, on the face of it, odd indeed to be quite so vehemently opposed to the idea of the role of the market within HE when, in fact, universities have done very well financially since high tuition fees were introduced for non-UK/EU undergraduate students from the early 1980s, the UK scooping a significant share of the global HE market and the fee income from such international students propping up the finances of many universities. Similarly, a flourishing market has developed in the past decade for taught Masters courses bought by both UK/EU and international students, and especially the huge fees charged for the Masters in Business Administration (MBA). For the 2013 entry, almost all English HEIs will be charging the full £9,000 per annum to new UK/EU undergraduates; and with only three below £7,500—including London Metropolitan University (LMU) at £6,850 as the cheapest traditional HEI (compared to the fees of the for-profits institutions at around £6,000, as explored in Chapter 11). The tuition fees for international undergraduate students average across all the UK HEIs at over £11k and about £13k for laboratory-based subjects—with variation from £9,000 at LMU to over £20,000 at a few.

The market for postgraduate taught (PGT) courses averages £6k for UK/EU students—but double that for international students, and with peaks of *c.*£21k for the latter in some laboratory-based disciplines at Cambridge and UCL (and with over £27k for some courses at the LSE). The MBA market ranges from well below £10k at several HEIs to over £40k at Oxford, averaging £15k. All this demonstrates active and developed markets in all student areas and all types of course, except for UK/EU undergraduates; and that high global ranking for the HEI clearly translates into high brand-value and hence the freedom to charge high fees/prices in the PGT and international student markets (notably at Cambridge, LSE, Oxford, and UCL—the Coketown MBA might well be extremely well-taught but it will never command the premium fee at Oxford's Saïd Business School and even were the teaching at the latter to become dire the fee would probably not need to be reduced to reflect that). Such marketization in the PGT arena and for the international students seems to be utterly uncontroversial compared to the anxieties triggered by the whole concept of the introduction of UK/EU undergraduate tuition fees just before 2000 and then their tripling a decade ago, before another tripling from 2012–13. Thus, we have an extensive and complex HE market sub-divided into the new UK/EU undergraduate market (and potentially with further sub-markets, such as the Oxford PPE brand commanding a premium fee), a well-established PGT market (with sub-markets such as the MBA), and the long-standing international student market.

That said concerning (so far) the non-market in UK/EU undergraduate tuition fees, there does appear to have been an increasingly competitive market around the edges for the 2013 entry with even some of the Russell Group players having to compete on entry offers. It also seems iPads, laptops, rent reductions, scholarships, and even actual fee discounts are on offer during 'clearing' as the, as it were, HE annual sales—and even tickets for exclusive extra guest academic-celeb lectures being offered (*Sunday Times*, 11 August 2013: 'Universities woo elite students with cash and iPads'). This market competition applies as ever for those HEIs simply trying to fill places with almost any applicant, dropping entry grades as needed; but now there is to be a frenzy to get ABB applicants since such are beyond the HEFCE cap on numbers if an HEI is keen to expand (as did, for example, notably Bristol in 2012 in gorging on additional AAB applicants, the threshold being a grade higher last year—and possibly leading to under-recruitment problems at other Russell Group universities such as Southampton and Liverpool). Such fringe competition is as Kirp (2003) would predict from the US HE experience, but market competition by way of openly and aggressively reduced sticker-pricing has not broken out among the cosy cartel of high tuition fees US HEIs (although it may exist in disguised fee discounting by way of the award of merit aid and also in responding to student demands for 'pampering': 'They see themselves as savvy consumers, and in picking a college they are looking for the sybaritic pleasures of gated community suburbia. For them, monasticism is out and hedonism is in.'—Kirp, 2003: 118).

The same August 2013 release of A-level results that kicked off the clearing season also revealed what is happening in terms of the wider market aspect of what subjects young people are selecting at school, with a view to applying to university and taking a degree course that might enhance their employability. It seems that the trend is for them to become more instrumentalist and calculating, which is not surprising when they could be spending £27–36k in fees and a further £25–30k on living costs to acquire a degree (and when they must be aware of graduate un-(and under-)employment among the age cohorts just above them). Maths and the sciences are growing in popularity, having been in the doldrums for many years; 'soft' subjects such as media or tourism, and also modern languages (MLs), are in decline—the latter steadily for some time and now sharply so. And hence, understandably, a number of

HEIs are contemplating the closure of their MLs departments—although that could be premature since MLs in 2013 have begun to pick up at GCSE!

This raises the interesting question of whether there is a market failure here—perhaps these young people neglect MLs because of some information deficit—or whether it is simply a matter of demand and supply working just as to be expected within a market-place, and indeed to be welcomed by the neoliberals. The MLs lobby, of course, duly leans on government which, naturally, announces an enquiry. Will the HEFCE at the behest of the BIS next end up intervening in the HE market to correct for a lack of demand for MLs, and will HEFCE spend taxpayer money propping up MLs departments? Will government decide that MLs should be compulsory to age 16, even 18 as in the continental IB, in the hope of creating a viable HE market for MLs? Will anybody just accept and properly address the facts that MLs are often poorly taught, are difficult anyway, and that the average English teenager lacks the incentive to learn (randomly) French or German or Italian (as opposed perhaps to the potential usefulness of Mandarin or Spanish as widely used trading MLs in this century)—whereas his/her counterparts in all other EU countries really need the one ML, English, as the global *lingua franca* to access employment in international business, to access worldwide youth culture, and to travel to interesting places?

And also the study of MLs at HEIs is usually the study of literature, and if UK business needs MLs skills, it could probably supply them by incentivizing staff to take a crash course in 'Business French' or 'Marketing in German' (just as the middle classes soon brush up their pathetic schoolboy French once they need to communicate with a plumber about work on their villa in the Dordogne). The HE industry could respond, not by seeking subsidies for MLs and declaring the student customers to be wrong in not appreciating how good MLs are for them, but by giving the product a makeover in the same way that Latin and Ancient Greek were very successfully repackaged as 'Classical Civilisation' at a few HEIs (while closing down at others once schools stopped teaching them)—so, 'European Studies', or perhaps even more marketable would be 'European Studies with Management'. It is, presumably, such crude thinking that so infuriates the CDBU about HE floundering around within the agora; and the MLs case is certainly an example of a bigger problem for government in deciding on what basis it now intervenes in the HE market it has so enthusiastically espoused: for example, if government did elect to intervene in what it assumes is a market failure in the take-up of MLs, should it be to prop up the provision of French and German in universities as literature courses, or to encourage their replacement by Mandarin, Spanish, and perhaps Russian as strictly languages-for-business courses?

Given the HEIs' long experience with a market in international students and more recently in PGTs, why, then, is the concept of another new and explicit market for UK/EU undergraduates paying high fees in English universities suddenly so repugnant in 2012–13? Because tuition fees are to be up to £9,000 rather than £3,000 as since 2005–06 or £1,000 as first introduced in 1998–99? Because the taxpayer will have retreated from any direct funding of English university teaching costs other than providing a small subsidy for costly STEM subjects as degree courses in science, engineering, technology, medicine? Because the payment of high fees might engender consumerism on the part of the student-customer and challenge the academics' producer-capture of the ivory tower, requiring more and better teaching of undergraduates? Because students will select what they hope are degree courses offering employability rather than liberal arts Humanities subjects? And it is perhaps even more odd to be opposing these market 'reforms' when, in fact, they are pumping into academe, via the much higher fees and at least for the very many institutions merrily charging the full £9,000 (including for Humanities subjects), about an extra £600 per UK/EU undergraduate per year of the degree course—an increase of just under 10% on the total value of the lower £3,000 fees along with the former direct taxpayer subsidy of teaching by the funding council grant to universities, and after allowing for leakage of up to £1,000 of the £9,000 as the financing of access initiatives demanded under the HEIs' OFFA agreement (and such net extra funding comes into HE at a time of harsh 'austerity' for most areas of public spending). Finally, it is a not an unreasonable assumption that a good chunk of the CDBU's esteemed membership have happily funded their children through private schooling as an example of a market in another area of education where parental private investment in independent school fees is undertaken clearly to gain a market advantage for the child (whether by way of entry to an elite university or into the employment market)—while doubtless many a CDBU academic over the past 20 years has enjoyed a very successful career playing the new market in research output ushered in by the periodic RAE exercises dating from the mid-1980s.

Similar sentiments to the CDBU agenda are expressed more poetically by Fred Inglis (*Times Higher Education*, 14 March 2013: 44–47): 'The fruits of the spirit of the [public] university [are] integrity of scholarship, honouring the facts, determining the truth, cultivating doubt, protecting and guarding the culture, imagining the common good, defining justice, succouring mercy... To have care of these matters is to act not just as the best part of a nation's mind, its alter ego, but as the conscience of the state, let alone the government. A country's possession of itself, of how it should live well and do right, will be judged, advised and inflected by the many differing enquiries and conclusions of its universities... University authority is, naturally (the correct adverb), held in trust for the people. It cannot be the prophet of profit, for all that the parent state needs it to be profitable. A university, even in its most commonplace circumstances, ties the knot between the knower and the known, and discovers its own virtues in that tight configuration.' Amidst all this overblown rhetoric there is no explanation of why, say, the University of Law is supposed to be inherently unable—because of its private for-profit nature—to fulfil the requirement to care for 'the fruits of the spirit of the university' when teaching its undergraduates at a lower fee than many public institutions. Just as there is no clarity as to why Poppleton University, to provide a fictitious example, 'in its most commonplace circumstances', when teaching law or business studies, tourism, or golf studies, is simply by being not-for-profit and quasi-public automatically better at being able to tie 'the knot between the knower and the known'. Nor is it clear why a 'public' UK university operating a campus abroad, or several such, is still delivering a public good or in fact is indistinguishable from a for-profit supplier of HE expanding internationally in search of market-share and enhanced profitability.

And the likes of Professor Inglis do not tell us just how many universities, of precisely what kind and size, are needed and to be funded by the taxpayer at exactly what level to do quite what, so that they can be 'the conscience of the state'. Will less than 40 do the job as pre-Robbins, or perhaps it has to be around 80 as prior to the polytechnics becoming universities in 1992, or even well over 100 as today? Are they all to be given the same research funding per academic as they used to get teaching grant per student? The pious words of the CDBU and others help us very little in considering just what the country needs by way of tertiary education for 2020 and beyond, but they tell us a lot about the blinkered nature of the academic profession (or at least parts of it, perhaps at the older and more privileged end of it). The criticisms of Annan (1999: 295–296) apply as much to Collini (2012) as they did to his writings on HE back in the 1990s: Annan saw Collini as then suffering 'from a well-known donnish illness—inwardness' and accused him of also failing to 'even address the problems of diseconomies in university governance'; thus, Collini and his sympathizers lack credibility in that they end up 'by being a lobbyist who [does] not understand politics'. (It is interesting to speculate whether Lord Annan, as a paid-up member of the 1970s–1980s academic great and good, would have today joined the CDBU!)

There is a growing literature on the marketization of universities and their shift from the public sphere as they face a forced descent from the acropolis to the agora. The neoliberal transformation and restructuring of higher education is an increasingly global phenomenon (discussed further in Chapter 8), even if the English are now privatizing to a greater degree and faster than elsewhere. The notable contributors to the analysis are: Readings, 1996; Slaughter and Leslie, 1997; Marginson and Considine, 2000; Bok, 2003; Kirp, 2003; Geiger, 2004; Slaughter and Rhoades, 2004; Teixeira et al., 2004; Engell and Dangerfield, 2005; Hersh and Merrow, 2005; Washburn, 2005; Rhoades and Torres, 2006; McMahon, 2009; Tuchman, 2009; Schrecker, 2010; Brown, 2011; Regini, 2011; Teixeira and Dill, 2011; Conrad and Dunek, 2012; Brabazon, 2013; Brown and Carasso, 2013; Coaldrake and Stedman, 2013; Goodman et al., 2013; Rolfe, 2013.

In exploring the limits of markets in relation to HE, Sandel (2012: 107–110), for example, pointedly raises the case of 'the buying and selling of admission to elite universities' within the USA ('legacy preferences') as 'the admissions edge given to the children of alumni', which operate 'as a form of affirmative action for the affluent', noting that such practices give rise not only to issues of 'fairness' but also of the 'corruption' of institutional integrity. The same territory is covered in: Karabel, 2005; Golden, 2006; Kahlenberg, 2010. Karabel, for instance, cites Harvard in 2002 as admitting 40% of 'legacies' compared to 11% of other applicants, while at Princeton the figures were 35% and 11%; and Kahlenberg comments that the Princeton figure of 35% had reached 42% by 2009, which netted almost $55m from its alumni in 2007–08 alone. (On the broader social inequity hard-wired into US HE admissions see Radford, 2013.) The literature on marketization in HE usually recognizes that most countries face the challenges of increasing demand for HE and only a few oil-rich, small nations can afford to respond by expanding public provision (Heller and Callender, 2013).

Otherwise, it is a matter of selecting from among three key policy options: charge tuition fees to make up for constraints on the ability of the taxpayer to finance more HE at the going rate (this tends to be the policy option most frequently taken up, now as an extreme in England); reduce costs within HE so that more students can be taught with the same or fewer resources (another common policy, and the one deployed in the UK over the period from *c*.1975 to very recently); encourage, via deregulation and liberalization, the private provision of HE as a demand-absorbing mechanism (a route only since the 2011 White Paper being seriously followed in England, but one which sees around half of all students now within private for-profit HEIs in many Latin American and Asian countries)—or, of course, some combination of all three. All three options involve consideration of the potential trades-offs, and indeed political dilemmas about, quality and access or social equity, and also cost, within the supply of HE. In addition, the issue of quality control of the for-profit providers can be highly sensitive since there is often a simplistic assumption of an inevitable tension for the commercial supplier between quality and profit (with the latter allegedly always trumping the former). In fact, it may well be that the for-profit provider can simply function more efficiently than the public sector HEI, so as to be able to make a profit even when sustaining teaching quality and probably deploying a sizeable marketing budget, as well as by offering only the less expensive subjects (law, economics, business, accountancy rather than medicine, engineering, physics, chemistry)—which also happen to be more in demand. Notably, the for-profit institution will not be paying its academics to undertake research, nor offering them as generous pension schemes as in the public institutions; while the students will not be provided with the lavish campus recreational facilities typical of the modern public HEI. The nature of these for-profit providers of HE is explored further in Chapter 11.

If, therefore, the prevailing trend globally is towards retreat and cost-sharing (Johnstone and Marcucci, 2010; Heller and Callender, 2013), along with taxpayer substitution, the question arises whether it has gone too far in some countries. Carpentier (2012) comments: 'Strikingly, the UK mass higher education system of 2010 is as reliant on private funding as the elitist one of 1920'; and will be more so as the 2012–13 fees increase works through the student year cohorts, raising the question of 'stretching the cost-sharing strategy to the limit' (Carpentier, 2012). Whether or not some nations might be going too far too fast down the path of marketization, the trajectory is broadly the same worldwide. Slaughter and Cantwell (2012), for example, compare the USA and the EU, each seeking to bring HE closer to the market so as to be better able to compete in the knowledge-based economy, but each following a different route (the former characterized by being 'incremental' but going further faster; the latter rushing to catch up by a process of 'reverse engineering' the model out of an hitherto heavily state-controlled HE sector). In the EU, however, there has also been greater institutional and faculty resistance to American 'endless competition' and 'academic capitalism', a greater commitment to preserving the concept of HE as a public good/service. This point is made by Regini (2011) who notes how it was once possible for 'universities and companies' to ignore each other but how that has 'radically changed' as 'market elements' and 'market logic' have penetrated HE as 'largely the result of governments' incentives or pressures' (the start date for which is given as the Thatcher Government's cuts for UK HE in 1981). Yet, that said, (non-England) EU HE remains mainly publicly funded and hence there is no basis for 'theorizing a retreat of the state or a takeover by the market in the field of HE'— marketization, as experienced in England even before the 2012–13 fees hike, is 'simply not on the agenda in any [other] European countries'. The US home of 'academic capitalism' as a feature of 'the new economy' and of 'the knowledge society' is analysed in Slaughter and Rhoades (2004); and is added to by the exploration of entrepreneurial universities in Palfreyman, 1989; Slaughter and Leslie, 1997; Clark, 1998; Clark, 2004; Shattock, 2009—and the entrepreneurial academics contentedly operating within them (Stankiewicz, 1986; Perlman, 1988) who are broadly welcoming corporatism and markets, busily making fluid the boundaries between public and private as a traditional public good regime and the new academic capitalist regime 'coexist, intersect, and overlap' (the policing of the borders and fault lines being a task for government by way of judicious intervention in and regulation of the HE market).

Teixeira (2011), in reviewing 'the growing role of privatization and marketization in the EHEA' (European Higher Education Area), sees more of a threat to HE as 'a bastion of public service', noting that historically universities have had 'a hybrid public and private ethos' but with a much greater public dimension since the war. This public ethos is being eroded as 'European HE has experienced the growing influence of market forces' and the introduction of market mechanisms to create quasi-markets within HE. While in most EHEA nations public HEIs educate 90% or more of students, private HE caters for *c.*40% in Belgium, *c.*35% in Poland, and *c.*15% in Hungary. Across the EHEA governments 'are increasingly inclined to steer their higher educa-tion systems and institutions towards greater marketization and privatization', leaving it 'harder to distinguish between public and private institutions' in the context of 'a growing market orientation of public higher education'—not least as the introduction and increasing of tuition fees, and even of vouchers, moves higher up the public policy agenda in the face of Europe-wide austerity. In Teixeira et al. it was concluded that 'market forces are now intrinsic to the environment of higher education' as 'one important and viable instrument of steering higher education systems' (albeit as 'neither the magic potion that will solve all problems in higher education, nor the personification of evil'), and also that 'the most challenging policy issues are tuition pricing at the first degree level and academic quality assurance' (Texeira et al., 2004: 348–349). In short, can marketization ever achieve adequate competition that delivers good quality HE at a reasonable price? A few years later in Teixeira and Dill, it was acknowledged that the trend is 'to empathise the virtues of markets' and to denigrate 'the vices of public intervention in higher education' (2011: vii), but that market mechanisms have 'reshaped the reality of higher education' so that 'HEIs around the world are facing in their daily activities the implications of marketization' (2011: xvi–xvii).

Brown also carefully and comprehensively reviews the concept of a mar-ket within HE and the global trend towards the marketization of HE; but seems less accepting overall of the process, detecting and stressing negative aspects: increased stratification within the HE system, reduced diversity, risks to quality of provision, and the introduction into the academy of alien business and commercial values (as if they are not already there given, as already noted, the long-standing market in international students and the more recent mar-ket in taught postgraduate degrees, let alone also in research funding). Thus, Brown (2011) concludes with a chapter entitled 'Taming the Beast', putting forward the need for 'more appropriate public policies' that could achieve 'a better balance between these various benefits and detriments' of marketization (Brown, 2011: 158). 'A balanced higher education system' would, apparently, have a roughly 50:50 split between taxpayer funding of the cost of undergrad-uate education and the amount paid by the student in tuition fees. There is, however, no clarity provided as to precisely why a 50:50 split is preferable to 75:25 or 25:75, or indeed 0:100 as the current destination of English HE.

Here, of course, the issue is not about whether there are markets within HE, but essentially about whether the market should also now apply to non-international student undergraduate provision, and if so at what level of tuition fees. One pundit's suggested random slashing of the funding council block grant for undergraduate teaching is countered by another's proposed random reduction (or non-increase) in tuition fees; one pundit's recom-mended free market in HE is another's suggested government intervention in its provision. There simply is no right conceptual answer; the answer will vary according, as ever (Shattock, 2012), to the financial pressures faced by government in funding public services and just how much political clout HE can summon up compared to the health, schools, policing, pensions, transport, welfare, or defence lobbies—although there may well be from time to time an element of political ideology also driving a government's HE policy making (Tapper, 2007). At the time of writing, and in the context of the Coalition Government's austerity measures, English HE is a woefully weak lobby—students rioting over fees in 2010–11 was a mere passing moment compared to the potential ballot-box power of the pensioners in 'The Age of Aging' (Magnus, 2012). It is likely that across Europe, free public HE will steadily give ground to tuition fees as governments struggle with the adverse demographics and the spiralling cost of pensions during the next few decades—that is simply the global trend towards the student financing of HE (Heller and Callender, 2013), as well as a feature of the steady globalization of HE by way of marketization and commodification (King et al., 2011 and 2013).

Then there are those, besides the CDBU as discussed, who explicitly seek to fight a rear-guard action against marketization (for instance and notably: Brown and Carasso, 2013). They would wish to adjust backwards the public–private balance of funding sources (increasing the reliance upon funding council grants for teaching as opposed to charging higher student tuition fees) for HEIs so as to protect the public good aspect of the university and to reduce the steepness of the institutional hierarchy within English HE. In short, less stress on HE as a private economic good and an attempt to relocate HE back into the public sphere, away from market-steering and back to government-steering. The Coalition's variable full-cost tuition fees policy capped at £9,000 is seen by Brown and Carasso as 'the most radical in the history of UK higher education' (the average fee in 2012–13 has turned out to be £8,354)—and indeed 'amongst the most radical anywhere' (Brown and Carasso, 2013: 1). The £9,000 is the culmination of a long process of marketization beginning with the charging of full-cost fees to international students from 1980–81 (the number of such profitable students duly doubling by 2010–11) and exacerbated as HEIs struggled to deal with hefty cuts in public funding from 1981–82 (Kogan and Kogan, 1983)—a few by rapidly becoming entrepreneurial in a wide range of ways: on the University of Warwick as the 1980s pin-up entrepreneurial university see Palfreyman (1989) and Rushton, as ch. 16 in Warner and Palfreyman (2001); more generally see CUA (1992) and Clark (1998) and (2004).

Thus, the state's role, as successive governments viewed it, became to 'facilitate and extend the market' and this market competition 'is seen as the key safeguard of quality' rather than trusting the academic community (Brown and Carasso, 2013: 120–121). In a tally of the benefits of marketization, the authors recognize greater efficiency and enhanced service-orientation by way of responsiveness to stakeholders. This is, however, outweighed by 'significant detriments' in terms of reduced institutional diversity and enhanced stratification within the HE system, resulting from 'competition by emulation' (Brown and Carasso, 2013: 129–131) and also a (likely) declining equity in access to HE as well as quality (probably) being adversely affected by student-consumerism and institutional competition (although it is acknowledged that there is a 'lack of any serious study' of and 'very little hard evidence' on the relationship between the combination of market competition, plus reducing HE funding, and 'the quality of student learning and achievement'—Brown and Carasso, 2013: 150–152). They conclude that the marketization of HE in England has proceeded too far as an 'experiment' being pursued in spite of 'the copious evidence' showing 'the very clear limitations of markets as a means of providing an effective, efficient, and fair education system' (Brown and Carasso, 2013: 179).

Sadly, the internal contradictions within this overview of what little is known about HE and markets demonstrate that there is really no such 'copious evidence' to show that the risk of dramatic and public market failure in delivering HE is potentially any more detrimental to the student experience than the danger of long-term and insidious government underfunding of mass HE as a Galbraithian public squalor activity. Whether the market in undergraduate education can work in terms of the student-customer being an adequately informed consumer is another issue (addressed in Chapter 6). Yet, if he/she as a UK/EU student is not to be seen as an adequately informed consumer when now paying fees of up to £9,000 per annum, it has to be explained why those within UK universities have so happily taken fees at a higher level for many years from international students to prop up the ailing finances of UK HE given that, presumably, such students are, if anything, in an even weaker position to be well-informed purchasers. It is difficult to avoid concluding that the opponents of marketization within HE are selective in determining which markets to denigrate—seemingly, the recent one for UK/EU undergraduates but not the long-standing one for international students, nor the fairly fresh one for postgraduate taught masters courses. Nor probably the two decades old RAE/REF competition for research funding where the riches are great for those successful as an institution or personally within an academic career in winning grants—and most acutely in the sciences as recorded in Berman (2012) who discusses the evolution of 'market logic' and 'academic entrepreneurship' within US academe since the 1950s as driven partly by the wider neoliberal agenda, partly by the seeking of 'economic rationalization' within institutions, and partly by the actual competitive spirit and careerist enthusiasm of the scientists themselves. In so far as economic theory offers any clarity at all on the relative merits of a free (or 'relatively free', quasi-) market as opposed to the public provision of HE it is probably the case that, while the Coalition Government has a greater attachment to the former ideology even than its recent predecessors, the main pressure for the 2012–13 reforms or experiment has been the desperate state of public finances that demanded austerity—along with a long-term shift in how HE is viewed, from being an exclusively public good (Pusser et al., 2012) to one now seen as substantially an activity offering a (supposedly) sizeable private benefit to the graduate.

In terms of struggling to reach an informed and evidence-based public policy decision on just what should be the optimum split between the taxpayer's share of financing undergraduate HE by way of grant or subsidy to the university compared to the student's payment of tuition fees, there is, as noted, very little concrete evidence to go on. This leaves scope for enjoyably sweeping assertions in the political debate about HE—and also for making heavy cuts in HE spending without any immediately discernible adverse effects (short of cuts that reduced the overall number of places) in contrast to how quickly, say, reductions in healthcare funding show as politically embarrassing increased waiting lists, or how fast potholes appear in roads starved of routine maintenance. We do, however, have some material on the assumed private and social benefits of HE that might suggest a rational split if one is able to accept the starting-point assumptions built into these economic models, especially concerning the imputed economic values for such non-market outcomes as the better health seemingly experienced by graduates as well as their being less likely to engage in crime (other than perhaps as bankers in white-collar crime), let alone whether they are happier, more cultured and tolerant, better parents, and so forth. McMahon (2009) argues that HE is such a good thing that government should spend more, since the social return exceeds the taxpayer cost, and he fully subscribes to the human capital or endogenous growth theory that ascribes high value to HE's provision of more graduates. He comes up with a proposed optimum 50:50 taxpayer-student/family split as being economically efficient, concluding that current public investment in higher education is 'significantly below optimum'.

Thus, while McMahon's assessment might mean the UK spending more overall on HE to reach the USA's *c.*2.5% of GDP, the almost equal taxpayer-student split as it was in England with fees at *c.*£3,500 certainly should not have shifted to nearly total funding by the student at £9,000: he would see England as having ignored his warning that 'privatization should not go much further if higher education is to remain economically efficient, which includes serving the public good'. In fact, since he allows for the cost to the student of earnings foregone while in HE also to be counted as part of the individual's contribution, arguably fees of *c.*£3,500 would be too high in terms of a 50:50 balance in dividing the cost of HE between taxpayer and student: hence, cost-sharing in US HE too 'may already have gone too far'. He would nudge US HE, and by implication even more so now English HE, firmly back into the public sphere—otherwise, sustained under-investment in HE 'puts the nation at risk'. A problem, however, besides the conceptual issues with such a line is that it fails to ask whether HE delivery at present is cost-effective at the prevailing levels of fees (that question will be addressed in Chapter 6). It could be that the cost-structure of universities is too high overall and/or the cost of HE via tuition fees is high because there is the subsiding of inefficiencies as well as the cross-subsidizing of research. The USA's cost of HE at 2.5% of GDP may just mean it is a massively inefficient industry compared to the UK's 1.1% spend rather than that the latter's HE is under-resourced, as may also be the case with US healthcare versus the NHS, where possibly commitment to the market has indeed gone too far in the former: see Callahan and Wasunna (2006).

Another difficult question is whether HE is actually value for money for the student at whatever particular fee level and whether the student via the payment of high(er) tuition fees should in fact be subsidizing the research time and activity of academics—perhaps because academics' research can be demonstrated as enhancing undergraduate teaching over and above the academic's professional duty to keep his/her scholarship updated in support of good teaching (so far, however, such a clear and strong link between active research and better undergraduate teaching is unproven for the bulk of courses/modules within an undergraduate degree programme); and/or possibly because the student in effect is 'buying' a more useful degree by way of it signalling improved employability via the brand-value of the university being higher as a result of its research output as the major factor in the global rankings of HEIs (as discussed in Chapter 8). If it really can, in fact, be demonstrated that being taught as an undergraduate by a research-active academic (as opposed to one whose scholarship is kept up to date) actually is a major factor in the quality and effectiveness of such teaching, then the HE sector will have to explain away the fundamental reality that most academics in most HEIs are not truly research-active, and not a few even in the minority of research-focused universities are at best between bursts of research (if not now permanently exhausted research volcanoes), and hence are not being entered into the RAE/REF submissions.

Even more of a discrepancy is the possibility that anyway many if not most of the very research-active faculty may not do much if any undergraduate teaching, their time being too precious to waste on students who are then increasingly left to be taught by casual academic labour. And, in terms of undergraduate tuition fee income not spent on direct teaching inputs but leaking away to cross-subsidize the research time (whether productively used or not) of the academic labour force, there is the scandal that some universities continue to operate an automatic or quasi-automatic generous full-pay one-year/term-in-seven sabbatical leave policy and hence are funding even more time that is difficult to show is research-productive in the case of some academics. Of course, if in truth the student is gaining significant employability simply by graduating from the HEI with the best brand-value (in terms of its global ranking based almost entirely on research output) his/her entrance qualifications can access, then the student may well not bother to challenge the HEI's neglect of undergraduate teaching as he/she pays the £9,000 per annum in tuition fees, so long as the university sustains or enhances its research rank (and the now ubiquitous 2:1 degree is duly awarded).

The real problem then is, where elite brand-value is not being achieved from the research productivity and where the undergraduate teaching input is not impressive in its quantum of contact hours and feedback, it becomes difficult to see, in terms of market theory, how the university will, in the long run, be able to get away with charging tuition fees at the full £9,000 end of the range—other than, in the context of HE as an imperfect market, by relying on HE being a Veblen good where high price is taken and assumed to indicate high quality in the absence of any reliable alternative information supplied to the student-consumer to assist him/her in determining the quality of what is being offered. And, in the context of SSRs of 1:20 or more, as well as so much undergraduate teaching being delivered by inexpensive casual/adjunct/zero-hours staff, it is, arguably, pretty nigh impossible for any university to demonstrate that the academic labour content in the delivery of the teaching quantum for most undergraduate degree courses exceeds, say, half of the average fee of c.£8,250 charged to first-years in 2012–13 (a figure due to increase as even more HEIs shift to the full £9,000 from 2013–14). The rest leaks away into the funding of glitzy buildings and bloated administration, as well as covering inefficiencies in the delivery of teaching (notably in terms of the HEI management's inability to address issues of incompetent and underperforming academic staff). Hence, so far, the resistance of HEIs to reveal such costing data, and hence the 2013 call from *Which?* that they should be made to show just how much of the tuition fee income is really spent on teaching.

A carefully detailed and helpfully clear analysis of the mechanics of the new HE funding regime and of the allegedly adverse impact of markets upon (and of the alien role of markets within) HE, as driven by the current Coalition Government, is McGettigan (2013). It fails, however, to put the latest ratcheting up of tuition fees in an overall historical context, and is essentially a polemic against supposed 'free market ideologues' driving HE reform by way of marketization by conducting an experiment as 'a huge gamble' that 'threatens an internationally admired and efficient system', using 'increasing competition and student consumerism as the battering rams with which to overcome university inertia': 'the creative destruction of mass higher education' as it is 're-engineered by stealth through a directed process of market construction'. Whereas over the messy decades since the mid-1970s, the need to reduce public expenditure has been the key driver of HE policy-making (albeit that there is often window-dressing by way of exhortations to achieve efficiency and introduce market competition), McGettigan argues that the Coalition has done the reverse in that it has hidden behind the search for 'austerity' while eagerly pursuing its marketization crusade.

Thus, McGettigan works hard to explain the arcane nature of public finances and to argue that the larger-loans-for-higher-fees arrangement will in fact cost the taxpayer far more over coming decades than it will save the public purse in the form of the previous HEFCE teaching grants to universities. Indeed he notes that the uncertainty over predicting the repayment or bad-debt rate— 30% or so as initially assumed but now looking like 40% or more—has so far stymied the attempts to sell off the student loans book (as also attempted by the previous New Labour Government) and/or to privatize the loans scheme—the terms of the loans may well need to change, to the disadvantage of the graduate making repayments, so as to enhance their attractiveness in the 'financialized' marketplace...). Even the otherwise soberly expressed views of the outgoing HEFCE Chief Executive (Sir Alan Langlands) are forthright in declaring that the current full-cost fees experiment is seen by the rest of the world as 'completely bonkers' (as reported in *Times Higher Education*, 25 April 2013: 6). Yet public policy that might seem crazy in just one country at one point in time has a habit of popping up and being applied elsewhere, and the evolution of policy can be rapid once a key principle is breached—say, the concept of HE as a free public good and hence no UK/EU undergraduate tuition fees in the early 1990s at English HEIs, but £1,000 by the end of the decade and £3,000 just five years later, with £9,000 being reached barely ten years after their (re-)introduction.

It is worth pausing to assess the comparable international data relating to the context of the English full-cost fees experiment. Taking the 2012 OECD's 'Education at a Glance', we see the GDP spend on HE as a wide range led by the USA at a little over 2.5%, about three-fifths being private (fees and donations) against the two-fifths public funding. South Korea, Canada, and Chile also come close to 2.5%, while the OECD average is 1.5% and with the UK at 1.25% (a tad ahead of Germany and a bit behind France or Japan as being on the average). The UK public–private split is about 45–55 compared to around 35–65 in Japan, to a broadly 50–50 divide in Australia, and a roughly 85–15 split in France and Germany. In terms of the growth of the private element of HE funding since 2000 and up to 2010, the UK leads the table at almost 40% against an OECD average of some 7.5%. Moreover, the higher fees in England from 2012–13 will clearly widen and accelerate that growth so as to increase the gap. Yet in considering these broad variations in how much is spent on HE (and in exactly how that amount is shared between the taxpayer and the student/family) and then also noting the relative economic progress of the nations concerned, it is really rather difficult to say that a high spend (the USA) is necessarily linked to economic success (cf Germany's below average spend), or that the balance of the public–private sourcing of the spend seems significant (France compared to the UK, and both equally sluggish economically relative to Germany).

Hence, whether it is indeed 'completely bonkers' to shift the UK 55% reliance on private funding of HE beyond even that of the 65% in Japan, the 60%

in the USA, or the 50% in Australia to an extreme reliance (80–90% by 2015–16?) on private funding is not clear in terms of there being any certainty by way of an adverse impact upon potential economic growth (the issue of the theoretical relationship between HE and economic growth will be addressed in Chapter 6). Moreover, the global market for HE (where full-cost tuition fees have applied for many years in most countries) is dominated by nations where the public funding of the HE is less than half—for 2010 the US has a 16.5% market share, the UK 13%, and Australia 6.6% (with next Germany at 6.4% and France at 6.3%); and since 2000 the USA and Germany have given up share to the UK and Australia. Doubtless the global university rankings are a factor (see Chapter 8) and surely teaching in English is a factor along with the politics of immigration and student visa policies, but it may be that HEIs better funded overall from a diversity of income streams (including the tuition fees of international students) offer the discerning global student a more vibrant institutional setting and indeed a better national brand within the global rankings than HEIs that risk being underfunded as part of an austerity-squeezed public sector. As more US HEIs face cuts in their state grants and perhaps find increasing resistance to hiking fees for in-state students as the automatic response, they may be keener to recruit internationally, conceivably growing the less than 4% of non-US students in US HE towards the 16% in the UK and the more than 20% in Australian universities: such, of course, is the nature of markets.

A more balanced assessment than that offered above by the many opposing and regretting how far policy has developed in relation to the provision of English HE through high tuition fees and marketization comes from Barr (2001 and 2012) and Barr and Crawford (2005). They see HE as optimally financed, in the context of reduced funding for and the competing demands within the Welfare State, as well as in terms of social equity and economic efficiency, by a cost sharing between the taxpayer and the student, the latter supported by a well-designed loans scheme. HE funded solely or largely by taxpayer subsidy is 'regressive' in unduly benefitting the middle classes and also risks being under-resourced given the competing demands for public funds, a competition in which universities and students will probably lose out to schools, hospitals, pensioners. Such provision of HE is then best delivered 'substantially' through market forces operating efficiently within HE via the use of tuition fees (but perhaps with a ceiling on their level) as the vital price-signalling process needed for the proper distribution of resources in a capitalist economy—and indeed also inside mass HE where 'the polite myth' of all universities being assumed to be of equal quality can no longer be sustained. Barr and Crawford are comfortable that the HE applicant-student can be an adequately informed consumer within this competitive marketplace, and anyway it is 'not clear that a central planner would do better' in determining which courses should be offered, in what quantities, and at what fees/prices: such 'consumer sovereignty' is 'a useful instrument' while central planning of HE 'is no longer feasible or desirable' (Barr and Crawford, 2005: 104 and 141).

They do not, however, argue for a totally free market; while there must be a shift from the central planning of HE, they call for 'a suitably regulated market' (Barr and Crawford, 2005: 104), not least in terms of some government intervention being needed via grants for poorer students and schemes to raise aspirations for potential applicants from poor backgrounds so as to ensure appropriate fair access and widening participation, but also government intervention in the market-place is vital in ensuring that 'satisfactory quality assurance is in place' to protect the student-consumer (Barr and Crawford, 2005: 293). Thus, they welcomed the £3,000 capped variable tuition fees introduced by the 2004 Higher Education Act (getting through the Commons by only five votes, despite Labour's 100+ majority) as 'a cause for celebration' (Barr and Crawford, 2005: 291), but warned that the cap should not remain too low for too long. Since 2012–13 it has been £9,000 and it remains to be seen whether this is 'high enough to ensure a competitive regime', and, as already noted, time will also tell as to whether the blanket 'expensive and regressive' interest rate subsidy for the loans scheme is sustainable (Barr and Crawford, 2005: 303)—and the SLC loan book is approaching £50bn at 2013…

Interestingly, the decades-long discussion over the interaction between universities and the market (as detailed earlier and with Thompson (1971) as an early contributor) and also of the individual academic's ability to be entrepreneurial within the market-place, is nicely reflected in the campus novel (Davies, 1986 and 1988; Parkin, 1986; Bradbury, 1987; Lodge, 1989) as a much more enjoyable way of following the history of the market idea and ideal within HE trumping the public good concept of the university—or rather of the university as once run for the convenience of its professors (Amis, 1951) and later of its lower-status academics (Bradbury, 1975), rather than by its managers and increasingly for its student-consumers (the decline of donnish dominion discussed in Halsey, 1992). It is indeed ironic that Thompson's 1971 criticism of Warwick University as being too close to Midlands industry saw the same institution well-established as 'the entrepreneurial university' by the late 1980s (Palfreyman, 1989; Clark, 1998 and 2004) and hence being duly castigated as such (aka the University of the Lowlands) in the two novels and the related TV series by Davies (a former lecturer at the Coventry College of Education taken over as a teacher-training college by the adjacent University of Warwick in the early 1980s).

The life of the contemporary managed academic as a far cry from Bradbury's *The History Man* of 1975 (and even further from the privileged closed-world of Snow's *The Masters*, 1951) is portrayed in the trilogy by Anonymous (2006, 2007, 2008), while the life of the new lecturer *Crump* at Thames Metropolitan University (Vanston, 2010) is not perhaps that different from the experience of the hapless *Lucky Jim* as a junior academic two generations before (Amis,

1951). For both the hapless Jim and the naïve Crump there is bitter disappointment about life in academe: the former ends up at a dull, unintellectual redbrick of the kind criticized by Truscot (1943 and 1945) while the latter finds himself at a 'market-led' university that is 'just a business like any other' (to recruit and retain students there is 'massive grade inflation and a terrible dumbing down' as 'a corrupt sham and scam on an enormous scale'). Sadly the massification of UK HE over the past twenty years has not yet found within the university novel genre the equivalent literary quality of Bradbury and Lodge from the 1970s and 1980s. Modern student life is shown in the TV series *Fresh Meat* (2011–2013) as somewhat different from 'the student experience' promised in the marketing hype directed at potential applicants and their parents in the prospectus and at open days.

For the wider history of the post-war British 'Welfare Consensus' and of 'Consensus Corporatism' see Harrison who also observes in relation to HE that the 1950s/1960s were 'a bonanza time for British universities, a brief interlude between austerities' (Harrison, 2009: 370). For the ending of this era of HE's 'rapid and well-funded expansion' and of 'generous funding' (Harrison, 2009: 370) came along with the broader unravelling of the post-war consensus as 'Corporatism in Crisis' and the discovery of 'A Free-Market Alternative' as well as 'Free Market Consumerism' (for instance, does anyone regret the passing of the General Post Office's (GPO's) monopoly of the supply of telephones and the months'-long wait to secure a connection?). In the words of Harrison the 'Universities profited from the state's advance after 1945 but suffered from its retreat after 1979' (2010: 395). On just how golden the golden interlude of the 1960s was for UK HE note Marwick (1998: 286–287): UK students 'were better treated than anywhere else in the world'—'For almost all students not only was tuition free, but public grants almost met living expenses. Teacher-student ratios were remarkably low, and the systematic education provided was far ahead of the casual lectures in overcrowded halls too frequently delivered in the other three countries [France, Italy, the USA]'.

It could not, and did not, last. For the beginning of the end by way of the hastening economic decline of the early 1970s see Sandbrook (2010), who then paints a grim picture of economic crisis in the mid-1970s (Sandbrook, 2012) by when Britain was the 'Sick Man of Europe' with inflation reaching almost 35%, interest rates at 16.5%, an 83% marginal tax rate, and VAT jumping to 25%, and coupled with the 'national humiliation' of an International Monetary Fund (IMF) bailout sounding 'the death knell for Keynesianism' even before Mrs Thatcher swept to power in the 1979 election following the 'Winter of Discontent' by which time Britain was said to be ungovernable in the face of rampant trade union power as 'the British Disease'. The subsequent 1981 cuts by the first Thatcher Government were seen as the nemesis of the universities (Young, 1991), to be followed by the 1985 vote (738:319) by Oxford dons against a proposal to award Mrs Thatcher an honorary degree

(Young, 1991, ch. 18, 'Treason of the Intellectuals'; and see also Campbell, 2003). Indeed, the funding of the expanded elite UK HE system of the 1960s may well have been too generous; certainly, the later curtailed generosity arising from national economic crisis and also HE massification, with marketization and managerialism thrown in, seemed even more of a fall from grace because of the earlier state largesse. What government now wanted were plentiful performance indicators, meaningful metrics, accurate accountability, and a credible contribution to economic progress (to what later became 'the Knowledge Economy'—Temple, 2012).

The universities, once a cosy, quiet, vaguely quasi-public backwater of the Welfare State at the time of *Lucky Jim* (Amis, 1951) educating some 2% of the age cohort, were bereft of public support when the axe fell in the 1981 cuts after some two decades of expansion, and when they were then charged with inefficiency in the 1985 Jarratt Report (Sandbrook, 2012: 289–300). The tweedy, pipe-smoking conservative 1950s student had become the long-haired, hippy, revolting student by 1968 (Searle, 1969) and was ensconced in a career as a denim-jacketed radical academic by the mid-1970s—Dr Howard Kirk, aka *The History Man* (Bradbury, 1975), as a sociology lecturer and, according to Sandbrook, 'the most repellent fictional monster of the decade', full of 'intolerant self-righteousness' and 'narrow dogmatism'. The focus of student (and faculty) late 1960s activism had shifted by the mid-1970s from the LSE and Warwick to trendy Essex and the rather more gritty Polytechnic of North London (now London Metropolitan University), with Middlesex Polytechnic not far behind. When universities appeared in the media, it was 'in terms of strikes, sit-ins and general absurdity'—even at Oxford where in 1973–74 there were occupations by students (Palfreyman included, but for one chilly night only in the cavernous and draughty Examination Schools) convinced that, by winning the right to a student union building (a Central Students Union, and 'C-C-CSU' was the chant as we bravely faced the Proctors and Bulldogs, lapdogs of capitalism). Supposedly taking on the might of the Oxford Establishment would help to liberate Britain's exploited masses, and the Junior Common Room (JCR) of Queen's College duly voted its solidarity with the miners. Sadly, nobody took these militant students 'as seriously as they did themselves' and the general public 'deeply resented being lectured by middle-class youngsters', albeit led by 'comic, even ridiculous figures'. That said, there was on campus as ever the silent majority, (very silently) enjoying being 'far better treated than their counterparts overseas' and being 'taught in small classes and seminars, not in gigantic Continental-style lecture theatres'. Morgan (1999: 296) states simply that the student antics of the 1960s/1970s 'led to the vogue for higher education embodied in the Robbins Report rapidly losing its sheen' and this was one factor, along with the others explored, whereby the universities (having in the 1960s 'acquired a public esteem unique in British history'—and the consequential generous public funding) by the 1980s came to illustrate 'the gulf between the old professional order and the new Thatcherite ethos' to which they seemed 'complacent', 'managerially incompetent', and 'lacking in account-ability' (Morgan, 1999: 480)—the Iron Lady soon had them 'in visible retreat' (Morgan, 1999: 518), along with even the miners.

In fact, faced with an increasingly difficult jobs market by the late 1970s, students once again became conservative as anger became apathy—but the status of the universities had been lastingly damaged in public opinion, not least because it was still, as Morgan comments, 'in the common room, not in the student union bar, that the flame of revolution burned brightest' and 'with the fire of moral indignation' most intense among the young self-styled Marxist lecturers (some of whom by the 2000s had been tamed or matured as very well-paid Vice-Chancellors). Lodge (1978, 1985, and 1989) captures some of the era's obscure intellectual fashion very adroitly, which Sandbrook describes as 'its obsession with subcultures, minorities, and plural abstrac-tions, its abasement before French critical theory, its devotion to jargon, its scorn for readability, and above all its towering, world-class earnestness' (2012: 289–300). Burleigh makes much the same point about the late 1960 student/lecturer protests: 'In various European centres, juvenile revolution-ary sectarians turned forests into a flurry of leaflets, while throwing up a few toy barricades... [Some] professors tried to curry favour with the insurgent young... junior-ranking academics often behaving with the customary amor-alism of the desperate... [and these 'formerly militant students' went on to ensure the universities] thenceforth were dominated by people with little or no experience of what is popularly (and properly) called "the real world"... they inhabited a peculiarly trans-temporal space where the quest for vicarious rejuvenation often meant remaining juvenile into one's retirement...'. Yet the Kirks of HE remained influential on into later decades, as the intellectual ideas pioneered by his 'real-life equivalents shaped generations of scholars and stu-dents alike' (Burleigh, 2006: 359–360).

And not just in universities, where confined to the seminar room 'the Howard Kirks of British academia would have been no more than an eccen-tric distraction from the grim challenges of the 1970s', for 'plenty of idealistic young intellectuals were determined to get involved in the political process and duly colonized the Labour Party...' (Burleigh, 2006: 302), thereby neatly despatching it into the political wilderness until Blair's New Labour landslide of 1997. It is interesting to speculate that the most scathing criticism of mar-ketization in English HE perhaps comes from the now somewhat ageing Kirks of academe, rather than from the younger generation of academics who have adapted to corporatist and managed HEIs, a few of whom may in fact prefer a pluralist market-based HE model to an underfunded Cinderella public sector fate (as could await Scotland's universities, and probably also those in Wales).

In considering what drove the New Labour Governments of 1997–2010 into introducing and then increasing tuition fees for UK/EU undergraduates with

the Coalition Government moving to full-cost fees, the most likely explanation is to ease the burden of mass HE on the taxpayer by sharing the cost of HE
with the student, a global trend as noted (Heller and Callender, 2013); the alternative being under-funded continued Galbraithian public squalor. The latest
shift to full-cost fees seems to be the result of the new Coalition Government's
austerity policy demanding even greater cuts in public finances. Underlying
the stark funding issue, there is indeed much rhetoric on the need to encourage competition through the marketization of HE and by empowering the student. The funding climate for HE, in the UK and indeed across Europe, will
depend by 2020 on the unfolding political battle between the 'Austerians' and
the 'Spendarians' (aka the Keynesians), on whether the latter can achieve a
reversion to the 1990s and early 2000s policy of 'tax-a-bit-less' (compared to
the 1960s) but 'borrow-a-lot-more', so as to enable publicly funded institutions 'to-spend-as-ever' in terms of sustaining the European welfare model,
of which free or at least low-fee public sector HE has long been a component.
Certainly, in the context of post-2015 government finances the prospects for
HE seem bleak, at least according to the Institute for Fiscal Studies (IFS Report
R86, November 2013, 'The Outlook for Higher Education Spending by the
Department for Business, Innovation, and Skills', at www.ifs.org.uk).

It is perhaps too cynical, but it is also still fun to speculate that there is
a clever Coalition Government conspiracy. Government cannot afford to
finance mass HE at the generous rate as was the case for a system barely
one-third the size of some twenty-five years ago, when taxpayers paid far
higher levels of tax; but thinks (probably correctly—see Mazzucato, 2013), and
certainly hopes, that the science and technology research undertaken within
universities will be successful in engendering economic growth by supporting research and development in industry via intellectual property exploitation and technology transfer. And it wants the country's top-ten, world-class,
elite universities to remain internationally competitive, yet there are political difficulties over too overt a policy of pushing extra funding at them, as
happens now in many other countries (Palfreyman and Tapper, 2009; and as
explored in Chapter 8). Thus, by charging students the supposed full cost of
their education (which cannot possibly cost £9,000 to provide given the actual
quantum of teaching—see Chapter 6), in fact the flow of money into research
has been sustained compared to what has happened to many other parts of
public spending which have been severely cut. Moreover, the student paying
fees above £6,000 contributes up to around 30% of the amount above £6,000
to the access and widening-participation efforts of universities (which often
take the form of bursaries to poorer students), so government also ensures
its policy to enhance social equity in HE is funded by another party, the hapless student paying in effect a redistribution tax of some 10% on a £9,000 fee.
Thus, in short, the young undergraduates of the 2010s are left individually
facing high fees and incurring high debt; and the latter student loans debt if

some 40% is never to be fully repaid will be a further collective burden on their generation by the time they reach middle age. And the fee income fails to provide them with value-for-money in terms of the quantum and quality of teaching. It is used to prop up a costly and moribund HE model, is diverted to subsidise research activity of varying social, cultural, and economic value, and is needed to offer some degree of social equity in HE admissions to meet the guilty conscience of their elders.

The fact that the student loans system needed to finance the fees will have to be increasingly heavily subsidized is perhaps just about acceptable if the indirect result is a welcome support of science and technology research as potentially HE's main contribution to national economic productivity and prosperity. The fact that economically unproductive humanities research probably also gets subsidized from student fees is perhaps just about palatable to some (and for many at least the history books are far more readable and enjoyable than whatever emerges as journal articles from the labs). Yet the financial long-term burden upon the 'pinched generation' arising from a decades-long obligation to repay official student loans for tuition fees and for living costs while in HE (let alone any private borrowings for such living costs) is surely another example of unfair intergenerational equity compared with the (authors as) baby boomers' earlier enjoyment of free HE and generous student grants, and compared with an even older generation where its richer members still benefit from free bus passes and winter fuel grants (Willetts, 2010; Howker & Malik, 2010). The means-tested student award, at almost the maximum level, received by Palfreyman in the early 1970s would have been worth in 2012–13 money something like £5,000 per annum, and it was then still possible also to sign-on for weekly cash at the Labour Exchange in all three vacations! That said, whether or not in the Age of Austerity the wealthier pensioners should lose benefits, the savings would hardly finance mass HE with a 45%+ age-participation rate (APR) compared to a 1970s expanded-elite HE system of *c*.15% APR. Indeed, even before the age of austerity, hardly any nation could afford to fund mass access to free higher education (or at least to a reasonably resourced free HE).

6

The Student as Consumer: Legal Framework and Practical Reality

Abstract: The fact that the funding of teaching in English higher education is now overwhelmingly underwritten by the fees that students (and/or their parents) are required to pay inevitably generates pressures that recast higher education as a product and students as consumers. This chapter explores the current legal framework which guides higher education institutions in their provision of teaching and learning. The judicial deference to academic judgement acts as a strong defence of institutional behaviour and limits both the regulatory function of the Office of Independent Adjudicator and the contractual rights of individual students. Moreover, there is no clear evidence as to whether prospective students are acting as informed consumers when selecting what university to attend. Do they have sufficient information to make an informed choice? Are they guided more by the perceived ranking and status of a university rather than its competence in delivering academic programmes? What are the criteria they should employ when making their selections? How do they calculate the potential returns from higher education? In pursuing these concerns, this chapter draws also upon the literature on US HE where there has been an established market in fees for a long time but also the absence of a strong regulatory framework to protect students as consumers.

INTRODUCTION

In this chapter we consider the 'Student as Consumer', outlining the legal context and framework within which English universities operate in terms of the business-to-consumer (B2C) relationship clearly identified by law in the form of the implicit (albeit not usually in the form of a detailed and explicit written) contract-to-educate between the student-consumer and the university-business supplier of the teaching and learning, assessment, and degree-awarding service. We stress that, in considering pressure for change impacting upon the university, it is crucial to have some understanding of the legal status of the traditional institution as, in the main, a private charitable corporation. Traditional universities may behave like entities within the public sector but, in English law, they are not technically public bodies or authorities unless specifically designated so in certain statutes such as the 2000 Freedom of Information Act or the 2010 Equality Act. There are also now the newly created entrants as the latest wave of HEIs if not actually always universities, in the form of the private for-profit limited companies supplying higher education.

In each and every case, the contractual duties under consumer law towards an HEI's fee-paying students are exactly the same. Moreover, for government seeking to enhance consumer protection for the student as supposedly being at the heart of the university by way of its commitment to teaching, it is vital to recognize that, unique among all business suppliers of a service, universities possess a valuable get-out-of-jail-free card in the refusal of the courts to second-guess and review decisions based on the proper exercise of expert academic judgement—just as the Office of the Independent Adjudicator (OIA) is barred by its founding statute from receiving and adjudicating student complaints, and involving academic judgement in, say, lecture content, assessment, and marking, or degree classification.

We also contemplate the English HE—or indeed TE—landscape of 2020 from the perspectives of the student-consumer, of the institutional provider, and of the academic profession (or, if that term is in fact now too grand for what is in effect tertiary education delivered in various ways within a wide range of diverse institutions, perhaps a more appropriate term is 'the academic labour force'). It will be a messy and fuzzy landscape, more Monet than Constable and much less like a system. There will be implications arising from this process of profound structural change for legal concepts such as academic freedom and university autonomy, but also in terms of the practical reality for the academic career and for what is now termed 'the student experience' of his/her 'teaching and learning' (once higher education). In looking at the question of whether undergraduate education is value for money for the student-consumer paying high fees, we are especially concerned with the issue of cost control and pricing within HE and the problem of the under-informed consumer regarding high fees as the proxy for high quality teaching and learning—or at least of the brand-value of the degree in terms of its signalling power concerning the graduate's employability. We ask in this chapter whether, as a matter of practical reality in the context of other large-scale areas of economic activity, the university's special protection from judicial scrutiny can really be defended, given that students-qua-customers are not only now paying high tuition fees but also increasingly doing so to commercial profit-making institutions (as encouraged by government policy to enter the HE market as the providers of vocational courses supposedly enhancing the private rate of return through the graduate's hoped-for increased employability, as opposed to the Robbins concept of studying for a degree as something that also provides a social rate of return through its cultural and citizenship aspects).

It is also necessary to consider not only who actually pays for undergraduate education (now a burden falling pretty well entirely upon the student/family given taxpayer retreat since the almost total removal of the funding council block grant to HEIs for undergraduate teaching and the related virtual trebling to £9,000 of the cap on variable tuition fees), but also who should pay in terms of a fair balance in cost sharing between the taxpayer and the student based on any hoped-for economic and social gain for the nation in adding graduates to its human capital as opposed to the assumed private benefit for the individual graduate by way of enhanced employability and earnings. In Chapter 8 we consider HE as a globalized commodity and its marketing to international students consuming the now clearly established university brands thanks to the fairly recent development of the world-ranking league tables, and how British universities seek to operate within this global market. In that chapter we also return to the question raised within this chapter: how might HE begin to deliver more by way of rigorous and well-resourced undergraduate teaching, while at the same time charging less by way of tuition fees (the quality–price balance) in the increasingly normal context of the student now financing HE, an issue HE will have to address in terms of its affordability both for the individual student paying fees and for the nation funding student loans. This is an issue that will force universities at some point to face up to their long-standing inefficient operating practices, not least in possibly carrying a number of underproductive academic staff, where academics are meant to be research-active or where alternatively the non-active are not being redirected towards teaching loads. Chapter 11 explores the growth of the for-profit commercial suppliers of HE as part of the marketization process within English HE and indeed globally, as well as its potential role in driving down the cost of HE provision. And in exploring all these issues it is inevitably necessary to contemplate in some detail the US HE experience as being the nearest analogue to the policy path now being pursued in English HE.

LEGAL FRAMEWORK

This section provides a brief summary of the legal context within which the English universities operate under English law (Farrington and Palfreyman, 2012—as updated online at: oxcheps.new.ox.ac.uk). The vast majority of universities are 'public' in the sense that they are (or rather used to be) substantially funded via annual block grants from HEFCE (previously the UFC and UGC) for the provision of undergraduate teaching to UK/EU students and for research, and in the sense that they are not-for-profit charitable entities. They are not publicly-controlled, publicly-owned public sector institutions in the way that, say, local education authority schools are or as for public services such as policing, (much of) the NHS, and (most) prisons. They usually take the form of chartered or statutory corporations aggregate, but some are set up as charitable companies under the 2006 Companies Act (Farrington and Palfreyman, 2012: chs 1–3); they are all subject to the remit of the Charity Commission under the Charities Act 2011 (although their prime regulator for the purposes of the Act is HEFCE—Farrington and Palfreyman, 2012: ch. 7). They are, under English law, all private corporations in the same way that US private universities and colleges such as Dartmouth, Harvard, Princeton, and Stanford are, as opposed to public US universities such as Berkeley which are, at varying degrees of being arms-length, owned, funded, and controlled by the US state in which they are located (Farrington and Palfreyman, 2012: ch. 24)—similarly, almost all universities in the rest of the EU are public sector institutions, albeit that they have been awarded greater autonomy from government control over recent decades (Farrington and Palfreyman, 2012: ch. 25). In contrast to the traditional 'public' universities in England, there are now a few for-profit commercial universities and colleges which are commonly referred to, loosely, as 'private'—they are set up as companies under the 2006 Companies Act and are subject to broadly the same regulatory regime (Farrington and Palfreyman, 2012: ch. 4) as for the 'public' institutions by way of the use of the university title, the power to award degrees, and quality assurance via the QAA (there is more discussion of these for-profits in Chapter 11). The 1983 University of Buckingham is often said to be 'private' in contrast to the 'public' universities, but as a chartered charitable corporation aggregate it has exactly the same legal status as (say) Warwick, Birmingham, or Bristol; it was thought of as 'private' because it did not receive UGC (or later, UFC/HEFCE) block grant as public/taxpayer funding.

The chartered universities have a Visitor, whose role is now residual, and are as such eleemosynary: having a Founder who set the entity up to distribute his alms/charity and who then appoints a self-perpetuating Visitor to oversee the entity's governance (for example, William of Wykeham, Bishop of Winchester, was the Founder in 1379 of New College, Oxford, and the Visitor is the Bishop of Winchester). Most nineteenth-century civics or 1960s Robbins universities were 'founded' by the King/Queen as in effect the creations of their civic communities aided by government funds (local in the case of the civics and national via the UGC for later creations, although the relevant local authorities will have donated land as the site for the Robbins new universities). The formerly LEA-created, -owned, and -controlled polytechnics became independent statutory higher education corporations in 1988 and then were retitled universities after 1992—they are the 'post-1992' universities as a later wave of 'new universities' but, apart from their means of creation under legislation rather than charter, their legal status is the same in that they too are private and charitable, albeit as statutory rather than chartered, corporations.

All these institutions are governed by lay-members as the majority members of their councils in the chartered universities or their boards of governors in the statutory universities (Farrington and Palfreyman, 2012: ch. 5), or as their directors on the board of the company in the case of the for-profits; but their professors and other faculty in the chartered universities via the Senate have some formal constitutional powers over academic matters, and usually a wider influence in the governance of the pre-1992 'old' universities than academics have within the post-1992 'new' universities. The lay-members, since the Jarratt Report (Committee of Vice-Chancellors and Principals, 1985) and via such bodies as the CUC (1995), have reasserted their constitutional power and authority (Moodie and Eustace, 1974; Shattock, 2006; Shattock, forthcoming) as were so clearly dominant at the time of the creation of the civics in the 1890s/1900s and as yielded during the age of donnish dominion in the 1960s (Halsey, 1992), giving rise to a shift from academic demos and collegiality expressed in the departmental meeting and faculty boards to the managerialism of the more assertive vice-chancellors and their management teams working closely with key lay-members as formal officers of the corporation (Tapper and Palfreyman, 2010; Farrington and Palfreyman, 2012: ch. 6; and Chapter 4 of this book).

This process of the adjustment of relative actual power within the university, while the technical constitutional position has been broadly unchanged since the modern model of governance was set by the creation of the civics more than a century ago, has not applied at Oxford or Cambridge (Tapper and Palfreyman, 2011) since their collegial governance structures as self-governing medieval academic guilds and that of their colleges as autonomous sovereign collectives or corporations of their fellows are unique within the UK and indeed globally (in the USA, the lay-trustees/overseers have formal control like the lay-members in the UK (Duryea, 2000); in the European universities beyond those in the UK there are remnants of the medieval guild of masters in that the rector and deans are often elected, but they are in effect state entities. The declining status and authority of (and trust in) the academic profession relative to managers and governors is, along with concerns over the commodification and marketization of HE, part of the ever-growing literature on and an element in the Zeitgeist of the modern university—just as audit and accountability is part of the Zeitgeist of the New Public Management of recent decades (Power, 1997; Pollitt and Bouckaert, 2004). The individual academic (leaving aside Oxbridge college fellows) is simply, in law, an employee covered as for any employee by the body of employment law arising from the common law of contract and the various statutes offering employment protection (Farrington and Palfreyman, 2012: chs 10 and 11)—except that, while academic tenure has now been abolished as part of the 1980s reform of universities, there is some degree of protection of academic freedom that is specially applicable to faculty within universities (Farrington and Palfreyman, 2012: ch. 13).

The student in any English HEI, charitable or for-profit, is in English law a party to a contract-to-educate, the other party being the institution 'public' or 'private'; this contractual interpretation of the relationship between the student and the university dates back to English, Scottish, and American cases from the 1870s–1890s (Farrington and Palfreyman, 2012: ch. 12). Disputes concerning this contract are generally justiciable in the courts, but only once all the HEI's internal appeals or complaints/grievances mechanisms have been exhausted (the Visitor's exclusive jurisdiction over such disputes in the eleemosynary chartered institutions having been removed by the Higher Education Act 2004). Where the post-1992 HEI is allegedly misapplying its regulations, the student can also seek urgent judicial review for it to be ordered to proceed properly (the post-1992 former polytechnics, having been created by legislation rather than royal charter, are subject to public law or administrative law as applied via judicial review). Some aspects of the contract, however, are deemed 'unsuitable' for adjudication in the courts 'because these are issues of academic or pastoral judgment which the university is equipped to consider in breadth and depth, but on which any judgment of the courts would be jejune and inappropriate' (Court of Appeal in *Clark v University of Lincolnshire and Humberside,* 2000). Thus, the courts (whether in the context of a dispute under the private law of contract or in the process of public law judicial review) will not second-guess such academic decision-making, providing the HEI has duly and properly followed its published processes and procedures, which must be generally compliant with the expectations of natural justice and match the requirements of contractual fairness. In fact, this judicial deference to the exercise of expert academic judgement is long-standing in every common law legal jurisdiction and amounts to a now almost unique special protection for the university (and its academics) at the expense of the consumer protection rights that would otherwise usually apply in full (similarly the legislation creating the OIA in 2004 specifically precludes it taking on student complaints that involve 'academic judgement'). This, as it were, 'get-out-of-jail-free card' for HEIs will be considered further in due course. And indeed this HEI-student contract is deemed to be a business-to-consumer contract (B2C) covered by consumer protection legislation. We will discuss just how informed a consumer the 16/17-year-old can be when shopping around within the HE market for what is potentially a £50k investment over three or four years of his/her life, and also exactly what the degree of consumer protection is available in the HE market-place compared to buying the other large-ticket items in life such as a house/flat or a pension plan, and spending, say, half that sum on a car or a tenth on a holiday, as the other major purchases.

Suffice to say now that, while the student is, in law, clearly a consumer of a service provided by the university/college and is increasingly seen to be such by politicians, by the public, and (reluctantly) by academe and HEIs (as well as students now being more likely to perceive themselves as such), he/she is hard-pressed to be certain as to what precisely are the terms of this consumer (B2C) contract with the HEI, since most HEIs do not (yet) use a formal detailed written contract (for a suggested model template see Farrington and Palfreyman, 2012: 443–447). This seems, as discussed later, to be ever more untenable as HE becomes steadily commercialized and commodified, as marketization ushers in for-profit providers, and as fees climb to £9,000 per annum. In short, the 1982 Supply of Goods and Services Act requires the HEI to deliver the service of teaching and examining 'with reasonable care and skill' (s13) and further consumer protection legislation such as the 1977 Unfair Contract Terms Act and the 1999 Unfair Terms in Consumer Contracts Regulations also applies, along with the 2008 Consumer Protection from Unfair Trading Regulations, to limit the HEI's use of exemption and disclaimer clauses in whatever form of contract-to-educate it might explicitly have or in the material such as the prospectus and course regulations that might be absorbed into an implied contract. Sadly, there are some English universities that have in use an egregious contract that almost certainly has within it terms unfair to the student in seeking to exclude or limit the institution's liability to the student in the event that it fails to deliver its side of the bargain (Farrington and Palfreyman, 2012: ch. 12). And the recent EU Consumer Rights Directive—with its renewed emphasis on fairness and transparency—has duly triggered a review of UK consumer protection legislation and already resulted in a proposal for a Consumer Rights Bill that will probably tidy up into one Act all consumer protection law as noted, and which also in turn might mean universities having to be much more explicit over the exact quantum of teaching provided for the fees/price so that applicants can make fully informed choices. (See the discussion below of the 2012 and 2013 HEPI/*Which?* surveys of undergraduate teaching provision and students feeling short-changed on arrival at university, having, they claim, been under-informed if not actually misled when applying. Almost 10% of respondents referred to alleged misrepresentations by the HEI in the exciting promises and offerings of its recruitment message compared with the on-campus mundane reality of provision.)

If the economic theory discussed in Chapter 5 is to be applied in the increased marketization of English HE and without alarming market failures arising as feared by many, an important condition for it to work effectively is whether the HE market can really be said to have adequately informed consumers, and a key question arises as to the degree that the HE market (like any other market for B2C goods and services) is appropriately regulated by existing consumer law and other monitoring mechanisms. In the case of higher education, the former is not fully applicable given the issue of judicial deference to the exercise of expert academic judgement as noted, and the latter is not yet fully developed in the way that other economic activities have a regulator set up by legislation to protect consumer interests. Moreover, other economic activities often have an umbrella trade body that develops a voluntary but powerful code of practice and a related arbitration process (for instance, the used car retailers), and even sometimes puts in place a bond to protect consumers (for example, the travel and package holidays sector). It sometimes seems that HE in the 2010s is where, in consumer protection legal terms, the used car trade or the package holidays industry were in the 1960s! As HE is increasingly marketized and commodified, commercialized, and made profit-generating, for some HEIs it surely becomes more difficult to justify in public policy terms the historic hands-off approach of the courts where the allegation is of, say, the inadequate or poor provision of the teaching of a purely vocational degree course by a for-profit entity for which the student has paid some £6,000 per annum (as opposed perhaps to an arcane dispute over the quality of the Philosophy degree delivered for free by a public not-for-profit university where there are issues of academic autonomy about who judges what is an appropriate interpretation of and competent lecture on Kant's theory of this or that). See also Chapter 11 for the (potential) application of competition law to the HE market.

Notwithstanding the 2011 White Paper's aim of putting students at the heart of the HE system (or indeed HE industry), the English HEIs have some way to go in terms of voluntarily protecting students as consumers from the growing risk of misrepresentation as competition for students increases within the HE market-place and their marketing hype runs ahead of their operations capacity to deliver consistently and sustainably over the three or four years of the degree course just what was promised. In legal terms, the risk of an aggrieved student bringing an action for misrepresentation will grow as part of the steady marketization of English HE, and hence a combination of the HE sector, of the government, and a consumer body such as *Which?* needs to address the extent to which the HE market is to be a regulated market. Not that, from the legal context, the former provision of HE as an almost entirely quasi-public sector activity delivered by 'public' HEIs meant that the consumer protection legislation described earlier applied any the less (subject to the caveat already noted concerning judicial deference towards the proper exercise of expert academic judgement) or that there was not still a risk of misrepresentation as young people contemplated the offerings of the 'public' HEIs, most of which were competing for customers as much as now the 'private' HEIs compete with them in the enhanced HE market (it is, of course, the case that such UK/EU student-consumers did not have to pay tuition fees at all until 1999–2000 and then only at a modest level until the £9,000 fee cap applied from 2012–13).

The experience of the OIA over the past half-dozen years in handling a growing number of student complaints is salutary in terms of predicting what fees of £9,000 from 2012–13 may mean as against those of £3,000 prevailing so far in the history of the OIA (Farrington and Palfreyman: ch. 12). The OIA sees proportionately more complaints from students paying their own fees as postgraduates and paying higher undergraduate fees as international students. Students on vocational courses leading to the award of a degree combined with professional status and confirmation of fitness-to-practise or employability as a teacher, nurse, social worker, and so on, also tend to create proportionately more work for the OIA. Simply, the more the student has at stake in terms of fees incurred and/or career prospects, the more likely he/she seems to seek redress via the OIA when things do not work out. So, if UK/EU undergraduate tuition fees are now to be higher than for most taught postgraduate courses and also are getting towards being as high as for undergraduate international students, and if in addition high fees push students increasingly towards vocational degrees with anticipated better employability, it seems that the OIA will be ever busier—even assuming it continues to be barred from receiving student complaints relating to matters of academic judgement. The OIA experience suggests that consumerism increases as students pay higher fees, no matter that the interpretation of the relationship between the student and the university in blunt contractual B2C terms fails to acknowledge adequately the very prolonged and extremely interactive nature of the student-university teaching and learning process, one hardly akin to the routine purchase of products nor to the passive consumption of a service that is characteristic of the transactions envisaged under consumer protection law.

PRACTICAL REALITY

We turn now to the practical reality of universities operating within the market-place, as well as applicants exploring the market-place and students negotiating three or four years of sustained service delivery by their HEIs. There is also the interesting issue of how government HE policy can extract the benefits of market competition within a regulated market (assuming that a completely free market is politically and morally unacceptable) while also limiting the potential adverse excesses of such competition so as to protect the student as a consumer of a service to be delivered with 'reasonable skill and care'. The risk is that price competition leads to a resourcing gap for some HEIs unable to reduce costs as fast as the market drives down prices/fees, and thereby gives rise to market failures both by way of quality issues and disruptive restructuring within and among institutions. Another risk is that greater marketization and commodification of HE does not in fact give rise to an efficient market; that instead there is market failure because the applicant-student can never be a fully informed consumer and relies on high price to signal high quality (HE as a Veblen good): the HE market-place becomes an example of 'the market for lemons' problem because of hidden, incomplete, missing, incomprehensible (but hopefully not fraudulent) information. In terms of the degree of state regulation of the HE market, government will have to use competition law and consumer protection law to help it correct for potential market inefficiency and failure, as well as intervening where the market is unlikely to provide certain aspects of social welfare or equity and public good.

What will be the roles of the QAA, of the OIA, of OFFA, of HEFCE, of the NUS, and of *Which?*—indeed, will there be a new HE or even TE Regulator? Might the OIA end up as the *de facto* regulator in naming and shaming HEIs failing to deliver HE with skill and care, to deal properly with complaints? We need also to explore the cost structure of HE and the problem it has in efficiently controlling costs to ensure effective delivery of whatever is to be the teaching and learning student experience as promised at the time of recruitment and as then actually provided during the degree course. And we ask just what it is that the student gets for his/her payment of the now (post-2012/13) arguably highest tuition fees of all OECD countries. If the marketization of HE is as advanced and pervasive as its critics fear and as its proponents hope, the result should be that a combination of the student operating as a consumer (protected by consumer law as detailed above) and also competition engendered within the regulated marketplace will drive up quality in the provision of HE according to the theory discussed in the Chapter 5. If that were the case, why do we encounter a growing literature, much polemical but some carefully researched, on the alleged deficiencies in the delivery of HE as an over-expensive and poor value for money service?

This chapter, in exploring all these areas, has to draw heavily on the sizeable range of material concerning US higher education, where not only has there been more work done on university costs but also the longer tradition of (until 2012–13) higher tuition fees provides the nearest we have to an informative analogy for what is the English HE policy-experiment now underway. Over in the USA, there are exactly the same political issues as in England (as indeed in many OECD nations). What does it really cost to provide a year of undergraduate education? Is mass HE becoming unaffordable not only for the state but also for the squeezed middle classes in the same way that in the UK independent school fees inflation has run well ahead of salary inflation? On the squeezed middle classes Boyle (2013) notes that in the USA in the mid-1970s the top 1% enjoyed just under 10% of GDP but now the figure is almost 25% and that the position in the UK is not vastly different (see also Stiglitz, 2013); while Newfield (2008) considers specifically the fate of the public university as a middle-class perk within the fading American Dream. In terms of HE becoming unaffordable, is the national student loans debt (both for the USA as it tops $1 trillion—*c*.£200m in the UK—and for the individual graduate) now unsustainable as a drag on economic growth? In terms of the cost/price of HE, just what do universities and their academics do during the many non-teaching weeks of the university year? In terms of the value for money of HE and its efficiency, what do students actually learn in becoming graduates and are they better taught by a research-active faculty as often claimed? And the questions continue... Are students to be thought of, and are they increasingly thinking of themselves, as consumers? Does the law offer them sufficient consumer protection? Will there be disruptive innovation, perhaps via MOOCs, that can at last increase HE productivity beyond its medieval craft-industry constraints and reduce costs/fees? What is the optimum balance of public to private HE provision? What role do the for-profit suppliers of HE play, and what role should they play? How does HE contribute to society and to the economy in terms of social and public benefit as opposed to the student's private benefit, and how can we measure such benefit (both economic and also socio-cultural)? In the funding of HE should there continue to be taxpayer-retreat and cost-sharing, or cost-shifting to the student by way of higher tuition fees? If universities see their public funding reduced so that they are less state-funded and more just state-assisted or even merely state-located, what is the appropriate governance structure and management style for operating these businesses? How are the flagship public institutions such as Berkeley to be funded to compete with the private not-for-profits such as Stanford and MIT in the global rankings race?

Such questions indicate the many concerns over the efficiency and effectiveness of HE, as well as about the economics of HE delivery; and thus, in the US context, Sowell (2011: ch. 4, 'Academic Facts and Fallacies') challenges the allegedly producer-captured nature of US public universities run for the convenience of their rent-seeking tenure-privileged faculty, expensively teaching too little and only what they want to teach (their narrow research specialisms) when they want to teach it (not before 10am or after 4pm on three midweek days for some twenty-five weeks a year), while cleverly using accreditation processes to erect high entry barriers against competitive, new, for-profit providers of HE that might otherwise drive down tuition costs (and hence fees charged to students). The idea and ideal of a market in HE is distorted by the ranking of HEIs, which is based very largely on their research output and the student as consumer being unable to assess the quality of the teaching provided. Sowell questions whether 'going to college' as a key component of the American Dream has not now become so costly as to erode the supposed earnings gain for most graduates, albeit that there is a huge variation in the financial returns of having a degree qualification depending on the prestige of the institution attended and the subject(s) studied. The HEIs play games to enhance their rankings position—for instance, wasting time and money on huge admissions offices busily and cynically encouraging applications so as then to be able to reject them and stress the institution's selectiveness (Harvard rejects almost 95% of its applicants). The universities have a poor understanding of their cost structures given both the utterly 'arbitrary' allocation of faculty time between teaching and research, and also the few incentives to bother with cost control let alone cost reduction compared to the for-profits which 'tailor what they supply to what is in demand by paying customers, the same as other profit-based businesses do' (Sowell, 2011: 122).

Similarly, Reynolds (2012) writes of the bursting of the HE bubble as the end approaches for continued debt-fuelled tuition increases that avoid universities addressing cost curtailment, and doing so mainly by improving faculty productivity. He cites college tuition as inflating over the three decades since 1980 at 7.5% per annum compared to the Consumer Price Index (CPI) at under 4%, and even medical costs inflation at just less than 6% (over the 30 years 1978 to 2008 CPI increased 3.25 times, medical costs 6-fold, and HE 10-fold). For Reynolds (2012), the student loans debt is both insane and dangerous as the result of HE 'living high on the hog'—and hence 'major structural change' is needed and 'a major correction' is looming. Meanwhile, he advises potential students to think hard about whether going to college is worth the excessive cost and debt—and warns that universities should reconsider their costly building plans as well as facing up to 'curriculum reform and changes in instructional methods' so as to provide students with 'actual value for their educational dollars' (courses with greater academic 'rigour' and more use of online learning) as 'serious efforts to rebuild the higher education model'.

The polemical populist attack on American HE and on the tenure privilege of its academics egregiously neglecting undergraduate teaching has gathered pace over some twenty-five years: the analysis essentially unchanging (HE is too expensive, poorly managed, producer-oriented); the suggested reforms remaining pretty much the same (more teaching, better teaching, more coherent degree programmes, less stress on useless research, tighter cost control); the response of HEIs the same (with little happening by way of change as the HE gravy train contentedly trundles on along the track of increased costs and fees); and the language of the debate always strident ('corrupt', 'scam', 'frauds', 'academic excesses', 'crisis', 'bursting bubbles')—albeit that the colours and the graphics of the book covers or dust-jackets get evermore colourful and stark. Thus we have items from, say, Sykes (1988), Kimball (1990), Schaefer (1990), and Douglas (1992) to (more recently, for example) Hacker and Dreifus (2010), Kamenetz (2010), Taylor (2010), Riley (2011), Bennett and Wilezol (2013), and Selingo (2013).

Selingo ('Editor at Large, Chronicle of Higher Education') gives a feel for this bitter polemical onslaught on US higher education: 'American higher education has lost its way'; 'costs are spiralling out of control and quality is declining'; 'American higher education is broken...beset by hubris, opposition to change, and resistance to accountability'; 'a systematic dumbing-down of college campuses'. And next from Bennett and Wilezol, the first billed as 'A former United States Secretary of Education': 'two-thirds of people who go to four-year colleges right out of school should do something else'; 'most of higher education fails most students'; 'too many people are going to college...studying irrelevant material that leaves them ill-equipped for the job market...[and] paying too much for tuition...[at these] overpriced and under-performing colleges and universities'; 'the frighteningly paltry amount of learning that takes place on some college campuses'...They continue: 'easy access to federal loans and grants has produced an increase in [HEIs' uncontrolled and excessive] costs'; the HE scam of colleges and universities 'falsely portraying high tuition fees as a metric of value', as equating to high quality teaching and degrees; 'underworked professors'; 'an ever growing amount of administrative bloat'; 'students are not being challenged'; HE 'has become exorbitantly expensive and inefficient'.

And, for an especially egregious example within academe of the professoriate's rent-seeking behaviour, see Tamanaha (2012) on the extreme exploitation by the USA's 200 or so law schools of the lucrative market in charging excessive fees to fund their underworked and overpaid academics; Bok (2013: ch. 13) makes many of the same points in a marginally kinder way. The law schools' quasi-cartel continues to be successfully protected by the self-referencing (and indeed self-reverential) accreditation mechanism run by the law professors as a mechanism to set high entry-barriers for any innovative and low-cost new competitors, and despite challenges by the US equivalent of the UK OFT (Tamanaha, 2012: ch. 1). The exposure of their 'aggressive massaging' of graduates' employment data to enhance positions and profiles in the dysfunctional rankings seemingly has no impact on law schools' tactics, which also spend some $1 billion annually 'buying' students with high SAT scores (which looks good in the rankings) by offering merit-based scholarships as fee discounts (Tamanaha, 2012: ch. 7). The UK's manufacturing of lawyers via the modest fees charged by the for-profit BPP University or the University of Law is by comparision with the technically non-profit US law schools a model of a competitive and effective market functioning rationally and with integrity. While the cynic will expect the for-profit HE provider to seek to rig the market, the naïve may be shocked to learn that the non-profit provider within the HE market is also just as likely to seek to do much the same given half a chance— and hence the sad necessity for the role of government policy in creating a well-regulated market.

What has changed over the past two decades of such attacks on US HE, however, is that recently more measured texts are also conceding and concluding that there is indeed something seriously wrong with US HE in terms of both the quantum and also the quality of undergraduate teaching. Lucas (1996) provided an early balanced assessment of the debate over the alleged failings of US HE, rather siding with the critics than the defenders. Indeed, one can go back further than Lucas to commentators already posing awkward questions about the sustainability of the traditional university as early as the mid-1970s. For example, Eric Ashby's essay (in McMurrin, 1976: 13–27) explored the need for the university 'to evolve without affront to its heredity' and is blunt about 'the forces which propel its evolution' as being 'three categories of customers' ('the students, the employers of graduates, and, in a state university, the legislature representing the public who foot the bill') and 'all three of these categories of customers have legitimate claims on the university'. Similarly, Gardner's essay on 'Forces for Change in American Higher Education' (in McMurrin, 1976: 103–123) noted the 'real, omnipresent, and foreboding' fiscal crisis afflicting US HE, including 'a startling loss of public confidence in the entire enterprise'; as well as observing that 'the influence of communication technology' will revolutionize the delivery of HE teaching (citing the 1972 Report from the Carnegie Commission on Higher Education 'The Fourth Revolution: Instructional Technology in Higher Education').

Well, US HE has, of course, survived and thrived its way through 1970s fiscal crisis to become the evermore and even more expensive commodity now under widespread and growing criticism; just as the then new forms of technology have so far failed to become the 'desirable modes of instruction for large numbers of students while being more cost-effective as well' and leaving the dominance of the medieval lecture and pattern of the academic year from the Middle Ages firmly in place across modern US (and UK) HEI campuses. We discuss in Chapter 11 whether the latest predictions about the ever less affordability of, and an impending IT/MOOCs revolution in, HE will unsettle the traditional university any more than did the threats of four decades ago, or whether as the Age of Austerity eventually ends HE will simply shrug off its critics and up its prices/spending—although one thing is perhaps certain, as Gardner noted back in 1976, the reaction of vested interests within HE to such threats of fundamental change will be 'as unsure [as] uneven' in the 2010s as in the 1970s.

Thus, in the past few years we have had some serious key texts that should not be just shrugged off: on how Harvard (and its ilk) have 'lost sight of' and 'forgotten' about teaching (Lewis, 2006); on how US universities are 'underachieving' as they 'accomplish far less for their students than they should' as the poorly-led and undermanaged faculty 'neglect pedagogy' under the guise of academic freedom and hence there remains intact 'the crust of inertia and complacency that keeps most colleges from challenging accustomed methods of teaching to become genuine learning organizations' (Bok, 2006: 330); on the slow and low completion rates within US public universities (Bowen et al., 2009); on the need for colleges 'to engage in some serious self-examination' and recover their commitment to teaching (Delbanco, 2012); and on just how 'academically adrift' and disengaged the undergraduates are today as they put in such little effort, mainly because the professoriate requires so little of them given its negligence in designing and delivering effective teaching (Arum and Roksa, 2011—whose depressing study of national data also concerns Zumeta et al., 2012).

The last item paints a grim picture indeed of 'limited learning on college campuses' based on an extensive research project funded by the US Social

Science Research Council (this is not some hysterical polemic to be brushed aside by the HE establishment): students' 'academic effort has dramatically declined in recent decades' from some 40 hours per week in the 1960s to about 27 in the 2000s, and 'the faculty cultures and orientations' of 'the college professoriate' has much to answer for, since they have struck 'a disengagement contract' with their students (along the lines of 'I don't want to have to set and mark much by way of essays and assignments which would be a distraction from my research, and you don't want to have to do such course work as a distraction from partying: so we'll award you the degree as the hoped for job ticket in return for compliance with minimal academic requirements and payment of high fees'; and on the 'Party Pathway' through HE as some US HEIs come to resemble country clubs see Armstrong and Hamilton, 2013). But all may not be lost—paying higher and higher tuition fees might 'serve to impose a new sense of self-discipline on students' and to refocus their attention upon academic activities as they seek value for money just like any other consumer; or, that said, it may mean that they are even less concerned with pure academic content as long as the course delivers 'its instrumental value' by way of the desired credential as a signal of employability (Labaree, 1997). Arum and Roksa (2011) continue: the depressing testing and monitoring data shows that three semesters into HE and there is but 'a barely noticeable impact on students' skills in critical thinking, complex reasoning, and writing'; these students just are 'not learning much' and this should 'give pause to the recent emphasis on "college for all" policies'. There is simply not adequate interaction between faculty and students; there is so little academic discourse by way of rigorous teaching by the former and the opportunity for engagement by the latter in fulfilling assignments which can be discussed with faculty. There really has been dumbing-down of at least the quantum of intellectual activity needed to achieve 'graduateness' as too many students 'have been left academically adrift on today's campuses' so that their academic gains 'are either exceedingly small or empirically non-existent'; all of which is 'sobering' and 'troubling indeed' as well as the fact that it 'should be a cause for concern' to the taxpayers, to the students, and to the families who have to fund this vast and costly HE scam.

And the reform urgently needed? Just the faculty doing their job properly: 'providing academically rigorous instruction' based on 'high expectations' of students putting in effort to complete coursework that is 'appropriately demanding' and with the faculty fulfilling its collective academic responsibility to address curriculum design. In short, as, in the UK, the recent Coalition White Paper on HE expressed it, 'putting students at the heart of the university' rather than the rent-seeking interests of academics and their managers! But reliance on the student being an empowered consumer and on the competition induced within the market model of HE alone is unwise for policy-makers: as part of the remedy for HE's shameful 'inattention to student learning' there must, argue Arum and Roksa, be 'the implementation of externally mandated accountability systems' similar to the ones used in the provision of schooling (and as proposed in the US federal government's Spellings Report (Spellings Commission, 2006)—and as, of course, promptly and universally derided and rejected by most of the US HE interests!). Indeed, Arum and Roksa talk of the need for 'some form of exogenous shock' to the 'entrenched organizational interests and deeply engrained institutional practices' of the US HE industry since universities' efforts have been so 'feeble and ineffective' in terms of grappling with the problem of 'limited learning' given that, sadly, 'undergraduate learning is peripheral to the concerns of the vast majority of those involved with the higher education system'.

In essence, if HE is to be a mass-going-on-universal provision, it increasingly amounts to TE and has to function more like a continuation of schooling than the pedagogic norm of the elite HE era; operating as a market may help, but it will be a regulated market not a free market since government has a duty of care to the unavoidably underinformed and underempowered student consumer risking a substantial amount of personal money as well as potentially never-to-be-fully repaid taxpayer loan money. In the UK, the development of the Office for Standards in Education (OFSTED) as a schools inspection regime has enhanced educational standards over the past decade, as has the introduction of the innovative and tightly managed chains of academy schools offering competition within London in particular, which might suggest a more powerful role for the QAA so avoiding UK HE going even further along the way of US HE as gloomily described by Arum and Roksa. How then is commitment to undergraduate teaching to be made central to the academic career? How to correct for the dreary scenario painted by Ward-Perkins (2005: Preface)?— 'The career structure and funding of universities in the UK currently strongly discourages academics and faculties from putting any investment into teaching—there are no career or financial rewards in it.' Yet, as he comments, the lively teaching of engaged undergraduates also helps the academic's research avoid 'obscurantism and abstraction'; a point made by another Oxford Don thanking his students: 'Over the years I have... gained no less from the comments and criticisms of generations of students; there can be no better testing ground for ideas than an Oxford tutorial, and no better way of winnowing wheat from intellectual chaff.' (Ibbetson, 1999: Preface).

How long before all undergraduates in English universities now paying hefty tuition fees receive the 'minimum' by way of 'teaching and learning' within 'the student experience' that was proposed in Palfreyman (2008: 40) when fees were but one-third of the prevailing 2012–13 levels?—teaching throughout terms 1, 2, and 3 of all academic years (not fading out by Easter of years one and two, leaving the student adrift for six months, as happens at some universities in some subjects); seminar sizes capped at 1:12 (not at 1:20–25 as in too many HEIs); each student to 'prepare and present' at least once in each seminar series (not able to remain speechless on the back row week-in and week-out, if attending at all); seminars to be led by 'full' academic staff at least 75% of the time (not by casually employed temporary adjunct staff or graduate students); each item of formally assessed summative course work to be preceded by two items of informal formative written work as 'practice' in the art of academic discourse (not leaving students receiving nominal feedback only in the next term on just the one marked assignment relating to the seminar series of the term before); each item of written work (whether formal or informal, assessed or not) to be the subject of a 15 minute 1:1 oral feedback session with the seminar leader (not merely a scrappy feedback on paper); all students to have an academic tutor providing a 1:1 session for 30 minutes each term/semester to discuss overall academic progress, options choice, and study skills. Such careful attention to teaching inputs should begin to justify the charging of £9,000 tuition fees by using more of the fee income in the direct provision of undergraduate teaching, as well as potentially enhancing employability for graduates across the jobs/careers spectrum by ensuring they are articulate critical thinkers and adaptive lifelong learners: otherwise, the £9,000 fee should be greatly reduced. And even the non-vocational Humanities graduates would benefit as do the Oxford students: see the 2013 Oxford University Report on 'Humanities Graduates and the British Economy: The Hidden Impact', where over recent decades such graduates are shown to be sought after by employers because of being intensively taught and fully stretched by the Oxford tutorial teaching format, which provides opportunity for engagement in the liberal education process (whatever the subject area—Palfreyman, 2008). Moreover, the use of such face to face direct communication between student and academic about the former's written work would help to reduce the disturbing growth in cheating where students are now buying bespoke ghosted essays that the plagiarism-detecting software does not necessarily spot.

There were, of course, from the time of the earliest attacks upon US HE also its defenders, responding to the critics and lamenting the marketization of and the corporatism within universities (as also for UK HE as noted in Chapter 5: Hussey and Smith, 2010; Docherty, 2011; Collini, 2012; McGettigan, 2013—but also Holmwood, 2011; and Rolfe, 2013). For instance, over in the USA Smith (1990), Barber (1992), Soley (1995), and Readings (1996), all rather echoing Veblen (1918) and his critique that the university had become a business. Later, as noted in Chapter 5, came others: Bok (2003), Kirp (2003), Engell and Dangerfield (2005), Hersh and Merrow (2005), Washburn (2005), McMahon (2009), Tuchman (2009), and Conrad and Dunek (2012). And most recently there is Bok (2013) recognizing many of the growing criticisms of, but also offering a somewhat Pollyanna-ish defence of, the state of US HE which currently faces 'a bumper crop of complaints' and where the ability of HEIs to defend themselves is not helped by a 'lack of reliable knowledge' or by 'fuzzy and uneven knowledge' about their performance—a weakness not assisted by the fact that rankings and ratings are 'not a reliable yardstick for measuring progress'. And this dearth of understanding applies especially to any attempt to monitor and manage teaching, given also 'the curious lack of attention paid by most college faculties to the large body of empirical research on teaching and learning': hence faculties have been 'notoriously sluggish in changing their curricula and the ways in which they teach' and in addition 'college instructors have yielded to the desire of students by making diminishing demands on their time'. The end result is simply that 'many college courses are woefully inadequate'. That said, Bok sees real 'Prospects for Reform' (ch. 10), and even extending to long-needed proper training of academics as teachers (238–246) and he also anticipates much-needed improvements to undergraduate teaching (404–407); thus, (almost) all will (eventually) be better... Similarly, Lane and Johnstone (2013) detect improvements in US HEIs' efficiency and effectiveness, accountability and productivity.

Yet it is still hard not to feel that the critics of US HE do not have a point, and also that the same degree of detailed examination of UK HE would not reveal many of the same issues and problems. The limited material we have so far for UK HE does indeed echo some of the concerns being so vehemently and increasingly expressed in the USA. For example, the HEPI Report No. 57 on 'The Academic Experience of Students at English Universities—2012 Report' reveals cause for worry over the rigour of undergraduate degree courses at many HEIs in terms of the somewhat minimalist study effort seemingly needed for success. In fact, way back Eliot (1909) recognized that: 'A very important function of a faculty [the academics collectively] is to determine the normal number of weekly exercises for which each registered student shall be responsible... everything depending on the standard of work by the student for each weekly appointment... [and hence a faculty also needing to exercise appropriate control] over the methods of instruction [and] over individual eccentricities [amongst academics]' (Eliot, 1909: 109–111).

The HEPI 2012 data shows (HEPI, May 2012): that there is 'considerable continuity' with the surveys of undergraduates undertaken in 2006, 2007, and 2009—to which the response of 'the university establishment' had been 'defensive' with 'an unwillingness' to engage with the 'uncomfortable' issue of just what students get by way of teaching and are expected to put in by way of academic effort; that there is, however, a 'refreshing' new environment where universities are beginning to provide more information to applicants; that in 2012 students receive some 14 hours of weekly teaching, varying across subjects from over 20 to less than 10—predictably (and probably as ever) much higher in medicine (thankfully and reassuringly) and the sciences compared to the humanities and social studies; that students express dissatisfaction with low contact hours; that the related 'private study' input does not balance out the variability in contact hours across subjects and hence some students overall simply work less on their academic activities than others (an average of *c.*14.5 hours on top of the 14 contact hours gets us close to the 27 hours that alarms Arum and Roksa (2011) as being a significant decline for US students from some 40 hours in the 1960s, although that figure of 14.5 is at least up by an hour on the earlier HEPI surveys); that while the medics might clock up a 35-hour week as if in a full-time job, academic life for most students 'resembles part-time employment' (sometimes at barely 20 hours per week—and for only about 30 weeks each year); and the amounts of effort required to earn an undergraduate degree varies not just across subjects but also dramatically amongst universities (being generally highest in the pre-1992 'old' universities), which when in addition account is taken of the higher study hours in other European countries 'raises potentially awkward questions' along the lines discussed earlier for US HE. While the students in the 'old' universities may put in more hours, they are, however, more likely to be taught in larger groups and more by graduate students—presumably the pre-92 academics are more distracted from undergraduate teaching by the demands of research than those in the 'new' post-92 and less 'research-focused' institutions. Some 15–25% of students record in the HEPI survey that they see their HE as 'very poor' or 'poor' value for money—this is, of course, before the 2012–13 fees hike for UK/EU undergraduates.

Perhaps the new £9,000 fees will see an increase in the quantum of teaching provided and also a greater commitment to study by the paying consumer, but the HEPI survey finds that the increase to the £3,000 fee in 2006–07 did not lead to improved teaching provision by way of, say, smaller groups or more sessions ('the increase in fees has led to no change')—despite students and government expecting the new money to fund improved staff-student ratios and more teaching; and so one can indeed speculate what the extra income was spent on and what might happen to the additional tuition fees income from 2012–13. (And Willetts (2013: 38 and 47) makes the same point: 'The pendulum has swung too far away from teaching...Looking back we will wonder how the higher education system was ever allowed to become so lopsided away from teaching.') Thus, this valuable and disturbing HEPI survey data for 2012, as for the earlier reports, again raises the same questions 'concerning the intensity and extent of what is offered to and demanded of students', ones still being mainly 'unanswered' and ones still leaving the HE sector under an obligation that they 'should now be addressed properly'. As in the USA, the HE industry is adept at evading criticisms about its efficiency and effectiveness, its value for money in public policy terms; concerns that almost all other areas of the public sector and quasi-public sector have been forced to address, let alone the way that the private sector has responded to more competitive global markets and increased consumerism. Indeed, now, in the context of stringent austerity, even the military is under pressure to get to grips with their dire record on procurement. Can US HE, and as now followed along the same high fees path by UK HE, really continue to remain aloof from (quasi-) market and consumerist pressures as its costs spiral and its prices surge? What does government need to do to regulate the HE market so as to ensure HEIs are responsive to the market-place?

The 2013 HEPI Report, in conjunction with *Which?* (HEPI, May 2013), as the latest update on 'The academic experience of students in English universities', goes even further in presenting disturbing data that is an indictment of English undergraduate HE in the twenty-first century: students are not getting a better teaching and learning experience by virtue of paying fees, whether as initially introduced at £1,000 or as increased to £3,000 and nor so far for the first year students paying now £9,000. The 2013 report starkly declares that 'there is no sign that as students pay more they are receiving more for their money, and that is reflected in a sharp increase [for the 2012–13 survey] in the proportion of students who feel that they are not receiving good value for money'. Also universities are poor at explaining to students 'why it is that they may be receiving less contact than they might have expected' as well as at being 'transparent more generally about what students can expect' (and even the new much-vaunted block of KIS data 'is partial and does not give students the full picture' about the quantum and style of teaching). Moreover, there is huge and 'disquieting' variation in terms of just how much academic work a student is required to do subject by subject across universities, which 'raises questions about the comparability of standards in different institutions' which have 'never been seriously addressed'. While the QAA might believe a degree needs some 1,200 study hours per year, the average at English universities is in fact only some 900 hours and hence 'on average the standards of degrees are not as has been assumed' (some HEIs demand an input of 45–50 hours per week over 30 weeks or so, others as few as 15–20, and with a median at around 30).

Thus, the report comments: 'It is unlikely that on average students studying for less than half the time studied by other students in the same subject will achieve the same outcomes. And yet almost all obtain degrees, no matter the differences in the amount of studying they have done.' Of course, it helps the HE industry that, as the supplier of the service, the university is usually in full control of deciding the output/result via degrees awarded, whereas a hospital, say, has far less ability to present a botched medical procedure as a success— and, of course, the patient-consumer can sue for medical negligence in a way that the student-consumer is not (yet) able, given the unique protection for academe in the form of judicial deference towards the proper exercise of expert academic judgement (as discussed). But students can detect sloppy teaching practices: almost 60% of those surveyed felt the academic experience had not met expectations, with nearly one-third saying that contact hours had been fewer than hoped for, while even more felt that the course was 'poorly organized'. And ominously for universities, the new £9,000 first year students are twice as likely to think their courses are 'poor value for money' than the 2006 cohort when fees were at £3,000—indeed, the responses of these first years now mirrors the usually greater dissatisfaction of overseas students regarding value for money since they have paid the equivalent of £9,000 or so for some years. Whether by 2020 universities will still be able to fob off such criticism of their neglect of undergraduate teaching and of the student-consumer complaints remains to be seen.

The *Which?* report of the same 2012–13 survey on 'The Student Academic Experience' (May 2013) is perhaps even more blunt than HEPI in criticising HEIs: 'some interesting and challenging findings' that show just how 'stark' is 'the need for clear upfront information about what students can expect from their academic experience', with 21% of students surveyed thinking universities' information was 'vague', 9% even finding it 'misleading', and with 30% of the 2012–13 first-year students considering their course 'offers poor value for money' (indeed, 'the high levels of discontent with value for money may in fact be an underestimate'). Thus, *Which?* calls for 'better information about academic study' so that a there is data on university websites about 'the amount and type of scheduled contact time' (which should become part of the KIS 'as soon as possible'—and this is data the HEIs, of course, deliberately did not include in the KIS as currently in place). The consumer body also demands urgent 'investigation of variability in study time' by the QAA and BIS (the report shows, for instance, Oxford Law students clocking up almost 40 hours of private study time against some eight hours of scheduled teaching as one extreme, compared to Leeds Metropolitan's Business Studies students at six and ten hours respectively at the other end of the scale; in History the variability is a total of barely 20 hours overall at Northumbria and Essex, compared to about 27 at UCL and Sheffield, and around 33 at Oxford or Cambridge). Nothing suggests that students at one university are lazier than at another: it is a function of what is asked of them by way of the weekly workload and also of what attention is then paid to their response to such demands (see the discussion in Palfreyman (2008) of the Oxford Tutorial as constituting a low contact time but high private study and intensive feedback model of undergraduate education). The report, in addition, is critical: of the sloppiness of academics in providing useful, consistent, and timely feedback—barely 25% of students benefit from face-to-face feedback on assigned/marked work; of their incompetence in organizing courses; of their teaching quality; and of the lack of action across the sector in terms of improving teaching provision as fees have increased over the past decade. Moreover, 'there needs to be greater transparency over expenditure levels' in terms of explaining just how the course fees charged relate to the actual cost of course delivery as fewer than 40% of students view their courses as value for money—'it will be particularly important to ensure that it is possible to distinguish how much money institutions are spending on teaching versus other activities' (data as indeed now being collected under HEFCE's TRAC(T) requirement for greater transparency in HEI expenditure but data that, one suspects, many universities will be very reluctant to release!).

Other surveys of students come up with the same increased emphasis upon their growing demands: 'Students appear to be becoming more serious and professional about their studies.' (UNITE Group plc, 'The Next Generation 2013: A report into applicant and student expectations', www.unite-group. co.uk). Similarly, the PA Consulting Group in surveying HEIs' managements ('Charting a Winning Course: How student experience will shape the future of higher education', 2013, www.paconsulting.com/highereducation) notes 'the beginnings of a sea change in the strategic priorities of leaders across the HE sector' as they increasingly focus on 'the competitive battle for fee-paying students and the imperative to offer attractive and rewarding learning experiences'. That survey also detects 'some scepticism' about the much predicted potential impact of MOOCs as massively disruptive and fee-reducing (see Chapter 8); while foreseeing the rise of the HE market as triggering 'substantial restructuring and rationalization among current institutions' (more by way of HEIs merging rather than just disappearing into insolvency). The 2012 OIA Annual Report (www.oiahe.org.he) also stresses the ever-growing student expectations of what the HEI should offer and deliver by way of the teaching package; it notes (again) a 'significant increase in the number of complaints received', indicative of a rising 'challenge' for HEIs 'in terms of managing expectations and delivering a high quality student experience' (the complaints graph for 2012 indicates 'another record year' where 'the upward trend shows no sign of slowing down'—and this before the higher fees regime applies to all UK/EU undergraduates…). On the broad international attempt to enhance quality in HE, see Land and Gordon for a comparative review, and especially Gorling, 'Quality Enhancement in England' (Land and Gordon, 2013: ch. 5).

As in the US literature, we have criticisms of the declining state of British HE. Naylor (2007) rages against how the newly corporatized universities are 'dishonest' in pretending that they are any longer adequately resourced to deliver effective mass undergraduate education as the unit of resource has fallen, and as the focus on RAE performance has brought neglect of teaching, let alone whether there really are well-paid graduate careers awaiting the increased output with its loans burden. Brabazon (2007) takes aim at the managerialism of 'men in shiny suits' duly awarded the 'vanity' title of professor who unleash a 'mudslide of management speak' and where 'clicking replaces thinking' within an under-resourced teaching process struggling to cope with students woefully 'ill-prepared' for university, all deficiencies which the management ignore and hide. She sees academic management as the problem, not the academic profession, in neglecting undergraduate teaching, in not allowing more students to be expelled 'for not doing the reading'. That said, in the context of mass HE 'academics must become proactive and experienced teachers, trained in pedagogy' (perhaps more like school teachers than Oxford dons!). So, does it matter if some Media Studies students coast through to graduation on less than 20 hours work a week, as long as medics and engineers are worked hard so as to be competent? Should everything be left to as free a market as possible, where HE is mainly a consumption good rather than a matter of personal and social investment, or is regulation needed to avoid a crafty mutually convenient disengagement contract among distracted academics and lazy instrumentalist students?

Yet it should be remembered that the 1990s/2000s criticisms of US HE discussed in this chapter were nothing new for back even in HE's halcyon days there were academics who had 'become less and less preoccupied with educating young people, more and more preoccupied with educating one and another by doing scholarly research which advances their discipline' (Jencks and Riesman, 1968: 13). But there is a convenient 'mutuality' in this new relationship with students in that they are less pressured as formerly demanding education gives way to quasi-automatic certification and credentialism, and HE becomes simply 'a social sieve'. And along the way, universities spend more and more in unaccountable ways as they offer lavish amenities on their students and throw money around 'to assemble, support, and pamper a faculty of gifted scholars' for whom any interest in and commitment to undergraduate teaching will not lead 'to greater prestige and influence than mediocre teaching', and for whom there is no 'professional training program that develops pedagogic skills in a systematic way'. Thus, the same old criticisms not after all for a mere twenty-five years as suggested but in fact dating back almost fifty years as US HE, according to Jencks and Riesman, slipped into its wicked ways during the 1960s, a route arguably followed by UK HE from the mid-1980s as it built into its structure financial incentives to pursue research at the expense of neglecting teaching and as massification reduced the unit of resource. Perhaps, in fact, it has ever been such, bearing in mind Truscot (1943 and 1945) tackling the dullness of teaching and the laziness of professors—and noting also the polite complaints made by the NUS to the UGC in 1960 about too many lectures and too few tutorials/seminars where there could be active dialogue between student and teacher (cited in Ashby and Anderson, 1970: 100–101).

Sadly, maybe it is simply that the academic profession is just as likely to become a conspiracy against the laity as any other and is very adept at getting around the supposed discipline of the market-place and of the supplier-consumer relationship. Certainly Adam Smith assumed this to be so: 'In every profession, the exertion of the greater part of those who exercise it, is always in proportion to the necessity they are under of making that exertion. This necessity is greatest with those to whom the emoluments of their profession are the only source from which they expect their fortune... [and preferably earned] where the competition is free [and against] the rivalship of competitors...' (Smith, 1776: Book V, ch. 1, Part III, Article 2d). Certainly Smith would have had no concerns about competitive markets in higher education, and hence it would be preferable that in some universities (such as at Glasgow where he held a chair) 'the greater part' of the teacher's income 'arises from the honoraries or fees of his pupils' so that 'he still has some dependency upon the affection, gratitude, and favourable report of those who have attended upon his instructions' as earned and deserved 'by the abilities and diligence with which he discharges every part of his duty'. In other universities, however, the salary was the whole income and hence the teacher is tempted 'to neglect' altogether his duty or at least 'to perform it in as careless and slovenly manner' as he can get away with—and especially where the only 'authority' over him is a corporate body 'of which he himself is a member', since then all the members 'are likely to make a common cause, to be all very indulgent to one another, and every man to consent that his neighbour may neglect his duty, provided he himself is allowed to neglect his own'. Commenting on Oxford, where Smith was a student for a time, 'the greater part of the public professors have, for these many years, given up altogether even the pretence of teaching'. Smith would indeed have welcomed the 2011 White Paper on HE that seeks to empower the student-consumer for otherwise: 'The discipline of colleges and universities is in general contrived, not for the benefit of the students, but for the interest, or more properly speaking, for the ease of the masters'.

Riesman (1998, original edition 1980) again stressed the cynical mutuality of the academic-student cosy arrangement: 'Even the most shoddy, cut-rate, and cut-throat degrees are not necessarily frauds on the student consumer. They may, in fact, be examples of collusion between academic vendor and student buyer to secure a credential at some monetary cost but almost no cost in time or effort' (Riesman, 1998: 117). He did not see consumer protection legislation as likely to help the student because government lacks the resources to police quality in HE while 'court actions are also too uneven'—as already noted, judicial deference towards the proper exercise of expert academic judgement shields universities and hence such judicial comments as that of Judge Plotkin dissenting in a 2002 Louisiana case are rare: there has been 'a continued and prolonged lack of oversight and accountability ... [whereby the courts] abrogate judicial responsibility to protect students [when] with the ever increasing price of higher education, universities now aggressively market themselves to would-be consumers [and] with the use of [such] marketing tactics by universities comes added responsibility and accountability to the consuming public' (quoted in Farrington and Palfreyman, 2012: para 12.88). Indeed, Riesman (1958) had called for much more information about HEIs to be made available so as to create the informed student-consumer: 'some impartial yet fearless agency' to 'issue vivid and candid reports' as does the 'Consumers Union' on goods such as vacuum cleaners' and to do 'research on the qualitative aspects of education from the student's point of view', acting as 'a respected clearing house for penetrating reports' (although one should not 'underestimate the resistance colleges would put up to this kind of investigation'). As already discussed, the 2013 *Which?* Report calls for much the same improvements to the imperfect British HE market so echoing Riesman from more than half a century before, and time will tell whether the English HEIs can shrug off such demands as did the US HE industry for the subsequent decades.

But, perhaps, and only half a century later—and indeed as recently (re-) urged in the 2006 Spellings Report on US HE and also as prominently flagged in the 2011 White Paper on UK HE—we will begin at last to see, for English HE at least, some progress towards the student-consumer becoming genuinely informed as the QAA and the OIA sharpen their regulatory axes, as the KIS data is unleashed (and hopefully improved), and as the *Which?* HE website goes live ('*Which?* University' at www.university.which.co.uk—in conjunction with the NUS, and covering around 30,000 courses at over 275 HEIs; see also the website www.bestcourse4me.com): let alone as the BIS digests the 2013 calls from *Which?* to force HEIs to be more forthcoming with informative data for applicants. Certainly the *Times Higher Education* Student Experience Survey 2013—'Student Satisfaction: What matters most to undergraduates'— in surveying some 12,000 students at 105 institutions across 21 dimensions of university life comments that 'reforms ramping up levels of competition' have made 'improving the student experience' into 'an even more pressing concern' for universities, reflected in more movement within the top ten than in past years: the University of East Anglia (UEA) in reaching number one for contented students has, for example, reduced class sizes and made academic staff more accessible as an example of how the importance of teaching is being recognized and its status enhanced (Lancaster, for instance, now has a maximum seminar size of 15). The impact of even higher fees since 2012–13 has yet to show up in such surveys, as also recognized in the HEFCE report 'Higher Education in England: Impact of the 2012 reforms' (March 2013: 2013/03 at HEFCE, www.hefce.ac.uk) which notes that the reforms are intended to achieve 'increased dynamism and student choice' but that at present 'it is impossible to separate short-term volatility from longer-term trends'.

By 2020, assuming the full-cost fees policy has not been reversed, it should be clear whether the student really has been put (back?) at the heart of the university, and whether, in the words of the 2011 White Paper, there has been 'a renewed focus on high quality teaching' offering 'better quality at lower cost' and 'making it harder for institutions to trade on their past reputations while offering poor teaching in the present' as well as whether HEFCE's proposed new role 'as a consumer champion for students' with 'a new explicit remit to promote the interests of students' has really put 'more power into the hands of students' and has been able 'to restore teaching to its proper position at the centre of every higher education institution's mission'. Indeed, the May 2013 advertisements seeking a new CEO for HEFCE duly stressed HEFCE's consumer protection function: it is implied that, in fact, it has long had 'a remit that has protected the student' (really?) and it is clear that it will be 'advocating for student interests' as 'stakeholders' in HE (and even if thereby student interests are brought into direct conflict with, say, academics' and HEIs' research priorities?). And, as elsewhere in this book where we compare the US and the UK, we note from Kaplin and Lee (2013: 3) that 'student consumerism' is evolving in the USA in the context of the contractual relationship between student and HEI, and in relation to ever increasing tuition fees: 'Students' and parents' expectations have increased, driven in part by increases in tutorial fees and in part by society's consumer orientation.'

It would seem unlikely, however, that the student will ever again end up quite as central and powerful as at the medieval University of Bologna which epitomized the student-focused model rather than the masters-centred model that prevailed at Paris, Oxford, and Cambridge (on medieval Oxford and Cambridge see Cobban, 1988). As described by Cobban (1999: 49–50), the Bologna students had 'a highly developed contractual view of university life' which saw the institution as simply an agency 'whose services and staff were open to hire like any other business' and which should operate in the best interests of the paying customer, the student community exercising control over the academic staff 'for every aspect of their professional lives': the hapless academics being reported to the rectors by student-elected spies and duly fined for starting a lecture late or for running over time, or for poor quality lecturing. All in all a system 'based on mutual mistrust and antagonisms' (similarly, Rait (1918: 24–28) talks of the masters being 'subject to numerous petty indignities'). Rashdall (1936: vol. 1, ch. 4, Section 4) notes how the Bologna professors were under 'the discipline' of 'their domineering pupils', and were 'treated as absent and incurred the appointed fine accordingly' if a minimum audience was not achieved; if the lecture got under way, the lecturer was 'regulated with the precision of a soldier on parade or a reader in a French public library', a deposit being forfeited if his lectures failed to cover the academic territory at the required pace.

Turning to the question of cost control in HE and its affordability, again more is known and discussed about US HE. The popularist and polemical books by Hacker and Dreifus (2010: ch. 7) and Kamenetz (2010: ch. 3), for instance, explore 'why college costs so much' as HEIs 'continue to run on myths and mantras, illusions and delusions' while refusing to undertake 'self-scrutiny' (Hacker and Dreifus, 2010: 258–259); and they discuss how to tackle the 'unsustainable cost spiral' that is mainly driven by taxpayer-retreat and cost sharing in the public institutions combined with the fact that HEIs are loath to address cost-cutting (Kamenetz, 2010: 50). Similarly, Bennett and Wilezol (2013: ch. 1) explore 'The Borrowing Binge' that has fuelled hikes in tuition fees and enabled US HE to avoid bothering with cost control let alone cost reduction as achieved in almost all other areas of US economic activity (except perhaps for the military and in healthcare).

There are, however, other more academic and sober studies of the cost structure and the 'cost disease' of US HE: Bowen (1980), Clotfelter (1996),

Ehrenberg (2000), Massy (2003), Vedder (2004), Archibald and Feldman (2011) and Martin (2011). The Archibald and Feldman volume is defensive, wringing hands about HE costing so much and concluding there is little to be done about it; while the last three volumes are scathing in their analysis and their remedies stark: market competition and discipline is needed to force cost control and innovation within inefficient and unresponsive universities, undergraduate fees should not be subsidizing faculty research, research might even be hived off into institutes so as to end the massively expensive prestige arms race based on research output (Brewer et al., 2002), faculty teaching loads need to increase, public institutions must be privatized, administrative bloat has to be addressed (Ginsberg, 2011), the principal-agent problem within HE has to be dealt with (there is nobody in charge who is made answerable to the consumer), a much better and deeper understanding of the teaching and learning process is required, other kinds of providers of undergraduate education should be encouraged so as to develop competition and drive down prices, blanket and excessive public subsidy could be replaced by fees vouchers as student-centred funding that would empower the student-qua-consumer. (West also argues for privatization and vouchers in ch. 5 of Sommer, 1995.)

Martin (2011) is perhaps the most robust in his assessment, talking: of 'extravagant increases in cost' matched only by the neglect of teaching that results in 'a secular decline in quality'; of the fact that HE 'has the worst record of any sector in the economy' for cost control; of innovation being 'stagnant'; of academics wanting to, and being allowed to, teach only what suits them as 'an egregious governance failure' and 'serious agency abuse on the part of faculty'; of faculty failing to discipline the shirkers among themselves; of 'an expansion in the output of research with dubious value' at the expense of teaching and of increased costs; of HE in fact happily and greedily embracing market opportunities while its defenders see 'nefarious capitalist values' impacting upon the campus. It is not a pretty story: it is one of producer-capture, of rent-seeking behaviour, of the exploitation of monopoly, of weak management, of poor governance, of grossly overpaid CEOs, of inadequate competition, of incumbents erecting accreditation hurdles for new entrants, of inefficiency and incompetence, of groupthink, of Luddite behaviour, of neglect of the prime teaching mission of the university, of classic conspiracy against the laity, of potential hubris should the middle class eventually and successfully rebel against the increased unaffordability of tuition fees and if market forces manage to deliver disruptive innovation by way of MOOCs.

Part of the affordability problem in US HE, however, is a decades-long price surge driven by cheap borrowing to fund the payment of fees; the student-consumer became insensitive to price given the availability of low-cost debt combined with the assumption that high fees might hopefully signal high quality, as well as the message that not gaining a degree left one doomed to a lifetime of no or low-pay employment. The result leaves the US facing another kind of sub-prime mortgages bubble (the one that triggered the global financial crisis of 2007–08) as graduate loan debt reaches $1 trillion spread over some 40m US citizens, 2m of whom are unemployed as the interest on their debt accumulates (Collinge, 2009) and exceeds auto loans debt or credit card debts (an analogy is the similar spiral in the fees charged by UK independent schools over the past decade or so, which were also often funded by parents borrowing at low interest rates against seemingly ever-rising house prices). There are worries that this massive US graduate debt burden is a brake on the economy as it dampens consumption spending and home purchases among the indebted.

Perhaps Professor Barr, as noted in Chapter 5, is right to suggest that UK HEIs should not be allowed to set uncapped fees funded by unlimited loans: that would encourage the same wastefulness within UK HE, as found in US HE, and also would become a crippling burden on the economy. Ways just have to be found to make HE less costly and to improve its productivity (although at present it is hard to find agreement on how to even measure HE productivity let alone enhance it—see Sullivan, 2012). Even if fees stick at around the £9,000 capped amount for some years yet, US average student debt of some $24k (c.£18k) is less than half of what will potentially be the English norm of about £45–50k (three or even four years fees at, say, £9k per annum plus three or four years of living cost loans at over £5k per annum). In the US, President Obama's 2013 State of the Union address has called upon Congress to amend the Higher Education Act so that affordability and cost/fees control becomes a factor in accreditation as well as encouraging for-profit providers to deliver lower cost HE than the public sector HEIs seem capable of doing. Conceivably HE will in due course face the equivalent of the no-frills airlines challenging incumbent legacy carriers as a for-profit easyJet or Ryanair enters the game (see Chapter 11 on the for-profit HE providers). There again, perhaps both US and UK HE can shake off the criticisms and calls for reform as they have for the last 50 years or so...

One issue in students' contemplating the 'affordability' of HE is their perception of the financial return on the investment by way of the graduate premium as the extra lifelong earnings, often said somewhat simplistically in the context of the 2012–13 fees hike to be a headline-grabbing '£100,000'—a figure which as an average hides a mass of variation in terms of being a graduate in what subject from what university, and of whether an individual's wider social and cultural capital is contributing to employability (or indeed his/her unemployability). The BIS has, in fact, recently issued a new analysis putting the pay-off (after allowing for student debt based on the new higher fees of £9,000) at £168k for men and £252k for women (presumably reflecting the latter's especially poor pay for those without a degree), but such figures still, of course, being only a crude average across all subjects/HEIs (BIS Research Report 112, 'The Impact of university degrees on the lifecycle of earnings: Some further analysis', August 2013). There are doubts (Brown et al., 2011; Blacker, 2013) over the ability of HE to continue to deliver for the consumer as it may have done in the past as the over-expansion of over-costly HE has left too many over-indebted graduates chasing declining opportunities for traditional graduate careers within 'congested labor markets' and hence they face the evermore 'visible and painful' reality of 'a broken promise' hitherto neatly linking 'education, jobs, and rewards', an end to the 'fairy tale' of HE and 'the narrow-minded (human capital) view of education as an economic investment'. All as something of 'an inconvenient truth' about the 'education explosion' in terms of the HE sector seeking and governments profligately providing public funding for HE on the basis of its supposed contribution to economic growth and also in terms of HE selling its expensive services to student-consumers on the basis of promises of enhanced employability within well-paid graduate jobs—and hence, of course, the concerns already discussed over the percentage of graduates who will never earn enough to repay their student loans...

Similarly, Wolf (2002) questions 'the great secular faith' of 'education spending in [promoting] economic growth' as HE now churns out many more graduates 'who have, on average, been considerably less well and intensively educated' than those of a generation ago: Wolf recommends ensuring that primary and secondary education are adequately funded as a much greater priority over HE. Helpman (2004) also notes the very limited role of the human capital theory in explaining 'the mystery of economic growth', stressing that the real contribution of HE to the economy may well be much more by way of its intellectual property creation and exploitation (see in addition the papers collected in Wolf and McNally, 2011). Much the same point is made by Alvesson (2013) who challenges the US and European over-expansion of HE, noting the reduced employment prospects of the graduate output, as well as grade inflation and dumbing-down across academe: 'never before have so many studied for so long and learnt so little' (Alvesson, 2013: 75). He could have added, and nor have they eventually emerged from full-time education with so few job/career opportunities while burdened with so much debt having, especially in the USA and now particularly in England, paid so much in tuition fees. That said, there is the much more upbeat BIS Report 110 (August 2013), 'The relationship between graduates and economic growth across countries', which argues that 'at least one-third' of UK labour productivity growth of some 35% over 1994–2005 is the result of HE churning out more graduates as it massified—although the report also concedes that 'providing estimates of the impact of HE on growth and competitiveness is a major challenge'. There are also others—Lane and Johnstone (2012)—who see a clear link between investing in HE and economic progress; as also overall did the Dearing Report (NCIHE, 1997: Reports 7 and 8), although it noted that there is 'no consensus' on the causes of economic growth and there are 'wide margins of uncertainty' (in Paragraphs 2.32 and 2.33 of Report 7), while the direction of causation is 'unclear' in terms of more HE means more economic growth or in fact vice versa (Paragraph 11 of Report 8). And, in bold contrast to the BIS latest report, there is the polemical critique of HE as simply (and allegedly) a huge waste of money for so many graduates, coming usually from extremely successfully self-made business entrepreneurs (for example, Dolan, 2010). In fact, in the US data is available in some states on the precise value of a specific degree from a particular HEI (for instance, in Virginia at www.esm.collegemeasures. org/esm/Virginia; and see more generally www.payscale.com/best-colleges/ degrees.asp/, and www.cew.georgetown.edu/collegepayoff). The UK is some way behind, the under-informed applicant once being told, as noted, a rather simplistic, perhaps misleading, story about a degree being worth on average around £100k over a lifetime of extra earnings—and with little explanation as to just what range such an average hides, exactly what variation there is across different HEIs (and among different courses/subjects), whether that tempting headline figure is after the payment of fees for and the funding of living costs during HE (and still less whether the opportunity cost of earnings foregone while in HE is factored in, let alone allowance for interest payments on the student loan debt). Yet there is hope for the UK HE applicant trying to make informed and judicious decisions about the spending of several years of fees at up to £9,000 and living costs of more than £5,000: the BIS message is to be updated, again as noted.

And, perhaps more usefully, data from Her Majesty's Revenue and Customs (HMRC), the Student Loans Company (SLC), and the Higher Education Statistics Agency (HESA) is being mined and compared in an interesting and important research project funded by the Nuffield Foundation that is the work of three academics (Dearden, Shepherd, and Vignoles: 'Estimating the Human Capital of Graduates'). The release of this data in 2014–15 or so may well be transformative in debates about, and in facing up to issues such as, the affordability of HE (both for the nation/taxpayer and for the student/family), the funding of HEIs, the value for money of HE courses, and the viability of individual HEIs and of subjects/disciplines within the regulated HE market over the next decade or so. It could even lead to the state in effect offering a voucher to cover the loan of, say, only £6,000 per annum by way of a voucher towards tuition fees and leaving it to those HEIs which elect to charge more to find for themselves private capital willing to offer additional loans towards the higher fees with the capital markets duly testing whether the HEI's record of producing employable and sufficiently well-paid graduates justifies the risk of bad debt within such a private loan-book (see Lleras, 2007, on a capital markets approach to the financing of students paying fees). The data should also con-tribute to informing the university applicant on what is the likely private rate of return on specific degree course X at annual fees of £Yk at particular uni-versity Z, as against the crude averages bandied about as the lifetime graduate earnings premium. Certainly, the ONS Report on 'Graduates in the UK Labour

Market 2013' (November 2013 at www.ons.gov.uk) does not provide encouragement for the belief or hope that an expensive degree automatically leads to a well-paid career, let alone to the hoped-for graduate premium: half of recent graduates are employed in 'a non-graduate role' and this is 'an upward trend' since 2001; while a third of graduates five years on are still in 'a low skilled role'.

Thus, we have the concept of the student as a consumer in terms of 'the impact of the consumption model on universities' (Williams, 2013), which has seen the instrumentalist and infantilized student consumer emerge as a result of 'a number of social, political, and cultural trends' over several decades rather than simply because of the recent (re-)introduction of tuition fees barely a decade ago—and also see Barnett, as ch. 5 of Callender and Scott, 2013, for a critique of the 'questionable' concept of the student-qua-consumer: the White Paper's policies 'are liable to lead to an impairment [rather than the expected enhancement] of the student experience' (86). A process marked along the way by such as the 1993 'Charter for Higher Education' which referred to 'customers' and 'standards of service'; and then by the Dearing Report (1997) focusing on the student being at the centre of HE (see ch. 3 of the Dearing Report). A process also aided by the growth of student satisfaction surveys that oblige academics 'to avoid making intellectual demands of their students' for fear of earning a low score from what are now to be viewed as 'vulnerable customers' within the 'therapeutic' university (Ecclestone and Hayes, 2009). Williams (2013) urges HE to move 'beyond entitlement', to rediscover the idea and ideal of 'a community of scholars' engaged in an 'intellectual collaboration' that inevitably brings 'elements of social, emotional, or intellectual risk' and where universities are no longer to be 'held to account for the emotionally arbitrary satisfaction levels of their students'; to move beyond the 'intellectual passivity' of the contemporary student experience. As, of course, with the vague 'manifesto' of the CDBU discussed in Chapter 5 the problem is, however, that we have a mass HE system that is in effect a TE system of wildly differing institutions serving the very variable needs of widely different types of students in terms of their motivation and fitness for higher education, and it is not going to go away so that academe can revert to the halcyon days where students are no longer consumers, customers, or clients but are once again junior members of the academic enterprise; the genie of massification, marketization, and managerialism is not going to be put back into the bottle.

Yet, clearly, the market model, marketing discourse, and the consumer metaphor have their limitations in describing and guiding the student-university relationship, whether in terms of what it is in legal theory or what happens in practical reality. Even if, 'both global forces and historical precedent point to an inevitability of marketization' as 'an encroachment of market machinations', as 'unstoppable' and indeed as welcomed by significant parts of academe 'seduced by the consumerist culture' and willingly embracing 'the market logic' of, say, competitive research funding (Molesworth et al., 2012: ch. 18).

Such limitations include the fact that HE is a process requiring active and prolonged participation by the consumer, and one where the customer simply cannot always be assumed to be right since he/she may need to be failed, and also where the students inevitably may not all be satisfied all the time with the pace of their progress along the sometimes convoluted and difficult road of learning for which simplistic evaluation methods drawn from other areas of commercial activity for measuring supposed satisfaction are inappropriate.

For the various reasons (discussed in Chapter 5) the public role, character, and value of the university began to be called into question after the golden interlude (detailed in Chapter 4), leaving the universities to become market spaces and face the often unexpected and unintended consequences of having to operate within these new HE markets, and to encounter the student-as-consumer (with his/her irritatingly varied and sometimes only dimly perceived needs) which may involve the HEI cynically hyping the non-academic consumption elements of the campus offerings (a careful tour of the glitzy new recreational and residential facilities, having skipped past the understocked library and avoided detail on burgeoning class sizes—Slaughter and Rhoades, 2004: 297–302). At the same time as universities struggle with markets and consumers, government retreats from being the direct and main funder of English undergraduate teaching and hence needs to determine its residual role in regulating the HE market-place so as to ensure a degree of consumer protection for the not always adequately informed and fully empowered student-consumer deploying what is in effect his/her 'voucher' valued at up to £9,000 (or rather £27,000 or even £36,000 counting all three or four years of a course).

One aspect of creating such a regulated market is whether enhanced competition of HE provision and/or major changes in the way higher education is delivered can be used to drive down price (fees) in the context of the student increasingly financing HE (Heller and Callender, 2013). Interestingly, in their book on government failures King and Crewe (2013) count among their many egregious examples the Coalition Government's tuition fees policy in that there has not (so far) been any sign of the price competition that was expected to make the charging of £9,000 exceptional and to result in an average fee of *c*.£7,500. Allegedly, government has 'bungled in a big way' in that the policy is also not reducing the cost of higher education for the taxpayer obliged to fund student loans to pay fees. We will return to these issues in Chapter 8 (the delivery mechanism within higher education) and Chapter 11 (the provision of greater competition within higher education).

7

The Rise of the Research Agenda: Redefining the Academic Mission

Abstract: Integral to the English idea of the university was the inextricable link between teaching and research. However, increasingly it has been argued that teaching needs to be informed by a commitment to scholarship (rarely carefully defined), and the growing reality is that some academics have contracts to pursue only research (although they may supervise graduate students), while others are contracted to undertake only teaching duties (although they may also have their own limited research agendas). Within this broad context, the purpose of this chapter is to analyse the structural development of English higher education with particular reference to the evolution of the Research Assessment Exercises since their instigation in 1986. The argument is that in terms of quality research, English higher education is composed of a number of sectors that, although they overlap at the edges, form a hierarchical whole. It is neither a straightforward bipolar model nor a sharply structured pyramid. While research excellence is widely spread, nonetheless there are different levels of institutional commitment as reflected in the overall quality profiles, the quantity and range of research outputs, and the academic focus of those research commitments. The chapter concludes that, while in English higher education the commitment to research is indeed widespread, the funding mechanisms (which are politically controlled) that have accompanied the Research Assessment Exercises have been manipulated over time to construct an increasingly differentiated institutional model. It appears that the intention is to create an elite cadre of research institutions by restricting funding to those 'units of assessment' that have been assessed as demonstrating only the very highest research quality.

INTRODUCTION

Integral to the traditional idea of the English university was the understanding that the transmission and expansion of knowledge were but two sides of the same coin. Consequently, the established assumption was that academics had a duty to be engaged in both undergraduate teaching and expanding knowledge. The Robbins Report reiterated probably the best view of the classical perspective:

> There is no borderline between teaching and research, they are complementary and overlapping activities. A teacher who is advancing his general knowledge of his subject is both improving himself and laying foundations for his research.
>
> The researcher often finds that his personal work provides him with fresh and apt illustration which helps him to set a subject in a new light when he turns to prepare a lecture.
>
> (Committee on Higher Education, 1963: para 557, as quoted in Shattock, 2012: 170)

Although the pursuit of research may have enhanced qualities that made you a better teacher, it is impossible to assert that one's particular research interests would always have had a direct input into one's teaching. In many fields the researcher is at the disciplinary boundaries far removed from the staple fare that is likely to be the diet of the average undergraduate, but the demands of doing good research, perhaps above all a commitment to rigorous critical thinking, was arguably the very quality that made for good teaching.

In practice, the degree of synergy between teaching and research would undoubtedly vary, ranging from the broad claim that at their best they were both driven forward by a commitment to common values to the possibility of a very direct liaison in which you taught a course related to your research field, which in that case it was even possible your own personal research could form part of the course. Moreover, even if there should be no *direct* link to the precise focus of one's research, the relationship could be established by placing a specific course in the broader scholarly tradition of the discipline in which it was embedded, with the assumption that academics could locate both their teaching and their research within that tradition. In effect, both teaching and research would be seen as two interactive halves of a common intellectual tradition.

Even the push for the idea that universities can be dedicated solely to teaching genuflects to the claim that its quality at the very least will be informed by research. For example, the 2003 White Paper argued that:

> It is clear that good scholarship, in the sense of remaining aware of the latest research and thinking within a subject, is essential for good teaching, but not that it is necessary to be active in cutting edge research to be an excellent teacher.
>
> (Department for Education and Skills, 2003: 54)

On the other hand, this could be interpreted as little more than a commonly expressed platitude to assuage the reality that a new model of the university was taking shape, one in which the functions of research and teaching were steadily being separated.

The reasons for the attempt to construct a synergy between teaching and research may be interpreted more mundanely: as a politically convenient social construction rather than the proclamation of a pedagogical truth. The academic profession in England took root in the latter half of the nineteenth century, which witnessed *The Revolution of the Dons* (Rothblatt, 1968) as the clergymen gave ground to the dons (Engel, 1983). It was important for the Oxbridge dons to define their roles in a way that would distinguish them from the masters of the public schools with which many of the colleges retained close ties, including an entwining of the careers of schoolmaster and don. Incorporating into the academic role the idea that the don was charged with the responsibility of enhancing scholarship meant an escape from the implied drudgery of being a mere schoolmaster. Moreover, at Oxford (Tapper and Palfreyman, 2011: 26–28) the alleged synergy formulated a bridge between the idea of the college as providing a liberal education for the nation's emerging elites (Newman, 1959) and the incorporation of the colleges into the university by becoming headquarters for its faculties (Sparrow, 1967). The social construction, therefore, was of the academic as both a tutor and a scholar, which was accompanied by a political compromise that saw the university, and not just at Oxford, as a base for research as well as teaching.

The propagation of the idea that within the university teaching and research should interact to form a synonymous whole has been reinforced by the argument that both pursuits should be steered by the academic profession. The academy is seen as the guardian of high-status knowledge, which it controls by determining both how it is to be taught and expanded. But this is to present the argument far too starkly. Inevitably the universities adjusted their degree programmes to accommodate changes in society as most clearly seen in the incorporation of the expanding professions (Perkin, 1989) and the burgeoning sciences (with particular reference to Cambridge's Natural Sciences Tripos, see Macleod and Moseley, 1980). And for both the professions and science there was a need to satisfy the interests of the professional associations and scientific bodies. Moreover, the state from at least the First World War onwards (note the creation of the Department of Scientific and Industrial Research in 1916) has taken a persistent interest in research and more particularly in constructing a policy for science (Salter and Tapper, 1994: 155–181). Indeed, it could be argued that the most potent forces for the very foundation of the University of London and the nineteenth-century civic universities were the pressures exerted by the presence of an expanding professional class and a growing manufacturing base. The question then is how were these pressures accommodated by the universities? To what extent did the pattern of accommodation vary and how are those variations to be explained (Barnes, 1996)?

This chapter examines the pressures upon the evolution of the research agenda in contemporary English higher education, essentially since the UGC's decision to allocate its funding of research through the Research Assessment Exercises. Recent developments will demonstrate the attempts to steer higher education research through a combination of political pressure and the funding mechanisms established by the quasi-state, that is by both the funding and research councils. The intention is to examine the implementation of the Research Assessment Exercises and analyse their evolution. In the process of achieving these two goals, the chapter assesses their significance for decision-making within higher education institutions, their impact upon academic faculty, and their reshaping of the funding council model of governance. It will conclude by an extensive evaluation of their impact upon the overall structure of the university system. As the steering of the system's academic profile still remains heavily dependent upon the willingness of institutions to comply with the implied rationale of the politically driven policy implementation strategies, in Chapter 10 we show how a range of individual institutions of higher education have responded to these pressures.

THE PRESSURES FOR CHANGE IN ENGLISH HIGHER EDUCATION AND THE IMPLEMENTATION OF THE RESEARCH ASSESSMENT AGENDA

In addition to the rise of mass higher education and the funding pressure this has generated, there are two broad pressures that have shaped the overall pattern of higher education development in recent decades. Firstly, there is the need for the universities to demonstrate that they provide sufficient value in return for their receipt of public expenditure (value for money), and, secondly this value is measured by their ability to meet certain social and economic goals deemed to be vital to the welfare of the wider society. There are no objective measures to ascertain whether or not universities are achieving value for money in terms of meeting these goals, for this is determined by political judgements with different governments arriving at their own (and possibly varying) conclusions. Until recently the social goal has revolved around the widening participation agenda, but the current Coalition Government has reinterpreted this by requiring higher education institutions to promote social mobility. The economic goal is to provide teaching that matches the manpower demands of the evolving occupational structure and to undertake research that enhances the productive process. Thus, the purpose of higher education is defined by changing political interpretations of its societal relevance.

We have already briefly considered four initiatives pursued by the University Grants Committee (UGC) as in its latter years it pursued a markedly more proactive role in shaping the development of British higher education. Firstly, the founding of the 1960s new universities, which the UGC saw in part as an initiative to promote the restructuring of knowledge, both its content and academic management. Secondly, the attempt to monitor and steer though its subject sub-committees the evolution of the overall academic map with particular reference to the proliferation of more specialized knowledge areas in which Russian Studies was the cause célèbre. Thirdly, its decision to distribute selectively the funding cuts imposed in the early 1980s by the then Secretary of State, Sir Keith Joseph. Fourthly, its instigation in 1986 of the first Research Assessment Exercise (RAE) designed to distribute selectively core public funding to support research. Henceforth, while the principle that the universities received a block grant from the Council would be preserved, it would be clear what percentage of a university's income was dependent upon the assessment of the quality of its research output. The RAE (to be known as the Research Excellence Framework—REF—for the 2014 evaluations) is worthy of special attention not only for its potential long-term impact upon the structure of the system, but also because of its profound implications for how we are to interpret the idea of the university. Can the RAEs be seen as the necessary precursors of the idea of 'the teaching-only' universities as the logical conclusion of the increasingly selective funding of research?

The origins of the RAE have been well documented (Salter and Tapper, 1994: 173–179; Shattock, 1994: 37–44; Kogan and Hanney, 2000: 96–103; Tapper, 2007: 188–189; Brown, 2013: 43–46; Shattock, 2013: 173–175). Broadly speaking, there are two entwining explanations. Firstly, Shattock presents us with the politically pragmatic case. He notes that with reference to the distribution of its recurrent research funding grant prior to the first RAE: 'The UGC did not reveal the basis of its decisions on the grounds that this might jeopardize universities' autonomy of decision-making in distributing resources so the differentiation was camouflaged or simply lost in quinquennial expansion targets' (Shattock, 2012: 170–171). Moreover, this was accepted by the Committee of Vice-Chancellors and Principals (CVCP) because it believed such revelation could lead to greater UGC control along with internal conflicts within universities over the distribution of their research funding. However, in the context of political pressure for greater openness in the distribution of public funding, coupled with more sympathy within the research councils for the selective allocation of resources, it was increasingly difficult to sustain such a stance. The outcome was the instigation in 1986 of the first RAE. All commentators agree that Peter Swinnerton-Dyer, the then Chair of the UGC, was the primary mover in the instigation of the new allocation model, but Shattock claims that he did not see it '... as anything other than a short-term mechanism for redistributing funds. There was no indication that this was to become an apparently permanent feature of the funding and differentiation of UK higher education' (Shattock, 2006: 138).

However, while it may have been a political fix for Swinnerton-Dyer, there was clearly a body of opinion that wanted both less opaqueness in the distribution of resources and believed as a matter of principle that research funding should be allocated selectively. In order to sustain the output of quality research it was important to reward those who were responsible for most of its production, which would also put pressure on other less research-active universities to up their game. In the words of Kogan and Hanney:

> The majority of the policy makers or policy influencers whom we interviewed either believed that selectivity and the resulting stratification were inevitable or that the policy was right in principle.
>
> (Kogan and Hanney, 2000: 101)

Moreover, they go on to suggest that Swinnerton-Dyer's appointment as Chair of the UGC was in part due to his 'known preference for excellence and stratification' (Kogan and Hanney, 2000: 96), which suggests that his construction of the RAE may have been more than a 'short-term mechanism for redistributing funds'.

More important than cavilling over the role of Swinnerton-Dyer is to understand the broad guidelines which underwrote the operations of the first RAE. Although the pressure for selectivity in the distribution of its core research funding may not have come from the UGC (or indeed from the universities), it assumed, under the auspices of Swinnerton-Dyer, the lead role in the instigation of the process. Nonetheless, certainly after the UGC was replaced in 1989 by the funding councils, there was always the possibility that governments could intervene to impose their own policy demands. Therefore, even if the instigation of the RAEs was a political fix to resolve a contemporary malaise, the fact that it was amenable to government pressure has helped in fact to ensure its longevity.

While the RAE was devised as a mechanism that enabled the UGC to distribute the public funding of higher education research while fending off its critics, it also pointed the way to the Committee becoming a regulatory body, a mantle that clearly has been assumed by its successors the funding councils. In a letter sent to Lord Chilver, the first Chair of the Universities Funding Council (UFC), the Secretary of State laid out 'broad guidance' on how he understood the relationship between the Council and the Government in which he asserted:

> Within these constraints, it will be for the Council itself to devise appropriate means of allocating funds between institutions. I shall however expect to see

two key features. The first is a means of specifying clearly what universities are expected to provide in return for public funds. The second is a systematic method of monitoring institutional performance. I attach particular importance to the latter...

(Secretary of State, 31 October 1988)

Thus the UGC replaced its internal mechanisms for the distribution of its research funding with a process open to public scrutiny, but at the same time it had to respond to the increased government demand for greater accountability, which it alone at the time could put into operation. For the higher education institutions the consequence was that they would have to put into effect research strategies, which would be public documents subject to public scrutiny.

While the RAE kept direct government intervention at bay, it also helped to legitimate the selective allocation process in the eyes of the academic community by basing the exercise upon peer review. It was possible, therefore, to see this as a form of self-regulation which was firmly under academic control. Moreover, it embraced the whole of the UK system of higher education (post-devolution the national funding councils carry out a joint research assessment exercise and, although there is agreement on the assessment procedures, the individual councils determine how they will distribute their own funding). Furthermore, it incorporated the whole range of disciplines, although some had argued that it was not an appropriate mechanism for measuring research quality in the humanities and social sciences. But not to be incorporated raised the fear that research in the excluded disciplines could be seen as of less value. The decision whether to participate or not in the evaluative process was made by the individual universities, but almost inevitably this was 'Hobson's choice' for not to partake meant forsaking the possibility of obtaining research funding and sent out the message that you were not a research-active university no matter what evidence you might present to the contrary.

What was equally significant for the universities was that they determined what research outputs should be submitted—whichever the departments (units of assessment) and the academics deemed eligible. The point is that the assessment process did require active institutional and academic participation, providing an opportunity for the universities to establish their identities and reflect on how they would like them to develop. The RAEs, therefore, were integral to the process of establishing institutional missions. For the academics it became critically important to be seen as research-active; for many it was a key ingredient in finding a post, securing internal promotion, or instigating a move to another university. Moreover, it has enabled some academics to secure contracts that did not oblige them to engage in teaching, especially undergraduate teaching.

Perhaps the most important feature of the initial RAE is that, although it was designed to secure the selective distribution of research funding, it was not a 'winner-takes-all' model in which a relatively small number of universities would secure all the funding while the majority were left empty-handed. The assumption was that, although research excellence would tend to be located in some universities, there would be at least pockets of excellence throughout the system. The evaluation was of the comparative performances of different departments rather than of different universities. This did not preclude the possibility of a university obtaining the highest rating across all its departments while other universities demonstrated small pockets of excellence. As we will see, over time the debate moves on to whether the allocation process for research funding should shift from a model that encourages selectivity to one that embraces concentration. But what made the initial drive for selectivity widely acceptable was the evaluation of departmental performance as opposed to assessing the overall capacity of a university to provide research excellence.

Not surprisingly, although the operation of the 1986 RAE went relatively smoothly, it was not without its hitches and in particular the fact that not all of the panels adopted the same grading scale smacked of incompetence. Trevor Smith's judgement that it was 'deeply flawed' and 'by any test this was a pretty rough and ready lash of techniques'(Smith, 1987: 303–309, as quoted in Tapper, 2007: 101) is reflected in other assessments, although not so stridently expressed (Phillimore, 1989). But at least the technical proficiency of the review process could be improved, and the Roberts Review of the exercise post-RAE2001 concluded that by then, 'The system was, we believe a qualified success. The grades commanded great respect and helped to drive improvement in UK research, which has helped to maintain the UK's position as one of the leading research nations' (Roberts, May 2003: 41).

But more significant than the operational efficiency of the process is how two key variables have evolved over time: the evaluative scale (including its component parts and the relative weights attached to them), and how the scale relates to the distribution of funding. Both variables have changed over time, reflecting a combination of political pressures and inputs from the academic community. As a broad generalization it can be said that the evolution of the scale has been controlled more by the academic community acting in conjunction with the UGC/funding councils, while its impact upon the distribution of funding has been driven more by negotiation between government and the UGC/funding councils. It is the shifts in the construction of these two variables that determine whether the assessment of research has led to either selectivity or concentration in the funding model, so resulting in either the emergence of a highly stratified system of higher education or one that still retains a strong measure of a shared purpose.

THE EVOLVING RAE MODEL

Although they reach different conclusions on the impact of the research assessment process on the structure of UK higher education, both Shattock (2012: 175–183) and Brown (2013: 46–54) provide a reasonably detailed overview of its development between 1986 and the present—with assessments occurring in 1986, 1989, 1992, 1996, 2001, 2008, and now the Research Excellence Framework to be concluded in 2014. Between 1989 and 2008 the evaluative scale went through three phases (note in the 1986 RAE the assessment panels constructed different scales, although overall they broadly followed the model employed in 1989 and 1992):

1. The 1989/1992 exercises: a five point scale ranging from '…international excellence in some sub-areas of activity and to obtainable levels of national excellence in virtually all others' to 'research quality that equates to attainable level of national excellence in none, or virtually none, of the sub-areas of activity'.

   (Universities Funding Council, 26, 1992)

2. The 1996/2001 exercises: a seven point scale (a 5* rating has been added and the third rating divided into 3a and 3b) which ranges from 'research quality that equates to attainable levels of international excellence in a majority of sub-areas of activity and attainable levels of national excellence in all others' to 'research quality that equates to attainable levels of national excellence in none, or virtually none, of the sub-areas of activity'.

   (RAE96, 1/1996; RAE2001, 4/2001)

3. The 2008 exercise: a five point scale (from 4* through to 1*) which ranges from 'quality that is world-leading in terms of originality, significance, and rigour' to 'quality that falls below the standard of nationally recognized work'.

   (RAE2008, 23 April 2013)

RAE2008 represented a clear break with the past in the sense that rather than presenting a finite score for each unit of assessment: 'Results were published as a graded profile…to allow the funding bodies to identify 'pockets of excellence' and reduce the abrupt grade boundaries which had previously had significant funding impacts' (Brown, 2013: 51). The impending Research Excellence Framework will follow the 2008 model (with more standardization of both procedures and criteria, and a reduction in the number of sub-panels from 67 to 36, but still dependent on peer review rather than a metrics-based mode of assessment) but the most controversial new element is the 'requirement that departments demonstrate the "impact" of their research—its benefits to the economy, society, and culture beyond the academy' (Gibney, 1 November, 2012: 41).

But what has been the impact of the assessment exercises upon the public funding of research in higher education? In the words of Shattock:

> The significance of the 1985 resource allocation process was the way it established a direction of travel towards a more differential system.... 1985–86 established an escalator, upwards or downwards, which very few institutions were ever able to escape... The RAE represented the operation of the 'Mathew Principle' in its purest form....

> (Shattock, 2012: 177)

The concentration of funding appears to have increased steadily between 1986 and 2008, with decisions to remove over time any funding from the lower-graded departments and to increase the differentials amongst those with higher scores. That this was at least in part a result of political intervention is most clearly seen in the government's 2003 White Paper, *The Future of Higher Education*:

> ...a further Research Assessment Exercise is not due until 2008, and we believe that there is a case for more discrimination between the best before then.... We will ask HEFCE, using the results of the latest Research Assessment Exercise, along with international peer review of additional material, to identify the very best of the 5* departments which have a critical mass of researchers—'6*'—and will provide additional resources to give them an uplift in funding over the next three years.

> (Department for Education and Skills, 2003: 30)

In spite of HEFCE putting its objections on the record, the departments were duly selected and their enhanced funding was forthcoming (Tapper, 2007: 197).

But that was far from the end of the matter. The methodology employed in the 2008 RAE (the presentation of profiles of research excellence within the units of assessment as opposed to awarding an overall score for each unit of assessment) demonstrated 'that research quality is far more widely spread than might previously have been thought, and shows that much of the research produced in institutions where research funds have been concentrated is not particularly high quality' (Adams and Gurney, 2010: para 27). The consequence, therefore, of RAE2008 appeared to be a reaffirmation of the principle that research funding should be distributed selectively on the basis of measured quality. However, as we will see when we analyse the rise of the mission groups in UK higher education, RAE2008 has generated a very significant political struggle. On the one hand, there is the Russell Group (by and large its members have been the major beneficiaries of the selective allocation of research funding), which has started to argue that, if the UK wishes to remain at the cutting edge of research, then resources need to be concentrated upon a limited number of universities. Whereas the other groups, although advocating the continuation of the selective allocation of funding, insist that funding should follow wherever research excellence is to be found.

Under government pressure, HEFCE has already moved to undermine the somewhat wider distribution of research funding that RAE2008 implied. Firstly, it has used 'revised weighting factors to shift the balance across 1*/2*/3*/4* units from 0/1/3/7 to 0/1/3/9 so increasing the concentration of resources towards the research with the highest impact' (Adams and Gurney, 2010: para 28; see also Corbyn, 11 February 2010: 12). Subsequently, it has shifted the balance further still by removing 'all funding previously allocated on the basis of 2* research: QR income will now be determined solely on the basis of 3* and 4* research—with 4* continuing to account for three times as much as 3*' (Jump, 29 March 2012: 7). One may question the very purpose of the Research Assessment Exercises if there is a broadly based political drive, embracing governments of differing persuasions, to ensure the increased concentration of research funding. In this respect, HEFCE appears to have become little more than a conduit for government policy, a surrogate for the government of the day.

A NOTE ON THE RESEARCH COUNCILS

This apparent attempt to stratify the system into different sectors has also been reinforced by the funding strategies pursued by the research councils, the second arm of the dual support system for the sustenance of higher education research. The distribution of research council grant funding between 1995–96 to 2007–08, with reference to the top 4, top 15, and top 25 universities, although demonstrating stratification, has been relatively static over time: four universities received slightly more than a quarter of the funding, the top 15 just over 50%, and the top 25 close to 70% (Shattock, 2012: 185). However, Brown (2013: 67–74), with reference to funding designed to replenish the research infrastructure and support graduate students, shows that the distribution of these resources has favoured the elite universities and notes, in particular, the impact of the RAE's QR ratings in the making of these decisions. However, while '...at the *institutional* level, total quality-related (QR) cash from the Higher Education Funding Council for England and total research council funding are highly correlated is neither new nor surprising', however, 'at the *subject level* it is typically weak' (Diggle and Chetwynd, 18 April 2013: 39, emphasis added). In other words there is not a strong correlation of research council and RAE funding for research in particular subjects, which suggests the presence of a measure of research diversity within the overall system.

While both the RAEs and the research councils have impacted upon UK higher education through the mechanisms they have employed to allocate research funding, an important distinction between them is that the purpose of research assessment has been to evaluate the quality of outputs whereas the research councils have a long history of shaping the inputs into the higher education research agenda (Salter and Tapper, 1994: 155–181). Thus for the RAEs the focus is upon outputs, for the research councils it is upon inputs. Working under the auspices of Research Councils UK (RCUK), there are seven independent research councils:

Arts and Humanities Research Council (AHRC)
Biotechnology and Biological Sciences Research Council (BBSRC)
Engineering and Physical Sciences Research Council (EPSRC)
Economic and Social Research Council (ESRC)
Medical Research Council (MRC)
Natural Environment Research Council (NERC)
Science and Technology Facilities Council (STFC)

(Research Councils UK, 18 April 2013)

Although, in the words of RCUK: 'The Research Councils fund research on a competitive basis employing independent expert review' (Research Councils UK, 18 April 2013), they also give a strong steer to the kind of research they are likely to fund. For example, the Arts and Humanities Research Council states: 'Our strategic programmes address issues of intellectual and wider cultural, social or economic urgency that the Council considers are best supported by concentrated and coherent funding initiatives' (AHRC, 18 April 2013). In parallel fashion, the BBSRC remarks that it '...has a set of Council-wide strategic priorities. These reflect the major priorities set out in the BBSRC *Strategic Plan 2010–2015* and set out topics or activities within these that the Council wishes to particularly encourage and promote' (BBSRC, 18 April 2013). Therefore, not only is the funding of research a powerful leverage for the institutional fragmentation of the higher education system but also a means for shaping its precise research goals.

RESEARCH FUNDING AND THE SHAPE OF THE SYSTEM

In his assessment of the impact of 'market based policies on UK higher education' Brown has claimed: '...there has been a significant increase in vertical institutional differentiation, which the Coalition Government's reforms will further increase. Research selectivity has played a crucial part in this' (Brown, 2013: 163). In apparent support Shattock has argued that: 'From 2001 the selectivity process was deliberately used to reinforce institutional rather than subject differentiation' (Shattock, 2012: 182). But Shattock goes on to claim that the UK model of higher education is more complex than conforming to a straightforward hierarchy defined by research success. Although there may be a pinnacle of four internationally rated research-intensive universities (Cambridge, Oxford, Imperial College, and University College), there are at least 35 universities that have 'a reasonable claim to be regarded as research-intensive' (Shattock, 2012: 184). Moreover, he points to the development of research traditions within many of the post-1992 universities and concludes that 'appeals to institutions to define themselves as teaching-only seem likely to fall on deaf ears' (Shattock, 2012: 186).

But, if the distribution of research funding (including also grants awarded by the research councils) has not ushered in a model of higher education within the UK that can be neatly defined, is it so complex that the only appropriate labels to define it are either diverse or variegated? If we accept Shattock's claim that there are in the UK four world-class research-intensive universities, with some 35-plus institutions in all embracing a strong research mission, then what does this say about the rest of the system, the other some 130 institutions of higher education? And how is the overall shape of the system to be interpreted? Although the mission groups Million+ and University Alliance (effectively the representative bodies for the post-1992 universities) are forthright proponents of the message (clearly underwritten by their interpretation of the evidence presented by RAE2008) that first-rate research is to be found across the English system of higher education, how much substance is there to this claim? What is the most apt label to describe the model of English higher education as determined by the outcomes of the Research Assessment Exercises? We will explore this question with reference to RAE2008, because, at the time of writing, it was the last overall evaluation of research quality in the United Kingdom, and for the first time the methodology of presenting quality profiles for the units of assessment was employed. The intention is to examine the distributions of quality research that the exercise found and only then comment on the consequent funding decisions that have depended so much upon political intervention.

RAE2008

The evaluations arrived at by RAE2008 were made by 67 sub-panels of experts, one for each unit of assessment, who 'worked under the guidance of 15 main panels' (RAE2008, 23 April 2013). The profiles 'present in blocks of 5% the proportion of each submission judged by the panels to have met each of the quality levels defined below'. These quality levels were as follows (RAE2008a, 23 April 2013):

4*   Quality that is world-leading in terms of originality, significance, and rigour
3*   Quality that is internationally excellent in terms of originality, significance, and rigour but nonetheless falls short of the highest standards of excellence
2*   Quality that is recognized internationally in terms of originality, significance, and rigour
1*   Quality that is recognized nationally in terms of originality, significance, and rigour

Unclassified Quality that falls below the standard of nationally recognized work. Or work which does not meet the published definition of research for the purposes of this assessment

The UK overall percentages at the various quality levels were as follows: 4* (17%), 3* (37%), 2* (33%), 1* (11%), and unclassified (2%). With such a positive picture of the nation's research strength, it was almost inevitable that at least pockets of research excellence would be widely distributed. However, it should be noted that the picture is probably less rosy than it appears to be as the institutions controlled the selection of faculty for the submission process rather than being required to enter all those who were eligible. Inevitably there would be a temptation to submit only those departments and academics whose research was likely to be positively rated, although—as we have noted—there are constraints on institutional game-playing.

A total of 159 institutions submitted evidence to demonstrate their research quality: 126 located in England, 18 in Scotland, 11 in Wales, and 4 in Northern Ireland (RAE2008b, 23 April 2013)[1]. A significant minority of the institutions, some 25 in all, have a specific academic focus and made very restricted submissions, usually to only one of the sub-panels (for the main source of our analysis see, RAE2008b, 23 April 2013). Most of these institutions fall into one of two groups. Firstly, there are the schools/colleges/institutes of art/agriculture/business/drama/music/zoology that occupy particular niches within the overall higher education system. Secondly, there are also focused submissions from some of the constituent members of the University of London, which provides them with a broader institutional base. These latter include: St. George's Hospital Medical School (which in fact made submissions to eight sub-panels, mainly—as one would suspect—in the field of medicine), the Marine Biological Station as Millport (now closed), the British Institute in Paris, the Courtauld Institute of Art, the Institute of Cancer Research,

---

[1] The analysis of the evidence is restricted to the listed 126 English institutions.

Heythrop College, the Institute of Education, the London School of Hygiene and Tropical Medicine, and the School of Pharmacy—now incorporated into University College, London.

There is a second group, numbering some 35 institutions nearly all of which are post-1992 universities, which made submissions to up to ten sub-panels. Unsurprisingly, as they have no medical schools, few of them made submissions to any of the medical or related sub-panels (the one exception was the sub-panel 'Allied Health Professions and Studies'). Their submissions to the science, engineering, and mathematics sub-panels were also restricted (although there were a few for the sub-panels 'General Engineering and Mineral & Mining Engineering', and 'Computer Science and Informatics'). The assessments that do appear are disproportionately: 'Communications, Cultural, and Media Studies', 'Sports-Related Studies', 'Art and Design', 'English Language and Literature', 'Business and Management Studies', 'History', and 'Social Work and Social Policy & Administration'.

This second group merges into a third, composed of some 30 institutions all carrying the university label but predominantly post-1992 universities, which made submissions to between 10 and 25 sub-panels. Of the older foundations, four of them (Goldsmiths College, School of Oriental and African Studies, London School of Economics, and Royal Holloway College) are part of the federation of the University of London and have established academic reputations in a relatively limited range of academic disciplines: that is also true of the University of Essex, with its powerful base in the social sciences, which also belongs to this group. A special mention needs to be made of Imperial College (with submissions to only 21 sub-panels), which also falls into this group but is rightly considered, by Shattock amongst others, as one of Britain's four world-class, research-intensive universities. Because of the relatively confined academic focus of Imperial, its submissions fall overwhelmingly into the fields of medicine, chemistry, physics, mathematics, and engineering. But it should also be noted that in comparison with most other universities, the academic numbers submitted by Imperial to each sub-panel were very substantial. With respect to the post-1992 universities that belong to this third group the biases, both in favour of or not making submissions to particular sub-panels, are parallel to those that occurred with the second group, although there is a somewhat greater likelihood of submissions to the engineering and social science sub-panels.

There are some 35 English higher education institutions, which submitted to 25 or more sub-panels. Several of the 1960s new universities (UEA, Kent, Sussex, Warwick, and York) in the company of Queen Mary College London and the post-1992 university, Plymouth, made between 25 to 30 submissions. While a mixed bag of civic universities (Liverpool, Leicester, Liverpool, Newcastle, Reading, and Southampton) along with King's College London, Durham, and Exeter each made between 30 to 45 submissions. This leaves nine universities that made over 45 submissions (Birmingham, Bristol, Cambridge, Leeds, Manchester, Nottingham, Oxford, Sheffield, and University College London).

Although categorizing institutions by the number of units of assessment they made to RAE2008 is only part of mapping the research excellence of UK higher education, it does shed some light on the overall character of the system. A distinction needs to be drawn between focused research excellence and excellence that has a wide disciplinary range. However, as only some ten universities made submissions to over 50% of the 2008 RAE sub-panels, there was a clear tendency for research output to be reasonably concentrated within most of the institutions. A critical discriminating variable is whether or not the university has a medical school. Those institutions without a medical school made very limited submissions to the medical sub-panels, especially those located in Main Panel A (RAE2008b, 23 April 2013). For the post-1992 universities, the sciences along with mathematics were also restricted fields of research, although engineering (presumably reflecting an early academic focus) figured reasonably prominently. Interestingly 'Sport-Related Studies' figured in a wide range of submissions, but not in those of either Cambridge or Oxford, both of which made submissions to the 'Classics, Ancient History, Byzantine, and Modern Greek Studies' sub-panel where they were joined by just 16 other institutions.

The figures are reflecting two variables: the extent to which a discipline has become embedded within particular institutional settings, and the relative costs of expanding the current disciplinary range. If the intention is to establish a strong research output then to expand some areas of knowledge simply requires large resources, dependent upon the need to attract leading figures in the field as well as construct appropriate facilities with the right equipment. There is a natural tendency, therefore, to build upon what you already have rather than to create a new, possibly costly, disciplinary profile. Or if you should decide to expand, it is probably easier do so in fields where the major costs are incurred by the input of human resources rather than the building of state-of-the-art laboratories. The implication is that the outcome of RAE2008, at least with respect to the assessment of research quality, would both reflect the findings of previous assessment exercises, and set a mould for the 2014 Research Excellence Framework, unless the inclusion of measuring research impact is going to alter significantly the evaluations.

Broadly speaking, the number of sub-panel submissions that institutions made to RAE2008 determined the overall size of their total input of academic staff: the greater the number of sub-panel submissions, the larger the cohort of academics deemed to be research-active. However, there are examples of large submissions to a single sub-panel which are more substantial in terms of academic numbers than the input into several sub-panels made by many post-1992 universities. For example, the specialist colleges and institutes of the University of London are especially heavy-hitters in comparatively narrow research areas (for example, the Institute of Education, London School of Hygiene and Tropical Medicine, and the Royal Veterinary College). The post-1992 universities were also inclined to have one significant input with smaller inputs from a range of other units of assessment, presumably building their research output around a traditional core identity. Noticeable amongst the larger inputs of the post-1992 universities were the following sub-panels: 'Art and Design', 'Allied Health Professions and Studies', 'Business and Management Studies', 'Communication, Cultural, and Media Studies', and 'Social Work and Social Policy & Administration'.

Very few of the post-1992 universities entered more than 200 full-time equivalent academic staff in RAE2008, and many comfortably under 100. The exceptions are: the Universities of Brighton, Central Lancashire, De Montfort, Kingston, University of Arts London, London Metropolitan, Manchester Metropolitan, Nottingham Trent, Oxford Brookes, Portsmouth, and Sheffield Hallam, with Plymouth and the University of the West of England as the leaders, each submitting over 300 full-time equivalent faculty members. In comparison, all of the pre-1992 universities that made submissions to less than 25 sub-panels submitted by a wide margin over 200 faculty members including those (for example, Essex, the London School of Economics, SOAS, and City University London) offering only a restricted range of disciplines. There are also some heavy-hitters in this category: Lancaster and Loughborough, each submitting the research of over 600 faculty members, and, moreover, these two universities made substantial submissions to particular sub-panels: 'Business and Management Studies' at Lancaster, and 'Mechanical, Aeronautical, and Manufacturing Engineering' at Loughborough. As previously observed, a special note has to be made of Imperial College, which couples its comparatively limited focus upon particular sub-panels with the entry of significant faculty numbers to almost all the units of assessment to which it made submissions. Comfortably over 1,000 research-active academics fell within Imperial's remit, which is significantly higher than all the other individual institutional submissions in this group.

We have divided the heavy-hitters (in terms of number of submissions to the units of assessment) into three groups: 25 to 30, 30 to 45, and more than 45 submissions. All nine universities with entries to more than 45 units of assessment each submitted over 1,000 academics in RAE2008 with the heaviest inputs from Cambridge, Manchester, Oxford, and UCL. Indeed, Cambridge and Oxford each entered more than 2,000 faculty members. It is also noticeable that these four universities had very large entries (over 100 academics) in particular disciplines: Cambridge ('Biological Sciences', 'Physics', 'General Engineering and Mineral & Mining Engineering', and 'History'), Manchester ('Biological Sciences', and 'Business and Management Studies'), Oxford ('Physics', 'Law', and 'History'), and UCL ('Other Hospital Based Clinical

Subjects', 'Biological Sciences', and 'Physics'). As we have noted, the only other higher education institution in England that matches these numbers is Imperial College. Ironically they are mirroring the pattern found in many of the lesser research-active institutions—large core inputs supplemented by a small range of submissions.

With the exceptions of Southampton (with over 100 academics entered in its submission to the sub-panel 'Other Hospital Based Clinical Subjects'), and King's College London (with over 200 academics entered in its submission to the sub-panel 'Psychiatry, Neuroscience, and Clinical Psychology'), none of those universities that made between 30 and 45 sub-panel submissions had single entries of a comparable size. Moreover, both Southampton and King's College had total submission numbers of over 1,000 whereas the other universities in this category ranged from some 600 to 800+. In terms of the third category (25 to 30 submissions), the input varied from some 400 to 600+ academics, with Warwick being the exception in two respects: an overall larger entry (some 900) and with one major submission of over 100 to the 'Business and Management Studies' sub-panel.

Without, as yet, any reference to the evaluation of research quality, what the data is showing is a very varied picture within the English higher education system in terms of its research output. While universities may be keen to avoid the teaching-only label, the outcomes of the apparent widespread commitment to pursue a research agenda can be seen as *in practice* internally differentiating the system as much as it may *in theory* suggest an almost universal adherence to a common idea of the university. Obviously, the shape of the research commitment is in part determined by the different academic profiles of institutions—their disciplinary range, the size of their departments, and the research interests, as well as the motivation, of their faculty. Of course these are variables that can be reshaped by funding, which can be used both to reinforce and extend current research commitments and incentivize faculty motivation. However, the 2008RAE data point to considerable variation with respect to both the range and size of research missions: from very focused outputs reflecting the research of a comparatively few individuals to very diverse outputs made up of the contributions of hundreds of individuals, with several steps between these two extremes leading to the possibility of constructing several different groupings within the system depending upon where you draw the lines in terms of the range of inputs to the sub-panels, the variations in their academic composition, and the volume of faculty this embraces.

In view of the very positive overall evaluation by RAE2008 of the quality of research output (54% classified as falling in either the 4* or 3* categories), it can be confidently asserted that high-quality research is being undertaken across the system at large. While the purpose of the research exercise was to evaluate units of assessment rather than overall institutional research profiles, the temptation to produce an institutional quality ranking list and, furthermore, to correlate it with funding awarded by the research councils was overwhelming. The *Guardian's* list was based on average ranking scores in terms of the 4* to 1* scale across all institutional sub-panel entries (*Guardian*, 1 May 2013), but excluded institutions making less than five sub-panels submissions (mainly those with a one-dimensional academic focus, which includes several members of the federation of the University of London). Some selected rankings scores are as follows:

University of Cambridge	2.975
University of Warwick	2.799
King's College London	2.693
University of Kent	2.598
City University	2.476
University of Brighton	2.372
St. George's Hospital	2.279
Roehampton University	2.198
University of Huddersfield	2.096
University of Teesside	1.990
Bath Spa University	1.891
UC Plymouth St. Mark and St. John	1.082

There is, therefore, a steady decline in ranking scores from the University of Cambridge at the top of the list to UC Plymouth St. Mark and St. John at the bottom. But what the scores for the units of assessment reveal is that very few sub-panel submissions failed to record at least some research graded at 3* and, more often than not, at 4*.

CONCLUSION: THE MODEL OF THE SYSTEM

This chapter has analysed the research record of English higher education with reference to three particular variables: its disciplinary range, the institutional commitment as defined by the number of academic faculty considered to be research-active, and the evaluation of the quality of research outputs in RAE2008. While there is strong evidence that high research quality is widely spread within the system, it is also true that a lot of that quality comes in small packages. In sharp contrast at the other end of the scale there is a core of institutions which have a considerable range of research that has been classified as 'quality that is world-leading in terms of originality, significance, and rigour'. In between these polar points there are a number of overlapping sectors.

It is impossible to give a straightforward answer as to how many sectors there are because it depends on how the defining criteria (academic range, the size of the input, and the ranking of quality) are weighted. For example, in the

Guardian's presentation of the outcomes of RAE2008, the London School of Economics is ranked third (after Cambridge and Oxford) in terms of the combined ranking scores of its sub-panel submissions. However, it made inputs into only 14 sub-panels, the same number as the University of Essex, which was placed ninth in the *Guardian* list. Moreover, neither the LSE nor Essex entered more than 500 FTE faculty members in RAE2008. The more academically specialist institutions of the University of London, which were excluded from the *Guardian*'s ranking list, also raise the problem of how their overall position within the system is to be interpreted. Indeed, the issue is most clearly illustrated by the obvious research excellence of Imperial College, although it has a notably more confined academic range than, for example, the University of Manchester.

Obviously the easiest way to define the sectors is to construct them on the basis of one variable and then introduce any qualifications that need to be made in any discussion of their composition. Drawing our own lines through the *Guardian*'s ranking list in which a perfect score would be all entries averaging out at 4.000, we end up with the following sectors:

> Average ranking 2.800+: Cambridge, Oxford, LSE, Imperial, UCL, and Manchester
>
> (6 English institutions)
>
> Average ranking 2.800 to 2.600: University of Warwick to the University of Sussex
>
> (20 English institutions)
>
> Average ranking 2.600 to 2.400: University of Kent to the University of Hertfordshire
>
> (14 English institutions)
>
> Average ranking 2.400 to 2.000: University of Brighton to the University of Wolverhampton
>
> (31 English institutions)
>
> Scores below 2.000: University of Teesside to UC Plymouth St. Mark and St. John
>
> (22 English institutions)

The introduction of the two other variables (academic range and the size of institutional inputs) obviously would complicate the picture and, moreover, it is important to stress that the sectors are not as sharply defined as the presentation suggests, but rather merge at the boundaries. But the most important qualification is that the purpose of the Research Assessment Exercises was not to measure the quality of research output by comparing institutions, but rather to measure research quality with reference to units of assessment against a defined standard. While the RAEs point to a relationship between quality research output by units of assessment and institutional profiles, it is not equally strong across all academic areas, and it also shows a fairly general spread of at least pockets of research excellence.

The evaluation of research output suggests a model of different sectors that overlap at the boundaries. It is far from a bipolar model and some way from conforming to a neat hierarchy. However, while it may be proving difficult for governments to persuade some universities that they should be teaching-only institutions, it is evident that a large segment of the tertiary sector is devoted *primarily* to teaching, and that research is a marginal activity for many of the faculty. At the other end of the continuum are those universities which have a genuine claim to be seen as world-class, research-intensive universities. In these institutions, research will at the very least vie with teaching both in shaping self-identities and determining the direction of academic careers. For institutions it is a question of money and status; for academics it is self-fulfilment, personal advancement, and the recognition of one's peers.

It can be argued that the purpose of the Research Assessment Exercises has been perverted by political intervention; that a process designed to reward research quality wherever it was to be found increasingly has resulted in the targeting of public funding to secure an institutional concentration of research output. The clearest recent move in this direction has been the decision to restrict public funding to only those units of assessment graded either 3* or 4* in RAE2008. While this will almost certainly result in a further concentration of research, it is not an illogical decision. In a time of protracted pressure on funding there is an argument that it should be directed at those units of assessment with only the highest RAE scores. While the consequence of this may be a greater concentration of funding, there remain powerful voices that this is best way of securing the long-term future of the UK's research base, and that the dissipation of funding will steadily undermine an enviable national record. There is also no doubt that if funding were to be directed at the core of the pre-1992 universities then it would be more focused upon underpinning the traditional areas of knowledge, and less likely to be directed at, for example, 'Nursing and Midwifery', 'Town and Country Planning', 'Library and Information Management', 'Social Work and Social Policy & Administration', 'Sports-Related Studies', and 'Communication, Cultural, and Media Studies'. To some extent the model already has this bias built into it by weighting the funding returns by the unit of assessment, but it is possible to go further down this road.

The most potent reason for the shift from research selectivity to greater research concentration is due to the fact that the RAE was always a political fix and, especially since the emergence of the funding council model of governance, major developments in higher education have been underwritten politically. While it may be admirable to assert that public funding should be distributed in a manner that enables institutions with less-developed research bases to enhance their research profiles, governments have wider considerations to take into account. Moreover, it is important to consider why distribution on the basis of the current evaluations of research quality should be considered to be an equitable policy. If equitability is to be the overriding concern, then surely it would be fairer to distribute funding according to faculty numbers—so much per faculty head, perhaps weighted by a disciplinary differential because research in some areas generates higher costs than in other areas? If particular imposed values are to determine the model for distributing research funding, then arguably it is more reasonable to maintain that they should be the values that drive the duly elected government of the day, which if it is wise will pursue its policies in close consultation with those interests that pervade the higher education sector.

8

The Globalization of Higher Education: Coping with Rankings and League Tables while Delivering More and Charging Less

Abstract: While the proliferation of league tables purporting to rank the global status of higher education institutions has been lambasted in certain quarters, they are undoubtedly here to stay. It is virtually impossible for those designated as the leading world-class universities to avoid the pressure of sustaining their 'iconic' status. But it has to be recognized that the dominant input into securing such an elevated status is the quantity and quality of a university's research output. And yet, certainly in the contemporary English context, the most prevalent political pressure is to increase the quality of the students' teaching and learning experiences. The chapter, with considerable reference to the American experience, explores the possibilities of achieving the latter goal, while retaining the aspiration of maintaining (or becoming) a world-class university. To this end it raises the possibility of exploring the MOOCs option to reduce costs, implementing American-style 'honors programs' to sustain quality teaching, increasing competition by enabling additional providers to enter the higher education market, and an enhancement of the powers of the regulatory state to reinforce consumer (student) protection (which in the United States may mean the federal government assuming a greater role in the affairs of higher education).

In earlier chapters we have discussed the rising concerns and criticisms, notably within the USA but now increasingly also in the UK, about the affordability of HE (for the economy, for the taxpayer, for the individual student) as HEI spending climbs remorselessly and as tuition fees are steadily inflated (and hence graduate debts spiral). There is, in addition, ever-more anxiety and doubt over the value for money of costly mass HE (costly whether to the taxpayer by way of subsidy or to the student/family by way of the introduction of and the steady increase in tuition fees as a worldwide policy trend—Heller and Callender, 2013) in relation to the quantum and depth of the learning offered and gained, and in terms of graduate un/under-employment. In this chapter we explore whether, when, and how HE may yet be forced to address such issues within the areas of the quality of 'teaching and learning' (Land and Gordon, 2013) or of what is now termed 'the student experience' (Kandiko and Weyers, 2013) by—at last—finding ways to deliver more while charging less: unless, of course, there is a return to the financial circumstances prevailing during the decade or so to the 2007–08 crash, which might mean that HE yet again is let off the hook as an industry able to avoid the normal demands of market-driven innovation and price competition. The research-focused universities, however, while also having to learn how to deliver more undergraduate teaching and value for money with perhaps less by way of tuition fees, would still need to be responding to the growing pressure of the global rankings game that is largely based on metrics and performance indicators to do with research output and that are the dominant factor via the league tables in the establishment of brand value within internationalized HE.

With respect to the latter group of universities, there is also the interesting concept of the Emerging Global Model (EGM) of the Super Research Universities (SRUs) as a very small sub-set (Palfreyman and Tapper, 2009: 203–218) whereby, arguably, only two dozen or so global elite SRUs are able to afford the cost of competing within the HE premier league (Salmi, 2009). They will have far more in common managerially with each other than with the rest of the HEIs within their national sector—in relation, say, to the academic contract and tenure, to how research is funded and managed, to attitudes on academic freedom and collegial governance, or to intellectual property exploitation and technology transfer, as these elite institutions compete for faculty as well as for graduate students on the international merry-go-round of the academic research career, but also collaborate on research projects (Anderson and Steneck, 2011; Sakamoto and Chapman, 2011). And leaving aside whether the creation of such SRUs is more than simply a matter of a government throwing money at a few HEIs at the apex of the national pyramid, and whether there may be also complicating factors such as the link with 'creative clusters' made up of HE activity, of media companies, of high-tech industries, of generally the professional and creative classes coming together as a critical mass in a given and attractive area (Florida, 2005 and 2008)—such as in the case of Harvard and MIT being located in Boston; Berkeley, Stanford, and CalTech in/around San Francisco; UCL, ICL, Oxford, and Cambridge in/around London; and probably in coming decades for Hong Kong, Shanghai, Singapore, Munich, Tokyo, and Toronto. Certainly some nations are investing heavily in the race to create world-class universities. (See Altbach and Balan (2007) for an analysis of Asian elite research universities, and Palfreyman and Tapper (2009) for government attempts explicitly to identify and provide extra funding for universities in Germany, China, and Japan that aspire to join this elite stratum—while, arguably, the UK's RAE mechanism (see Chapter 7) has been an indirect and implicit way of promoting elite HEIs in this global rankings game).

The HE rankings and league tables industry (with origins stretching as far back as the 1900s in the USA) really took off a decade ago as an aspect of the globalization of HE, and they are now a significant factor in HEI strategic planning and management as HEIs cope with their impact upon how they are perceived by potential faculty and students or by alumni, and how they are judged by government and other funding agencies; they are also a major factor in government HE policy-making. Yet there is (so far) comparatively little literature analysing their methodologies, their accuracy, their use, their effects (King, 2009; Hazelkorn, 2011 and 2013; Altbach, 2013). As Altbach comments: 'In the era of globalization, accountability, and benchmarking, university rankings have achieved a kind of iconic status... [albeit that they] vary in quality, focus, and in the specifics of their methodologies... They are an inevitable result of higher education's worldwide massification... [being used as] an important tool in the global knowledge race' (Altbach, 2013: 26). But a key—perhaps some would assert *the* key—aspect of the university's purpose in the form of teaching 'is largely ignored in all of the rankings, since we have yet to develop comparable measures of its quality and impact even within countries, much less across them' (Altbach, 2013: 27). Thus research activity dominates the rankings methodologies and processes—as easier to measure and compare (even if such comparisons are often partly based on rather fuzzy surveys of institutional 'reputation' as perceived by a small sample of geographically concentrated academics, and even if citations data favours the hard sciences and material published in English), and as having vastly greater prestige than humble teaching for the HEI and for the individual academic's career (Brewer et al., 2002).

There is, then, some well-founded scepticism and indeed cynicism about the rankings game, but they are undoubtedly here to stay: if they do not produce the right answer for HEI X or Y, or indeed country X's HE system, a new, more appropriate methodology can always be invented to give better results (as indeed the European Commission is trying to do as it spends millions of Euros on its 'U-Multirank' in the hope of locating some non-English EU universities within the top-twenty of some ranking or other: Vught and Ziegele, 2012). And as might Oxford or Cambridge, say, via a new ranking of 'Quality of University Lawns' in which they would be guaranteed easily every year to beat the far richer Harvard given the shoddy state of Harvard Yard! The current ten or so major global ranking systems are listed by Hazelkorn (2013: 3), their evolution and proliferation during the 2000s driven by concerns over accountability, transparency, consumerism, and value for money in HE policy-making and funding. They are widely used across more than 60 nations, many of which also have another 60 or so internal national league tables (and several of which global and national tables are now readily available as smartphone apps). Yet, as Hazelkorn (2013: 4–7) notes: while 'there is no such thing as an objective ranking... [and] no agreed method on what is or how to measure academic or educational quality...', it has not prevented their annual publication creating 'a feeding frenzy that is sending shock waves throughout the higher education system worldwide', and their being used 'as a strategic tool and management instrument' within HEIs (and indeed by individual academics 'to boost their own professional standing')—with many HEIs 'gaming' the rankings process as best they can, and sometimes simply cheating in supplying or interpreting data. And, thus, all the world's 16,000 [*sic*] or so HEIs spread across some 180 countries are straitjacketed into a global rankings methodology 'based on the top 100 [EGM, SRU] universities internationally': an 'undue focus on a small, elite group of 'world-class universities' [that] has led to a spiralling reputation race' which is affecting HE 'both positively and perversely, and in both intentional and unintentional ways' (a race engaged in by individual HEIs and also by governments seeking to propel at least a couple of their HEIs into the global top 10, 25, 50, 100; while, within this competitive and costly zero-sum game, the USA, the UK, and Australia seek to retain their current disproportionate dominance of the top 100).

The 'growing obsession with university rankings'—which overall 'elevate and fetishize particular conceptions of status' (and especially where based on reputational surveys 'prone to being subjective, self-referential, and self-perpetuating') and which are 'accelerating the marketization of higher education in the belief that free markets and competition are best'—ignores the conceptual fallacy at the heart of the entire league tables industry, whereby the rankings '(over)emphasize research at the expense of teaching and learning or the full bandwidth of higher education endeavour' and also ignores the reality that in fact for governments 'the policy choice is framed as one between world-class universities vs world-class [HE] systems' and that their unwise and indiscriminate use of such 'crude' and 'imperfect' input/output indicators 'to inform policy carries many risks' (all quotes from Hazelkorn, 2011: 4, 18, 75, 183–185, 204). King offers much the same criticisms of and concerns about the 'imperfect instruments' (2009: 144) of the rankings as being 'overly simplistic in their compression of many variables into one overall system of numerical ordering' (2009: 135), but he recognizes that the league tables 'strike a chord with the new moods of consumerism' in the world where, 'as students and their parents are paying more and more for the privilege of attending university, they want value for money' (2009: 145). These global and national league tables 'seek to make the world of higher education more knowable, more orderly as markets, and more amenable to a pattern of governance suitable for the marketized, competitive, and increasingly transnational organizations that universities have become' (2009: 162); they are 'a form of bounded rationality that offer a variety of stakeholders a set of simple heuristics with which to comprehend an increasingly complex but less directly knowable world' (2009: 212–213). Thus, as King argues, the rankings become part of a new and extensive global, informal, and private regulatory-governance structure for an increasingly marketized and commodified HE industry, substituting for outdated and clunky public and legal compliance mechanisms.

Alvesson (2013: chs 4 and 5) sees the rankings as distorting the meaning and the purpose of the university, while also triggering a neglect of teaching in the relentless pursuit of research kudos and prestige: leaving HE characterized by 'a wealth of examples of grandiosity and illusion tricks' within 'the triumph of emptiness'. Similarly, Shin et al. (2011) also see the rankings as problematic in their methodology and perverse in their misuse and abuse within HE policy-making as well as in HEIs' strategic decision-making; as does Bok in dismissing them as 'not a reliable yardstick for measuring progress' (2013: 38), albeit that we have only the most 'fuzzy and uneven knowledge about the performance of universities' (Bok, 2013: 3) which face 'a bumper crop of complaints' about their expense and accountability.

The simple fact is that these league tables duly establish HEI brand-value, which—as noted in earlier chapters—can possibly enhance graduate employability whatever may or may not be the actual quantum and quality, efficiency, and effectiveness of the student teaching provision. The student may well be content, therefore, to pay high fees for high brand-value, while tolerating the neglect of undergraduate teaching as HEI resources are focused on the prestige and kudos of the research arms race (the brand-value being translated into graduate employability as employers use it—along with the 2:1 minimum degree standard—as an initial filter for dealing with a high number of applications). It is, however, a grim indictment, both of the rankings industry and also of the whole HE industry (and its vast and expensive academic audit and quality control apparatus as evolved over the past two decades or so) that, as Altbach notes, there is still no agreement on what constitutes any standardized and comparable level of academic achievement for 'graduateness' in most subject areas (other than on obvious ones, such as a reasonable clarity and consensus on just what are the skills and competencies of the medic or engineer), still less of what quantum and even less of what quality of undergraduate teaching (never mind how to record and measure so as to create comparable metrics, and let alone also the accurate monitoring and recording of what students input by way of private learning time) is needed and expected for delivering any such minimum standard of degree and what is to count as 'graduateness'. The undergraduate teaching and learning aspect of the modern university is as underdeveloped and neglected as the research dimension in some HEIs, and the management function in most is bloated and expensive.

There is, indeed, scarcely any understanding of and consensus over just what is 'higher' about and within the process called 'higher education', let alone any consensus on exactly how quality in delivering HE teaching is achieved, sustained, and preferably also enhanced. And so, sadly (and as explored in earlier chapters), the student-consumer is left assuming (hoping) that high price signals high quality (HE as a Veblen good), while the low quality or low value for money HEI can thereby (at present) get away with overcharging in such an imperfect market where the consumer is unavoidably underinformed and vulnerable, and where consumer protection in HE is (as yet) woefully underdeveloped. At the same time, the HEI is facing the consequences of the globalization of HE and also coping with negotiating the rankings and league tables game, while perhaps (as we next explore) soon being obliged in the context of disruptive innovation and market competition to deliver more by way of teaching so as to address the quality deficit in undergraduate HE—and also charging less by way of tuition fees so as to address the affordability and the value for money issue within undergraduate (and indeed postgraduate) HE.

That said, there may be at least a straw in the wind: the OECD is discussing an international testing process for HE along the lines of what has been developed for measuring comparative achievement in school systems by a three-year cycle of testing 15-year-olds in maths, science, and reading (PISA, the Program for International Student Assessment)—where, usually, the US K12 system performs dismally (like, it now seems and as discussed in earlier chapters, also does much of its HE system: Bok, 2006; Arum and Roksa, 2011), the UK not much better, and with the best results coming from the likes of Shanghai, Singapore, and Seoul (triggering school reform proposals for the USA—Tucker, 2011), as well as giving momentum to the academies trend in the UK (Adonis, 2012). The OECD's chief education advisor (Andreas Schleicher) commented that such PISA tests in HE could counteract the emphasis within the existing HE rankings upon research: 'We need some language to talk about teaching quality and learning outcomes that isn't tied to research. If we don't have a way of measuring teaching, then we are going to have to rely on reputation—which only tells you about the past.' (*New York Times*, 'Should University Systems Be Graded Too?', 21 July, 2013: at www.NYTimes.com). It remains to be seen whether the proposed AHELO (Assessment of Higher Education Learning Outcomes) will have an impact (even if the OECD allegedly has spent some $13m on developing it). There is similar talk in the USA about a national standardized testing regime for HE graduates, but—predictably—the US HE Establishment has already spoken out against it, especially if each HEI's score were not kept cosily anonymous (see the response of an official of the American Council on Education as quoted in the same *New York Times* article cited earlier) and particularly if based on the US Collegiate Learning Assessment test that has exposed the campus learning deficit seized on by Arum and Roksa (2011) and to which the academy has responded by claiming that it is methodologically suspect. In the UK it seems that no HEIs want to apply the easy and obvious experiment of having sample examination scripts, assignments, and dissertations re-marked by a panel of outsiders to see if a 2:1 in Astrology at Coketown Met really does match a 2:1 in the same subject at the University of Barchester, and nor indeed within the same HEIs is there much scrutiny of the sometimes wide variation in the percentage of 1sts/2:1s awarded across academic disciplines.

But what are the prospects of any serious changes to how HEIs deliver, fund, and price teaching? At present there is much talk (for instance Wildavsky et al., 2011 and notably, Christiensen and Eyring, 2011, from whom the following quotes are taken) of impending 'disruptive technologies' and of 'disruptive competitors' hitting the comfortable, complacent, costly, medieval pattern of university activity, forcing the traditional HEIs to 're-engineer their institutional DNA from the inside out' and to confront 'disruptive innovation' from 'alternative forms of higher education' by using 'new and much less expensive technology for educating students' via online learning. A few Oxfords and Harvards, UCLs and MITs, may be safe within their elite bubbles from such change, but not the many HEIs 'stuck in a dangerous competitive middle ground, neither highest in quality nor lowest in cost'. This squeezed middle embraces a lot of HEIs that may have to abandon the hitherto strategy of choice of attempting to emulate the US Ivy League or the top upper dozen of the UK Russell Group universities, which becomes impossibly difficult as the cost of prestige seeking rockets.

Thus, the focus will be on using online teaching assisted by carefully managed and monitored 'skilled instructors' to reduce the cost of a degree to 'less than half the price' currently set by the public producer-oriented HEIs. The authors compare the online courses 'to the cars rolling off the line at a Toyota factory', with the traditional university professor as 'a weekend enthusiast who builds custom cars' (in effect, comparing the productivity transformed industries of the modern globalized economy with craft guilds of the Middle Ages—and with HE seen as still lodged firmly in the fifteenth century). In this brave new world of 2020 HE, and as also reflected in the Coalition's 2011 HE White Paper, the student-customer is indeed king ('The Student as the Primary Constituent': 'The student-centred university is the exception today. In the future, no other kind is likely to succeed.'). The range of subjects/courses is rationalized (even culled) and hence narrowed to focus on students' choice which is driven by their perception of what is vocational and enhances employability; the academics are no longer collectively indulged in their pursuit of 'scholarly effort into research', but face a plethora of new incentives within a complex modernized and managed career structure based on a rich diversity of individualized (research-only, teaching-only, and mixed research and teaching commitments, etc.) contracts as the 'hard choices' and 'trade-offs' of operating within a competitive market are painfully addressed. While all this may sound a tad depressing for the UUK and the Universities and Colleges Union (UCU), Christiensen and Eyring are 'cautiously optimistic' about the traditional university adapting to compete with the more market-responsive and flexible for-profits using low-cost teaching technology to achieve the productivity breakthrough that has so far eluded HE. Thus, the traditional university may yet avoid the fate of the oversubsidized automakers and legacy airlines of the 1970s and 1980s once they become unable to simply overprice their way out of a commercial and competitive reality driven by technological change and globalization.

And the disruptive technology for HE is online teaching, usually expressed as the arrival of MOOCs, Massive Open Online Courses: BIS, *Massive Open Online Courses and Online Distant Learning,* Research Paper 130, 2013; Paolucci, 2013; plus, more broadly, Bates and Sangra (2011), Bowen (2013), Miller et al. (2013), and Shattuck (2013) on higher education in the digital age. Indeed, as of August 2013, the word MOOC has been entered into the Oxford English Dictionary (OED) as 'a course of study made available over the Internet without charge to a very large number of people'. There are several emerging platforms or consortia through which such MOOCs are being offered, and we are also beginning to see deals with publishers to offer free access within a MOOC to online excerpts from leading textbooks and also to rent use of textbooks for the duration of the MOOC (for instance, 'Coursera' with OUP, SAGE, and Wiley, amongst others). So far the other major providers of MOOCs are: 'FutureLearn', 'Udacity', and 'edX' (the first linked to the UK's OU, the second to Coursera and Stanford, the third to MIT and Harvard; and thus each is linking up with elite HEIs). Udacity and Coursera are for-profit venture capital-funded entities while edX is a not-for-profit outfit backed by $30m each from MIT and Harvard. Moreover, 'NovoEd', again involving Stanford faculty, has been launched in 2013; while it is said that Google is also looking at the MOOC concept. And there is now 'iversity' as a Germany-based operation, as well as 'OERu' (Open Educational Research University) located in New Zealand, 'Veduca' in Brazil, 'Edraak' (Jordan), and 'Xuetang' (China). Yet it is early days—the world of MOOCs being barely three years old—and the business model for how MOOCs might be priced for routine use within HE undergraduate teaching has yet to be fully developed, as opposed to their being at present an exciting free novelty and/or a useful *pro bono* offering.

They may end up being used widely within certain subjects to cover the basic teaching material currently provided in often (over-)crowded and sometimes (over-)dull lectures and seminars, for which the HEI would pay the MOOC provider a usage/lease fee for its students' enrolment and also assessment/certification fees. Or perhaps some would be sponsored by the relevant industry seeking appropriately well-taught MOOC 'graduates'; or even financed by the MOOC provider selling access to the best-performing students to potential employers of such graduates. The HEI would, of course, seek to justify a premium tuition fee (over and above the cost of a collection of MOOCs) for added face-to-face contact, for some modules delivered in the traditional way, for its lavish infrastructure of sports and entertainment facilities, (perhaps even) for its quaint library, and (of course, as its valuable monopoly power) for its packaging of all the teaching and learning into a degree-awarding process. But in using MOOCs it could obviously save money on teaching costs and could elect to pass some of the savings to the customer. Clearly work is needed on how such courses could be accurately assessed and cheating or impersonation avoided: but already Coursera (now with more than 30 HEIs signed up and over 200 courses on offer, and in excess of two million users) has evolved 'keystroke biometrics' ('Signature Track') to verify Student X is indeed at the terminal, while other MOOC providers require physical presence at some 4,500 supervised testing centres run by Pearson VUE globally when students want official credentials. From the point of view of the IT-literate and social media-savvy 2010s student, the potential MOOCs-ization of (or some part of) undergraduate teaching probably would be welcomed over trudging to 9am chalk and talk lectures; for the academics relief from having to take a turn delivering 'Calculus 101 for Engineers' or 'Economics 101 for Business Studies' would doubtless have its appeal—unless MOOCs meant redundancy so as to pass on cost savings by way of reductions in tuition fees!

The jury is out as to whether MOOCs are to be 'the Napster moment' for HE, the disruptive innovation that reduces cost and price so as once again to make HE more affordable in the USA and UK (on the failure of such early 2000s HE open-access online ventures such as Fathom and AllLearn see Walsh, 2011). While there are undoubtedly pedagogical and quality issues in relation to the uncritical and random adoption of MOOCs (as indeed for all digital-learning and student use of digital information: Brabazon, 2007 and 2013), MOOCs are now being increasingly used within HEIs (but not necessarily earning the student formal course credits as opposed to being a teaching aid), as they have in effect been the prime teaching method used so successfully in a prototype form to deliver OU courses for decades (hence the potential credibility of the OU's FutureLearn with another dozen or so UK HEIs already attached to it). But MOOCs could signal the radical unbundling of HE, as the Minerva Project (backed by some $25m of venture capital, yet still needing much more to launch as Minerva University in 2015) is gambling on its business plan to reduce the cost of a degree by at least half, with the students taking MOOCs and other online courses over the four years and working together (and with tutors) online, as well as spending residential spells in different major worldwide city locations on a Minerva campus. The online process will deliver the factual content; the online student-tutor and the residential student-tutor gatherings concentrating on developing critical-thinking and lifelong-learning, although core first-year courses will focus on broad generic academic skills that, Minerva asserts, traditional US degree courses only randomly develop (if at all) in their students where there is little by way of robust pedagogy underpinning course structures and delivery. Minerva's claims are made with typical American (indeed Silicon Valley dotcom startup) hype, not least by invoking the concept of the Oxford 1:2 tutorial (while actually proposing to teach in 1:19 seminars) and also in stressing that it will be taking on the US Ivy League head-on (at least on price if not on a better quality learning experience), delivered in part, it says, by retired or disaffected former Ivy League and even Oxbridge academics with a strong interest in and commitment to teaching—while being given space still to pursue research.

The UUK and UCU are publicly guarded in expressing their views on the threat of MOOCs-ization to the traditional HEI business model—while privately possibly either rather negative and even Luddite, or indeed hubristic in dismissing another scare story about the arrival of technology-driven, low-cost HE. Others, however, such as the think-tank the Institute for Public Policy Research (IPPR) are warning of (and indeed welcoming of) MOOCs as 'An Avalanche is Coming: Higher Education and the Revolution Ahead' (Barber et al., IPPR 2013, at www.ippr.org). Thus, referring to and drawing upon both US and UK HE, the IPPR Report argues: that 'deep, radical, and urgent transformation' is needed across HE since 'the traditional university is being unbundled'; that the university has to respond and adapt to a market where 'the new student consumer is king', while governments 'will need to rethink their regulatory regimes'. Furthermore, HE costs are rising too fast and fee-paying undergraduates are being expected to finance a too-high cost base, some of which by way of research activity is 'irrelevant to their experience' (and even sometimes 'detrimental'); that all this is at a time when 'the value of a degree is falling' and for-profit competition within HE is 'heating up'. Disruptive innovation will arrive courtesy of MOOCs as a tipping point at a time when traditional HE is beset by issues of quality and cost control, of demonstrating value for money and of affordability; while the global and national rankings, along with the accreditation process for university status, are unreasonable barriers to innovative new entrants to the HE market. Universities are thus 'everywhere facing intensifying consumer pressure' over such matters as the unreasonable variations in teaching quality within and across HEIs and subjects; and 'for traditional universities, a dramatic rethink of how faculty use their time and how they interact with students will be central to future success'. HE must become much more flexible, offering shorter more intense degree courses, mingling full-time and part-time study periods, mixing online and classroom delivery; and 'the warped logic that has locked price and quality together [in the HE market] needs to be broken ... [there is a] need to find ways to reduce cost while increasing quality'.

Barber et al. (2013) foresee: a few elite EGM/SRU universities largely unchanged but now using MOOCs within their teaching and also being the provider of high status MOOCs for use in other HEIs; a few global mass universities using online teaching, trading on their value for money and flexibility; a handful of expensive niche universities such as the US liberal arts colleges, the New College of the Humanities in London, the new for-profit UK

University of Law, and the global online Minerva University; the local university, using teaching content from the mass universities and perhaps certification by the elites but delivering a localized in-person contact in such subjects as medicine and laboratory/workshop-based subjects; and the lifelong-learning institution. These five types of HEI arise from 'unbundling the classic university' and then 'rebundling the elements' in different ways for this century and for a globalized world. In the context of a global HE market, just 'as an avalanche reshapes the mountain, so the changes ahead will fundamentally alter the landscape for universities'.

Similarly, the Hudson Institute has issued 'Beyond Retrofitting: Innovation in Higher Education' (Kelly and Hess, 2013, at www.hudson.org). Their argument is that the accreditation cartel in US HE will block technological innovation such as MOOCs and the vested interests of the incumbent HEIs will be protected from new and innovative entrants to the HE market, leaving only minimal retrofitting to give the illusion of progress ('repackaging a largely familiar product at a familiar price'). Hence a radical 'deregulation' of the HE industry has to happen so that the focus is on the outcomes rather than the process of delivery, there is openness to new providers, and unbundling can occur to offer students flexibility and portability of learning. The arrival of MOOCs alone will otherwise not trigger the changes needed to address quality and price issues to the advantage of the student-consumer; instead 'a new, more vibrant higher education market' is needed and one that can be created only by government intervention to break the inertia and the lethargy of, and wrest power and control from, 'the existing web of colleges and universities' since 'technology does not always equal innovation', especially in 'less competitive and more heavily regulated markets' and where, in the case of HEIs, the interests of the academic employees trump those of the students as the paying customers. Thus, MOOCs will be captured within the traditional HEIs' 'credit monopoly', being 'readily co-opted into the existing system' unless the HE cartel is broken up and its accreditation process opened up, unless the 'regulatory capture' prevailing within HE is ended in favour of a functioning market as deregulation did for 'trucking, airlines, and telecommunications' in the USA as also in the UK with, say, bus travel, air travel, telecommunications, utilities. (See also in similar vein: Zemsky et al., 2005; Zemsky, 2009; and Zemsky, 2013.)

And, while MOOCs may or may not prove to be the catalyst for radical change in the delivery of HE, another innovation from US higher education which has in fact been around far longer and has already been widely adopted within some 1,000 US HEIs (but also to be found in other countries, especially in Japan and Holland) is the concept of the Honors Program (the National Collegiate Honors Council at http://nchchonors.org). Here, as a 1960s/1970s response to the early timing of massification within US HE (1950s) compared to its belated late 1980s arrival in UK HE, a selected 10–20% of undergraduates, at extra cost to the HEI but (usually) with no additional tuition fees, receive further and more personalized teaching. Might some such innovation arrive in English HE as the fees climb and concerns about value for money are expressed? The factors behind the spread of the US Honors Program (HP) are probably a mix of: luring some applicants who might otherwise have gone to liberal arts colleges renowned for their relative intensity of and commitment to undergraduate teaching; ensuring at least some students maximize their Grade Point Averages (GPAs) to their own personal benefit by enhancing their employability and also increasing the possibility of progressing to graduate activity at prestigious universities. All of course, then show up to the university's advantage within the league table data (as well as potentially producing more affluent alumni with fond memories of their student teaching and learning experience, who duly donate more). Perhaps there is even an element of institutional guilt at just how little quality teaching students would otherwise receive as massification and the research emphasis short-change undergraduate teaching; as well as providing greater professional satisfaction to those faculty willing to deliver extra teaching to truly hard-working, bright, enthusiastic, and engaged students.

In a European (except seemingly Holland) context, however, an American-style Honors Program may well not be acceptable for reasons around the need for demonstrably equal and fair treatment. A fully-fledged HP could mean high-ability, highly-motivated students being taught in smaller and special classes alongside other such students (as in effect 'streaming' of ability that causes such angst in comprehensive schools), and in courses/classes not otherwise offered to all the student intake. That said, clearly in the context of a developing HE market, where competition is preferably not to be simply on price or rankings prestige as brand value, there may over time emerge and spread an English version of the American HP—which could mean that up to one in five students would be getting the better quality teaching that high fees should provide.

So, while clearly, and for better or for worse in the globalized market of HE, many English universities have to try to play the rankings and league tables game (even if the rules with their emphasis on research outputs in the global rankings are biased against the majority of players), there is still some uncertainty as to whether the evolving HE market will really bring greater competition from new for-profit entrants delivering innovative and lower-cost HE on a scale to threaten the traditional public-in-all-but-name HEIs residing comfortably under the blanket of a state-sponsored virtual monopoly and hence able at present to fix tuition fees at close to the £9,000 maximum in a cartel-like way while resisting any real exercise of consumer power within an imperfectly working market. As in the US, there is further to go—not towards a completely free and unfettered market that would bring with it the risk of unacceptable market failures—but towards a state-regulated market, operated in favour of the student-consumer rather than the university-producer; and that might mean the removal of the £9,000 cap so as to fully deregulate pricing within the HE market while at the same time loosening up controls on supply within the HE market so that new entrants can compete on price, flexibility, and teaching delivery via the use of disruptive technology such as MOOCs and online learning more broadly.

The Browne Report ('Securing a Sustainable Future for Higher Education', 2010) led to a set of proposed changes that were then watered down into the 2011 White Paper and are now partially implemented (short of using legislation) to speed up the pace and widen the extent of deregulation and of market reforms. An HE Bill could have dealt with the current shortfalls in consumer protection for undergraduates deploying what is potentially almost a working lifetime of debt, a debt level that could be reduced through effective price competition and at least made more palatable if greater consumerism in the HE market meant less chance of the quantum and quality of teaching delivered feel like poor value. However, what we may find is that the incumbent HEIs shake off any competition from the for-profits as new entrants and also internalize to their advantage any supposedly disruptive technology by way of MOOCs. We may well have to wait a long time for a no-frills 'easyUni' or for the MOOCs frenzy really to impact upon the medieval university model in a way that the digital age has upon the newspaper industry or the music business. Bowen (2013), however, does see MOOCs-ization as, eventually, the potential partial answer to (US) HE's cost disease, its productivity issue, and its affordability problems—partly addressing the 'rising tide of anger and resentment' (Bowen, 2013: 26) over the ever-escalating price of going to college as part of the (fading) American Dream: 'the broader structure of higher education is likely to change quite profoundly' through 'at least a partial unbundling of activities' (Bowen, 2013: 66; see also Kelly and Carey, 2013).

Along with Vedder (2004), one of the most persistent and perceptive of the scholarly critics of US HE is Robert Zemsky (Zemsky et al., 2005, Zemsky, 2009 and 2013). Zemsky ruefully notes that: 'For three decades now, higher education's truth tellers and prognosticators, including me, have been predicting that American higher education is about to change because it has to change...For all these decades, however, the money bet has remained the same: higher education will change little if at all...For thirty years, the very thing that each wave of reformers has declared needed to be changed has remained all but impervious to change.' (2013: 2 and 15). Thus, Zemsky is forced to admit: 'My unhappy conclusion is that reform will not come to higher education until and unless the federal government becomes an active sponsor of change.' (2013: 17). As English HE with its now near-universal £9,000 tuition fee becomes more costly directly for the student and indirectly for the taxpayer funding the loans system, the same issues arise as for US HE: what needs to be done to ensure the new HE market is efficient and is regulated effectively to the benefit of the student-consumer and of the nation? Zemsky wishes he could rely on the faculty to see the pressing need for and to make radical reforms to the 'economically unsustainable and educationally dysfunctional' curriculum (2013: 82), but they are collectively blinkered, self-ish, and inept (enmeshed in 'faculty deliberations that are endlessly circular' 2013: 37). He also wishes the federal government would not simply fuel HEIs' inefficiency and neglect of cost control by hiking federal grants and loans so as to provide ever-greater subsidy of the wasteful lifestyle, and would now assert its potential regulatory power so as to address the current 'regulatory quag-mire' (2013: ch. 4) and 'to compel higher education to change' (2013: 55). The curriculum needs to be re-engineered 'to constrain both student and faculty choice' (2013: 85)—just as, say, London Metropolitan University has rational-ized its degree courses and now offers the lowest-cost undergraduate degrees among the traditional English HEIs.

Zemsky offers a route for the academics to assert themselves profession-ally before it is too late, as—this time—the pressure for change really is over-whelming because: 'the states' disinvestment in public higher education' is now irreversible (2013: 161—see also, for instance, Ehrenberg, 2007). There are at last some powerful voices being heard amidst the 'moribund' and 'unrespon-sive' traditional HEIs, in the 'aggressive' form of the Gates Foundation and the Lumina Foundation calling for US HE 'to fix itself, choosing leaders and managers who know how to corral reluctant faculty and move forward with an agenda' (2013: 163–165); and 'the emergence of a market-savvy for-profit higher education sector is making change possible' (2013: 167) as it industrial-izes and standardizes the delivery of vocational HE, and develops in a way that 'could, over time, become the dominant model for postsecondary education, save that which is offered by major research universities and elite liberal arts colleges' (2013: 168), one also likely to be taken up by the 'community colleges and the less selective public comprehensive universities' (2013: 169).

These 'dislodging events' might actually now mean that US HE can no longer shake off the demands for change, and, as change happens across HE, the traditional faculty can either 'remain passive, pursuing their own interests and careers separately' or 'grow more petulant, lamenting ever more loudly that academic purposes and the life of the mind are too easily being dismissed' (Zemsky, 2013: 171)—see the discussion of the UK's CDBU in Chapter 5 for the UK's CDBU as an example of such 'petulance'. Or the faculty could get their collective act together and once again take their teaching duty seriously, and deliver a competent curriculum based on sound pedagogical thinking and using online learning processes (Zemsky, 2013: ch. 11).

The role of the federal government, however, is crucial to rescuing US HE: it has 'to fix, fund, and facilitate' (Zemsky, 2013: ch. 12); not least by 'regularly as well as forcefully' asking 'the basic questions' that have little to do with those posed by the sadly ineffective accreditation bodies; viz 'Does the institution practice "truth in pricing" and "truth in lending", and does its advertising make false claims guaranteeing remunerative employment?' (Zemsky, 2013: 209). This is the new, meaningful, and necessary role of the regulatory state rather than that of the historic (post-war) provider-state; and it will involve more than just student-consumer legal protection in that the federal government will also need 'to fund a national testing regime documenting undergraduate learning' (Zemsky, 2013: 212). Zemsky is also sceptical of the validity of the testing process currently used, and hence calls for a more sophisticated and comprehensive federal mechanism along with the need 'to establish a new federal agency responsible for monitoring institutional compliance with the rules and regulations governing the disbursement of federal student aid' (Zemsky, 2013: 215—note, the allocation of these monies being the crux of potential federal power over and control of HE). And Zumeta et al. (2012) echo Zemsky in calling for HE to 'operate in a more systematically efficient and publically accountable way' (28), not least by fully embracing 'promising practices in online learning' and 'innovations in the design, delivery, and assessment of higher education' (148–154) given that 'the patterns of public expenditures and tuition growth of recent decades are not sustainable' (161): there is a need for 'increased openness to new delivery models' (161) which 'need to be tapped more extensively than they have been' (190) rather than a simplistic reliance on forever hiking tuition fees—which have grown from being a *c*.22.5% share of HE costs in 1985 to over 45% by 2010 (20).

And such calls for HEIs to engender innovation in teaching and to (re-) embrace a commitment to teaching are not confined to the USA and the UK: Fallis (2013) proposes comprehensive reform for Ontario's HE system which would, inter alia, address how 'the prestige of research' has 'overwhelmed undergraduate education' (while at the same time 'undergraduate tuition has been rising', making the teaching content of the degree course even worse value for money), an unfortunate process that is now 'a serious problem' where undergraduate teaching as 'the primary task of universities' has thereby failed for some time to 'get the support it needs' (2013: 271). The remedy is 'to require that universities be more transparent about how resources are allocated', about 'how much is spent on undergraduate education' (2013: 272): which, Fallis recognizes might be difficult, since universities have weak financial systems and do not necessarily know what expenditure serves which purpose, especially when it comes to assessing the deployment of costly faculty time among undergraduate teaching, graduate teaching/supervision, research, consultancy, scholarship updating, administration, and civic engagement duties. Moreover, HEIs should also be obliged to deploy any extra 'revenue from increases in undergraduate tuition toward [only and directly] improvement in undergraduate education' (2013: 274), rather than it leaking away to prop up research activity, administration, and glitzy campus infrastructure.

However, concerning the need for and the potential for the federal government to seize the initiative on US HE reform given the deep inertia and profound complacency within the HE sector, President Obama's August 2013 proposal to develop and apply metrics to assess HEIs' value for money to the student and taxpayer (and then to use them in deploying federal financial aid to students) has, predictably, met an immediate wall of opposition (*Times Higher Education*, 29 August 2013, 'ObamaRank: US Academy up in Arms Over President's Plans'). Indeed, the liberal professors within academe, roused to defend their vested interests, appear unusually (Gross, 2013) to be united with right-wing Republican politicians fearing that Washington bureaucrats will in effect be setting HE prices—although some student groups have welcomed the President's attempt to curb tuition fees by forcing HEIs to address costs. The President is quoted (*New York Times*, 22 August 2013, 'Obama's Plan Aims to Lower Cost of College') as stating that 'it's past time that more of our colleges work better for the students they exist to serve'. One suspects, however, that Mr President will have as much political trouble tackling the scandal of the US HE industry via 'ObamaRank' as he did taking on the similarly powerful and selfish interests of the hugely costly US health industry in promoting 'ObamaCare' (Halvorson, 2009; Persily, 2013). It is towards this interesting concept of the regulatory state and its potentially more significant involvement in the emerging English HE market, and also the important issue of the entry of the for-profits at a competitive price and innovative element within the undergraduate market, that we turn to in Chapter 11.

In this chapter, as also in Chapter 6, we have, therefore, drawn heavily on the extensive analysis, some of it undoubtedly polemical, of US higher education as a more developed example of marketization within HE. However, the Australian experience in the introduction of tuition fees and loans, and very recently of the uncapping of student numbers (with discussion now of uncapping fees) clearly provides important developments with potential policy-making implications for English HE. In the context of the globalization of higher education there is direct and fierce competition between the top SRUs of the USA and the UK with a further stratum of elite research universities consisting of counterparts drawn from Australia and the Far East as well as the second tier of British and American research elites. Beyond the 20 or so UK universities that belong to these two strata, the remaining British HEIs (like their counterparts everywhere) need to find their strategic positions along the research-active to the teaching-only spectrum, and to set their fees competitively within a complex, increasingly global market-place, having addressed the issues of cost control, delivery innovations, productivity, and quality control as identified in the review of the literature on the political economy of HE set out in this chapter and Chapter 6.

Part III

Responding to Change: Organizational Fragmentation

9

The HE Industry: Speaking with More Than One Voice

Abstract: The institutional diversity of English higher education has given rise to, and in turn helped to intensify, a more open and pluralist politics of higher education in England. The first empirical section of the chapter analyses Universities UK (UUK), because it can be described as the main body claiming to represent the interests of the higher education sector as a whole. It then proceeds to examine what it describes as 'the mission groups': GuildHE, Russell Group, the recently demised 1994 Group, Million+, and the University Alliance. The endeavour is to present profiles of these groups and analyse their policy positions with respect to four key issues: research funding, the regulation of higher education, the widening of access, and the introduction of variable student fees. It evaluates their relative political effectiveness and posits the question as to whether their purpose is more to define their institutional identities rather than to influence the direction of policy.

THE CHANGING POLITICS OF THE GOVERNANCE OF ENGLISH HIGHER EDUCATION

Although in formal terms the UGC was part of the machinery of government for much of its history—arguably until the 1970s—it was very much on the outer rim of the state apparatus. It inhabited an enclosed domain dominated by senior figures from the academic world, frequently headed by those with strong Oxbridge connections, and was served by Treasury officials. It was enmeshed in a socio-cultural elite cemented by common career lines, class and educational backgrounds, and membership of the London clubs where as much committee business could be discussed as in its formal meetings. And, not surprisingly, much of the history of the UGC has been written as if its policy development was overwhelmingly driven by the efforts of its more eminent leaders—Walter Moberly, Keith Murray, and Peter Swinnerton-Dyer, to name but three. Obviously the closed domain would open up to incorporate other parties into the decision-making process in which the most frequent participants were the Committee of Vice-Chancellors and Principals (CVCP), the Association of University Teachers (AUT), the National Union of Students (NUS), and between 1970–1993, the Committee of the Directors of Polytechnics (CDP) representing the so-called public-sector institutions. However, this was a relatively enclosed world and conspicuous by its absence was a strong political input, including that of the Treasury, which until 1964 was the arm of government with formal responsibility for overseeing the UGC.

From 1945 onwards, and more especially from the 1970s when financial constraints and more explicit political pressure started to make themselves felt, the politics of the governance of higher education changed. The UGC became more open to parliamentary scrutiny (especially the gaze of the Public Accounts Committee), needed to co-ordinate more closely with the officials of the Department of Education and Science, and had to respond to government policy initiatives of which the most pressing was the cutting of public funding. The politics of higher education policy-making was subjected to a much broader inspection and more closely integrated into the Government's Comprehensive Spending Reviews orchestrated by the Treasury (see Shattock, 2012 for an excellent historical overview of these developments). This was a more open politics marked by greater conflict, which proved difficult for the UGC to control. For example, the failure to discuss publicly the criteria that determined how the Committee had distributed the cuts to its grant in the early 1980s owed much to the desire to contain grass roots opposition from the universities. Nonetheless, the politics of the governance of higher education was not only slowly opening up, but also becoming more conflictual in its nature.

As we have noted, thanks to the 1988 ERA, the Secretary of State assumed responsibility for the policy development of the English higher education system, while the funding councils (with national remits) acted as distributors of public funding and various regulatory bodies steered the policy implementation process. Henceforth, the pattern of change in higher education would be driven by the interaction of government policy and the implementation strategies of the funding councils. Clearly government is the dominant force in the relationship, possessing the authority not only to form policy but also to impose additional demands on the established regulatory regime. Nonetheless, it is in the interest of government to sustain the credibility of HEFCE in the eyes of the higher education institutions, and if it were constantly to impose its own will this would merely undermine the Council's standing. However, although the Council has the legislative right to communicate policy advice, it is unlikely to carry much weight given that governments are more likely to be persuaded by their own internal party interests and values.

Higher education is, therefore, a policy arena which is now very much in the public domain. While state power, accompanied by greater government control, has increased, it is important to remember that the era of the funding councils has seen an expansion of political engagement in higher education, which has been in part stimulated by its very model of governance. The shift to the new public management model of governance in continental Europe was seen as an attempt to lessen the stranglehold of the central state upon the universities (Magalhaes and Amaral, 2009), and in Britain it has been widely interpreted as resulting in the 'hollowing out' of the state (Rhodes, 1997, 2000, 2000a). However, it is important to note the different historical traditions: the university in the continental Europe—most clearly seen in the Napoleonic model—existed to serve the dominant interests of the state; in England its destiny was more under its own control, while at the same time genuflecting to the paramount societal interests while rarely threatening the demands of the central state. The contemporary politics of the governance of English higher education is underwritten by the fact it is a mass, diverse system that still remains heavily dependent upon public funding, and as such it will inevitably be subjected to those same pressures that impact upon all the significant areas of public policy. Undoubtedly the structure of control represented by the funding council model of governance has lessened the autonomy of the universities, but also it has made the struggles over the future development of higher education more open, and arguably more democratic.

If, therefore, the first explanation of the change in the politics of English higher education (from corporate governance to pluralism) is dependent upon the instigation of a new model of system governance, then the second is the fact that the university system itself has changed out of all recognition. Even prior to the 1992 Further and Higher Education Act that permitted the polytechnics to acquire the university title, post-1945 the university sector had been diversified by the incorporation of the colleges of advanced technology (CATs), the foundation of the 1960s new universities, and the creation of the Open University, all of which helped to reshape a model already composed of the collegiate universities, the large nineteenth-century redbricks, and the smaller twentieth-century civics. What the 1992 Act did was to put into the university pot a considerable number of institutions that explicitly had been given the polytechnic rather than the university label in part because they supposedly embodied a contrasting higher education identity. Although, as we will see, there have been important attempts to sustain the idea that the interests of English higher education are advanced best if they are furthered by one all-embracing representative body, it was almost inevitable that the growing institutional differentiation would within itself generate a mélange of interests, which if not actually competing with one another would advocate varying policy positions on key issues.

It is also evident that English universities see themselves as in competition with one other for public funding and private resources; a state of affairs that has been encouraged by successive governments. It has become important, therefore, for universities to establish positive identities that will help to ensure their future viability, perhaps even augment their reputations. Part of the process of institutional branding is the need to belong to the right group; one which matches self-perceptions and hopefully helps to secure a viable future. Thus, different groups emerge in part because of the need to establish a positive self-identity, and not simply out of a desire either to promote the interests of higher education as a whole or even to further particular policy goals. As we will see, this introduces an element of instability in the formation of the groups, partly because over time the formal status of an institution may change (for example, the acquisition of the university title) or a university may feel that it has outgrown its past identity and as part of its rebranding process it wants to secure membership of another group.

The emergence of the organized interests within the higher education sector is, therefore, a consequence of its very significant diversification over time to the point that, although there may be some widely shared policy concerns, segments within the sector believe they have particular interests that need to be defended politically and which help to define their identities within an increasingly competitive market. This chapter will examine this process of group formation at two levels. Firstly, by an analysis of Universities UK (UUK) that can best be described as the main body attempting to represent the interests of the higher education sector as a whole. Secondly, it will turn to the emergence of what we have labelled the mission groups: GuildHE, Russell Group, 1994 Group, Million+, and the University Alliance. However, it should be noted at the outset that GuildHE would see itself—like UUK—as a representative body rather than a mission group, but we will argue that its size and the character of its membership do not make this an appropriate label. The focus will be upon presenting profiles of these organized interests and examining their policy positions with respect to four main issues: the funding of research, the regulation of the higher education sector by the quasi-state, the widening of access, and the introduction of variable student fees. The chapter concludes by evaluating and explaining the relative policy effectiveness of the various mission groups. It also raises the question of whether group membership is more important for defining institutional self-identity rather than acting as a means of influencing policy, and should that be the case, what are the implications for the future of the one truly representative body, Universities UK?

REPRESENTING THE HIGHER EDUCATION SECTOR: UNIVERSITIES UK

In 1993, following the ending of the binary line, the Committee of the Directors of Polytechnics (CDP) was absorbed into the Committee of Vice-Chancellors and Principals (CVCP), which in December 2000 was renamed Universities

UK (UUK). Currently, UUK claims to have 134 members and sees itself as the main representative body for British higher education:

> In 2012, Universities UK's 94th year, our membership truly reflects a vibrant, successful and diverse sector, but our mission on their behalf remains largely unchanged. For over 90 years we have spoken out in support of the higher education sector, seeking to influence and create policy, and to provide an environment where our member institutions can flourish. Today Universities UK remains the essential voice of our universities—supporting their autonomy, celebrating their diversity.
>
> (Universities UK, 22 January 2013)

Reflecting the United Kingdom's devolution of the political and administrative structure of the British system of higher education, UUK has two autonomous national councils—Universities Scotland and Higher Education Wales. Inevitably the different national policy trajectories within the United Kingdom require UUK to shape its policies in ways which will harmonize with the established political boundaries as well as the contrasting traditions of higher education they sustain. While this was a reality that the CVCP always had to face, the post-1992 devolutionary process has intensified the necessity for Universities UK either to adopt policy stances that are tailored to differing national circumstances or simply to refrain from engagement in issues that are strongly influenced by the contrasting national political contexts, and, as we will see, this is a quandary that has been further exacerbated by the emergence of the mission groups.

While the presence of a range of internal factions makes it difficult for UUK to adopt a policy position on all issues that enables it to speak with one co-ordinated voice, the fact that its membership is all-embracing does give its claims to be *the* voice of the British higher education sector considerable legitimacy. This is reinforced by the fact that it is assuming the mantle pursued by its direct predecessors, which provides a clear historical basis to its claim. Regardless of how effective the impact of the CVCP and CDP upon the higher education policy-making process may be judged to have been, at the very least they both had a serious consultative role to play. Both the University Grants Committee and the National Advisory Body for Higher Education had several members with institutional bases that would have been represented in either the CVCP or CDP. Moreover, the present-day funding councils incorporate many academics into those procedures by which they fulfil their regulatory functions. For example, both the research assessment exercises and the quality assurance of teaching and learning draw heavily upon the academic labour force. Almost inevitably, therefore, the policy implementation process involves consultation with UUK as the sector's representative body.

Furthermore, although the funding council model of governance places policy-making in the hands of the government, it remains the case that it is still a process that continues to be dependent upon the interaction of government and the higher education sector interests. The classic example is for the government to propose broad policy initiatives and then seek out the sector's responses, which was the course followed by the current Coalition Government with respect to its White Paper, *Students at the Heart of the System* (Department for Business, Innovation, and Skills, June 2011). Indeed, the document contains an annex, which explicitly invites 'consultation on our proposals for reform', an invitation to which UUK was quick to respond. Moreover, committees of enquiry into higher education, with either broad or specific remits, will invite interested parties to submit evidence and, as we have noted the CVCP gave evidence to the Dearing Inquiry.

However, to be consulted about the direction of higher education policy is not the same as having a voice that determines what that policy will be. Furthermore, the advice presented by Universities UK will be but one of several inputs, and it has to be recognized that, with the clear political control of policy-making, those inputs are likely to be considerably less influential than when higher education policy was more in the hands of the those bodies (notably the UGC and NAB) that not only performed a regulatory function but also had a real say in the distribution of public funding for higher education as well as a significant input into how the system should evolve. The point is that higher education policy is now more closely enmeshed in the general framework of government policy and more clearly shaped by its economic strategy and broader policy goals (for example, the perception of higher education as an economic and social resource) that have been pursued by successive governments of different political persuasions (Shattock, 2012).

What are the ways in which UUK pursues its goals of seeking, to use its own words, 'to influence and create policy and to provide an environment where our member institutions can flourish'? On the political front, besides its input into government thinking on policy development, and the evidence it presents to official enquiries into how higher education should evolve (the Dearing Inquiry, for example, was meant to present a model of higher education that would last for the next twenty years), it has a strong parliamentary presence. It presents evidence to those parliamentary committees in both the Commons and Lords, which monitor those departments that are formally responsible for administrating higher education. Secondly, through parliamentarians who are sympathetic to its policy stance, it can have an input into those debates that are triggered by the passage of government legislation. Of course, parliamentary debates take place at a very late stage indeed in the policy-making process and it can be expected that government proposals (into which the higher education interests would have had an input) will prevail. However, it is recognized that the debates in the House of Lords on the higher education clauses of the 1988 Education Reform Act were influential in persuading the government to introduce changes that explicitly recognized academics had the right to exercise freedom of speech, and that this input was orchestrated by the CVCP (Crequer, 1989; Tapper, 2007: 120–123).

While the political dialogue in which UUK engages is central to its policy-influencing role, it is also committed to presenting to society at large a broadly positive image of British higher education. In fact it is a publicist for the cause of higher education, demonstrating how universities contribute to the general good of society, and thus merit public support, and particularly public funding. To this end it produces a range of publications, prepares briefings for the media, and also organizes conferences and workshops. Often in conjunction with other stakeholders, it will undertake research and produce policy documents that are designed either to have a specific policy impact or inform the more general debate about the future direction of British higher education. Finally, complementing its policy and publicity-generating roles are the services it provides to its members. For example, it is prepared to offer advice to universities that are contemplating amalgamations, exploring the possibility of franchising higher education programmes or which want to enhance their links to their local communities.

While the evaluation of the performance of these three roles (policy input, publicizing the merits of British higher education, and service to members) is open to debate, UUK does appear to be an effectively governed and managed organization. This is important given UUK's claim to be *the* representative body for British higher education, and, moreover, in view of the emergence of the mission groups, what would be the attraction to the universities of UUK membership if were a poorly functioning organization? Not surprisingly, given the structural differences in higher education and the changing political context, UUK does not operate in the same way as its predecessors the CVCP and the CDP and, furthermore, its *modus operandi* has changed somewhat since its foundation, as the lessons of steering a large and diverse membership have been absorbed. Its current structure of governance is as follows:

1. The main formal decision-making body is the UUK Board, consisting of 24 members including the President who is elected for two years.

2. The UUK Board has a five-person sub-committee known as the Executive, which assumes responsibility for policy decisions between Board meetings.

3. All members meet four times a year, including at an annual conference.

4. There are two autonomous national councils, one representing Scottish and the other Welsh members.

The daily administration of Universities UK is under the control of a Chief Executive (appointed by the Board) and the team of some 100 staff is organized into four groups: Communications, Policy, Member Services, and Resources (Universities UK, 22 January 2013a).

We have claimed that the emergence of the mission groups was encouraged by three interrelated forces: a new model of governance in which policy was placed under political control, the need for universities to brand themselves more explicitly as they competed more aggressively for both public and private funding, and the steadily enhanced diversity of the system of British higher education which brought under the university umbrella institutions embodying varying traditions. In the light of the emergence of the mission groups, it is more difficult to sustain the idea of UUK as *the* voice of British higher education or at least to believe that it is capable of formulating policy positions that represent the interests of the universities across the board. As we will note, part of the identity of the mission groups is that they represent particular policy positions, and that on several issues there is policy divergence rather than unanimity.

The devolution of political and administrative responsibility for higher education had already confronted UUK with the problem of possible policy divergence but it could be contained by establishing the autonomous Scottish and Welsh councils, which in effect recognized that on many issues policy needed to follow national boundaries rather than be British in scope. However, the mission groups are not so easily demarcated by such clearly defined boundaries, and, therefore, could not so easily be contained within UUK as separately identifiable sectors. Moreover, and more importantly, UUK perceives itself as a unifying force and its character would change very dramatically if it were formally to become a loose coalition of different interests. As long ago as 1998, Martin Harris in his role as chair of the CVCP is reported to have said:

> The CVCP will need to represent to the government and society the fact that there are different strengths and priorities within our diverse system, and rather than articulate one common position it will be necessary to articulate a range of points of view which between them represent what institutions are seeking.

> (Tysome, 6 March 1998: 5)

While this was a realistic response to the changed circumstances, the problem with such a strategy is that UUK (as the CVCP was to become) could evolve into a forum for the expression of policy differences and in the process lose completely any effectiveness it might have as a lobbying body.

Provocatively, Wolf has seen the emergence of the mission groups as a signal heralding the possible 'salvation' of British higher education because they have the potential to be so much more effective lobbyists than large umbrella groups like Universities UK (Wolf, 21 January 2005: 13). A more charitable interpretation is that, rather than become a divided policy advocate as suggested by Harris, the purpose of the UUK is now defined more in terms of its trumpeting of the merits of British higher education and the services it provides to its members rather than by its input into the policy-making process. However, it can continue to sustain broadly defined policy positions that are widely supported, of which the need for enhanced public funding is the most anodyne, but it cannot readily take sides where sharp institutional conflict is likely to arise. Interestingly, this will also impact on its input into policy implementation for, while there is considerable consensus on issues such as the selective public funding of research, the need for publicly controlled quality assurance mechanisms, and the importance of the widening participation agenda for higher education, there is real conflict amongst institutions on how these policies should be put into operation. Organizational unity, therefore, is built around the advocacy of broadly-defined policy goals as opposed to their detailed implementation coupled with UUK's role as a service provider and promoter of British higher education as a vital national product.

While Universities UK may not exercise the authority that was commanded by its predecessor the CVCP, nonetheless, it can be argued that it is doing a creditable job in very different and difficult circumstances. Not surprisingly, there are periodic claims that its internal tensions have reached breaking point, and that it is on the verge of losing a segment of its membership (Hill and Fazackerley, 9 December 2005: 2; Fazackerley, 28 April 2006: 2; Newman, 4 December 2008: 10), however—as we will see—it is the membership of the various mission groups that appears to be more fragile. It seems as if British higher education needs a single reference point and UUK continues to fulfil that role. A more difficult conundrum to resolve is how significant the membership of UUK continues to be for those who belong to it. If in part institutional identity is defined by being a member of a mission group, then to belong also to UUK may be little more than a gesture; that it is like joining a club because you are expected to be a member rather than belonging to it because you intend to play a major role in shaping its affairs. Membership, therefore, is more symbolic rather than important in shaping either institutional identity or signifying policy commitments.

THE MISSION GROUPS: SELF-IDENTITIES AND POLICY POSITIONS

GuildHE

GuildHE was founded in 1967 as the Standing Conference of Principals (SCOP) with the change of name instigated in 2006 (GuildHE, 23 January 2013). It sees itself as a representative organization because as SCOP its membership embraced the principals and directors of the colleges and institutions of higher education, and indeed when post-1992 the polytechnics acquired the university title and the Committee of the Directors of Polytechnics was absorbed into the Committee of Vice-Chancellors and Principals, SCOP remained a separate organization. Moreover, although GuildHE and UUK now share premises and often engage in joint activities (such as preparing reports and submitting evidence), they are still formally different bodies. Periodically there is talk of GuildHE joining UUK but retaining within it a separate identity that would specifically represent 'the interests of smaller specialist institutions' (Tysome, 22 September 2006). The problem from Universities UK's perspective is that, although devolution has forced it to adopt a federal structure, it would be quite another matter to reorganize itself to accommodate formally differing internal interests that defined their own identities. In effect it would become little more than an amalgam of a range of groups, an umbrella body for contrasting sectors rather than a forum for forging unity across the system.

It was the extension after 1992 of the university title to some of the colleges of higher education (thus following the same path as the former polytechnics) that brought about the change of title from SCOP to GuildHE. As the colleges acquired the university title, some of them decided to leave SCOP and seek membership of Universities UK. Currently GuildHE has 27 members and 9 associate members (GuildHE, 23 January 2013a), including ten institutions that the Department for Business, Innovation, and Skills, with strong support from GuildHE, recommended to the Privy Council on 27 November 2012 should be awarded the university title (GuildHE, 16 November 2013). It is composed overwhelmingly of smaller institutions pursuing specialist academic interests in art and design, teacher training, agriculture, music, and drama. In effect it has become (perhaps always was) a mission group representing a particular institutional segment within British higher education, although it identifies its membership as being both diverse and distinctive. Like UUK, GuildHE has an input into the policy-making process and provides services for its members, although—not surprising in view of its specialized membership—it is more inclined to celebrate the diversity of British higher education rather than trumpet its supposed virtues as a system. It also pursues these goals in parallel ways (publications, links to the media, presenting evidence to parliamentary committees, submissions to enquiries, as well as holding its own conferences and organizing events) and, furthermore, has a broadly similar structure of governance and administrative support staff, albeit operating on a smaller scale than UUK.

While it seems logical to argue that there will be a continuing role for an organization which represents the interests of smaller, specialized institutions of higher education, it is evident that the membership of GuildHE is constantly threatened by possible shifts in the overall structure of the system. The designation of the university title and the accruing of the right to award degrees undoubtedly impacts upon an institution's self-perception. As their identities change so there is pressure upon them to consider their group allegiances, but this is a fact of life for all the mission groups. The implication is that the recent awarding of the university title to ten of its members (strongly supported by GuildHE) ironically makes it more vulnerable to a loss of membership, although as small, academically specialized institutions, GuildHE appears to be their natural home.

An unresolved issue for GuildHE is the evolution of its relationship to Universities UK. If UUK becomes a service organization for its members, and couples this with the broad promotion of the apparent virtues of British higher education while sticking to the advocacy of widely agreed, general policy agreements (thus avoiding taking positions on either the detailed implementation of policy or the development of new policies), then it is possible that these two self-labelled representative organizations could merge but that would require a change in the role of both bodies, with UUK defining its input into the policy process in narrow terms and GuildHE relinquishing its claim to be a representative body. As this chapter has argued, Universities UK has already moved significantly in this direction and the question for GuildHE is whether it wants its role to be formally recognized in a federally structured UUK or whether it is prepared to act as a mission group (which to all intents and purposes it has become) while its members join UUK on the same terms as those universities that belong to other mission groups.

The Russell Group, the 1994 Group[1], Million+, and University Alliance

Each of these four groups came to represent a particular segment of British higher education, although how distinctively different the identity of institutions in any one group is from the identity of institutions in another group is not always that obvious. Indeed, the shifting patterns of group membership and the changes in some of their titles would suggest that some uncertainty pervades both the groups and their members. However, this may simply reflect pragmatic responses to changing realities. Groups may require new labels because they believe this will enhance their effectiveness, and universities may change their group membership because they want to assert a new identity.

Each of these four mission groups constructed strong, if overlapping, brand images. The Russell Group, which has expanded in size from 18 members at its foundation in 1994 to a current membership of 24, sees itself as comprising the major research universities in the United Kingdom, those institutions which, in the words of one of its in-house papers could claim to be 'world-class universities' (Russell Group, 2012). The 1994 Group, which unsurprisingly was also established in 1994, brands itself as bringing together the smaller 'internationally renowned research-intensive universities' (1994 Group, 24 January 2013).

---

[1] As our manuscript was being prepared for publication, the Board of the 1994 Group issued a statement—released on 8 November 2013—dissolving the Goup.

However, in view of the serious leakage of members in 2012 (its website listed a membership of 11 at its demise), it certainly needed to establish a broader identity in order to augment its support base if it were not to dissolve as a group.

Million+, which started life in 1997 as the Coalition of Modern Universities only to become Campaigning for Mainstream Universities before it acquired its present title in 2007, explicitly labels itself as a university think-tank, which would suggest that it sees its role as transcending that of a mission group working on behalf of its members, although all of its current 21 listed affiliates are post-1992 foundations (Million+, 24 January 2013). Million+'s mission statement is interesting, given that it attempts to bridge its think-tank and mission group roles in order 'to develop and shape public policy and funding regimes on a non-party basis' with the purpose of: widening access to universities, promoting institutional collaboration on a broad front in order 'to enhance social and economic outcomes', and celebrating 'the strength and diversity of the UK higher education sector' (Million+, 24 January 2013a).

In contrast to Million+, University Alliance (formed in 2006 as the Alliance of Non-Aligned Universities but adopting its new title in 2007—Newman, 19 November 2009: 35) clearly sees itself as first and foremost representing a particular university brand:

> University Alliance brings together 24 major, business-engaged universities committed to delivering world-class research and a quality student experience around the UK...Alliance universities have innovation and enterprise running through everything they do and deliver...
>
> (University Alliance, 24 January 2013)

But, like all the other groups, University Alliance believes that its brand signifies its members are making a very positive contribution to 'the wider public and economic benefit of the UK'.

The mission groups, therefore, communicate conflicting messages about their identities. On the other hand, they assume UUK's role by portraying British higher education as a diverse system that incorporates across-the-board a range of positive qualities (excellent research, high-quality teaching, and productive economic and social links to the wider society including their local communities) while, on the other hand, in the reported words of Cuthbert of the University of the West of England: 'They are pressure groups, pure and simple' (Newman, 19 November 2009: 36). As pressure groups they have to act as policy advocates, supporting proposals that coincide with the interests of their members but which may be opposed by the membership of other groups. They are pressure groups because their purpose is first and foremost to support their members' interests rather than attempt to work out policy lines that could benefit the system at large, but undoubtedly they would argue that they see the promotion of their group missions as the most viable way of enhancing British higher education; that there is no conflict between their members' interests and the welfare of the wider system. Moreover, it is through their policy positions that they define their own identities and to act as effective pressure groups obviously aids their own survival.

The different policy positions that the mission groups have advocated provide good evidence of their pressure group role. Our analysis focuses initially upon the public funding of research because this is the policy area which most sharply differentiates the mission groups, and it is their research funding that provides the sharpest financial contrasts. Furthermore, although almost all universities trumpet their commitment to high quality teaching, very few of them are prepared to embrace the teaching-only role. Many of the post-1992 universities are keen to claim they are research-active almost as if this were needed to justify their university title.

There is agreement across the mission groups that the public funding of research should be distributed on the basis of proven research excellence. In the words of the Russell Group: 'Concentration of research funding, based on excellence, is necessary to sustain the breadth and depth of the UK's research strength', and leaves little doubt that this is best achieved by funnelling most of the available resources into the research conducted by its own members: 'The Russell Group is concerned that the recent reduction in concentration of research funding…risks damaging the UK's research base and compromising the sustainability of our leading universities' (Russell Group, 2 February 2013). The three other groups argue that the public funding of research should be allocated selectively, but not necessarily channelled into a limited number of universities:

> The 2008 Research Assessment Exercise (RAE) demonstrated, without a doubt, that world-leading and international excellent research takes place across all our universities. It also demonstrated that there is no clear relationship between the size of an academic team and the excellence of the outputs they produce.
>
> (Million+, 17 May 2011)

> Our report also demonstrates why there is no significant correlation between productivity and research unit size. The data provides clear evidence that funding should always follow excellence where it is found, as any metric based on scale would not improve productivity. Indeed it could have the effect of excluding some of the very best units.
>
> (University Alliance, 12 July 2011)

> We should continue with our widely distributive funding policies, funding which rewards excellence wherever it is found supported by a strong core of Government support to national research and higher education.
>
> (1994 Group, September 2011)

Over time, the general trend in the distribution of public resources (both by the research councils and through the RAEs) to support both research funding and postgraduate students has become a more selective allocation process. Although it is not a uniform trajectory, particular universities and their academic departments have steadily gained the lion's share of resources. It is obvious, therefore, why the Russell Group should wish to counter any apparent move that bucks this trend and why the membership of the other groups should want to prevent a further concentration of resources that follows a straightforward institutional demarcation. However this is a struggle that the Russell Group universities appear to be winning:

> The total budget for QR research funding will remain steady at nearly £1.6 billion [for 2012–13], but the proportion that goes to Russell Group members will increase from 70.2% to 71.3%. The allocations of all the other mission groups will fall.

> (Jump, 29 March 2012: 7)

Although all the groups in part pitch the defence of their research role in terms of serving the national interest, it is clear that they are also bidding for a share of the research cake that can impact significantly upon their funding as well as shaping their own self-identity. All the mission groups see their membership as containing at least pockets of research excellence, but for both the Russell and 1994 Groups' research success and funding has been central to how they define themselves.

While interest group politics is most clearly at work in defining the mission groups' policy stances on research funding, it also intrudes—albeit more subtly—into other policy areas. Following the 2011 White Paper, the government required HEFCE to carry out a consultation exercise on 'A risked-based approach to quality assurance' (HEFCE, October 2012). Central to the review was the proposition that the current six-yearly cycle of reviews could be lengthened for providers who had already had two successful reviews, while for those providers who had yet to go through the review process it could be shortened to a four-yearly cycle. In fact HEFCE decided to retain the six-yearly cycle for current providers, and this had been supported by both University Alliance and Million+ while the 1994 Group reportedly argued that 'the sector should only support a move to a longer cycle if it is clear that the "triggers" for ad hoc intervention are sufficiently robust' (Morgan, 16 August 2012: 9). The Russell Group in its evidence to HEFCE's consultation had argued for a ten-yearly cycle and in response to the decision to retain the status quo Wendy Piatt, its Director-General, is reported to have made the following observation:

> We are disappointed that HEFCE has not taken the opportunity to adopt a genuinely risked-based, light-touch quality assurance regime – especially since the higher education White Paper made a commitment to substantial deregulatory change.

And she allegedly concluded that,

> Russell Group universities should be subject to considerably less inspection and bureaucracy.
>
> (Morgan, 1 November 2012: 9)

The split in university ranks over the regulatory framework for higher education in fact reflects divisions that have existed since the very introduction of the state-steered quality assurance agenda (Brown, 2004; Tapper, 2007: 167–186). Ironically, it is in part the claimed intention of the current government to put 'students at the heart of the system' that up until now has helped to shore up the regulatory regime. In the context of requiring students to pay considerably higher fees, it would have been politically difficult for the government to have moved significantly in the direction of deregulation. At least in the short-term it was necessary to convey the impression that the government would do its best to ensure that students received value for money, and sustaining more or less intact the existing regulatory framework was a politically cost-effective way to accomplish this. Clearly there would have been some risks involved in moving towards a ten-yearly quality assurance cycle for proven providers of higher education, but it is a matter of judgement as to how great these would have been. By leaving it to HEFCE to make the decision, the government was able to avoid formal responsibility and at the same time cover its political back. Moreover, at least in terms of size if not status, it was able to placate the largest wedge of universities and their mission groups, if albeit for only a short time.

However, all was not lost for the Russell Group on this policy front. The Quality Assurance Agency (QAA) has been invited by the HEFCE to target its efforts 'where they are most needed, tailoring the intensity of individual reviews and reducing the burden on providers which can demonstrate a strong track record in managing academic standards and quality. . . . Any variation in intensity of review for individual providers must be based on sound evidence and not prevent our reviewers from investigating the key issues affecting students and other stakeholders who depend on our work (QAA, 28 January 2013). The consequence is that the QAA launched a consultation process that lasted until 22 April 2013 and led to the publication of a revised Higher Education Review handbook with reviews commencing on a new basis in January 2014. One can only guess at the politics which led to the reopening of a policy issue that had apparently been closed by HEFCE in 2012. Regardless, QAA's remit strongly suggests that a risk-based regulatory model will be introduced and, although it may not be precisely to the liking of all the Russell Group's members, it appears that it will follow in its general policy direction.

The groups are also divided by two further important policy issues, the widening participation agenda and variable undergraduate student fees, both of which are even more enmeshed in the wider political milieu. Attempts to broaden the social composition of the undergraduate student intake have received almost universal political support and been embraced across the higher education sector. Both University Alliance and Million+ place considerable emphasis upon the social heterogeneity of their members' undergraduate populations, and it is not an exaggeration to say that they see a socially inclusive university as integral to their vision of higher education. For the Russell Group, 'widening access' is one of the policy areas which it specifically highlights, and the 1994 Group produced the policy brief, *Widening Participation Through Targeted Outreach Programmes* (1994 Group, December 2010). Both the Russell and 1994 Groups emphasize the point that it is up to their individual members to decide their own means for widening access and to set their own targets, with the Russell Group explicitly issuing a plea that the Office for Fair Access (OFFA) should 'recognize the limitations of the HESA performance indicators as a measure of institutional success in widening access' (Russell Group, 2013). The sceptic may wonder whether the widening participation is taken so seriously because if universities want to charge annual fees of over £6,000 they need to reach an 'access agreement' with OFFA, and they have no wish to face the possibility, however remote, of imposed access targets, although currently there is no legislative basis for such a move.

Neither University Alliance nor Million+, although proclaiming the social diversity of the student populations of their own members, have advocated publicly the setting of access targets to embrace the student recruitment of all universities. Not only would this be seen as at least an implicit attack on other universities, but would also infringe very severely the principle of university autonomy to which both government and all British universities pay at least lip-service. What does autonomy mean if an institution cannot determine for itself how it selects its student body? How far is government prepared to go in its effort to steer university decision-making in order to achieve its policy goals? Ironically, by allowing fees to be raised to a ceiling of £9,000 per annum, and even more so by not placing restrictions upon the number of students who could be recruited with A-level grades (or their equivalent) of AAB for the 2012 entry and ABB for the following year, it is the government itself that may be undermining the widening participation agenda. Many departments in the Russell Group universities receive more applicants with at least these grades than there are available places, and if there are no penalties for over-recruitment, then the temptation is to expand numbers to meet the demand. And all the evidence shows that academic achievement in pre-university qualifications favours heavily those from the more socially privileged segments of society.

Million+ goes as far as accusing the government of being obsessed with trying to ensure that a few additional pupils in receipt of free schools meals secure an Oxbridge place, rather than taking a deeper approach to understanding the importance of university access across the sector for enhancing social mobility (Million+, 19 September 2011). Although this interpretation of government priorities may be valid, the lesson is that the policy positions of the mission groups need to feed into the current concerns of the incumbent government, otherwise they are likely to be simply ignored. The Coalition Government's emphasis in relation to the widening participation agenda is more about the social diversity of the undergraduate population of the Russell Group universities than, for example, the proportion of mature students at post-1992 institutions.

Matching its significant enlargement and increasing institutional diversity, the most notable change in English higher education since 1945 has been the introduction of student fees. Shattock convincingly shows how 'it was the CVCP, stiffened by its new CDP membership, which forced a way forward', and how in response to the decision of its Executive Committee 'that a "special levy" of £300 be charged to the 1997–98 student entry' (Shattock, 2012: 130–134) the government set up the Dearing Committee. We have already examined how, although the process was haphazard, the Dearing Committee's recommendations eventually led to the introduction of variable student fees to be repaid by income-contingent loans. Over time, a broad policy consensus embracing all the mission groups has emerged which accepts the principle that students should contribute to the payment of their fees, and the differences between them are more about how the principle should be put into effect.

The most hostile criticism of the current income-contingent student loans scheme has been made by Million+ in its publication, *Fair, Progressive and Good Value?* (Million+/London Economics, November 2010), and in one of its earlier publications, *Graduate Tax: Would it Work?* (September 2010), it presented for consideration a sympathetic overview of one of the main alternative repayment mechanisms to income-contingent loans. And the Russell Group, commenting on the Browne Review, applauded its decision not to recommend a cap on fees, but realized that the best that could probably be hoped for was its incremental removal (Russell Group, 12 October 2010). Generally speaking, however, there is broad unanimity across the groups: students should make a contribution to meeting the costs of their tuition, it should be set at a level that does not deter would-be applicants, it should incorporate both full- and part-time students, there should be no upfront payments, there needs to be a system that is both easily understood and administratively straightforward, and there should be grants to cover at least some of the fees and living costs of students from lower-income families, although there is dispute as to whether the resources funnelled into bursaries/fee remissions as a result of the agreements reached with OFFA should be administered nationally or by the individual universities. The main explanation of the considerable measure of consensus across the higher education sector over this issue was the realization that in the context of a mass system of higher education, sooner or later no government would commit itself to underwriting the costs of student fees and living costs. Moreover, this new context has been reinforced by the economic realities that have pre-vailed since 2008. In effect this is a policy arena that is tightly controlled by a politics driven by economic pressures, which means that, if the mission groups are serious about influencing the direction of policy, their room for manoeuvre is severely limited. Their input is confined to influencing how an income-contingent loans scheme should function rather than challenging the principle of the policy.

CONCLUSION: INTERPRETING PRESSURE GROUP POLITICS

Whereas for much of its twentieth-century history, the development of the British university system was shaped predominantly by the interaction of the University Grants Committee and the Committee of Vice-Chancellors and Principals, since at least 1988 policy direction has been in the hands of the government and increasingly steered by a combination of economic con-straints and the priorities of the governing party. Although the CVCP was a body that the UGC essentially consulted, there was also a value consensus that underlay their interaction. They understood the purpose of the univer-sity in similar ways and broadly agreed on the course of its evolution. Not only is higher education policy now under direct government control, it is also strongly shaped by the idea that the central purpose of the university is to serve economic and social goals as defined politically. This is the context within which the mission groups have emerged, and in policy terms the best they can hope for is to be consulted. Inevitably, therefore, at this level they can be little more than pressure groups; organizations that provide evidence and advice, or rather are invited to make submissions to the government and branches of the quasi-state apparatus as policy is formed. Obviously, to be an effective pressure group it helps to be well resourced, competently governed, and efficiently administered. However, in terms of actually having an impact on policy, as opposed to being consulted or invited to provide evidence, the most important asset for a mission group to possess is to be in tune with the general direction of current government policy.

Since 2010, the years of the Coalition Government, the direction of higher education policy has generally followed the line advocated by the Russell Group. Although research funding is selectively allocated and determined by the assessment of its quality, the distribution model has become increasingly discriminating and now differentiates more sharply along institutional lines with the Russell Group universities as the net winners. Furthermore, although a light-touch regulatory regime has yet to appear, it is only a matter of time before the QAA puts an appropriate model into operation. All institutions accept the widening participation agenda and have made serious attempts to put it into effect, but both the pace and mechanisms of change are driven from below, with the state providing little more than relatively meagre financial incentives, which is a strategy that coincides with the interests of the more elite pre-1992 universities. Finally, although the undergraduate fees that the universities can charge for home-based and EU students are capped, they have been raised to £9,000 per annum with no limit placed on the recruitment of highly qualified applicants. Therefore, although the Russell Group universities function within publicly imposed financial constraints on fee levels, these are considerably less demanding than those faced by many institutions in other parts of the system, with the gap widening in recent years as the government struggles to create a market in tuition fees.

The logic of our analysis is that in terms of shaping policy outcomes, the mission groups are no more effective than the CVCP used to be. Indeed they are less influential because the CVCP had a consultative role to play with a policy-making partner (the UGC) with whom it shared a broad consensus of values. Although we have concluded that the Russell Group universities appear to have exerted the greatest policy influence, it is impossible to substantiate this conclusively. Would the higher education policies of the Coalition Government have been substantially different if there had been no input from the mission groups? In fact the main lines of higher education policy (variable fees, widening access, quasi-state regulation of the universities, and the selective allocation of research funding) have been in place for some years. What the Russell Group has been able to do is not so much to determine the direction of policy but rather to influence how it is implemented. But what success it may have had is none too surprising given the imperatives that have underwritten government policy: the need to control public expenditure (thus increased emphasis on tuition fees), the search for 'value for money' in the distribution of public expenditure (thus the increasing selectivity in the allocation of research funding), the continuing insistence that the university system has an obligation to enhance social mobility while respecting institutional autonomy (thus the widening access agenda), and the desire to encourage new providers of higher education while lessening the regulatory constraints where deemed appropriate upon current providers (thus the push for a lighter-touch regulatory regime).

The significance of the other function of the mission groups—their role in shaping institutional identities—is easier to evaluate. Each group presents a positive interpretation of the values and purposes of its membership while at the same time outlining how it operates to sustain their interests. Changes in the names of the mission groups (with Million+ experiencing two name changes) suggest attempts to clarify both the identities of the membership and how the group will function to further their interests. Decisions either to leave or join a group are indicative of a university attempting to re-establish its identity and this is likely to be of greater significance for the institution than any aspiration it may have to exert a policy influence. Therefore, although the pressure group role may be central for the mission group as an organization, for its individual members merely belonging may be considered a worthwhile end in itself because it provides a desired identity that affirms its position in the market. Indeed it may even help to embellish the image that the institution is attempting to create for itself. For example, can all 24 of the members of the Russell Group really be world-class universities at the cutting edge of research, or is there only an inner sanctum which can be so described? A clear indication that group membership is about shaping institutional images is that the acquisition of the university label has been a major driver for leaving one mission group and joining another. Arguably, therefore, the emergence of the mission groups is less about the formation of pressure groups and more about the need for universities to form positive self-images as part of their branding.

While the two explanations for the emergence of the mission groups are both plausible, they also imply significant messages for interpreting the likely future role of the representative body, Universities UK. While UUK may portray itself as the voice of British higher education, it is composed of such widely divergent internal interests that it cannot establish clearly defined policy positions. It is now a pressure group only in the sense of advocating the cause of higher education *vis-à-vis* other public policy issues. Thus, it is very keen to express the strength of the financial claims of higher education as the Comprehensive Spending Review (CSR) process unwinds, and generally to act as a bold advocate of the overall positive qualities of the system. But for policy positions regarding particular issues, the universities will look to their mission groups to represent their interests. Furthermore, although in comparative terms there may be a relatively confined reputational range amongst British universities, the need for institutional badging has intensified in recent years, driven by a combination of heightened diversity within the system and a greater need to secure a marketable niche. Again the universities will use their membership of a mission group in conjunction with their own branding to establish favourable identities. This is not something that Universities UK can do for them. Many British universities may come to the realization that membership of UUK has little to offer them and take the decision to withdraw, although—as we have noted—in recent years this possibility has been raised on many occasions and yet it still continues to survive, but as a cheerleader rather than as a pressure group. The future, however, appears to be in the hands of the mission groups but whether they can make an input into the policy process beyond presenting evidence and offering advice is another matter.

Furthermore, as the demise of the 1994 Group illustrates, group membership may not convey a sufficiently strong sense of identity for the individual university as it changes over time. Group fragmentation is always a possibility, reinforcing the need for the university to make sure that its own house is in good order, which should include fostering working relationships on precise projects with other universities both within, as well as external to, the mission group to which it belongs.

10

Responding to the State-Regulated Market: Higher Education Institutions Under Duress

Abstract: Central to the governance of the English model of higher education is how the HEIs respond to the state-regulated market. This chapter examines the responses of six institutions to four central policies. The six institutions are: University College London; London Metropolitan University; the Universities of Manchester, Southampton, Warwick, and the West of England. The policies are: fee-setting, patterns of student recruitment, the pursuit of a research agenda, and the means for evaluating quality control and enhancement. There is an examination of the changes in the rules governing the operation of the regulated market in each policy area (designed to further government preferences) and how the six institutions have adjusted to those changes: the attempt to manipulate the fees set by higher education institutions, shifting the emphasis away from student recruitment to student retention, distributing more selectively the core funding of research, and the intention to incorporate a stronger 'student voice' in the quality assurance process. While responding to the state-regulated market is clearly demanding in terms of the commitment of time and financial resources, the chapter concludes that it is a process that all these institutions have, at least for the most part, successfully negotiated. Although there is pressure for 'lighter-touch' regulatory regimes (to a limited extent implemented in terms of the procedures to evaluate quality assurance and enhancement), the conclusion is that the regulatory state is here to stay.

THE IMPORTANCE OF INSTITUTIONAL DECISION-MAKING IN THE REGULATED MARKET

This chapter analyses some examples of how a number of universities have responded to the pressures of the state-regulated market, and in conjunction with Chapter 11 on the expansion of the privately financed sector, presents an analysis of the steady reshaping of English higher education. Our examination of how the English system of higher education is governed emphasized the increasing attempts to control politically its overall development. The quasi-state apparatus now performs an essentially regulatory function while successive governments control the direction of policy and attempt to steer the way the system evolves. However, to have policy control does not mean that governments can dictate unilaterally the course of development or determine the precise outcomes of policy initiatives. Government policy control prevails in a context in which the higher education landscape is reshaped by the regulatory framework of the quasi-state along with the decisions that individual institutions and actors make in response to those pressures.

This, therefore, is a model of system development that permits an institutional input into the various stages of the change process: indirectly with respect to policy formation and implementation strategies (mainly an input made within the context of a pluralist policy struggle incorporating the organized higher education interests), and directly by charting the specific institutional responses to the pressures of the regulated market, which are determined by the decision-making procedures embedded within each institution. In this chapter it is the response of institutions to the demands of the regulated market that is the focus of attention. How do institutions act when there is no more room for manoeuvre? For the analyst of institutional behaviour, the task is to understand the decision-making process: the pressures for change, their interpretation within particular institutional settings, and how their formal structures of governance orchestrate the required responses.

In view of the powerful legacy of institutional autonomy within the British system, it is critical for governments to be seen as keeping themselves at some distance (at times, arguably, too distant) from attempting to determine specific courses of action for individual universities. Although there may be a political view of the desired model of the higher education system, which incorporates a clear understanding of its component parts and the differing functions they should perform, governments never directly dictate to individual institutions. In theory the overall system model is a consequence of the accumulation of the decisions made by individual institutions. However, institutional autonomy is bounded by the fact that the resources shaping responses to the state-regulated market are not equally distributed. There are three main areas of differentiation:

1. Institutional prestige of which academic reputation is the main but not the only component
2. A viable funding base comprising both the levels and sources of funding
3. A supportive organizational network within both the academy and the wider society

Although undoubtedly the distribution of resources amongst universities has an impact upon the response patterns to the regulated market, there should be no reason not to expect anything other than competent institutional decision-making arrived at through positive structures of governance working in harmony with astute leadership. Indeed, what one would hope for are institutional strategies which aim to augment the resources (prestige, funding, and support) that permit strong control over the demands of the state-regulated market—to be in a position to exercise choice rather than simply respond to pressure.

The state-regulated market embraces at least four complex areas, each representing a policy field, which requires higher education institutions to make firm policy commitments:

1. The setting of undergraduate fees for home-based, EU, and overseas students
2. Decisions impacting directly upon the pattern of student recruitment
3. The pursuit of a research agenda
4. The promotion of a positive image of teaching and learning

In each of these areas, higher education institutions are formulating policy within a context that is shaped by the interaction of state regulation and market pressures. It is our intention in this chapter to examine the institutional policies of six selected universities. The instigation of the variable fees regime has allowed higher education institutions to charge fees of up to a permitted maximum level which is currently £9,000 per annum. What has to be evaluated is the impact of two pressures: the need for institutions intending to charge a fee of over £6,000 per annum to secure an 'access agreement' with the Office for Fair Access (OFFA), along with the government's manipulation of the distribution of the student access numbers to secure lower fees. That manipulation also has a potentially direct impact upon student recruitment thanks to the decision to permit the unfettered recruitment of students with grades of AAB (now ABB) at A-level (with further relinquishment of control in the pipeline). There is further political intervention into student recruitment thanks to the decision to protect the science base by continuing some public funding for the teaching of STEM subjects (science, technology, engineering, and mathematics), to which should be added the continuing public underwriting of fees for trainee medics and dentists. This close interaction of fee-setting and student recruitment necessitates a joint analysis of the two issues. Furthermore, it should not be forgotten that student recruitment has also been impacted upon by the widening participation agendas of successive governments, which is now mainly pursued through the necessity of securing OFFA access agreements in order to charge fees of above £6,000 per annum.

The determining of fee levels and student recruitment operates within a market that is clearly regulated by the state, and leads to the distribution of an amalgam of public and private resources (albeit the latter supported mainly by publicly financed income-contingent loans to students). The public funding of research, certainly with reference to resources made available by the research councils and the periodic research assessment exercises, is determined by organized competitive procedures that will decide the distribution of funding. In effect the state regulates a competitive process to determine the distribution of public funding with the outcomes dependent upon an evaluative peer review process. As we have noted, governments with respect to the public funding of research have been more inclined to shape both inputs into the process (thus the designation of priority research areas by the research councils), and also the distribution of resources in relation to research outputs (thus the recent decision to restrict funding to only units of assessment graded either 4* or 3* in RAE2008), rather than attempt to determine the evaluative process itself—although with the inclusion of the essentially politically inspired measurement of the impact of research, that will change somewhat with the Research Excellence Funding (REF) exercise that is currently under way. Obviously such intervention impacts upon institutional decision-making. Is it, for example, strategically sensible to engage in the research assessment process when funding is going to be so focused upon only a narrowly defined interpretation of excellence?

If the setting of fee levels and student recruitment take place within the framework of a state-regulated market, while the distribution of public research funding is determined by an organized competitive process controlled by the quasi-state apparatus but open to government intervention, then what are the forces that shape attempts to promote positive images of the teaching and learning process? It is to be expected that all higher education institutions would like to see themselves as representing a strong tradition of quality teaching, and hope that their own self-images are shared by the wider society. One practical ramification is obvious: the need to ensure the recruitment of a continuous supply of adequately qualified students, critical to the lifeblood of teaching and learning. In view of the significant rise in student fees, accompanied by the removal of most public funding to cover teaching costs, not to mention the rise of the private sector with its tailor-made programmes, universities are in a market situation when it comes to student recruitment and need to demonstrate that they provide value for money. But this is a market that has been stimulated by prolonged and significant government intervention.

For some 20 years the academic performance of higher education institutions has been monitored by quasi-state institutions operating an evolving pattern of mechanisms designed to measure quality. This has been reshaped by the current Coalition Government which is determined to put 'students at the heart of the system', and to reinforce the commitment that universities make to the provision of high-quality teaching. The aim is to make the student, especially the prospective student, an informed consumer who—by examining a battery of information that the universities are now required to provide on their websites, consulting the national student satisfaction surveys, and examining the demands of undergraduate teaching imposed by different courses and institutions—will shop around to ensure that the best purchase is made. On the one hand, therefore, there is straightforward regulation under the auspices of the Quality Assurance Agency, on the other hand, government attempts to foster a market situation in which the student is encouraged to act like an informed consumer. This is not so much a state-regulated market but rather an example of government supplementing the quasi-state regulatory apparatus with measures designed to stimulate a market input that will supposedly enhance the institutional commitment to achieving high quality academic provision.

THE SELECTED INSTITUTIONS

The empirical heart of the chapter will draw upon six case studies to evaluate the responses of higher education institutions to the challenges posed by the demands of the various forms of the state-regulated market: University College London (UCL), the Universities of Manchester, Southampton, Warwick, London Metropolitan University (LMU), and the University of the West of England (UWE). Clearly this is not a cross-section that represents all sectors of the current English system of higher education and certainly not one that could claim to be proportionately representative. However, it does embrace some of the critical elements within English higher education, including a representative (UCL) of the largest federation of British universities (the University of London), of the traditional civics (Manchester), of the newer civics (Southampton), of the 1960s so-called new universities (Warwick), and of institutions that acquired the university label post-1992 (LMU and UWE). Each of the universities are differentiated somewhat in terms of their academic prestige, funding, and supportive organizational networks, and we will tease out what significance, if any, these variables have in shaping policies for each of the four main issue areas that we have argued are encompassed by an interactive, if somewhat varying, combination of state and market pressures.

THE STATE-REGULATED MARKET IN ACTION

The Setting of Fees, Student Recruitment, and Retention

As we noted, the concrete movement towards the imposing of student fees upon home-based and EU undergraduates had been put into operation by the recommendations of the Dearing Inquiry, although since 1979 the universities had been obliged not to subsidize the fees of overseas students. Subsequently, the 2003 White Paper was followed by the 2004 Higher Education Act, which replaced the fixed £1,000 per annum fee that had been imposed by the first Blair Government, with a variable fee of £3,000 per annum. McGettigan (2013: 25) sees this as a top-up fee because it was meant to supplement the then existing public funding of teaching. But perhaps of greater significance is the fact that £3,000 was the maximum fee that a university could charge, and unsurprisingly all but a very few English higher education institutions (Leeds Metropolitan, Greenwich, Winchester, and Northampton for only local residents) immediately imposed that maximum. In other words, far from being a variable fee, in effect a ceiling was set beyond which the universities could not go. While the government may have hoped for much greater variation in the imposition of fees (to reinforce the repeated calls for a more diverse system of higher education), the comparatively low ceiling would inevitably restrict the range of institutional differentiation. In reality it was more of a political manoeuvre to augment the funding of undergraduate teaching without technically increasing public expenditure, the input of which had been steadily decimated over the some previous 20 years.

The raising of the maximum fee level to £9,000 per annum (put into effect for 2012 entrants) by the current Coalition Government, while building on the 2004 legislation, is a more significant innovation. Firstly, with limited exceptions (mainly the medical and laboratory-based sciences) the direct public funding of undergraduate teaching has been removed; secondly, with a significantly higher maximum fee level the government undoubtedly anticipated greater variation in the imposition of fees, and that there would *not* be a universal move to impose a £9,000 fee. The Department for Business, Innovation, and Skills is quoted as claiming that, 'We have consistently said that we believe graduate contributions of £9,000 should apply only in exceptional circumstances. Institutions would need to charge considerably less than this to offset reductions in HEFCE funding...' (McGettigan, 2013: 27–28).

But, perhaps unsurprisingly, the Department's expectations were not realized and the government resorted to the manipulation of its control over student numbers in an attempt to bring about the desired reduction in fees. In the words of Brown and Carasso:

> ...a 'margin' of 20,000 places was to be created, by a proportional reduction across institutions. Those charging fees of no more than £7,500 (after any fee waivers) would then be free to bid for an allocation from those 20,000 places.

And they continue:

> This was a clear response to the large number of institutions that had indicated their intention to charge the maximum fee or very close to it.

Moreover, it appears to have had some impact:

> ...once the details of this policy had been announced, 24 universities and one college took the opportunity that was offered to revise their Access Agreements, and lower their fees, to enable them to bid for places from the margin.
>
> (Brown and Carasso, 2013: 93)

However, for 2013–14 entrants 'there will be a reduced pool of 5,000 margin places' (which will be allocated rather than distributed by institutional bids) and, moreover, 'ninety-four higher education institutions out of 122 that want to charge undergraduates more than £6,000 will set their maximum annual tuition at the £9,000 ceiling...' (Morgan, 26 July 2012: 6–7). But it should be noted that to date the ceiling remains at £9,000 with no increase to allow for inflation, and certainly no movement towards the recommendation of the Browne Review that there should be no fee cap. Furthermore, it is possible that, if demand for places does not meet expectations, then some higher education institutions will start to revise their fee levels downwards or increase the funds they devote to student bursaries.

While the introduction of the core/margin model to distribute undergraduate numbers was a clear attempt by the government to influence the level at which institutions would set fees, the decision to allow the unrestricted recruitment of students with high A-level grades or their equivalent (AAB for entrants in 2012 and ABB for entrants in 2013) had a more complex policy rationalization. It was a genuflection by the government in the direction of easing the state's stranglehold over the steering of higher education. It imposed no additional burden upon expenditure, with the policy simply entailing the possible redistribution of students amongst the higher education institutions. The Coalition Government has also moved more towards embracing the idea that higher education should promote social mobility rather than simply widen participation. The implied assumption is that by removing restrictions upon the recruitment of the most qualified applicants this would encourage the expansion of student numbers at the most prestigious universities, and thus possibly help to further social mobility. It was a question of attempting to widen the individual's choice of university rather than making it possible simply to pursue a degree programme. And, furthermore, it could help to bring down fee levels should the less prestigious institutions make the decision to lower fees in order to increase their chances in competing for the most qualified applicants. The prospective student would then have a choice to make, and it is possible that the respective costs of the programmes would be the deciding factor.

At the centre of our analysis is the dissection of the OFFA access agreements because they represent the most concrete manifestation of the regulatory state in action. They sanction the fees that the university intends to charge and how it will fulfil its obligations with regard to broadening access and improving retention. In effect the access agreements combine two central government policy objectives—the private funding of the teaching and learning process with the requirement that higher education institutions still need to pursue a widening participation agenda. To gain OFFA's approval for your access agreement, it has to be sure that on both fronts your proposed course of action is acceptable. Moreover, the recently appointed Director of OFFA, Les Ebdon, has urged institutions to be more strategically minded by monitoring, evaluating and, if necessary, modifying their approaches to securing change (OFFA, 12 June 2013). The implication is that institutions need to be constantly evaluating the effectiveness of their strategies.

None of the six institutions whose access agreements we are highlighting wanted to change their access agreements in 2012–13 'to bring them within the criteria to bid for student number places from the "margin" ' (OFFA, 5 June 2013), although it has to be said that LMU had already set its fees at a level that made it eligible to be allocated students from the 'margin pool'. Of the 25 institutions that followed this route (including one further education college), the overwhelming majority were universities that had acquired the title post-1992. In other words, the institutions competing for students from the 'margin pool' were drawn from a particular segment of the overall system. The 2013–14 per annum fee data for our selected institutions is shown in Table 10.1.

The overall expenditure on activities designed to enhance access as a proportion of the fee income above the base fee (£6,000) was: 16% (LMU), 22% (UWE); 26% (Warwick), 28% (UCL), 30% (Southampton), and 32% (Manchester). Some of the financial support to lower fee levels is provided by the National Scholarship Programme (NSP) which was first operational in the academic year 2012–13, and designed to replace the funding previously

Table 10.1. Fee Data: 2013–14

	Estimated average fee	After fee waivers	After financial support
	£	£	£
All HEIs	8,615	8,363	7,985
London Metropolitan	6,883	6,714	6,714
UCL	9,000	9,000	8,252
Manchester	9,000	8,842	7,975
Southampton	9,000	8,110	7,920
Warwick	8,921	8,661	8,202
UWE	8,908	8,908	8,501

Source: OFFA, 12 June 2013a.

provided by the AimHigher programme. Once the funding of teaching and learning became primarily the responsibility of the student and his/her family, then it was almost logical to place accountability for the delivery of the widening participation agenda upon the higher education institutions and further education colleges. The National Scholarship Programme, like OFFA itself, can be seen as a political gesture to sweeten the movement away from public funding. HEFCE informs us that: 'The government's contribution to the programme will be £100 million in 2013–14 and £150 million from 2014–15' (HEFCE, 2012: 5). The institutions are required to provide at least matching funding with the government's input directed at providing scholarships for first-year students 'from disadvantaged backgrounds' of not less than £3,000 (HEFCE, 8 June 2013: 5).

With the exception of LMU (which sees itself as championing 'affordable quality education'—OFFA, 9 June 2013), these universities have set fee levels that are either close to the national average for English higher education institutions or somewhat higher. Again excluding LMU, these are fee levels that would rule them out of any allocation of student numbers from the 'margin pool'. Neither UCL nor UWE have opted for fee waivers while LMU, with its comparatively low average fee, has made the decision not to provide additional financial support beyond limited fee waivers.

If the first, and certainly the most upfront, purpose of an access agreement is to set fee levels that will be approved by OFFA, then the second is to put forward the institutional strategies that justify the level at which the fee is set. The access agreements need to demonstrate institutional commitments in two key areas: steps taken to broaden the social range of access with particular reference to students from disadvantaged socio-economic backgrounds, and the measures pursued to enhance retention and academic performance. The retention agenda has been extended somewhat by the incorporation of a growing emphasis upon the need to prepare students for the job market, and in particular the high-status professions. It is also important to demonstrate the centrality of these goals in the overall commitments that institutions make, which invariably means outlining the change of command with explicit references to the involvement of student representatives in the preparation of access agreements, and showing that responsibility for implementation resides ultimately in the hands of the university's most powerful decision-making body. Although there has always been an emphasis on monitoring and evaluation, it now appears (following the appointment of Ebdon as Director of OFFA) that this will feature more prominently in any future access agreements with the clear implication that universities will need to adjust their strategies in the light of what seems to work best for them.

With respect to access there is a very strong emphasis in all the agreements on the social variables that have figured prominently in the various benchmarks formulated by the Higher Education Statistics Agency (HESA): state school/college attendance, family's socio-economic status, residence in low-participation neighbourhoods, and receipt of the disabled student allowance. Moreover, HESA presents separate statistics for mature students, while the universities themselves frequently refer to the access patterns for students from ethnic groups.

Not unexpectedly all six of the universities, with the occasional confession of the need to do better, defend their access records. LMU in this respect has a particularly self-congratulatory access agreement, seeing itself as having a strong record in terms of fair access and widening participation, which it credits to the strength of its neighbourhood recruitment stimulated by the partnerships it has formed with local schools and colleges. For LMU the central issue is how to improve retention and student performance (OFFA, 9 June 2013). The other post-1992 university (UWE), while retaining a strong emphasis on enhancing the access of target groups, stresses that it is using its bursaries not so much as a marketing tool but rather as part of a strategy (the UWE Student Progression Framework) that integrates access, retention, and employment. Like LMU, UWE places strong emphasis upon outreach activities within the local community to widen access. Whereas for LMU that community extends to the greater London area, for UWE it is the west of England (OFFA, 9 June 2013a).

The four other universities in the group of six whose OFFA access agreements were appraised (UCL, Manchester, Southampton, and Warwick) are all members of the Russell Group, which is a clear measure of their undoubted prestige. Obviously, they have to take the presentation of their access agreements seriously but their different positions within the higher education system are reflected in the tone of their agreements. It should be noted that all four of them are committing a higher percentage than either LMU or UWE of their fee incomes to widening access and enhancing retention. They have the financial resources, incorporating higher fees, which makes this possible. They are also prepared to contextualize their agreements in a way that implies there is no one standard against which they should be evaluated. Thus UCL states that it aims 'to recruit and retain the academically brightest students who share our values and will thrive in the rigorous teaching and learning environment that UCL provides' (OFFA, 9 June 2013b). For Warwick, the comparative reference point is the ten most highly selective English universities in terms of undergraduate recruitment (it claims to be the ninth most selective). While Warwick accepts that it needs to broaden the social composition of undergraduate access, it asserts that compared to these other highly selective universities it recruits the highest proportion of state school students, is second best at admitting students from the lowest socio-economic groups, and third best in recruitment from neighbourhoods with low participation-rates in higher education (OFFA, 9 June 2013c). Both Manchester and Southampton make parallel selected comparisons with other Russell Group members and, unsurprisingly, these also place both universities in a favourable light (OFFA, 9 June 2013d and 2013e).

The two major strategies, therefore, to widen access have been the offering of financial support in the form of bursaries and fee waivers (or a combination of the two) mainly to students from low-income families (defined predominantly as an annual income of below £25,000 per annum), and outreach activities that are directed mainly at the schools and colleges within the local geographic region and focused primarily (although not exclusively) on 16-year-old+ school students. While the access agreements demonstrate considerably more than a genuflection to the need to widen the social basis of recruitment, it is important to stress that they also symbolize the fact that this is an institutional responsibility. The universities have to respond to the political pressure (also economic pressure given the need to secure agreements if fees are to be higher than £6,000 per annum) but they are left to determine their own strategies. If they made the decision to prioritize improvements in their widening participation performance indicators above all other considerations they could do so. However, there would then be questions about the implications of this for student retention rates and achievement levels, not to mention whether such a strategy would simply negate the role of academic authority in the selection process. Interestingly, Warwick's access agreement mentions that it is exploring the possible use of contextual data in the selection of applicants—a route that Southampton claims that it has already implemented. While this may be an effective way of widening participation, it implies a possible move towards positive discrimination, which will upset in particular those organized groups whose interests are likely to be negatively affected (mainly schools in the fee-paying sector). But this may be deemed to be a price that is worth paying.

In view of its comparatively poor record, as demonstrated by the evidence on student progression, LMU devotes more of its access agreement to the issue of retention. There is explicit recognition of its weaknesses and it aims to make improvements with respect to both retention and academic performance guided by established performance indicators and benchmarks. The expectation is that improvements will follow 'the root and branch' revision of its undergraduate degrees (it now offers a portfolio of some 160 courses, reduced from around 600) and the reorganization of its teaching provision around modules that last 30 weeks with an increase in average class contact time for full-time students from 288 to 360 hours (OFFA, 9 June 2013). While the other universities mention the importance of formulating a retention strategy, the emphasis is essentially on presenting evidence to demonstrate their prevailing commendable outcomes and to pledge increased expenditure. For example, UCL points to its excellent retention rate but is honest enough to admit that 'there is still a relatively low proportion of students from under-represented groups' (OFFA, 9 June 2013b), and, therefore, recognizes that increased expenditure on outreach activities will necessitate a parallel increase in efforts to maintain a high retention rate through on-course student support. However, the only mention of a precise programme is UWE's reference to its Peer Assisted Learning programme offered to selected first-year students. Clearly it is going to be insufficient for universities to expand the social base of their student access without steps to monitor both the retention rates and academic success of those students admitted from disadvantaged backgrounds. UWE points to the obvious way forward—focus in particular on first-year students, identify those who are likely to be most at risk, and offer enhanced support programmes. Once again the political issue is likely to be why the university should direct funding to favour explicitly certain social groups, but this is unlikely to generate as much hostility as the attempt to engage in positive discrimination at the point of access.

The State-Regulated Competition for Public Research Funding

The state regulation of the public funding of research is different from the regulatory framework that guides fee levels and shapes access policies, because there is no requirement upon universities to compete for research funding. Indeed as far as governments are concerned, it would undoubtedly be preferable if the competition were less fierce; if some higher education institutions saw themselves as engaged essentially in teaching and providing services for their local communities including the expansion of student access, and that they disavowed, at least in practice if not publicly, a research role. However, that would almost certainly mean pursuing a commitment to only undergraduate teaching and forsaking the recruitment of graduate students. Moreover, it would mean accepting the idea that to be labelled as a university does not require the fulfilment of a research role, and that is not a path that higher education institutions in general seem prepared to follow.

In Chapter 7 we examined, with particular reference to the outcomes of the research assessment exercises (RAEs), the overall research profile of the English system of higher education. How widespread was the distribution of quality research amongst the English universities? In this chapter we will analyse for our six selected universities their inputs into the 2008 Research Assessment Exercise. Although there will be a small amount of overlap with Chapter 7, the intention is to present an overview of the demands made by the research assessment process and how the selected institutions have responded to them rather than to analyse the evaluation of the quality of their research. The fact that the evaluative process was controlled by the funding councils acting in consultation with the academic community, and incorporated a significant element of peer review, almost certainly encouraged institutions to make detailed submissions. Moreover, the incentive to participate would have been reinforced by the fact that *the range* of research quality within each submitted unit of assessment was to be evaluated, so enhancing the possibility of universities being able to demonstrate that there was within their midst at least some pockets of research excellence that could be expected to attract public funding. But what demands does the evaluative process place upon the participating universities? What light does it shed upon the operation of this state-regulated competitive process?

While the access agreements obviously expect the universities to address a particular set of issues, the priority they give those issues (for example, the relative attention to access as opposed to retention) and the form in which they address them (their strategies designed to improve their performance) are determined by the individual higher education institutions. For RAE2008, with the important exception of institutional control of whose research would be submitted for evaluation 'the process was highly structured'. The submitting institutions were required to make available the following information:

RA0/RA1 staff information
RA2 research outputs
RA3a and b research students and studentships
RA4 research income (from 2000–01 to 2006–07)
RA5 research environment and esteem indicators

(RAE 2008, 18 June 2013)

Naturally it was the written commentaries elicited by RA5 (one for each unit of assessment) that encouraged the most diversified inputs, and because they provide insights into the intensity of the commitment to research, and indications of future plans are in some respects the most revealing.

Table 10.2 is constructed from the 'overall staff summary' (RAO/RA1) information provided by the institutions and the external research income data (RA4) that are part of the submissions accompanying each unit of assessment. The data reinforce the map of the overall system's research structure that was established in Chapter 7. Differentiation in the evaluation of research quality appears to be broadly reflected in the quantity of the inputs into the assessment process. Unsurprisingly, those universities with favourably rated research records are also the institutions which tend to have the more developed research profiles. Research success appears to beget further research expansion. It can be argued that the demands entailed by making a significant input are worth the effort because of the rewards, both financial returns and academic status, which accompany the outcomes of the process.

However, even the collation of the data (and Table 10.2 does not contain all the required statistics) is a very demanding task, and it is a burden that all participating institutions (some of which may receive little funding from the RAEs) must bear. Moreover, while there is for each institutional participant 'an

Table 10.2. Submissions to RAE 2008

	Units of assessment	Full-time category A staff	Research assistants	Technicians	External research income
	Nos.	Nos.	Nos.	Nos.	(£m)
London Metropolitan	21	258	30	1	20.1
UCL	47	1,793	1,564	386	1,212.4
Manchester	53	2,160	1,424	428	838.4
Southampton	33	1,070	698	120	403.2
Warwick	29	966	402	176	291.0
UWE	22	320	91	15	41.9

Source: RAE2008, 20 June 2013.

overall staff summary', the individual units of assessment present more refined staff information: their own data on external research incomes, and, most significantly, individual statements of their 'research environment and esteem' (RA5). Although the latter vary both in terms of how they are structured and how much information they offer (obviously the larger the submission the more information they tend to provide), they all cover more or less a common range of concerns. The main shared ingredients are: research structure, staffing policy, outputs of the different research groups, the input of research students, research income, research strategy, and esteem indicators (for example, the various honours achieved mainly by the academic faculty and the editing of prestigious journals or a book series). Moreover, there is also some presentation of planned future developments, which invariably convey the intention of deeper engagement in an allegedly expanding research field. Indeed, many of the individual units of assessment describe their 'research environment and esteem' almost in as much detail, and certainly with as much thought, as their universities have put into their access agreements!

This is evidently a costly process, not only for the funding councils which jointly organize the evaluation of the research, but also for the universities and colleges making the submissions. For protracted periods of time it will draw many faculty members into an administrative role and make considerable demands upon support staff, probably located in a designated research office. The costs are incurred because the process by which research excellence is measured is complex and the intention is to reward departments with recognized achievements, which intensifies the desire to participate. The alternatives would have been to have a simpler process of evaluation (to operate with a different measuring rod), or—as has occurred—by manipulating the outcomes of the present process rather than simplifying the process itself. Furthermore, by adding the need to evaluate the impact of research, the 2014 REF will complicate the process.

The process is complex mainly because it revolves around peer review, and attempts to move towards a model based more on metrics is viewed with deep suspicion by many within the academic community. An alternative measuring rod would be to distribute resources on the basis of the grants awarded by the research councils (or even on the securing of external research funding from whatever source), but this would enhance the research incomes of a smaller number of universities rather than support the research of departments more widely distributed. Up to now, change has centred on the manipulation of the established RAE model through the modification of its resource distribution, which has benefitted most the more highly-rated units of assessments and a particular stratum of universities. While this is not an intrusion into the evaluative process itself, it has a direct impact on its intended purpose—the distribution of core research funding.

As we have shown, the Dearing Committee put forward the idea that there should be a partnership between higher education and the government underwritten by a compact. If there is a compact that guides the core funding of research then it is interpreted in different ways by the involved parties. Within the world of higher education there is a clear divide between those who believe that high-quality research should be supported wherever it is to be found, and others who feel that to ensure the future vitality of the overall research base funding needs to be concentrated upon those institutions where the evidence suggests that they have a broad and deep-seated research tradition. Is the purpose of the research assessment exercises to enhance pockets of excellence in institutions which are developing a research tradition, or to sustain high-quality research outputs in those universities where such a tradition is already implanted? It may be argued that either the restriction or enhancement of research funding to particular departments (units of assessments) is consistent with the idea that funding should be distributed selectively on the basis of evaluated quality, if measured quality is still the determinant of resource distribution and the departments their recipients. However, to deny all funding to research that is evaluated 2* (quality that is recognized internationally in terms of originality, significance, and rigour) or 1* (quality that is recognized nationally in terms of originality, significance, and rigour) in RAE2008 would be seen by many as far too harsh a judgement, especially as this decision favours a select range of universities.

While it may be expedient for the various parties to live with the current model for the distribution of core research funding (they can interpret the model on the basis of their own interests and simply complain when its outcomes do not favour them), it is important not to forget the costs in time, effort, and money involved in sustaining this state of affairs. If the academic community cannot reach a consensus on what are the purposes of the public funding of research, then these should be imposed politically and a model constructed that delivers them effectively. If the intention is to enhance the research profiles of higher education institutions that lack a deep-seated research tradition and in the process support quality research wherever it is found, then at least something like the current model, with all its demands, should prevail, and it should not be undermined by political decisions that distort its intended purpose. However, if it is believed that the overall vitality of the research base can be secured only by concentrating funding upon the established research-intensive universities, then the means should be devised to achieve this directly and effectively without resorting to the manipulation of the current model.

Evaluating Teaching and Learning: The Quasi-State and the Student as Consumer

Undoubtedly one of the most hotly contested disputes in the governance of the English university system has been the shifting of responsibility (with the key initial steps being made in the 1990s) for the maintenance of the quality of the academic experience from the institutions themselves to the quasi-state apparatus (Brown, 2001, 2004; Tapper, 2007: 167–186). In the words of Kogan and Hanney: 'The UK thus moved from a position in which the state had virtually no direct interest in assuring quality in universities and in which it delegated quality judgements in the public sector to an increasingly hands-off CNAA [Council for National Academic Awards] to one in which quality requirements were imposed by law' (Kogan and Hanney, 2000: 108). In 1997, after a comparatively short period of oscillation as to where the institutional focus of responsibility for quality matters should reside, the Quality Assurance Agency (QAA) emerged as the designated body. And, although the Agency's *modus operandi* has evolved over time, the QAA (with the necessary genuflections to devolution) still assumes this responsibility (see Brown and Carasso, 2013: 105–107, for the most important changes in its methodology over time).

The authority of the QAA derives from the fact that higher education institutions in receipt of public funding need to submit to the Agency's periodic quality audits. Moreover, the Agency will be called upon to offer its advice when privately funded institutions want to offer degree programmes or acquire the university title. It is clear that without the Agency's approval, such requests will swiftly run out of mileage. The most important expression of the QAA's authority is its reports on how individual institutions are meeting their obligations to assure the quality and enhancement of their academic programmes. These reports, now guided by a 'Quality Code for Higher Education', are drawn up after an institutional visit (lasting four days) which involves reviewing a large body of documentation and holding meetings with academic faculty, administrative staff, and students.

The 'Quality Code for Higher Education', which has been in operation since the academic year 2012–13, replaced the prior agreement on 'Academic Infrastructure' that had been arrived at by prior negotiation between the QAA and the major higher education interests. In effect the 'Quality Code' is an extension of the 'Academic Infrastructure' agreement. The latter explored two main fronts: whether 'confidence can reasonably be placed in the soundness of the institution's present and likely future management of its awards', and whether the same confidence could be placed in '... the quality of the learning opportunities available to students'. The 'Quality Code' is also concerned that adequate information 'meeting UK expectations' is 'provided about the available student learning experiences, and that the enhancement of those experiences also meets UK expectations' (QAA, 26 June 2013). The need to make sure that students and prospective students are provided with full information reflects the recent political push to augment the role of students as consumers, while the focus on enhancement (as opposed to assurance), picks up on an increasingly prevalent theme in the literature of the quality agenda.

Our analysis is restricted to the latest reports covering programmes offered at only the sample universities' home-bases (excluding, therefore, overseas provision), which is then followed by an additional note on the University of Southampton. The reports are as follows:

LMU: visited 22 to 26 November 2010, report published 1 April 2011
UCL: visited 9 to 13 March 2009, report published 31 July 2009
Manchester: visited 4 to 8 April 2011, report published 26 August 2011
Southampton: visited 11 to 15 February 2008, report published 18 June 2008
Warwick: visited 25 February to 1 March 2013, report published 24 May 2013
UWE: visited 23 to 27 March 2009, report published 14 August 2009

Excepting the very recent report for the University of Warwick, which was guided by the 'Quality Code for Higher Education', all the five other reports drew heavily upon the 'Academic Infrastructure' agreement, which was in operation when these universities were last audited.

The QAA's reports came to the conclusion that in all the five universities audited prior to 2012–13, 'confidence can reasonably be placed in the soundness of the institution's present and likely future management of...' both '...the academic standards of its awards' and '...of the quality of learning opportunities available to students' (QAA, 26 June 2013a). The more recent report for the University of Warwick made a similar judgment in terms of both these considerations but, following the new requirements, also confirmed that the university met 'UK expectations' with respect to both the information it provided students about the available learning opportunities and its commitment to the enhancing of those opportunities (QAA, 26 June 2013b). In each case, the reports made reference to features of good practice and recommendations for action (in some cases dividing these between the 'advisable' and the 'desirable').

The QAA was sensitive to the wider contexts that could have impinged upon the likelihood of the university experiencing a successful audit. For example, the reports for LMU and UWE briefly alluded to the former's financial difficulties (the fine imposed by HEFCE because of prior breaches of the regulations on student recruitment) and its conflicts with the Border Agency, and to UWE's leadership instability caused by a rapid turnover of vice-chancellors (QAA, 26 June 2013c and 2013d). While in both cases these may have had a negative impact upon the two universities (see Shattock, 30 May 2013: 39–40 for his analysis of the weaknesses of LMU's structure of governance in the early 2000s), the QAA at the time of these audits felt that both universities had responded positively to their problems and thus it could conclude they were offering quality degree programmes.

There is an element of ritual about the audit process with higher education institutions carefully following established, even if evolving, guidelines and then thanking the QAA for its report and the conduct of the audit visit, expressing pleasure at the commendations of noted good practices, and claiming to be already acting on its recommendations. However, the process does not always work that smoothly. The University of Southampton was visited by the QAA for an audit in the autumn of 2012 and the review was expected to be published in January 2013. However:

> The sector's standards watchdog [the QAA] has confirmed it has set aside an institutional review conducted last year into the University of Southampton on the advice of its appeals panel and will undertake a new review with alternative reviewers.
>
> (Grove, 16 May 2013: 6)

It is more than likely, however, that the new audit will find that the university has put into place procedures to rectify the shortcomings identified in the first review, and one can expect its report to be approved by all the interested parties. However, it does illustrate the point that the audit process is not automatically plain sailing for even prestigious universities. But this is an exceptional occurrence and Southampton in the words of the *Times Higher Education* '...has become the first university to successfully appeal against critical findings in a full review by the Quality Assurance Agency' (Grove, 16 May 2013: 6), although it has to be said that the appeal was directed not so much at the critical findings but rather whether the review team had followed the QAA's defined procedures.

Notwithstanding Southampton's recent contretemps with the QAA (and it should be remembered that its 2008 audit fell into the established pattern that we have outlined), the evaluation of academic quality was placed in the relatively safe hands of the QAA. While there may have been continuous hostility in certain university quarters to the intrusion of the QAA (time-consuming, intrusive, costly, and inducing game-playing) it was not immune to pressures for change (with probably the most significant shift being the move from departmental review to institutional audit—see Tapper, 2007: 180–184), and it established a regulatory framework that the universities could handle relatively smoothly. If LMU, given all the preceding internal turmoil, could come out of its 2010 audit relatively unscathed, then it seemed that the higher education institutions were capable of responding effectively to the presence of the QAA. Its activities may be resented as a perceived unnecessary intrusion into academic autonomy, but in practice it has been little more than a paper tiger. It was but another extension of bureaucratic intervention, and over quite some period of time, and with respect to a variety of issues, higher education institutions had become accustomed to dealing with such bodies.

The QAA audits, therefore, represented bureaucratic meddling and the only possible intrusion of a market dimension was the impact that the reports may have had on student demand. However, it is difficult to know how widely the reports are read by prospective students and what weight they carry *vis-à-vis* other inputs (for example: websites, the advice of friends and family, institutional reputation) into the decision-making process. With the arrival of the Coalition Government, there has been a move by the QAA to place a greater emphasis on enhancing, as opposed to checking whether there are mechanisms in place simply to assure, academic quality. In a complementary development, students are to be reconfigured as rational consumers who will make informed selections of a quality higher education programme that suits their current interests and aids their career aspirations. Moreover, the QAA itself, reflecting this shift, is placing more emphasis upon the extent to which students participate in ensuring the robustness of the procedures designed to sustain the institutional commitment to quality assurance and enhancement. The new strategy, entitled 'Higher Education Review' replaces 'institutional audit' with 'institutional review', although how much of a difference this will make in practice remains to be seen. There is also a move to two review cycles: a six-year cycle for those institutions with a record of providing successful quality and maintaining standards, and a four-year cycle for those with a shorter track record (for a concise overview of the new emphases, see McClaran's *Developing the New Higher Education Review*, 2 May 2013).

For students or prospective students to be rational and influential consumers they need to be provided with information, to be in a position to make public evaluations of the student experience, and to feel that they have an input into formulating the strategies designed to ensure the maintenance of academic quality. On these three fronts there has been government action. All higher education institutions are required to provide on their websites a link to the Unistats website where it is possible to find comparative information (some of which is drawn from the National Student Survey that has been in place since 2005) on patterns of study, costs and financial support, employment and salary data after the completion of higher education, and evaluations of the effectiveness of the local student union. These official moves have been complemented by other student surveys, of which the most notable is *The Academic Experience of Students in English Universities*, conducted since 2006 by the Higher Education Policy Institute (HEPI) that for its 2013 report joined forces with *Which?*, that provides would-be consumers with evaluations of the quality of goods and services that are sold in the United Kingdom. The focus of the 2013 HEPI/*Which?* report is partly upon the variations—controlling for degree course and institution—in formal teaching demands and how much time students actually devote to their studies. Furthermore, rather than attempting to evaluate academic quality it paints a picture of differences in levels of student satisfaction with their academic experiences (HEPI/*Which?* 15 May 2013).

Roger Brown has gone so far as to argue that the consequence of such inputs signifies a relative decline in the importance of the QAA's reviews:

> ...consider how much institutional effort already goes into preparing for, supervising, publicising and following-up the results of the annual National Student Survey. In effect, the NSS—and the Key Information Set (KIS)—has displaced QAA review as the chief quality assurance mechanism across the sector.
>
> (Brown, 2 May 2013)

But, as Brown rightly insists, neither the student surveys nor the provision of the Key Information Set are measures of quality, but rather they are the means of providing prospective students with more information when it comes to making decisions about their selection of a degree programme and at what university to study it. Moreover, there is the pressure upon the higher education institutions to account for the differences they may reveal.

In the sense that the NSS questionnaires contain student evaluations of their experiences of the teaching and learning processes, inevitably judgements about the quality of provision are being made. However, although the nature of these judgements may influence how institutions decide to respond to them, they cannot be seen as a reliable guide to measuring the quality of academic programmes. They are a means of providing prospective students with more information when they are planning their routes into higher education, but enhancing student choice may be seen as a more effective means of changing the experience of higher education than quality audits. Are universities more likely to provide a high-quality teaching and learning experience if there is pressure to ensure a viable student base rather than demonstrate to the quasi-state that their mechanisms to ensure quality assurance and enhancement are sound? Of course the two pressures are not mutually exclusive for, as we have noted, institutions are expected to give their students a stronger direct role both in assuring quality and making an input into the QAA's audit trail.

It is not inconceivable that QAA reports could become one of the channels through which a more informed student body is established if only, for example, by incorporating their main conclusions into the Key Information Set.

The six universities that we have selected for special attention in this chapter, along with the wider system, have no choice but to respond to the pressures resulting from the student surveys. In the context of variable fees, changes in central control over the distribution of student numbers, and overall demand for higher education that has been hit by the economic recession, it is critical to be seen as a university that offers a quality product. Moreover, it would be nonsense in the current circumstances to suggest universities should not be required to provide at least a standardized range of information about their academic programmes, and that students should not be allowed to pass judgement on the academic experiences that they encountered as undergraduates. Inevitably the universities have to respond to the pressures generated by these recent innovations because they may well have an impact upon future student demand. The implied government assumption is that this will force universities to offer quality degree programmes that are delivered effectively. But while student demand is not a direct measure of academic quality in higher education, is it not a more important pressure for the universities to respond to than the quality audits conducted by the quasi-state apparatus?

It may well be that in a market context the higher education system will come to be more relaxed about quality, and accept that the key concerns for many institutions are fee levels and student demand, and these may indeed become the indicators that signify the presence of quality. But, just as it took many universities an inordinate amount of time to accept the role of the quasi-state in regulating the quality of their academic programmes, so it is likely to take them as much time in accepting that they are operating in the context of a regulated market underwritten by variable fees and driven by student demand. But we have no reason to suppose that they are incapable of making the transition, which if Brown is correct about the institutional time and energy that goes into following up the publication of the National Student Surveys, is apparently already under way.

CONCLUSION: A NEW HIGHER EDUCATION LANDSCAPE?

What this chapter has illustrated is the sheer extent of the state's control over the higher education sector in England. The issue areas we have been examining—fee levels, student access, research funding, and quality assurance—are central to the functioning of the contemporary university and in all of them the state exercises the authority to steer institutional decision-making and to shape the overall pattern of how the system evolves. While the institutions whose responses to the regulatory state we chose to examine varied considerably in terms of their prestige, funding, and wider societal connections, and although they have at times resisted the state's tentacles, they are, nonetheless, firmly entrapped by its embrace.

Although the public funding of teaching and learning in higher education has shrunk sharply, and there is more flexibility in the steering of student recruitment, there is still close state control of the fees that can be charged and, for the time being, of the overall numbers of home-based and EU students who can secure access. Furthermore, higher education institutions have to sign access agreements if they want to charge annual fees in excess of £6,000 per annum, which require them to disclose their plans for widening the social base of their student bodies and ensuring student retention. While the parameters that govern access and funding represent the most complex example of the operation of the regulated market in higher education, the distribution of public funding to underwrite higher education research is more straightforward. Under the auspices of the government, institutions compete for resources within the regulatory framework constructed by the quasi-state. This is a straightforward competitive model to determine research quality with the consequent financial rewards determined politically.

The most interesting example of the regulated market in operation is the attempts to require higher education institutions to sustain and enhance academic quality. The system has moved from augmenting local responsibility resting in academic hands to supplementing this with teaching quality assessment (then to be followed by institutional audit), which has for the most part been under the control of the QAA. And now we have the apparent intrusion of market forces in the guise of students as informed and influential consumers, which we have seen as the addition of yet another layer in the evaluative process rather than one creating an entirely new model. Should it be a new model then it is more about augmenting student choice rather than measuring quality, and it has been more of a creature emerging from government decision-making rather than the market. The HEPI (and now HEPI/*Which?*) reports are but one example of the extension of this development beyond official circles, and while they may make many ponder about the institutional differences in the formal demands of the same degree programmes, along with the significant variations in the amount of time students are supposed to devote to their studies, they explicitly do not claim to be a guide for assessing, let alone measuring, academic quality (Bekhradnia, 17 May 2012: paragraph 9).

This chapter has illustrated the sheer weight of the regulatory framework that embraces the English system of higher education. The interaction between the state and higher education institutions is embedded in complex bureaucratic structures that function almost ritualistically. It can be argued that this is the price that publicly funded institutions, which have assumed the commitment to fulfilling a range of politically defined societal goals, have to pay if they are to survive. Ironically, however, even when public funding declines (as, for example, with respect to support for teaching and learning), the demands of the regulatory state grow more demanding rather than evaporate. For the universities it is more than a question of replacing public with private funding, for it is also necessary to regain control of the purposes of the university and to cut themselves free from the weight of the demands that have been placed upon them, which in truth they have frequently embraced.

If, however, this is a too optimistic (even naïve) scenario, then perhaps it is possible to think of ways in which the relationship between the state and the market can move away from straightforward state regulation as seen in the operations of OFFA, the QAA, and the Funding Councils with respect to the conduct of the RAE. They then move onto territory within which there is a mixture of unfettered institutional control (for example, universities make their own decisions about student fee levels and student recruitment) and more explicit state direction (for example, identify the research-intensive universities, fund them as such for a number of years, and then carry out a review), permitting the intrusion of the regulatory state only when the market suggests there are good reasons to suspect institutional malfunctioning (for example, a sharp decline in student recruitment or unacceptable dropout rates or poor undergraduate academic performance).

In Chapter 12, we will devote some space to developing alternative future scenarios for English higher education. In this chapter we have examined the impact of the regulatory state upon the system mainly through the prism of six quite different universities. Undoubtedly, market forces are beginning to impact upon institutional decision-making, although it is a market heavily underwritten by state regulation. Of course, the more general provision of goods and services is also underwritten by state-regulated markets, but the regulatory patterns that have been examined in this chapter would suggest that higher education is still perceived as a public good, the delivery of which needs to be firmly steered by public regulation. The price that the institutions pay for this (in resource expenditure, constraints upon action, and sheer institutional anxiety) are high, but it appears to be a straitjacket to which the system has adjusted reasonably comfortably. And, for many, better the devil you know....

11

The Descent from Acropolis to Agora: The Entry of the For-Profits

Abstract: We have seen in recent years the entry of a small number of for-profit providers into the English system of higher education. This has been stimulated by the Coalition Government in its attempt to diversify the provision of higher education. Government support has taken four concrete forms: new providers may be granted degree-awarding powers (DAPs) they can acquire the university title, they need to have no more than 1,000 full-time equivalent students to be eligible to claim that title, and their students can access the Student Loans Company for financial support to pay their fees. In return, the new providers enter the regulatory framework, which brings them closer to the publicly funded sector. Meanwhile, the publicly funded institutions increase their levels of private funding while some of them join with the for-profits to set up privately-funded 'offshoots'. The chapter, after covering these developments, goes on to examine the much larger for-profit sector in the US, raising the question of whether developments in England will follow a parallel course.

In earlier chapters we discussed whether neoliberal globalization and marketization within HE, and now the policy experiment in applying high undergraduate fees in England, should mean the entry of more for-profit providers of HE that could, in market theory terms, drive down the price of degrees while offering innovative responses to student-customer demand. One key way the affordability issue might be tackled by the for-profits is their unbundling of the delivery of teaching and learning from the cross-subsidization of research that goes on in some HEIs, as well as by focusing upon the low-cost vocational courses rather than offering the more costly laboratory and workshop courses. MOOCs as disruptive technology might lead to disruptive innovation, as considered in Chapter 8, across all types of HEI so as to help tackle HE's cost disease problem, but market competition from new for-profit entrants could also address the cost-price issue as they break up the semi-monopoly and cosy cartel behaviour of the quasi-public HEIs. As with MOOCs, opinions vary on the for-profits, and are often polarized: some vehemently dismissing both new technology and new entrants, whether from a reasoned analysis or from a simple Luddite stance; others wildly enthusiastic, welcoming both as symbolic of market forces driving much-needed change and progress, again whether from a reasoned despair over the current state of HE or from a simplistic and idealogical neoliberal viewpoint.

We have also explored the history of markets within HE, noting as have wise observers such as Bok (2003) commenting that the university is suspended between the acropolis and the agora, often with an academic foot in each. Indeed, as Kerr also has commented: 'The cherished academic view that higher education started out on the acropolis and was desecrated by descent into the agora led by ungodly commercial interests and scheming public officials and venal academic leaders is just not true. If anything, higher education started in the agora, the market, at the bottom of the hill and ascended to the acropolis at the top of the hill... Mostly it has lived in tension, at one and the same time at the bottom of the hill, at the top of the hill, and on the many pathways in between.' (as quoted in Zemsky, 2009: 45; and in Zemsky at al., 2005: 52).

The point about markets—when working efficiently—is that, usually, there are informed customers for whose cash businesses compete, making improved cars and TVs, or providing better holidays and flights, or whatever, along the way; and doing so at the same or even less cost. However, HE as a pure public service lacks such competitive innovation, just as once did the dying 1970–1980s British car industry in the days of state-subsidized British Leyland. As Zemsky et al. note, when discussing the growth of the for-profits within US HE over the past two decades: 'The University of Phoenix's success, both online and on its campuses, teaches us one lesson about how and why traditional higher education institutions so often misread the market. Phoenix knows exactly whom it serves and why—it has customers!' (Zemsky et al., 2005: 117). And as the for-profits compete, they offer flexibility of delivery and, to an extent, lower-priced options; and, yes, thus HE slips or even skids from being cosily located exclusively atop the acropolis or (to mix metaphors) inside the public sphere (Pusser et al., 2012) and down the hill towards the agora, having been so comfortably ensconced (albeit only for a few post-war halcyon decades) securely within the ivory tower: 'Citizens with rights to higher education become consumers of alternative educational delivery systems capable of purchasing choice.' (Rizvi in Priest and St John, 2006: 78).

But, of course, generally, government, through initially the deregulation and liberalization of economic activities and then the regulation of the market-place via competition and consumer protection laws, has to evict incumbents from the public sphere and remove entry barriers to new entrants bringing innovation and competition, and this we now see happening in English HE as the criteria for being granted degree-awarding powers (DAP) and for use of the title 'university' are duly relaxed as part of the policy experiment begun with the 2011 White Paper (see the legal framework at Farrington and Palfreyman, 2012: chs 3 and 4, and as discussed later in this chapter): and, naturally, the 'public' HEIs and their unions mutter about supposed weakened criteria and an alleged lack of control, while the 'private' sector asserts there are still barriers to be swept away.

The English truly commercial (fledgling) sector in HE is small (some half-dozen providers and less than 50,000 students on low-cost and relatively low-priced, no-frills vocational courses such as law, accountancy, economics, computing, healthcare, marketing, and business—HEPI, 2011), but it is growing and widening. The for-profit—and certainly not low-priced given its offering of many frills—London-based New College of the Humanities kicked off its £18,000 per annum [*sic*] liberal arts degree course with a 2012 entry. The notable major players, however, are the University of Law (as once the charitable chartered corporation College of Law, then selling its name and DAP badge to Montague Private Equity for *c*.£200m which instantly sought a title upgrade and duly commenced global expansion) and the BPP University (BPP College having been bought for some $600m by the US Apollo Group as the owner of Phoenix University and having in 2013 been awarded the title of BPP University). Temple (ch. 9 in Callender and Scott, 2013) explores UK private HE, and asks whether it is now 'a distinction without a difference?' to compare public and private providers: he foresees 'a more complex pattern of higher education developing, with intersecting fields of public and private provision and a wider range of overlapping institutional types... [so that increasingly] it must be open to question to what extent we can still speak of a single higher education "system" "sector"...' (2013: 171; see also Middlehurst, 2013).

Yet, as the 'public' HEIs begin to compete more for UK/EU undergraduates, just as they have over many years so comfortably and profitably operated a market for self-financing, postgraduate taught courses and also one for high-fees international students, the distinction between public and private, between not-for-profit and for-profit, between public good and commercial, increasingly blurs—and will do even more so as the traditional HEIs expand into overseas campuses and global joint ventures. Note the global expansion of the almost 200 international branch campuses as transnational HE delivery in the Middle East, India, China, and elsewhere—and already with some spectacular and costly failures! (McBurnie and Ziguras, 2007; Sakamoto and Chapman, 2011). And, following the example of the College of Law, it seems easy for (a perhaps insolvent) traditional HEI potentially to end up as a for-profit (with or without a name change, depending—as would be the price—on the remaining brand-value of the name and its DAP medallion), and hence some fear private equity companies as vultures circling weak, under-recruiting, low-status HEIs as sickly wildebeest exposed upon the veld. Just as likely, however, are collaborative ventures between entrepreneurial public HEIs and capital-rich commercial investors (for instance, already Laureate, Kaplan, and Pearson with Royal Holloway, Liverpool, and others)—and all as now encouraged, especially in terms of funding overseas expansion for UK HE plc, by the government (see the July 2013 BIS document, 'International Education—Global Growth and Prosperity'). There is talk of a £17.5bn HE export industry and the UK having 13% of the international student market, second only to the USA at 16.6%. (And on the need for a contractually rigorous Memorandum of Understanding when setting up and managing such ventures see Farrington and Palfreyman, 2012: ch. 17.)

The Coalition Government would argue that, short of enacting new legislation (as may well happen if the Conservatives win outright the 2015 election), the present regulatory mechanisms within HE are being used both to apply appropriate scrutiny of applications from new for-profit providers of HE for DAP and for use of the title 'University', and also to ensure that there are not unreasonable entry barriers unjustifiably protecting public incumbents: and an OFT 'market study' as discussed later may well test this latter proposition. The legal regime is described in HEFCE's July 2013 document titled 'Operating framework for higher education in England' from its Regulatory Partnership Group. Section 3 of which explains: 'how new providers can enter the higher education system in England, and on what basis'—'consistent with the government's aim of achieving greater diversity of provision, and the principle that all providers requesting access to HEFCE funding or with students who have access to student support funding have to meet certain regulatory requirements'; an approach which 'aims to balance the needs of a more open market for higher education with the absolute requirement for effective safeguards to protect the student and public interest'. Such new entrants, like existing ones, 'must meet required threshold standards, and they must be sustainable, well-governed organizations'. HEFCE will liaise 'in the collective interests of students' with the Student Loans Company, the Quality Assurance Agency, the Higher Education Statistics Agency, the Office of the Independent Adjudicator, and the Office for Fair Access in operating the framework and by 2014 provide 'a detailed register of designated higher education providers and a database of publicly available information about them'. This will include 'alternative providers' with DAP, such as the University of Law and BPP University (as opposed to traditional HEIs grant-funded by HEFCE) as entities which 'the government is keen to encourage' so as to inject 'further dynamism and student choice' into English HE.

Thus, there is in effect a vetting process ('to protect all parties, including students and taxpayers') that awards new entrants 'a status akin to having a licence to practise'. In short, HEFCE consults the QAA (which inspects the applicant) and then advises the BIS whether in turn to recommend the Privy Council to grant DAP for a six-year period. And similarly for the granting of the use of the 'sensitive' words 'university' or 'university college' via the Privy Council (as in the case of the chartered ifs School of

Finance recently granted university college status) or via the provisions of the 2006 Companies Act (as used in the case of both the University of Law and the BPP University as registered companies). The BIS seems now to be reorganized so as not to grant such extra status to an alternative provider whose six-year DAP term is just about to end. The 'alternative provider' is then signed up to 'a terms and conditions document issued by BIS' and to the QAA inspection regime (and might voluntarily join the OIA membership). The overall aim is 'to move to a position where HEIs, FECs, and alternative providers would be subject to a standard set of accountability requirements'—'but we are constrained by the existing legislation at the present time' (so, query: Will there be a 2016 Higher Education Act if the Conservatives win an outright victory in 2015?).

The 2014 HEFCE database will list the designated HEIs with their DAPs and authorized titles, whether they are in receipt of teaching and research grants from HEFCE, whether their courses are eligible for student support from the Student Loans Company (SLC), and only 'in exceptional circumstances' when clearly in 'the public and student interest' (since otherwise 'HEFCE's risk assessments are normally treated as commercially confidential') whether the organization has a red 'risk flag'. Then 'potential sanctions include the issue of an improvement notice, a freeze or cut in student numbers, or, exceptionally, the withdrawal of designation by BIS'. In effect, the BIS would be telling the SLC no longer to supply loans for any student at HEI X or for those students on specific course Y at alternative provider Z. The red-flagging of a provider would undoubtedly be a last resort, given the high chance that any entity so affected will contest the decision and perhaps seek judicial review of HEFCE's decision-making process. And, finally and crucially in terms of the step so far towards the deregulation of the HE industry, the threshold number of students for DAP and University status has been reduced from 4,000 to 1,000 full-time equivalents, so as more readily to let in new for-profit entrants as well as established small mono-subject colleges. This HEFCE 'operating framework' has been critiqued in HEPI Report No. 63 on 'The Future Regulation of Higher Education in England' (November, 2013, at www.hepi.ac.uk) as being overly complex, insufficiently comprehensive, and merely tinkering with current limited powers, confusing funding and regulation: thus, a 'more effective and more economical' regulatory model is offered, involving the creation of an OFHE (just as we have earlier postulated an 'OFTE') with a duty to protect 'the taxpayer, students, and other stakeholders' in terms of 'their investment in English HE' and in the context of 'the present moves towards a more market-oriented system' requiring 'an enhanced level of state oversight'.

There is as yet little sign of the for-profits lower-cost and shorter routes to a degree being mimicked by the traditional HEIs, but, in discussing DAP and the use of the words 'university' and 'university college' as deemed 'sensitive' by law, mention should be made of Coventry University College (CUC), which is wholly owned by Coventry University (CU) and was set up in 2011 as a trading operation with the legal status of a standard for-profit registered company (any CUC profits can, of course, be covenanted to CU free of corporation tax as is normal where HEIs run trading companies). Given CUC's link to the parent CU which validates its courses and the fact that the qualifications and degrees awarded are those of CU itself, the issue of separate DAP for CUC does not arise and nor probably the need for BIS approval for the use by CUC of the title 'university college'. The business functions from a building on the CU site, as well as having a London outlet. It offers courses, some at degree level, in, *inter alia*, accountancy, finance, engineering, law, biology, business; and the three-year degree fees are at just under £5,000 per annum (£6,000 in engineering) for which the CUC students receive separate teaching from those at CU but have access to (not borrowing rights from) the CU Library. The CUC students are said on its website to be ones not bothered about the traditional university student experience, and hence probably do not have (nor want) access to the CU Student Union and its gigs; while, on the other hand, presumably imbibing a teaching experience in, say, law or engineering (so as ultimately to earn the same CU degree certificate) that is not radically different, albeit dramatically cheaper and delivered by different staff in different teaching spaces (and perhaps with a higher online element).

This is, then, the interesting process of the unbundling of the product, of the mix of things that is the selling of the HE service of a university to its student-consumer: here for CUC compared to CU and other traditional English HEIs there is presumably no Student Union cost, there is less by way of library costs, there is perhaps lower-paid faculty (and probably not paid for research time), and whatever else is going on that might account for CUC being able to offer Law at £5,000 per annum (even less than the £6,000 at the true for-profits such as BPP University or the University of Law) compared with £7,800 per annum for Law at CU (CU is one of the few English HEIs not charging the full £9,000)—but almost certainly not yet using MOOCs to reduce teaching costs (see Chapter 8), even if the CUC website talks of online tutorials. So, from all this we might assume that the real cost of teaching and related support services for undergraduate degrees at traditional English HEIs across the board could be more like CU's £7,500 (or even LMU's £6,850, as noted in Chapter 5) than the £9,000 norm (arrived at via a pricing policy based more on what-the-market-will-bear than cost-plus, and perhaps assuming, even just hoping, that for prospective students high price signals high quality). Moreover, we might also assume that the cost of a no-frills version of a non-laboratory vocational degree such as Law can be as little as CUC's £5,000 (otherwise Coventry University College Limited will presumably soon go bust!) or at most BPP University's £6,000. And also assuming, of course, that all the degrees and all the teaching provided by all these different forms of HE player meet the same QAA minimum standards of quality, since otherwise the entities concerned will, as noted, from 2014 surely be red-flagged in the proposed HEFCE list of designated HEIs and alternative HE providers list!

For completeness in reviewing the at present rather limited sources of effective cost-price competition within the English HE market for the provision of UK/EU undergraduate courses, we should note that in the non-profit Further Education (FE) sector some 700 Further Education Colleges (FEC) deliver two-year Foundation degrees, HNCs/HNDs, and other HE activity to about 175,000 students as technically the students of HEIs in effect contracting-out their teaching and validating such teaching within their linked FECs. In addition, however, there are now around 10,000 HE student places directly funded in 50 or so FECs by HEFCE. It remains to be seen whether FECs as F/HEIs will seek DAP and whether the HEFCE directly funded numbers will grow, as government seems to be encouraging. This process could certainly help government in developing competitive cost-price pressure within the market by squeezing the lower end of the HEI range (as indeed in the USA the community colleges equivalent of the UK's FE colleges offer low-cost HE access—see Cohen et al., 2014). And one might speculate that some of the non-profit chains of academies that are transforming English schools may one day integrate upwards into FE or HE institutions.

Let us now explore further the concept of just how such an unbundling process might be encouraged, to the benefit of the student-consumer in driving down price and in terms of offering choice—looking first at possible regulatory intervention in the English HE market and then also at the experience of the growth of for-profit HE providers globally and especially in the USA, and having already noted the HEFCE 'operating framework' along with HEPI's alternative proposals for regulatory reform. For Stanfield (2009) and the Adam Smith Institute, the attempt by the BIS-HEFCE to standardize designation criteria and monitoring for all types of HE providers scarcely dents the existing public HEIs' £15bn monopoly of taxpayer subsidy for HE and still more is needed to create (Stanfield argues) 'full freedom of entry into the higher education sector' so as to prevent the current 'crowding out' of the for-profit institutions and of private investment—as well as weaning the once proudly independent HEIs off their over-dependency upon public funds by, in essence, the student having a voucher to purchase HE (as indeed now is in fact approaching reality as the student draws upon up to £9,000 per annum of SLC cash to pay tuition fees). All of which Stanfield believes is needed to engender 'competition and innovation' within HE as 'one of the least competitive sectors in the UK economy' (citing by way of support the University of Buckingham's and then BPP's innovative two-year degree courses ignored by the public HEIs and noting criticism in the *Economist* (from as far back as 1867) that Oxford undergraduates spent only 24 weeks of the year in university attendance—as indeed they still do!; and also to resist the 'special pleading by powerful interest groups for protectionist policies' and to promote 'free enterprise and deregulation' so as to 'foster innovation, spur competition, increase efficiency, and lower prices' in HE. (On accreditation as a formidable entry barrier within US HE, see Gaston, 2013.)

Thus, for Stanfield the future is a limited role for government in HE in terms of 'establishing a regulatory framework that will encourage a plethora of different institutions to compete and flourish on a fair and level playing field', and the future is a HE landscape of 'national and international, private, independent, autonomous, for-profit and not-for-profit institutions'. Moreover, there should be total deregulation of the use of the word 'university' for it is not for government 'to dictate who can and cannot use this word'. And, citing the OFT's 2009 'Government in Markets: Why Competition Matters—A Guide for Policy Makers', there should also be an OFT 'market study' of HE so as to test the current regime against the ideals of free competition operating in other sectors of the economy and as under the legal framework of the 1998 Competition Act and the 2002 Enterprise Act (Farrington and Palfreyman, 2012, paras 2.18–2.25, as updated at the OxCHEPS website) and from which HE should no longer be, in practice, substantially exempt.

The 2011 HE White Paper and the HEFCE 'operating framework' have taken HE so far along the road of the Adam Smith Institute's Report, but it may or may not be that a 2016 Higher Education Act (with perhaps the creation of an Office for Tertiary Education (OFTE), as a Regulator for Tertiary Education) will not only take English HE further down the liberalization route followed by so many parts of the economy since Mrs Thatcher's election victory in 1979, but also see the development of the regulated market for delivering HE and protecting students as consumers. The legislative model for an OFTE might be based on such regulators in telecommunications as OFTEL, in the water utilities as OFWAT, in the gas and electricity utilities as OFGEM, or as in the railways with ORR, and indeed in HE we already have OFFA. On the creation of regulators as part of the Zeitgeist of modern government as the welfare or provider state becomes 'a regulatory state' see Prosser (2010), who in his chapter 10, 'Regulating the Regulators', raises the persistent problem of *quis custodiet ipsos custodies*? (notably in the fiasco of the Care Quality Commission in relation to subsequent catastrophically failing hospitals and care homes seemingly having just been inspected and passed thanks to superficial procedures). Indeed, the October 2013 Report of the Higher Education Commission ('Regulating Higher Education: Protecting Students, Encouraging Innovation, Enhancing Excellence' at www.policyconnect. org.uk) calls for urgent legislation to achieve regulatory reform, creating a Council for Higher Education (CHE) to replace HEFCE, OFFA, et al., as well as proposing an insurance scheme (like, say, ABTA and ATOL in the travel industry) to protect students when an HEI fails: this CHE would include an 'Office for Competition and Institutional Diversity' which would presumably link in some way to the OFT/CC (as being combined into the CMA). The Commission urges all political parties to pledge in their 2015 general election manifestos to legislate along these lines.

The Office for Fair Trading (OFT) Guidance Document 519 (June 2010) outlines why and how it undertakes a market study, and the Competition Commission (CC) Guidance Document CC3 (April 2013) shows how it conducts a market investigation (in fact, the OFT and the CC are merging to create the CMA—the Competition and Markets Authority—which is expected to be more robust in enforcing anti-trust and competition legislation, as well as tackling market inefficiencies generally). From OFT 519 and CC3 it is important to note: the extensive investigatory powers of both the OFT and the CC; the overall concern of both bodies as to whether there are 'reasonable grounds for suspecting that a feature or combination of features of a market in the UK is preventing, restricting, or distorting competition' (Competition Commission, April 2013: para. 22): and the processes described in OFT 519 and CC3 could easily stretch over two years. Interestingly, CC3 (April 2013: para. 107–129) talks of 'price patterns' and 'pricing strategies' as 'indicative of competitive conditions', as well as of 'price-cost margins', 'profitability', and 'quality, innovation, and other non-price indicators', and also of 'information asymmetries' especially in relation to the customer assessing quality in the case of 'infrequently purchased goods' or of 'credence goods' where the quality is difficult to verify even after purchase (April 2013: para. 311–3.12)—and of the possibility that market players are 'tacitly' co-ordinating a course of action on pricing simply by the rivals within a stable market repeatedly interacting so as to 'be able to anticipate each other's future actions' as opposed to any obvious and direct attempts at forming an illegal pricing cartel (April 2013: para. 239).

What could be the parameters of possible OFT (or even CC) interest in HE, an interest certainly now being displayed by *Which?* as a powerful consumer body and as discussed in earlier chapters? The OFT is concerned with consumer choice and efficient market competition; hence it might wonder why almost all English HEIs are charging £9,000 when their prestige and brand-value are clearly spread over a wide range, when a few are charging much less for degrees supposedly of similar standard, and when the operating costs of HEIs must vary, at least to some degree, according to local labour rates for non-academic staff and in relation to local land/property values that dictate the cost of space. It could conceivably query whether the restriction to five choices on the Universities and Colleges Admissions Service (UCAS) form is anti-competitive and limiting of student choice, as perhaps also the requirement to apply to only one of either Oxford or Cambridge as a selection procedure undertaken in advance of the general UCAS admissions process. Then there could be concerns over the September clearing process in terms of, say, what time limits are imposed for the applicant to make a decision, whether when making such a decision the applicant can be said to be adequately informed, whether the applicant should be free to renegotiate the original offer from HEI X having been made a new offer by HEI Y. The OFT also has the duty of overseeing consumer protection law, as entirely applicable to the university-student, business-to-consumer (B2C) contract-to-educate discussed in Chapter 6 (and as detailed in ch. 12 of Farrington and Palfreyman, 2012).

The HE industry may, of course, be able to show that any constraints are to the overall benefit of consumers in that (say) the fast-moving and high-volume clearing process needs some order. The young HE applicants might, however, be seen as 'vulnerable' consumers (in consumer protection terms), needing greater protection as they make decisions to spend towards £50,000 on the next biggest lifetime transaction after whatever houses or flats and perhaps pension fund they may eventually buy; and also needing better protection in a market where price may be seen simplistically as the proxy for quality. And the OFT could be intrigued that this chunky financial transaction usually is not backed up by any detailed contract as with almost all other purchases of goods and services. (See ch. 12 on the student-HEI contract in Farrington and Palfreyman, 2012, and also on the application of consumer protection law to the student-university contract-to-educate, with in addition a suggested specimen or model student-university contract set out in the Appendix.)

Finally, questions might be asked about the HEIs' get-out-of-jail-free card by way of judicial refusal to review the exercise of expert academic judgement as applied within the university-student contract (Farrington and Palfreyman, 2012, Section D of Chapter 12; and as discussed here in Chapter 6): although that would take the OFT into deep public policy territory, given also that student complaints relating to academic judgement are off-limits under the legislation setting up the OIA (its method of calculating compensation, however, where it finds in a student's favour could perhaps be another area of OFT interest in terms of reviewing legal protection for the student-consumer). Indeed, the HE industry might yet seek proactively to get ahead of such potential scrutiny (and subsequent enforcement action) by doing what other sectors (such as the sale of used cars, holidays and travel, double-glazing, car hire, and even shoe repairs; along with the famed egregious behaviour of estate agents) have done in creating a voluntary Approved Code of Practice for its UUK member HEIs (and the alternative for-profit providers), duly agreed with *Which?*, the NUS, the OIA, the QAA, et al., under s8 of the Enterprise Act 2002 and in accordance with the OFT's guidance for its Consumer Codes Approval Scheme (as suggested in Farrington and Palfreyman, 2012: para. 12.95). Universities could soon be heading towards employing Compliance Officers (like banks), just as once in far-off innocent days they did not have costly Directors of Marketing, of Press and Media Relations, and of Human Resources, nor Deputy Vice-Chancellors for Teaching Quality. For the record, the OFT has so far had very limited involvement in HE (as have, locally, trading standards departments across the country): asserting competition law in vetting the Manchester-UMIST merger; scrutinizing and criticizing some HEI student residential accommodation contracts; querying some elements of the contract-to-educate at one or two HEIs; (at present) reviewing how some HEIs (unwisely) use that contract (by withholding degrees) to enforce the payment of bad debts under the residential contract or by way of minor library/disciplinary fines under the contract-to-educate, and noting the possible application of the public procurement rules to HEIs (Farrington and Palfreyman, 2012: respectively paras. 2.25, 20.01–20.14, 12.89, 20.15, and 2.13–2.15).

If the OFT were to become much more involved in HE, it would be applying the principles set out in its 2009 'Government in Markets' document, as referred to earlier: 'Well-regulated competitive markets can maximise consumer welfare...effective competition provides significant benefits for consumers through greater choice, lower prices, and better quality goods and services...Government sets legal and institutional frameworks for markets and companies to operate in...[since it] has a legitimate role in intervening in and shaping them...[and it] also intervenes more widely in markets to achieve other policy goals and correct market failures.' And government acts via the OFT whose 'mission is to make markets work well for consumers...[which] happens when companies are in open, fair, and vigorous competition for consumers' custom'. That said, intervention to address potential market failure can itself cause problems: 'One of the biggest challenges for policy-makers is to identify unintended consequences of regulations...[and also to guard against] 'regulatory capture' [when regulation ends up benefitting the industry regulated rather than the wider public] for instance, high entrance barriers to new, innovative. and competitive players' (OFT, 2009). And the OFT also considers the impact of government policy on the competitive efficiency of a market: perhaps, for example, asking whether the £9,000 cap on UK/EU undergraduate tuition fees is too low in that HEIs find it too easy to cluster at the maximum rather than engaging in price competition.

It is, however, important to remember that HE is a deeply complex, highly interactive, pretty unpredictable, and often unduly prolonged (and hence an even more costly) process compared to consumers purchasing most other goods and services—all as discussed in earlier chapters. But at this point we should again note Riesman, commenting on the massification and consumerization of the US, cautions that thinking of students 'as simply or merely consumers is a distortion...[since they] are at once the producers and the consumers of their own educational development...we do not 'buy' an education in the way that we buy an automobile that has a defect requiring recall or a household appliance or a pharmaceutical product...' (Riesman, 1980: 361). Thus, there can be a cosy convenient conspiracy between the student-consumer and the academe-provider: 'Even the most shoddy, cut-rate, and cut-throat degrees are not necessarily frauds on the consumer. They may, in fact, be examples of collusion between academic vendor and student buyer to secure a credential at some monetary cost but almost no time in cost or effort.' (1980: 177). And we must recall that, even earlier than his perceptive 1980 analysis, it was also Riesman (1958) who pointed out the utterly inadequate information upon which students made (and still make) momentous decisions about HE and HEIs: indeed, the search for an appropriate regulatory regime for HE dates back at least fifty years, and the potential abuse of the HE market was identified by Adam Smith more than two hundred years ago!

It is, then, perhaps timely for the English HE market, unusually complicated and *sui generis* as it may be, to be tested against the theoretical and practical working of other markets in different areas of the economy, as well as for the OFT's principles of choice and competition to be applied across several major dimensions of the HE market. If one key to effective markets is the arrival of competition for the traditional incumbents from lower-cost new entrants, then in English HE can the for-profits indeed enter and compete on a level field? If another key is the uninhibited spread of innovation to drive down costs/prices or to improve convenience and quality for the consumer, can English higher education's incumbents too easily block such developments as MOOCs? If a third key is the consumer having adequate information, does the combination of the HE industry's KIS along with, say, the *Which?* website and other material in the media such as national rankings (see Chapter 8), yet do the trick for the young and perhaps in consumer law terms 'vulnerable' HE consumer? And, if usually regulation is needed to guard against market failure, is the next step for English HE to have its 'OFTE' and 'DegreesWatch' ushered in by a new Higher Education Act, rather than the cobbled-together oversight of HEFCE, QAA, OIA, OFFA, et al.? Or is it even time for the HE industry to agree its own (adequately enforced and properly enforceable) Approved Code of Practice with the OFT and all other major players in providing for the interests of the student-consumer so that, either way, the student really is (re-)placed at the heart of the modern university?

Not surprisingly, the supposed poor graduation rate and other inefficiencies, and indeed even alleged corrupt recruitment practices, in the US for-profit sector are cited by those opposing its entrance into and growth within UK HE, as well as their raising the fundamental issue of student tuition fees (almost entirely publicly funded by grants and loans from the taxpayer) being used to finance profits for the private businesses owning such for-profit chains. These issue are explored by Kinser (2013) who talks of the 'astonishing' US for-profits growth to a $30bn-plus industry that now absorbs some 25% of US grants and loans to students, a doubling since 2000 of what were once known as 'trade schools' (in Heller and Callender, 2013: ch. 6). In effect, there would and probably could be no sizeable for-profit HE sector without the US generous student federal grant and loan regime (in contrast to most counties in Asia with substantial private HE and where fees are usually privately/family-funded).

Kinser shows that the student financial aid subsidy per credential/degree earned is similar for the private for-profit and not-for-profit HEIs at c\$36–37,000, compared to c\$25,000 for public HEIs (which, of course, also enjoy state grants and subsidies; as do some private not-for-profits from substantial endowment income). Moreover, all the figures had more than doubled in just a decade, indicating the uncontrolled nature of US HE costs as driven in part by the probably over-generous US grant/loans system (as, of course, heavily influenced by the powerful lobbying of the US HE industry). This does not suggest that the for-profits are more inefficient in the cost of producing a graduate but rather are equally inefficient as the rest of HE. That said, while the for-profit sector may be 'demonstrably effective' as a demand-absorbing mechanism (and indeed as an access-widening process in that the for-profits enrol proportionately more minority, older, and low-income students) within US HE, the jobs and earnings that the graduates of the for-profits gain do seem to indicate that the loans taken out to meet the fees charged are not a good investment for the student/taxpayer, or are an even worse investment in terms of the fees/price and earnings/pay-off ratio than for much of public US HE, where at least the debt burden is reduced by the state's direct subsidy of public HEIs: 'This could mean that under current financial models, for-profit higher education is inefficient at training students for future employment.' (Kinser in Heller and Callender, 2013: 111). A problem made worse where students top up public debt with private loans, as in the early years of the 2000s, when cheap credit created legions of over-borrowers whether as students or as house-buyers.

At least in the case of the for-profits, however, the hard-pressed US taxpayer has shifted the whole cost of the provision of another source of (still over-expensive) HE onto the hapless student-graduate who ends up paying off the loans debt for life (compared to a 30-year sentence in the English loans system and with no escape route even via bankruptcy for the US graduate). As Kinser stresses, the government funding of HE and HEIs, whether directly via institutional subsidy or indirectly via grants and loans to cover tuition fees, needs to build in aspects that 'value students completing their programmes, at reasonable costs, and with appropriate returns in the labor market' (in Heller and Callender, 2013: 111). Vague proposals in the English case of only funding up to, say, £6,000 of an uncapped tuition fees range (and probably within the HEI also differentiated by subject/course)—and leaving the student and/or HEI to find private loan financing for any higher fee—might well concentrate the student's and HEI's mind on the real value of the degree in employability terms, meaning either fees drop or places are unfilled where the HEI's brand and the degree's employability-enhancing element do not command the provision of more-difficult-to-find commercial loan funds. Unless, of course, the HEI can sell the expensive degree course on the basis of its old-fashioned wider liberal arts and cultural value to students (or their parents) unconcerned about affordability, debt, and employability. And there doubtless needs to be much greater consumer protection surrounding the private loans business within US HE, as indeed if ever commercial private lending became a substantial factor in financing English HE alongside the SLC's provision. It is simply a moral imperative, as well as sound public policy as a duty of the regulatory state overseeing a regulated market in HE.

Turning to the business model of running for-profit HEIs and whether they are delivering reasonable quality HE at a lower cost than in the traditional HEIs, while still (of course) making a profit for their shareholders, and hence can be (or should become) the source of competition within an efficient HE market that drives down price to the long-term benefit of the student and the taxpayer financing the former's student debt to fund fees, we look at three studies of the US for-profits: Ruch (2001), Breneman et al. (2006), and Tierney and Hentschke (2007)—and for further analysis, see also Berg (2005) and Hentschke et al. (2010). Breneman et al. do not see the for-profits as unavoidably tainted: 'any organization seeking to thrive in a market heavily influenced by word of mouth endorsements from existing customers has little incentive to defraud consumers'; nor are they 'a significant threat to most of traditional higher education' since they enrol from 'niche markets in specific professional/technical areas' (vocational skills and competencies) of the HE market neglected by public HEIs. But the traditional institutions do need to learn from their 'clear focus on education and training for employment, coupled with an emphasis on the student as client, as consumer, rather than as supplicant' offering courses at convenient times in convenient locations 'with a minimum of downtime' (all significant elements for older students with family commitments or part-time students with work commitments) and where 'the student is sovereign' rather than the HEI being 'more faculty-centred than student-centred' (Breneman et al., 2006: x–xi). The University of Phoenix has indeed had a major issue over the incentives offered to its student recruiters (an area 'replete with opportunities for less-than-ethical behaviour'—Breneman et al., 2006: 89) and, without admission of guilt, settled the complaint by the US Department of Education with a payment of just under $10m in 2004 (a tiny 'penalty' compared to Wall Street banks settling with their regulators in recent years).

Ruch starts with an interesting thought: 'It is not clear, at least to me, when or how it became a virtue for a university to be organized on a non-profit basis instead of a for-profit one.' (2001: 8). This leads on to the question raised earlier in this book as to why it is seemingly fine for English universities to have a flourishing market in postgraduate taught courses and also one in international undergraduates, each of which generates 'surpluses' or 'excess revenues' on which tax is not paid by these non-profit charitable traditional HEIs as opposed to creating profits as would naturally be the case in the for-profits and on which corporation tax is paid? But evidently it is not acceptable, to some, to have a market in UK/EU undergraduates (other than in competition by way of admissions standards). As Ruch notes, perhaps the distinction should be between tax-paying and tax-avoiding HEIs (2001: 92); and he goes on to explore how the for-profits manage their faculty ('the presence of bosses' 2001: 15) and work them harder by way of heavier teaching loads, with an 'almost total lack of release time for research and minimal release time for governance' (2001: 17)—certainly no costly complications such as tenure, and 'a reliance on part-time, practitioner faculty' (2001: 26) paid 10–15% below comparative public HEI rates and with less by way of institutional pension contributions (but there is no pressure to research and publish).

Does all this—compared to (the often mere pretence of) being taught by full-time (supposedly) research-active academics in public HEIs—make the for-profits irredeemably 'Drive-Thru U' and purveyors of 'McEducation'? Or have the for-profits simply unbundled and reduced the business of higher education to its no-frills and less costly essence with precision management and reduced academic expenditure, and by being student-focused? Are they to be welcomed as 'EasyUni' competing with pricey and ponderous 'StateAir'? And at the same time they make a profit for shareholders while charging fees a little lower than or a bit above those at the neighbouring taxpayer-subsidized public HEI with its key labour force spending time on research, its lengthy vacations, and with not only its costly labs and libraries but also other non-educational infrastructure and amenities such as stadiums and leisure centres. And to this could possibly be added: its weak cost awareness and cost control, along with the bloated administration, and lack of economies of scale.

Of course, the profit motive means the for-profits are susceptible to greed and dubious commercial practices, and hence it is the task of government and its cartel/competition laws, along with consumer protection legislation, to control market abuse, just as government struggles with the abuses arising within producer-oriented public sector agencies by inventing costly inspection regimes of varying levels of effectiveness. Whatever may be the differences by way of taxed profits as opposed to untaxed surpluses, by way of efficiency, and in terms of academic tenure as well as shared-governance or collegial structures, an important question (the key question?) is whether what goes on in 'the classroom' where the vocational skills and competencies teaching takes place in both the for-profits and the humbler end of the range of non-profits is in fact at all different, given a similar reliance on hand-outs and digital resources (and little if any need for books from a library), along with similar (high) class sizes. And, indeed, there is probably no discernible or meaningful difference, argues Ruch (2001) other than that the for-profit working environment may well be neater and cleaner (in keeping with US service industry norms), and the incompetent or lazy teacher will not be ignored and in fact will not be tolerated within a more rigorous academic management hierarchy that does not indulge faculty. The student teaching and learning experience is broadly the same; the student experience in a more holistic sense is indeed different, but the typical for-profit older student is not at university to party or to mature over three to four years (even five or six in some US public HEIs).

The 'misunderstanding, even vitriol' between the for-profit providers and the traditional HEIs is noted by Tierney and Hentschke (2007), with the latter seeing the former as 'charlatans' and the former viewing the latter as 'antiquated'. But the authors predict that the distinctions will over time 'blur and blend' (2007: 2 and 9); and will do so more towards the for-profit provider model as the one driving disruptive innovation within HE ('the for-profits have embarked on an innovation that is unprecedented... an invention that could remake the postsecondary landscape', Tierney and Hentschke, 2007: 27). Like the trend towards the corporate workplace 'university' (notably AT&T School of Business and Technology, the Disney Institute, MasterCard University, Motorola University), the for-profits are a flexible and innovative response to a demand for no-nonsense vocational training. Furthermore, the for-profit providers often collaborate with large businesses contracting-out such activities as staff development needs (as is also now beginning to happen in the UK where Asda is linked to Middlesex University for degrees in retail and distribution, while KFC is connected to DeMontfort University). And, of course, all this is helped by the for-profit institutions having greater access to development capital than the public sector as mainly large publicly traded corporations expanding and investing to meet demand or innovating with new technology. They have investors who are rewarded by increased profitability via the classic commercial recipe of overall growth in sales/revenues (economies of scale) as well as squeezing margins between price and costs.

Tierney and Hentschke (2007: 83) estimate that of the then average annual tuition fee of c$13,000 in the early 2000s the operating profit was some $2,250 with free cash flow as 'arguably the purest form of profit' at c$1,600; and hence the teaching costs are some $10,000—about $5,000 below public HEIs, which, of course, do not always provide (or perhaps often even do not really know) their detailed teaching costs as opposed to total spend per student, including on various cross-subsidies such as on research, administration costs, and borrowings. As already noted above, a major factor in controlling and reducing costs is the less favourable pay and pension terms and conditions for academics, along with achieving greater productivity from them through higher teaching loads and probably better training (at some for-profit providers 'dress codes are even put in place' for the professors!—Tierney and Hentschke, 2007: 103); although in most universities there is anyway already a (scruffy) dress code operating as dictated by local cultural norms and 'the suit' is then readily spotted as approaching administration!

Finally, in considering the US for-profits experience, Kirp (2003: ch. 13) has a case study of DeVry University: its 'cheesy' TV commercials, its 'bevy of recruiters', its spending 10% of its budget on marketing, its salesmen allegedly 'skirting the border of misrepresentation'...Yet 'instruction is more intense than at most community colleges and regional universities'; 'and it is often better as well'; its graduates get 'jobs with a future'; weak teachers are fired; courses are not cancelled; and quality across the campuses is consistent. For its students 'it's no longer party time' and 'a sense of self-discipline is necessary'. But it is indeed all about getting a job rather than a liberal education concerned with learning how to learn (practicality trumps intellectual curiosity); and the carefully arranged job placements, company tours, and extensive mentoring help—it all sounds a bit like the HND route to an engineering career once available in the UK of the 1960s and 1970s, or the famed German hochschule-apprenticeship system. The 'DeVry students wield the power of consumers, especially when it comes to the quality of teaching, and they know it'. But even its supporters wish DeVry could shake off the 1970s trade school reputation and image, not helped by the tacky commercials.

Everything is closely controlled from the DeVry Illinois HQ, although there is a tension between the marketers' 'aggressive promotion' and the academics' concern with 'intellectual integrity', and it can be a matter of 'academic standards versus the profit margin' (where the professors, barely half of whom are full-time, almost always lose). Kirp concludes: 'By and large, DeVry does good by doing well'—delivering efficiently what its 'mainly working-class students, the first in their families to go to college' want and need (albeit that there is a high dropout rate of over 60%, a bit more than at the public community colleges as the equivalent of HE within the English further education colleges: 'The fact that DeVry loses too many students doesn't undermine the accomplishment of teaching marketable skills to a substantial number of people who otherwise would be working at Wal-Mart.'). But, asks Kirp, 'Is it Higher Education?' at DeVry and Phoenix. Are these 'nuts-and-bolts' HEIs 'really engaged in higher education'? Yes, he replies, since that is the way so much of US HE has gone since the 1970s (indeed Flexner was complaining about such a vocational dumbing-down of US liberal arts higher education compared with Germany and England way back in 1930); and the convergence of the public HEIs towards the for-profits model rather than the other way 'seems the likeliest scenario', but in that process there will be a loss of 'commitment to the idea of public service'. Similarly, Zumeta et al. (2012: 145 and 170) conclude that the for-profits, providing they are 'properly regulated', are important if US HE is to expand so as to deliver 'a well-trained workforce' since they 'have been innovative in offering efficient, student-friendly programs and services that are responsive to the market'.

The for-profits from over there will one day surely arrive over here—with the Apollo Group's purchase of BPP perhaps being the bridgehead for invasion—are clearly far from perfect. Their rapid growth of two decades in the USA may well now be slowing if not reversing (as also their profitability)—but neither are the traditional public US or UK HEIs; and, in fact, the for-profits and the non-profits, the tax-paying and the tax-avoiding, begin to look increasingly similar as the latter move closer to the former in their managerialism and corporatism, their entrepreneurship and generation of 'excess revenues'. So far there is little by way of for-profit activity in UK HE, just as was the case in the early 1990s in the USA compared with a decade later and now even more so twenty years on. Looking at the websites for the University of Law and for BPP University, we find the latter offering under-graduate degrees in (along with variations based on) Accounting and Finance, Business and Management, Human Resources Management, Law, Healthcare, and Marketing. BPP is located mainly in London with some offshoots in (so far) Birmingham, Bristol, Leeds, and Manchester; and at fees of £6,000 per annum full-time for three years or for accelerated completion over two years. The £6,000 being, of course, the most their students can borrow from the SLC compared with up to £9,000 at traditional HEIs. There are also part-time options—while international students are charged £7,500 per annum for three years or £11,250 per annum for two years. The University of Law is—of course—offering undergraduate degrees only in Law as 'a focused law degree for focused individuals'. Located in London and half a dozen other cities across England, its fees are £9,000 per annum over two years or £6,000 per annum over three years for UK/EU and international students. The non-profit ifs School of Finance University College offers undergraduate degrees in banking and finance at £6,000 per annum; and, similarly, the non-profit University of Buckingham offers two-year degree courses across a much wider range of sub-jects, with flexible three times a year start dates, for some £24,000 in total fees for UK/EU students compared with £27,000 at almost all traditional English HEIs and consequently with only two years of accommodation costs (hence its website quotes under £40k overall for a degree compared with a figure at least approaching some £50k elsewhere).

So, the for-profits are, of course, cherry-picking from and parasitical upon the public HEIs in the way that, in the UK, private healthcare is upon the NHS which undertakes most of the training of medical staff and does the really dif-ficult, uninsurable, costly aspects of the business. The for-profits in HE need the non-profits to do the research to create the new knowledge, to write most of the monographs and many of the textbooks underpinning the scholarship that informs their teaching, perhaps in the future to generate and 'credential-ize' the MOOCs used in such teaching, to supply the Masters and PhDs to the staff they recruit, and probably also to provide a source of moonlighting academics earning a few dollars extra (just as the Open University has for decades employed legions of part-time tutors who are otherwise supposed to be full-time faculty at other UK HEIs). All that activity at the English pub-lic HEIs used to be partly funded by direct taxpayer grants and subsidy, as is still the case in the USA, albeit at a reduced rate. Now the burden in England falls largely upon the undergraduate to pay the tuition fees to cover the direct teaching provision, to meet the inflated campus overheads, to cross-subsidize academics' time spent on research (or not as the case may be), and to face an OFFA tax of almost 10% of the £9,000 by way of a contribution to access and widening participation in the name of social equity—as well as paying what has quickly become the annual £9,000 norm in the hope that this high price signals high quality and high brand-value (and, of course, in the expectation that it will lead to a well-paid career).

Not surprisingly, the tightly managed for-profits can deliver the simple no-frills teaching and learning component of the degree cheaper (as noted earlier), and do so even after probably spending more on marketing and even allowing for making a profit; and, on the basis of US experience, with similar quality—or at least more efficiently and reliably—in the nuts-and-bolts, skill-and-competencies vocational courses which characterize much of modern mass HE, where 'Marketing 101' or 'Maths for Business' or 'Contract Law' or 'Introduction to Double-Entry Book-Keeping' is the same material and content whichever kind of HEI it is nominally taught within and whatever the fee paid. As with MOOCs by way of disruptive technology discussed in Chapter 8, it remains to be seen whether there will be disruptive innovation in terms of price competition on any kind of scale from new entrants, or much more price competition among the traditional HEIs as they unbundle the product and its costs. Certainly the current government lives in hope of such, as a way to create the elusive real market in tuition fees and to make the £9,000 no longer the norm it has so rapidly become but indeed the exception as was intended as far as the burden of HE upon the government and taxpayer is concerned, and in fact the regulatory regime for HE has duly been tweaked to encourage such new for-profit providers. The problem for government is that the incumbent HEIs and academe generally are likely to be pretty good at closing ranks against new entrants and at clinging to their treasured position within the acropolis, as well as at resolutely refusing to unbundle their expensive product and stripping out some of its costly component parts. In short, the traditional incumbent HEIs are not generally at all keen to join the for-profits in the agora (except, of course, when it suits them to operate so enthusiastically and profitably in the postgraduate taught course market and the international student market).

Part IV

Towards the Free Market:
English Higher Education 2020

12

From Public Good to Market-Place: From Provider State to Regulatory State

Abstract: This chapter presents to the reader three interrelated themes. Firstly, it provides a synopsis of our understanding of the concept of the state-regulated market along with an overview of what model of higher education it has been instrumental in creating and now sustains. Secondly, we examine two comparative issues: the challenge that the new model of English higher education poses to the traditional understanding of the idea of the university (a present and past comparison), and whether developments in English higher education are so very different from those in other national systems (a brief transnational perspective). Thirdly, it speculates on the course of future trends in English higher education and, in particular, addresses the question of whether the state-regulated market will continue to constitute the mechanism for relating government via the quasi-state to the HEIs in order to shape the overall character of the system of higher education.

INTRODUCTION

This chapter is organized around three themes. Firstly, it will present a synopsis of our understanding of the state-regulated market along with the broad contours of the English system of higher education which it has helped to shape and now sustains. Secondly, addresses two different comparative issues: the challenges posed by the emerging model of higher education to the established interpretations of the idea of the English university (past and present comparisons), and how the evolving English model is to be evaluated in the light of international trends in higher education (cross-national/regional comparisons). Thirdly, offers some reflection on future trends in English higher education. In particular we address the question of whether the state-regulated market is likely to be steadily replaced by a market increasingly untrammelled by political intervention.

THE STATE-REGULATED MARKET AND THE DIVERSIFIED MODEL OF ENGLISH HIGHER EDUCATION

In common with other analysts of the English model of higher education, we have traced a broad shift in how the system developed over time from the days of the University Grants Committee (acting as 'buffer, coupling, and broker' in shaping the relationship of the universities to the state—Moodie, 1983) to the funding council model of governance, instigated by the 1988 Education Reform Act, which ceded responsibility for higher education policy-making to the incumbent government while the funding councils undertook the task of policy implementation, which in practice meant the distribution of public funding and the pursuit of an ever-expanding regulatory function.

We have moved beyond the dissection of this critical shift in the governance of English higher education by offering the argument that at the core of the funding council model is the emergence of a state-regulated market. Although this mode of steering the system reflects the dominance of particular political values, its development has been both pragmatic and piecemeal and, moreover, it incorporates many of the traditional assumptions about how the English university system should be governed. It is far from a planned model, but rather the cumulative outcome of responses to pressures more often than not generated by the failure of the economy to provide the resources to meet either the expanding demand for higher education or to underwrite the enhanced outputs (more research, widening participation, service to the knowledge economy, or a stimulant for the local community) that it was burdened with achieving.

While there have been key changes in both the roles of the government (the clear recognition that it is responsible for determining higher education policy), and of the quasi-state bodies (their control of the regulatory apparatus with ultimate responsibility—excepting occasional political intervention—resting in the hands of the funding council), there has been an attempt to sustain at least the figment of autonomy, the idea that the individual providers determine their own development. Indeed, the emergence over time of a small number of higher education institutions, which with the wisdom of retrospective analysis seemed to be so poorly governed, has led some to wonder whether too much respect has not been paid to the sanctity of institutional autonomy. While the evidence may suggest occasional official complacency rather than an actual respect for institutional autonomy, the operation of a state-regulated market is more about the attempt to guide the overall development of the system rather than central government assuming responsibility for the welfare of each and every higher education provider.

In our judgement, the state-regulated market is a very convenient political form of control: it provides government direction of the policy-making process, and even of policy implementation should there be a desire to impose a narrowly defined interpretation of policy outcomes, and it delegates responsibility for the day-to-day regulation of the overall system to the quasi-state, while sustaining the idea of autonomous institutional decision-making. Although there is a complex regulatory framework that embraces institutional behaviour, it tends to work by offering incentives for compliance rather than direct sanctions for non-compliance. Perhaps the best example is the 'access agreements' that the higher education institutions are required to reach with the Office for Fair Access if they intend to charge fees above a politically defined level. At the core of the access agreements are commitments by the higher education providers to offer a percentage of their fee income to provide bursaries and/ or fee-waivers to undergraduate students (with a focus on first-year entrants and those from poorer families), and to engage in activities—usually in the local community and often in conjunction with other higher education providers—designed to broaden the social basis of their applicants. These steps are supplemented by moves to ensure student retention, and at the very least to monitor academic performance. It is critical to note that few specific targets are set which carry penalties should institutions fail to meet them, although it is expected that over time the social range of applicants will be broadened and the retention and achievement levels of entrants deemed to be from socially disadvantaged backgrounds will improve.

In terms, therefore, of undergraduate access to higher education in England there has been a very evident state-regulated market in operation to which, besides the regulations already mentioned, can also be added the former controls on overall student numbers, a maximum fee cap, the removal of restrictions on the recruitment of highly qualified applicants, the attempt to influence fee levels by reserving a number of student places for institutions charging lower fees, and requiring providers to charge overseas students at least full-cost fees. However, it should be noted that what we have termed the state-regulated market operates with different procedures for the varying areas of higher education policy with contrasting inputs from the government, quasi-state apparatus, and the institutions. In the research assessment exercises, higher education institutions in effect compete for core research funding with the rules of the competition controlled by the funding councils and with research quality (which determines the distribution of RAE resources) measured by peer review. For the most part, government intrusion has been confined to influencing selectivity in the pattern of resource distribution. Perhaps the most interesting policy arena we have examined are the procedures to assure and enhance academic quality in which the regulatory role of the Quality Assurance Agency has become somewhat lighter over time and possibly downgraded in importance. Although higher education institutions still need favourable QAA reviews of their academic programmes, it may well be that national student surveys, fee levels, and patterns of student demand are increasingly perceived as, if not proxies for measuring quality, then as meriting greater institutional attention. In this one policy area there are signs, therefore, of a decline in the significance of the regulatory state coupled with an increase in the influence of the market, although—ironically—it has to be said that it is market pressure that is a direct consequence of government action as expressed, for example, in the 2011 White Paper, *Higher Education: Students at the Heart of the System* (Department for Business, Innovation, and Skills, June 2011).

Moreover, it is important to recognize that there are pressures to do more than simply provide students with an enhanced voice as the means of ensuring academic quality. The Higher Education Commission, in its second report, called for legislation that would create a common regulatory framework to be enforced by the regulatory bodies (including the QAA) acting under HEFCE's control (to be renamed the Council for Higher Education). The intended goals are, 'protecting students, encouraging innovation, and enhancing excellence' (Higher Education Commission, 2013). But whether the post-2015 government decides to go down this route by way of legislation remains to be seen.

Although we have surrounded our analysis of the emergence of the state-regulated market in cautious terms (as an evolutionary process, strongly driven by economic pressures, and necessarily underwritten by a broad political front), it is important to say that it does provide for us a logic to the process of change in English higher education. Its emergence is closely associated with the widening appeal in recent years of reform strategies that embrace economic liberalism—the provision of social goods is better provided by the market than the state with the latter's role confined essentially to underwriting some of the costs of that provision as determined politically, but perhaps more importantly, regulating how services are to be delivered. The driver of change is not just economically determined (a central theme in Shattock's *Making Policy in British Higher Education 1945–2011*(2012)) because decisions about what to fund and how to fund it (the key economic questions for higher education) are undoubtedly underwritten by value preferences. As noted, the Kogan and Hanney text (*Reforming Higher Education*) adopted a different position:

> Our theoretical position will be seen to be that of eclecticism. We eschew general hypotheses but look to political and other social theory to illuminate and help us to classify the experiences undergone by higher education in the UK between 1975 and 1997.
>
> (Kogan and Hanney, 2000: 42)

However, in practice, Kogan and Hanney, in similar vein to Shattock, present a picture of pragmatic change to unfolding events, that there is no underlying logic to the policies that have reshaped the governance of English higher education.

Although we may differ from Shattock and from Kogan and Hanney by positing the idea that the process of change in English higher education is now driven by a central dynamic, there is common ground in our interpretations of the actual politics of that change process. While the policy agenda is set by government, there is consultation with both the state apparatus and the wider range of organized interests about the implementation of policy goals. While it has become clearer as to where formal control ultimately resides, the range of inputs into refining and evaluating the decision-making process has never been wider. Whereas at one time policy-making was ensconced in a relatively narrow and enclosed world, it now encompasses a much broader pluralist input. Undoubtedly the arrival of mass higher education, the widening of the higher education agenda, and the pressures generated by the regulated market have helped to stimulate a decision-making process that goes far beyond the confines of yesteryear which embraced the UGC, the Committee of Vice-Chancellors and Principals, the Association of University Teachers, and with the occasional genuflection to the National Union of Students—and scarcely much beyond that.

The 1992 Further and Higher Education Act, while terminating Westminster's central control of higher education policy by incorporating it in the devolution package, also created a unitary model of higher education in England. The Universities Funding Council and the Polytechnics and Colleges Funding Council (products of the 1988 Education Reform Act) were amalgamated to form the Higher Education Funding Council for England. Henceforth in England there would be a unitary model of higher education, and in a comparatively short space of time the polytechnics and colleges that had fallen under the auspices of the PCFC acquired the university title. Although a unitary model of higher education, there were repeated government calls to the effect that it should also be a model which incorporated universities that were pursuing divergent missions; a diversified but unitary model—almost a contradiction in terms.

In addition to the question of what shape the structure of the system should assume post-1992, there was also the very real problem of its diminishing financial strength (crisis is not too strong a description of the deteriorating situation) generated by the steady decline in the per capita funding of the rapidly expanding student intake. The Dearing Committee was created with in effect three problems to resolve: to suggest ways in which the funding malaise could be alleviated, to decide what the structure of the system of higher education should be, and to map out the future relationship of higher education to the state. Most commentators agree that by far the strongest part of the Report was its analysis of the financial dilemmas, with its recognition that because students gained a personal benefit they should make a contribution to the costs of their higher education, and, moreover, it recommended that payment should be made through a scheme of income-contingent loans (a step that Robbins regretted he had not recommended in his 1963 Report—Robbins, 1980). These proposals, although not implemented in that form by the then Labour Government, were a clear harbinger of the current system of variable fees.

However, the Dearing Inquiry broached the idea of a broad concordat (a compact) between the higher education institutions, state, and society. In return for continuous public funding (including underwriting the bulk of teaching costs), a somewhat internally variegated system of higher educa-tion (diverse but not too diverse) would be committed to achieving a range of socio-economic goals (as politically defined) with its performance closely regulated by the quasi-state apparatus. In the sense of determining the subse-quent course of the development of English higher education, the legacy of the Dearing Report—like the Robbins Report before it—was essentially problem-atic. At the core of the Dearing Inquiry's failure is the complete absence of a compact between the dominant institutional interests to materialize. Instead, what has emerged is a state-regulated market within which the character of the system evolves as individual institutions define their future profiles. This is not so much a compact but rather a structured framework within which the major institutional actors (government, quasi-state, and higher education providers) interact to steer the development of the system.

And what has been the outcome? What we have witnessed post-Dearing, and indeed was already in the process of evolving prior to the Report, is an increasingly differentiated and stratified model that turns to the market to augment its income (student fees, more collaboration with public and private bodies to undertake activities that are hopefully profitable, the augmenta-tion of endowments and funding through appeals, and deals to raise private capital). The student has become a fee-payer and, more arguably, a rational consumer of a valued commodity. Rather than securing post-Dearing the evo-lution of a less stratified system of English higher education, we have seen the emergence of a profile that is more hierarchical and diverse in character. If there is a system of English higher education, it conforms more to the tertiary than the traditional university model. It is composed of contrasting, if overlap-ping sectors delineated by differing academic profiles, with variations in both the focus and intensity of their research commitments, and encompassing a status hierarchy that reflects embedded institutional reputations.

Reinforcing the pressure of the regulated market has been the expansion of higher education league tables, making both national and international institutional comparisons. As much as league tables may be decried, there is no doubting that some English universities see themselves as belonging to, or aspire to be members of, that sector which comprises the elite, so-called world-class, research universities. In our chapter on the impact of the research assessment exercises we identified a group of five universities (Cambridge, Oxford, Imperial College, University College London, and Manchester) that could claim to be members of that global elite (perhaps also including the

London School of Economics, albeit with a more limited academic focus). Moreover, we have examined the pressures within the United Kingdom to distribute research funding more selectively. Indeed, as much as identifying the leading research departments wherever they are found, the research assessment exercises have become a mechanism that increasingly discriminates amongst higher education institutions in the actual distribution of core research income. Finally, it now appears that the National Student Survey, which in part can be used to rank higher education institutions by student satisfaction, is becoming a more critical concern as we shift from a model in which quality was assessed by the regulatory state to one in which student choice and evaluation is accorded greater weight.

A clear indication of the importance that higher education institutions attach to the assertion of their own identities is the emergence of the mission groups, which bring together those who see themselves as sharing common academic goals. Of special interest are the shifts in allegiances (of which perhaps the most significant has been the desertion in recent years of several 1994 Group members to join the Russell Group) because it signifies changing institutional self-perceptions. It is partly a formal recognition of the fissures within the English system of higher education—one way of identifying its internal divisions, but also indicates a search for allies as institutions respond to the state-regulated market. For example, as we have analysed, there are different mission group positions on both the distribution of public research funding and the functioning of the regulatory state with particular reference to access issues and quality assurance/enhancement mechanisms. Moreover, the mere act of changing mission group membership can be taken as a sign that the higher education institution perceives the need to establish a different relationship to the state-regulated market, one that it expects to improve its bargaining position.

What we are witnessing, therefore, is the emergence of not only a more diverse system of English higher education, now more appropriately labelled as a tertiary model, but also one within which there is more flexibility of institutional identities. English universities are now more tightly managed institutions which attempt to carve out for themselves viable niche markets. For the most part, this will require making appropriate responses to the demands of the state-regulated market, while in a few cases there is a need to reaffirm the university's reputation as a world-class institution and as a respected member of a small network of internationally recognized elite universities. Another strategy is for the university to recast its mould in order to establish itself as a member of a desirable club. The best-known contemporary example is the entrepreneurial university (Clark, 1998 and 2004) with the University of Warwick as the designated English member (Palfreyman, 1989). In an interesting analysis of the embracing of the entrepreneurial ethos by Denmark's Aarhus University, Pinheiro and Stensaker (forthcoming) refer to this as a global idea that is interpreted locally. It is institutional branding through the acquisition of a label which carries very positive connotations. But, of course, having acquired the brand there remains the task of ensuring its enhancement and effective delivery.

The state-regulated market, therefore, establishes the framework within which the English model is driven forward. The system has moved forward driven by internal propulsion, through increased government direction and state regulation, and now by the emergence of a state-regulated market. But this is to outline only the general direction of change, for at each stage there is also a reconfiguration of the relationship between the key institutional actors (government, state and quasi-state apparatus, the higher education institutions, and the organized interests) driven by the different dynamics inherent in any process of change (political action, bureaucratic regulation, pressure group engagement, and market forces).

TWO COMPARATIVE PERSPECTIVES: PAST AND PRESENT, AND THE TRANSNATIONAL DIMENSION

Although we have argued that the evolution of English higher education shows continuity with the past, this should not blind us to the extent of the changes that have occurred over the past 25 years. In a comparatively short space of time there has been a shift away from an elite model towards a mass system of higher education, which is only partially composed of the traditional university sector (as those universities in existence prior to the passage of the 1992 Further and Education Act). As we have argued, the so-called knowledge society comprises a mass system of tertiary education embracing a myriad of institutions, a considerable range of full- and part-time programmes not all of which conclude with the awarding of a degree, and very different forms of pedagogy including distance learning and extensive continuous assessment.

Not only has there been a significant change in the overall structure of higher education but the current order also encompasses a new idea of the university, although it is more accurate to think in terms of the abandonment of the traditional idea rather than its reconstitution. Obviously, the idea of the university has always been contested territory but now institutions recruiting comparatively few full-time students and offering only a limited range of programmes (often very vocationally focused) can be awarded the university title and the right to award degrees. We have also examined the expansion of the research mission which for some universities (mainly drawn from the pre-1992 sector) seems to have become more important than the teaching of undergraduate students, and incorporates in some cases the employment of faculty members formally contracted so they can avoid undergraduate teaching. At the same time there is the emergence of a lumpen proletariat of part-time faculty on short-term, teaching-only contracts, who may help to supplement the teaching provided by (hopefully) the more gifted graduate students intending to pursue academic careers. The idea that there should be a synergy between research and teaching within the university no longer holds sway.

Despite (to express the point diplomatically) a steady relaxation in the understanding of what is a university and a considerable blurring of what precisely constitutes a degree programme, until comparatively recently it was, nonetheless, accepted that higher education institutions were pursuing a public good: providing knowledge that led to a more enlightened citizenry and undertaking research which benefitted humanity at large. In fact the issue was rarely explicitly addressed, and it was simply assumed that higher education was a public good. However, much of the debate about whether students should be required to pay tuition fees has been driven by the argument that the decision to study for a degree in part reflects a desire to obtain a valued private good, which should at the very least enhance an individual's job prospects and earning capacity. Undoubtedly there are broad benefits for society at large in the sustenance of a thriving system of higher education: culturally via the enhancement of knowledge, socially through the promotion of social mobility, economically thanks to the expansion of an intelligent workforce, and politically because the educated citizen is more likely to be an informed participant. But it is difficult to ascertain how much of a contribution higher education actually makes to the furthering of these particular ends in comparison to other publicly funded institutions such as museums, libraries, and schools. Therefore, especially in the context of the recent global economic crisis, it is unsurprising to find governments evaluating the relative merits of funding higher education against the needs of other institutions that could also claim to be pursuing a public good.

It can be reasonably asserted that the opening up of the debate about higher education as a private good was driven by those who wanted to see students make a direct contribution to its funding. The motivations for the drive were mixed: higher education was facing a financial crisis and enhanced public funding was exceedingly unlikely to be forthcoming; it was a soft target in any attempt to cut public funding as there was an apparently viable source of alternative funding, and it was assumed that it would have a positive impact upon the student-university relationship—universities would take their commitment to teaching and learning more seriously and students would demand more from the university while studying harder. Although there are counter-arguments to these claims, the important point is that they are all part of a broad ideological shift: for the student, higher education is essentially a private good that brings personal enhancement and thus it is only fair (with reference to the Dearing Report) that as the beneficiaries they should make a contribution to its costs.

Accompanying the expanding debate about higher education as a private good, indeed even preceding it, was a protracted struggle to determine its public purposes. The charitable status of higher education institutions was dependent upon the fact that they were non-profit-making bodies, and the acceptance that higher education within itself was a charitable pursuit. Nonetheless, over time successive governments have challenged universities to demonstrate their public purposes. Thus we have seen pressures on higher education to widen participation and so enhance social mobility, train students to fit into the nation's changing economic infrastructure, and to undertake 'useful' research. Traditionally, universities would have argued that their primary purpose was to transmit and enlarge high-status knowledge, the definitions of which were controlled by the academic community. But now they are called upon to define their goals in more concrete, politically acceptable, terms.

Almost inevitably, the emergence of the idea of higher education as a private good (or rather, its re-emergence given the relative tardiness of the state's commitment to underwriting nearly all the costs of providing higher education, including student fees and maintenance grants) has resulted not only in the reintroduction of student fees but also the development of a privately funded sector, including for-profit providers. While at the moment it is only a comparatively small development, it represents the strongest challenge to the idea of higher education as a public good which is publicly financed. It opens up the idea of higher education as a commodity that can be purchased and sold in the market, like most other commodities. Although the distinctions are fine, presumably the ultimate purpose of the for-profit providers is to make a profit out of higher education as opposed to offering it as a public good. However, the privately funded universities (with the University of Buckingham as the first English example) can be designated as charitable bodies if they pursue the purpose of providing higher education but are not for-profit providers. There is, therefore, a potential merging of identities between the publicly and privately funded sectors, which is reflected in the University of Buckingham's membership of Universities UK, the umbrella body for British universities. Furthermore, as we have noted, the established public sector has over time sought out sources of income beyond its core public funding, and there is a move towards public sector universities setting up separate subsidiaries that function on the basis of attracting private funding.

However, in view of the fact that the development of English higher education is driven by a state-regulated market, it is important to remember that the new-found liberalization remains constrained by state regulation. As the publicly funded sector has found it necessary to respond to market-place pressures, so the emerging private sector has had to come to terms with the established order. There are good reasons for privately funded higher education institutions to acquire the university title for it brings with it a prestige that is likely to carry weight in the market-place. For the most part awarding the title is formally a decision made by the Privy Council, which will act in part on advice it receives, via BIS and HEFCE, from the Quality Assurance Agency. Moreover, although a higher education institution can award degrees without the university title, the unrestricted right to do so is associated with its possession. Furthermore, with the shift towards the payment of fees through the income-contingent loans scheme, which is underwritten by public funding, the question has arisen of whether those intending to study at privately funded institutions can draw upon these resources. While the political response has been in the affirmative (albeit up to £6,000 per annum rather than £9,000), it is much easier for institutions to assert their claim if their academic quality has been positively evaluated by the QAA. All three areas—the use of the university title, the right to award degrees, and student access to public funding—illustrate how the so-called private sector is also ensnared in the state-regulated market.

While the focus of this book has been upon contemporary trends in English higher education, purposely excluding for the most part developments in the United Kingdom at large, the drivers and trends we have discussed clearly apply in varying degrees across most other OECD countries, perhaps most notably in the USA where some very similar challenges to the traditional producer-oriented public model of the university are arising in terms of its affordability, cost controls, quality assurance mechanisms, privatization, marketization, and commodification. But the United States does offer a model in which private funding and diversification in terms of both system structures (that is of the state systems of higher education) and institutional purposes are already deeply entrenched. Indeed, California's Master Plan for Higher Education created a hierarchical structural model in which functions were formally differentiated and, moreover, legally sanctioned (Callan, 2012). By comparison the more robust steering of English higher education seems positively tame. Perhaps the most appropriate way of expressing the comparative US/UK dilemmas (Bok, 2013) posed by the pressures for change (to which we have paid considerable attention) is to see them as global in both their origins and the range of their impact, but the responses as defined nationally and regionally with, arguably, the US as processing a model more adaptable to change.

In the restructuring of English higher education we are conscious that its development may yet be influenced, even potentially directed, by any shifts within the European Union (EU) on its policy with respect to tertiary education. In other words, the English model could move more in the direction of Europe rather than the US. Pinheiro and Stensaker maintain that in the context of a perceived crisis, 'The European higher education landscape has experienced dramatic changes in the last couple of decades as a result of numerous reforms within the sector' (Pinheiro and Stensaker, forthcoming). However, as illustrated by the very case study they examine in their article (the restructuring of Denmark's University of Aarhus as an entrepreneurial university), much of the impetus for change is directed by the central state and there is precious little genuflection to market forces.

So far, higher education within the EU has been almost entirely a matter for the nation states, with the Bologna Declaration providing governments with the legitimation for driving change along what they consider to be desirable paths. While there is a commitment to create a European Higher Education Area, there is at present no EU body that can force the individual national systems into a centrally defined straitjacket; the emphasis is on harmonizing national systems rather than standardizing them. The Bologna Process, therefore, provides leverage for action by national governments rather than a common blueprint which is enforceable at the European level. In practice the Declaration has had virtually no impact in England where some would say, perhaps complacently, that the reforms which have emerged in its wake have essentially followed the English model. But this is not to say that circumstances will not change, with the possibility of extending harmonization to the point that standardization takes over, with the process underwritten by EU legislation and driven forward by a designated part of the dreaded 'Brussels bureaucracy'. In the event of this unlikely scenario then it can perhaps be hoped that the British government, at least for higher education within the English boundary, will ensure exemption.

A potentially greater European threat to British higher education is the increasing tendency for European universities to offer degree programmes (especially at the graduate level) that are taught in English. The consequence is that they become more effective competitors for overseas students. But this can scarcely be objected to, given that the initiatives reflect bold institutional decision-making, and intensify competition within the student market—very consistent, therefore, with the values that have come to underwrite English higher education.

THE FUTURE: ENGLISH HIGHER EDUCATION IN 2020

In keeping with the analytical framework around which this chapter has been organized, these concluding observations will consider: the likely evolution of the state-regulated market in the near future, possible further developments in the structure of English higher education, and—from a global perspective—in what direction this would take the system. Recently, Huisman and his colleagues approached a sample of 'higher education experts' to reflect on what the map of English higher education would look like in 2025, and concluded with the observation:

Of course, in 2025 our predictions will be proven wrong, but that is not the point. We hope that in the coming years the scenarios will stimulate a debate on the future worlds that academics, higher education managers, and students would like to live in.

(Huisman et al., 2012: 362)

Our purpose is quite different: to present a reasoned picture of the future model of English higher education, the world in which its institutional providers along with all those who participate in shaping how they function, will have to live. It is not so much about constructing a model in which the key institutional insider would like to live, but rather an attempt to define the world in which they will have to live. But that scenario is also open to debate.

Although we can expect the state-regulated market to change at the margins over time, future developments in its operation will be essentially an elaboration of how it currently works. While it is tempting to surmise that the state-regulated market will steadily give ground as a less restrained market emerges, there are good reasons, however, why a dramatic shift in this direction in unlikely. Firstly, for the foreseeable future there will continue to be a considerable direct and indirect public funding input into higher education. Directly, for example, by providing support for the teaching costs of the STEM subjects and underwriting most of the core costs of research—indeed in the current harsh economic climate research funding has been reasonably well protected. Indirectly, for example, by underwriting the operations of the Student Loans Company (SLC), which provides the resources to meet the costs of student fees, and we should not forget that there are still maintenance grants for students from low-income families. Moreover, the terms of the income-contingent loans scheme are such (no repayment of loans if income is below £21,000 per annum, and the cancellation of any unpaid loan 30 years after graduation) that it is estimated over 30% of the total bill will never be repaid, with some predictions going as high as 40%. Inevitably, this has led some to question how much of a saving to the public purse the current scheme actually represents, but perhaps a more significant ramification is that if there continues to be considerable public funding, the state will want to call at least some of the tunes.

Secondly, in the era of mass participation the political ramifications of higher education are considerable. With an enhanced political profile it is more likely that governments will want to be engaged in shaping higher education policy and in steering system development. While this leaves open the possibility of advocating a wide range of options to shape the relationship between higher education, the state, and the wider society, it does mean that government intervention in some form or another is almost inevitable. The marked political impact of higher education policy is illustrated perfectly by the current Coalition Government's decision to permit an increase in variable fees up to a maximum of £9,000 per annum. This was a particularly bitter pill for the Liberal Democrat members of the Coalition Government to swallow, given that the Party had fought the prior general election with the pledge to phase out fees if elected. While this can be dismissed as merely an isolated event, it is incontrovertible that higher education is now deeply embedded in the pursuit of both social and economic policy. Successive governments have attempted to impose on higher education institutions their definitions of the public purposes they need to pursue, and the means to achieve this have been the strategic employment of public funding and a state-regulated market amenable to government pressure. We see no reason why this will change.

Thirdly, and ironically, the pressure to sustain a state-regulated market comes from the higher education providers, possibly more so from the new privately funded institutions than those that at least since 1945 have been supported overwhelmingly by the public purse. For the publicly funded institutions, although there was some hostility to the steady emergence of the regulatory state, the major problem they faced was the inexorable decline in their funding in relation to their expanding student numbers, the wider obligations they were supposed to fulfil, and their own aspirations. However, a state-regulated market does allow for greater institutional control over internal development than straightforward state control, and is infinitely preferable to a steady increase in parsimony and a slide into bankruptcy. The new privately funded higher education institutions also have much to gain from state regulation, in particular the formal recognition of their status (the university title and degree-awarding powers) and also access for their students to funding that may help to finance their studies. Once they have demonstrated their ability to survive in the higher education market-place then the new providers need to secure their positions, and while they may claim that this is best achieved by continuing to offer a quality product that is responsive to the demands of the market, undoubtedly it also helps to have acquired the trappings that are the gift of the state.

If the state-regulated market is going to continue as the mechanism that relates higher education to state and society, then we need to interpret how it is likely to evolve; and also note that we are more modest clairvoyants than Huisman's 'higher education experts', predicting change up to only 2020 (rather than 2025), the likely year that the next government's term of office will terminate. We will organize our thoughts around the three policy fields that have formed the core of our analysis of the state-regulated market: funding and access, research selectivity, and quality assurance.

On funding, the key issue is whether the cap on variable fees is going to be lowered, raised, or removed entirely. What we think is most likely to emerge is a straightforward removal of the cap but accompanied by the decision to limit government support to underwrite student income-contingent loans up to the current maximum (or even the lower figure of £6,000), and those universities wishing to charge a higher fee will be required to seek out alternative sources of funding beyond the set value of, as it were, the taxpayer's voucher held by the student. While universities charging above this figure will generate additional fee income, they will take responsibility for meeting the costs of their schemes including underwriting any debts that are incurred. Already there is some internal institutional differentiation in fee levels and over time this will increase. The decisions will be driven by a combination of student demand (presumably the greater the demand the higher the fee), judgements about what rival institutions are likely to charge, and internal politics (possibly a decision to charge low fees in order to help a department augment student demand). A move in this direction is likely to generate greater departmental friction within higher education institutions but again these have to be resolved by their structures of governance.

In the context of uncapped fees, and the consequential likelihood of wider fee differentiation between universities and among courses, then fee levels can be predicted to have a greater impact on student demand. Moreover, the recently announced relaxation in the control over student numbers, with unrestricted entry from 2015, was not entirely unanticipated. However, the widening participation agenda will still retain some importance for governments regardless of their political persuasion and, indeed, the universities themselves will continue to insist that their intention is to recruit the most able applicants. Consequently, we can expect universities—especially those which charge fees towards the top end of the market—to offer more generous amounts of support for those applicants from the current targeted categories. OFFA agreements will, therefore, still have a role to play in determining student support packages. However, we can expect the focus to shift, as it is already, from financial support for new entrants to monitoring what particular programmes are applied for, what steps the universities are taking to ensure high retention rates, and what occupations graduating students enter. In each case, particular attention will be paid to entrants from the designated under-represented groups.

While with fees and access issues it is more a question of tinkering with the current features of the state-regulated market, in terms of the delivery of core research funding there is the possibility of more radical reform. Firstly, a key policy decision needs to be reached. If it is decided that the most appropriate way of securing a powerful research future for British universities is to implement a strategy that incorporates very wide differentials in institutional funding levels, then that should be pursued directly rather than, as at present is the case, by focusing funding upon only those departments with the very highest-rated quality. In fact it is not our judgement that this policy decision will be made by 2020 but rather we will see a continuation of basically the current model. However, we believe that, after the current REF, efforts will be made to modify the process: shift the balance of resource funding towards the research councils (or, more radically, either allow the councils to allocate *all* public research funding or replicate for core research funding the same overall pattern of institutional distribution arrived at by the research councils), offer greater incentives to institutions not to compete for core research funding (possibly a direct allocation of some research funding—based presumably on faculty numbers—to be distributed at the discretion of the university), and widen the differentials in the allocation of resources between research fields (some research brings even greater rewards than is already the case). But the general picture will be a continuation of the current policy: an assessment process that continues to measure quality in relation to a range of units of assessments but a funding strategy that more generously favours an increasingly restricted range of institutions. However, while there may be a move towards greater selectivity in the funding of research, there are limits to how far it is possible to go down that road without changing the complete understanding of the purpose of the assessment exercises. Some would argue that we have already reached that point and it is about time to implement a more honest assessment process: perhaps a national decision to fund explicitly an elite number of universities able to compete in the global research rankings.

With the movement towards a lighter-touch regulatory regime, coupled with the considerably increased emphasis upon providing prospective students with greater information, and along with the surveys in which students provide evidence on their workloads and evaluate their degree programmes, the shift towards new practices in assessing the institutional commitment to quality assurance and enhancement has probably moved as far as it is likely to. In effect, the wings of the QAA have been clipped, although it is too soon to say whether prospective students are becoming more discriminating consumers or student surveys are actually persuading the universities that they need to ensure their teaching is of a reputable quality and their degree programmes of a high standard. It may take some time for the student to become a rational consumer and indeed universities and degree courses may be selected because of their current reputations, and for students once within the system the incentive is to confirm, rather than denigrate, the merits of their chosen universities. Few are likely to want to parade the fact that they chose to attend what they now consider to be a poor university and they have obtained a degree that is little more than worthless. Nonetheless, the fear of negative student reaction, even if rare, coupled with the continuing supervisory role of the regulatory state, is likely at least to ensure a positive formal commitment to the provision of quality in undergraduate teaching.

Although our predictions about the immediate future of the state-regulated market are cautious, they do encompass a somewhat reduced role for the quasi-state apparatus particularly in the shape of the QAA, OFFA, and the RAE (REF). The lead regulator will be the Higher Education Funding Council for England and the other manifestations of the quasi-state will function under its umbrella. But that said, we have raised the possibility of HEFCE being replaced by an Office for Tertiary Education (OFTE or some similar entity)! Moreover, the somewhat greater exposure to market pressures will mean more precarious futures for some institutions and the overall structure of higher education will change to reflect this.

While there will continue to be a policy focus on widening participation, there is no great expectation that the overall size of higher education will expand greatly, in spite of the removal of the cap on undergraduate recruitment. In terms of participation rates, higher education may be approaching a saturation point and the stress in the immediate future will be more upon consolidation of past advances as expressed in the higher education routes that students are following (what degree programmes they decide to study), retention rates, and the jobs they acquire. Some increase in the size of the privately funded, including for-profit, institutions can be expected but more important will be a blurring of the boundaries between privately and publicly funded sectors. The notion that there is a system of higher education, which is underwritten by a widely shared idea of the university, is all but dead. We have a tertiary model of differentiated sectors with both competition and co-operation within sectors, but increasing stratification between them.

There is likely to be more selective co-operation on both the research and teaching fronts. The motivations will be to enhance opportunities (faculty research), to preserve teaching programmes (although this may mean shedding some faculty if teaching is shared), to sustain student choice, to preserve institutional stability, and even to augment income (or at least mitigate losses). There is also the possibility of more institutional amalgamations, although such amalgamations may represent little more than one higher education institution taking over another. Moreover, while it is unusual given the English historical experience, the possibility of institutional failure and closure should not be ruled out. Invariably co-operation on the teaching front will be local in its scope with research co-operation, at least for the conduct of specific projects, possibly embracing transnational ventures driven from below by teams of researchers. The precise patterns of institutional interaction will be determined by the particular identities of the co-operating partners and the trend will be for like to seek out like. It is important, therefore, for institutions to carve out well-defined identities for themselves; occupying a niche market is a precursor for determining who your allies and collaborators are likely to be.

It will be interesting to see whether a sector emerges, as it has in the United States, which is composed of universities that see themselves as dedicated mainly to the provision of high-quality undergraduate education with a strong liberal arts focus. The privately funded New College of the Humanities appears to be following this model but the question is whether there is likely to be sufficient demand to secure its replication, or even its own long-term viability. What is more likely to emerge is that within some universities, which perhaps officially may label themselves as research-intensive institutions, there would be some departments more dedicated to providing a high-quality under-graduate education (or perhaps some universities will introduce the 'Honors Program' approach to be found in many US universities), while others may seek to reduce teaching costs through the use of MOOCs. Within the context of students paying high fees, especially if the fee cap is removed, there are a range of viable options including the adoption of the liberal arts niche. Furthermore, not only is there the prospect of fragmentation within the university, there is also the possibility of fragmentation within departments with the intensifica-tion of the divide between those who teach and those who undertake research, each with their own contracts and clear monitoring procedures to ensure that they are honoured. Obviously, institutions will take different paths, and one can expect that the bulk of faculty, especially within the pre-1992 sector, will be hired on the understanding that they will pursue research while taking responsibility for teaching, including undergraduate teaching. But we should not close our eyes to the fact that there are alternative models of the university and they are already taking shape.

The structural development of English higher education will be steered by the interaction of institutional patterns of governance and the pressures exerted by the state-regulated market. For effective responses to external pres-sure there has to be competent leadership, both with respect to its personal qualities and the decision-making procedures through which it functions. The English idea of the university has embraced contrasting models of higher edu-cation embedded in different traditions of governance. Given that we have posited the emergence of a considerably more internally fractured model of the English university, its governance becomes both more precarious but more vital to ensuring its success. The pressure will be on to construct modes of gov-ernance that continue to reflect an institution's embedded tradition but which enable it to grapple effectively with the problems posed by its contemporary environment. This will require a broad hands-on approach from the centre but one which liaises closely, perhaps through intermediaries (deans, heads of schools, and departmental heads), with the grass roots academic and admin-istrative faculty. It would be naïve, however, to suggest that there will always be harmony, for there is no doubting that the state-regulated market can be a hard taskmaster and failure to respond constructively to its messages is the road to ruin.

But not all is doom and gloom in English higher education. The nation pos-sesses several of the world's leading research universities with more ranked in most league tables in the top 100. While the student surveys raise some critical questions about undergraduate teaching, most students are more than satisfied with their university education. Aided by the worldwide dominance of the English language, it remains a fact that many overseas students still opt to study in England. It is evident that many, if not all, national systems of higher education are under considerable pressure thanks to: the current world economic crisis, the continuous squeeze even in good times on resources, the recent massive expansion in student numbers, and the fact that increasingly national systems have to respond to their location within a global market-place. While there are different directions that English higher education could follow (we have seen the United States as a role model, while others point to the Scandinavian countries as a possible way forward), it may be that, through the aegis of the state-regulated market, we are plotting the most viable future for ourselves; and in the process have perhaps arrived at a mechanism for change that others could adopt to devise their own solutions to their current dilemmas. Perhaps the way forward, therefore, is to follow the English policy strategy!

Nonetheless, in spite of this optimism, this chapter concludes on an uncertain note. Higher Education marketization may be significantly affected by the intervention of the OFT (using its broad competition and consumer protection powers as discussed in Chapter 11) which has just completed a consultation exercise on the market efficiency of 'the undergraduate higher education sector in England', and 'how universities go about setting fees'. We await an announcement as to whether the OFT will either drop the issue or proceed to launch a market study as demanded by *Which?* in its detailed and damning response to the consultation. If a formal market study is undertaken, it will clearly signify that at least in England the provision of HE has become a marketized and commodified economic activity; a significant step towards 'The Rise of the Regulated Market in Higher Education' and the 'Reshaping of the University'.

This is a process of reshaping that will act upon the teaching/research balance within universities and the forging of academic careers, will engender greater innovation in the delivery of HE to the fee-paying student-consumer, will blur the HE and FE boundary with both as a part of TE, will leave the universities seeking cost reductions and engaging in price competition, but at the same time see more interaction and collaborative ventures between suppliers within the HE market-place, including across the public/private sector divide.

Conclusion

Abstract: This brief conclusion provides an overview of the book. With a range of comparative material (mainly to higher education in the United States) the book has analysed contemporary developments in English higher education with particular reference to its changing structure, its modes of governance, its regulation, and its funding. The intention has been to describe the shift in the role of government as provider to that of government as regulator. While we see it as a scholarly book, we have not been afraid to express our own personal preferences and predictions in favour of a diversified model of higher education, of universities as providing a private as well as a public good, of the inevitability of a higher education system in which teaching is for the most part privately funded, and of the preference for central steering through the operation of a state-regulated market rather the enmeshing of higher education within the state apparatus and driven by its overwhelming dependence on the uncertainty of public funding.

We have explored the globalization of higher education and its impact upon English universities, along with other key drivers of change such as massification, marketization, and managerialism—all leaving universities wrestling with and being reshaped by competition, commodification, commercialization, consumerization, and with corporate governance replacing collegiality. We have also argued that historically English universities have been much closer to the market-place than is generally assumed, and not always uncomfortably so; and that, even in the post-1945 period when the trend has been for greater dependence on public funding, in the most recent decades they have nonetheless embraced a market-place in offering profitable postgraduate taught courses and competing for lucrative international students.

They have also now entered what is at present an inefficient and messy market-place for UK/EU undergraduates as the provision of HE for such has shifted from being seen almost exclusively as a public good to an essentially private good, as the taxpayer has retreated from generously funding an elite university system to sharing the financial burden with the student/family through loans for mass higher education. And indeed, via the £9,000 fee cap of 2012–13, shifting the burden very substantially on to the student-consumer of what is portrayed as a commercial transaction where a variety of old and new, both quasi-public and private HE providers deliver a service of teaching and examining in increasingly fluid and flexible ways—some moderately innovative in format and even in addition also offering limited price competition within the evolving market. This shift has been only partly for pure ideological reasons by way of a belief in markets, and rather more simply as a series of responses to national financial exigency seeking the reduction of the cost of public services.

The provider state thus becomes the regulatory state as it engineers this process of change, but not yet in HE with any certainty as to the exact degree and detail of regulation that is possibly needed or perhaps desirable. At the same time, however, growing dissatisfaction with the quality and quantity of undergraduate teaching and learning, explicitly more so in the USA than (as yet) in the UK, drives consumerism—as do the ever-higher tuition fees. This necessitates the need for improved consumer protection for the vulnerable purchaser of HE as now an expensive private consumption and positional good. We argue that this process will be refined over the next five years or so as 'The Rise of the Regulatory State' in English HE, and perhaps also for US HE. Although, that said, we concede that a return to boom economic circumstances could once again relieve HE of such pressures to reform in terms of cost control, price competition, and innovative delivery; and, moreover, the potential intervention of the EU to force the harmonization of higher education across much of Europe could force a shift back towards English HE as a largely public service. Otherwise, we see a near-universal global trend in the opposite direction as nations travel the same broad trajectory.

We have attempted to present this picture of change in a scholarly fashion by adopting an analytical approach that we think makes sense of the change process. However, we have not refrained from expressing our own views on either the desirability of the overall direction of change or the more particular policy preferences which have accompanied it. We are pleased by the move over the past 25 years away from the idea, that was beginning to take root in certain quarters, of higher education as simply a public good that should be underwritten by Treasury funding and with universities operating as little more than public sector institutions. There is now an English system of higher education in which internal differentiation is quite clearly recognized and with its varying segments performing both overlapping and contrasting roles. For the better, we have moved away from a model in which at least implicitly every institution that carried the university label could pretend that its purpose was to reinvent itself as a leading world-class research university. It was almost as if it were something of a negative label to be called a polytechnic which served the local community by offering high-quality teaching and training in a whole range of vocational courses that would enhance employability. Thus, it is perhaps to be regretted that the current Coalition Government has extended the entitlement to use the university label to a wide range of both private for-profit providers and small colleges with very specialist academic goals. The university title now confers essentially a symbolic status, which may be gratifying for the new title holders, but has little meaning in terms of conveying an academic identity. However, in terms of the overall development of English higher education this extension of the university title should not prove to be too sharp a break on the move towards securing greater institutional diversity.

As has been consistently argued throughout the book, the current process of change in English higher education is underwritten by the development of a state-regulated market. The incumbent government sets the policy parameters, while the various quasi-state apparatuses determine (ultimately under the political guidance of the government) how those policies will be implemented. The role of the higher education institutions is to decide how they will respond to these constraints. Nonetheless, there is a considerable degree of interaction between government, the quasi-state, and the higher education institutions before the state-regulated market takes a precise form in shaping any policy area, and it is always subject to evolution either as governments change or lessons are learnt. Indeed, there may well be market inefficiency or even failure that requires government intervention to correct. This may necessitate future legislation or regulatory action to stimulate more effective outcomes in terms of price competition, innovative practices, and new entrants, as well as to enhance consumer protection for students.

The state-regulated market is a realistic model for analysing English HE. It recognizes the paramount role of government steering, which has not decreased even though the teaching and learning process has become considerably less dependent on public funding. It also reflects clearly the input of the Higher Education Funding Council for England as the chief regulatory body with the other regulatory bodies falling under its auspices. Although the process can be said to preserve institutional autonomy in the sense that universities will decide for themselves how they will respond to its demands, this is a very formulaic interpretation of the idea of autonomy. Universities will be driven by their financial needs and it is impossible for them not to compete for the various sources of available public funding. But there should also be a strong incentive to augment private income in order to ease somewhat the grasp of the financial tentacles of the government. Furthermore, the need for financial stability should also prove to be a strong incentive to prudent financial management (especially if price competition develops within the UK/EU undergraduate market and cost reduction is required). It is also important to raise the question of whether autonomy for the majority of universities has ever meant much more than institutional control over the right to make, for the most part, unpalatable decisions. Of course, university-led bodies—most notably the University Grants Committee—had considerable authority to shape the overall development of the system, but this was heavily dependent upon government funding, and universities had to accept the fact that there were constraints upon their aspirations. Their evolution was as much centrally guided as driven forward by autonomous decision-making.

Although it is impossible to deny that increasingly higher education is a global product, shaped by pressures that range from personal decision-making to action by international bodies, the book has directed its attention to the fact that it is also a product which is delivered locally. There is nothing new about this: for example, the Oxbridge collegiate, Napoleonic and Humboldtian models, while apparently incorporating universal truths about the nature of higher education, were adjusted to fit local social and cultural milieu as they steadily crossed national boundaries. Contemporarily it does appear that MOOCs will have a global impact but to gain a foothold they will need to impact upon how people decide to spend their time and will need to be widely recognized by employers. Do they have something relevant to offer? In this case the challenge may be global, and may require the established universities to demonstrate to students that they have something positive to offer (albeit at a price) that they could not obtain by following the MOOC route. Or the incumbent providers within the HE market may simply internalize and credentialize MOOCs as a means of reducing teaching costs (but not necessarily prices by way of reduced tuition fees).

It remains to be seen how the regulatory state seeks over the next few years to intervene in the HE market, which it has sought to develop as it shifted from being the provider state. In the book we have referred to HEFCE's proposed new regulatory framework, to calls from the Higher Education Policy Institute (HEPI) and from the Higher Education Commission (HEC) for comprehensive regulatory reform, and to the potential involvement of the Office of Fair Trading (OFT) in relation to competition and consumer protection law impacting upon HEIs. In addition, there is the constant exhortation from the Minister for Universities and Science to put 'students at the heart of the system'. The difficulty is balancing the freedom of an efficiently operating HE market with the state's need to see accountability for the use of taxpayer largesse in funding the student loan arrangements as well as meeting the state's concern over the student-qua-consumer and also the widening participation agenda (with the drivers of the regulatory state possibly transforming it into a controlling state). The contents of an HE Bill may well in due course give definitive guidance as to how the regulation of the HE market will develop.

In the meantime, the Coalition Government's English HE policy experiment continues apace as, in the Chancellor's Autumn Statement of December 2013, the abolition of the cap on UK/EU undergraduate numbers from 2015–16 was announced, with the extra £2bn annual cost for an additional some 60,000 students being met by the impending £12bn sale of part of the student loans book. The funding question mark over the long-term financial viability of the open-ended commitment to providing loans for UK/EU undergraduates in a market where almost all universities have drifted to the maximum capped fee of £9,000 per annum, and in which there is to be no control on student numbers, continues to generate considerable concern (Morgan, 12 December 2013: 6–7). Indeed, in the HEPI 2013 annual lecture, Bekhradnia labelled what he saw as, in effect, 'a voucher system' as being 'philosophically, economically, and socially untenable' as a funding arrangement that 'will not persist' (Bekhradnia, 26 November 2013: 8).

However, while the student loans book may eventually become unaffordable for the taxpayer (allegedly a fiscal black hole) if nothing is achieved by way of cost control and cost reduction by ensuring greater innovation and price competition amongst HE providers, and while a change to a Labour government in 2015 may see flirting with a reduced cap of £6,000 and a graduate tax (as seemingly at present is its evolving HE policy), we assert that the rise of the regulated (but never a truly unfettered) market in higher education will continue. Reversion to funding university undergraduate education as a free public good is simply unaffordable in the context of aging demographics; and this continued process of change will be reshaping the university for some years yet as the regulatory regime evolves.

Moreover, given that the costs of HE teaching will continue to be substantially borne by the student, there is, arguably, a moral obligation in terms of intergenerational equity upon universities to find innovative ways to reduce costs and hence tuition fees. They need also, of course, to respond to students as fee-payers becoming increasingly assertive and engaged customers as appears to be happening already as many HEIs overhaul their degree programmes and promise to take their teaching obligations as seriously as their research ('Must do better, university teachers warned'—*The Times*, 21 November 2013). It may yet be that a new and competitive market in undergraduate provision will at last prove to be the decisive factor in improving the quantum and quality of teaching.

In writing a book about contemporary policy developments, there is always a fear that something will break shortly after the publication of your manuscript that will undermine its major conclusions. For us it has been the forthcoming 2015 General Election, raising the prospect of a government of a different political persuasion, with vividly contrasting policy aspirations, coming to power. But, as those who have read this book will realize, this has always been little more than a marginal concern for us. A new government may readjust over time how the state-regulated market functions, but it will be no more than a modification of the established patterns of state-regulation. The next substantial challenge for English higher education will come from students acting as rational and increasingly demanding consumers, but that is something which has already been set in motion.

Bibliography

Adams, J. and Gurney, K. (2010), *Funding Selectivity, Concentration and Excellence—How Good is the UK's Research*, Oxford: HEPI Report Summary 46.

Adonis, A. (2012), *Education, Education, Education: Reforming England's Schools*, London: Biteback Publishing.

Altbach, P. G. (2013), 'The Globalization of College and University Rankings', *The Europa World of Learning, Volume 1*, London: Routledge, 26–29.

Altbach, P. G. and Balan, J. (2007), *World Class Worldwide: Transforming Research Universities in Asia and Latin America*, Baltimore: The Johns Hopkins University Press.

Alvesson, M. (2013), *The Triumph of Emptiness: Consumption, Higher Education and Work Organisation*, Oxford: Oxford University Press.

Amaral, A. et al. (2009), *European Integration and the Governance of Higher Education and Research*, Dordrecht: Springer.

Amis, K. (1951). *Lucky Jim*, London: Penguin.

Anderson (1960), The Anderson Report, *see Ministry of Education*

Anderson, M. S. and Steneck, N. H. (2011), *International Research Collaborations: Much to be Gained, Many Ways to Get into Trouble*, Abingdon: Routledge.

Anderson, R. (2006), *British Universities Past and Present*, London: Hambledon Continuum.

Annan, N. (1990), *Our Age: Portrait of a Generation*, London: Weidenfeld & Nicolson.

Annan, N. (1999), *The Dons: Mentors, Eccentrics and Geniuses*, London: HarperCollins.

Anonymous (2006), *A Campus Conspiracy*, Exeter: Impress Books.

Anonymous (2007), *Degrees R US*, Exeter: Impress Books.

Anonymous (2008), *The Whistleblower*, Exeter: Impress Books.

Archibald, R. B. and Feldman, D. H. (2011), *Why Does College Cost so Much?* New York: Oxford University Press.

Armstrong, E. A. and Hamilton, L. T. (2013), *Paying for the Party: How College Maintains Inequality*, Cambridge: Harvard University Press.

Arts and Humanities Research Council (accessed 18 April 2013), 'Strategic Programmes', <http://www.ahrc.ac.uk/Funded-Research/Funded-themes-and-programmes/Strategic-p>.

Arum, R. and Roksa, J. (2011), *Academically Adrift: Limited Learning on College Campuses*, Chicago: The University of Chicago Press.

Ashby, E. and Anderson, M. (1970), *The Rise of the Student Estate*, Cambridge: Harvard University Press.

Baatz, M. (2013), *English Universities, 1852–2012: From Freedom to Control*, Sherborne: Downland Publishing Company.

Bailey, M. and Freedman, D. (2011), *The Assault on Universities: A Manifesto for Resistance*, London: Pluto Press.

Baker, S. (7 April, 2011), 'Underlying Disorders', *Times Higher Education*, 35–42.

Baker, S. (22 December 2011), 'Split in Funding could lead to Sector Schism', *Times Higher Education*, 6–7.

Baldwin, W. and Palfreyman, T. (1547), *A Treatise on Morall Philosophie* (1620 edition: <http://www.archive.org/details/treatiseofmoralloobald>).

Barber, B. R. (1992), *An Aristocracy of Everyone: The Politics of Education and the Future of America*, New York: Ballantine Books.

Barcan, R. (2013), *Academic Life and Labour in the New University*, Farnham: Ashgate.

Barnes, S. (1996), 'England's Civic Universities and the Triumph of the Oxbridge Model', *History of Education Quarterly*, 36 (3), 271–305.

Barnett, C. (2001), *The Verdict of Peace: Britain between her Yesterday and the Future*, London: Macmillan.

Barnett, R. (2012), *The Future University: Ideas and Possibilities*, Abingdon: Routledge.

Barr, N. (2001), *The Welfare State as Piggy Bank: Information, Risk, Uncertainty, and the Role of the State*, Oxford: Oxford University Press.

Barr, N. (2012), *Economics of the Welfare State*, Oxford: Oxford University Press.

Barr, N. and Crawford, I. (1998), 'The Dearing Report and the Government's Response: A Critique', *Political Quarterly*, Volume 69, No.1, 72–84.

Barr, N. and Crawford, I. (2005), *Financing Higher Education: Answers from the UK* Abingdon: Routledge.

Barzun, J. (1991) *Begin Here: The Forgotten Conditions of Teaching and Learning*, Chicago: University of Chicago Press.

Bassett, R. M. and Maldonado-Maldonado, A. (eds.) (2009), *International Organisations and Higher Education Policy: Thinking Globally, Acting Locally?* Abingdon: Routledge.

Bates, A. W. and Sangra, A. (2011), *Managing Technology in Higher Education: Strategies for Transforming Teaching and Learning*, San Francisco: Jossey-Bass.

Bekhradnia, B. (17 May 2012), *The Academic Experience of Students at English Universities—2012 Report*, Oxford: HEPI.

Bekhradnia, B. (26 November 2013), *Higher Education in the UK – Punching Above Our Weight. Really?* Oxford: HEPI.

Bell, R. and Grant, N. (1973), *A Mythology of British Education*, London: Panther.

Bennett, W. J. and Wilezol, D. (2013), *Is College Worth It?* Nashville: Thomas Nelson.

Berg, G. A. (2005), *Lessons From the Edges: For-Profit and Non-Traditional Higher Education in America*, New York: Praeger.

Berman, E. P. (2012), *Creating the Market University: How Academic Science Became an Economic Engine*, Princeton: Princeton University Press.

Biotechnology and Biological Sciences Research Council, (accessed 18 April 2013), 'Strategic Priorities—BBSRC', <http://www.bbsrc.ac.uk/funding/priorities/priorities-index.aspx>.

Blacker, D. J. (2012), *The Falling Rate of Learning and the Neoliberal Endgame*, Alresford: Zero Books.

Bok, D. (2003), *Universities in the Marketplace: The Commercialisation of Higher Education*, Princeton: Princeton University Press.

Bok, D. (2006), *Our Underachieving Colleges: A Candid Look at How Much Students Learn and Why They Should be Learning More*, Princeton: Princeton University Press.

Bok, D. (2013), *Higher Education in America*, Princeton: Princeton University Press.

Booth, C. (1987), Central Government and Higher Education Planning: 1965–1986, *Higher Education Quarterly*, 41 (1), 57–72.

Bowen, H.R. (1980), *The Costs of Higher Education: How Much Do Colleges and Universities Spend per Student and How Much Should They Spend?* Washington: Jossey-Bass.

Bowen, W. G. (2013), *Higher Education in the Digital Age*, Princeton: Princeton University Press.

Bowen, W. G. et al. (2009), *Crossing the Finish Line: Completing College at America's Public Universities*, Princeton: Princeton University Press.

Boyle, D. (2013), *Broke: Who Killed the Middle Classes?* London: Fourth Estate.

BPP (accessed 1 November 2011), <http://www.bppbusiness.com/about_bpp/our_history.aspx>.

Brabazon, T. (2007), *The University of Google: Education in the (Post) Information Age*, Aldershot: Ashgate.

Brabazon, T. (2013), *Digital Dieting: From Information Obesity to Intellectual Fitness*, Aldershot: Ashgate.

Bradbury, M. (1975), *The History Man*, London: Secker & Warburg.

Bradbury, M. (1987), *Cuts*, London: Hutchinson.

Breneman, D. W. et al. (2006), *Earnings from Learning: The Rise of For-Profit Universities*, New York: New York University Press.

Brewer, D. J. et al. (2002), *In Pursuit of Prestige: Strategy and Competition in US Higher Education*, New Brunswick: Transaction Publishers.

Briggs, A. (1991), 'A Founding Father Reflects', *Higher Education Quarterly*, 45 (4), 311–332.

Brock, M. G. and Curthoys, M. C. (eds.) (1997), *The History of the University of Oxford: Volume VI, Nineteenth-Century Oxford, Part 1*, Oxford: Oxford University Press.

Brock, M. G. and Curthoys, M. C. (eds.) (2000), *The History of the University of Oxford: Volume VII, Nineteenth-Century Oxford, Part 2*, Oxford: Oxford University Press.

Brown, A. (2009), *The Rise and Fall of Communism*, London: The Bodley Head.

Brown, L. D. & Jacobs, L. R. (2008), *The Private Abuse of the Public Interest: Market Myths and Policy Muddles*, Chicago: University of Chicago Press.

Brown, P. et al. (2011), *The Global Auction: The Broken Promises of Education, Jobs and Income*, New York: Oxford University Press.

Brown, R. (2001), 'Accountability in Higher Education: The Case for a Higher Education Audit Commission', *Higher Education Review*, 33 (2), 5–20.

Brown, R. (2004), *Quality Assurance in Higher Education: The UK Experience Since 1992*, London: Routledge/Falmer Press.

Brown, R. (2011), *Higher Education and the Market*, Abingdon: Routledge.

Brown, R. (2 May 2013), 'Risk-Based Quality Assurance—The Risks', in HEPI, *New Arrangements for Quality Assurance in Higher Education*, Occasional Reports, No. 6, 8–13.

Brown, R. and Carasso, H. (2013), *Everything for Sale? The Marketisation of UK Higher Education*, Abingdon: Routledge.

Browne, J. (October 2010), *An Independent Review of Higher Education Funding and Student Finance*, <http://www.independent.gov.uk/browne-report>.

Burleigh, M. (2006), *Sacred Causes*, London: Harper Press.

Butterfield, H. (1962), *The Universities and Education Today*, London: Routledge & Kegan Paul.

Buxton, J. and Williams, P. (1979), *New College, 1379–1979*, Oxford: New College.

Callahan, D. and Wasunna, A. A. (2006), *Medicine and the Market: Equity v Choice*, Baltimore: The Johns Hopkins University Press.

Callan, P. M. (2012), 'The Perils of Success: Clark Kerr and the Master Plan for Higher Education', in Rothblatt, S., *Clark Kerr's World of Higher Education Reaches the 21st Century: Chapters in a Special History*, Dordrecht: Springer, 61–84.

Callender, C. and Scott, P. (eds.) (2013), *Browne and Beyond: Modernizing English Higher Education*, London: Institute of Education Press.

Campbell, J. (2003), *Margaret Thatcher: Volume 2, The Iron Lady*, London: Random House.

Carpentier, V. (2012), 'Public-Private Substitution in Higher Education: Has Cost-Sharing Gone Too Far?' in *Higher Education Quarterly*, 66 (4), 363–390.

Carswell, J. (1985), *Government and Universities in Britain: Programme and Performance, 1960–1980*, Cambridge: Cambridge University Press.

Carter, I. (1990), *Ancient Cultures of Conceit: British University Fiction in the Post-War Years*, London: Routledge.

Cassidy, J. (2009), *How Markets Fail: The Logic of Economic Calamities*, London: Penguin.

Chapman, A. W. (1955), *The Story of a Modern University: A History of the University of Sheffield*, Oxford: Oxford University Press.

Christiensen, C. M. and Eyring, H. J. (2011), *The Innovative University*, San Francisco: Jossey-Bass.

Clark, B. R. (1998), *Creating Entrepreneurial Universities: Organizational Pathways of Transformation*, Oxford: Pergamon Press.

Clark, B. R. (2004), *Sustaining Change in Universities: Continuities in Case Studies and Concepts*, Maidenhead: SRHE/Open University Press.

Clarkson, L. A. (2004), *A University in Troubled Times: Queen's Belfast, 1945–2000*, Dublin: Four Courts Press.

Clotfelter, C. (1996), *Buying the Best: Cost-Escalation in Higher Education*, Princeton: Princeton University Press.

Coaldrake, P. and Stedman, L. (2013), *Raising the Stakes: Gambling with the Future of Universities*, St Lucia: University of Queensland Press.

Cobban, A. (1988), *The Medieval English Universities: Oxford and Cambridge to c.1500*, Aldershot: Scolar Press.

Cobban, A. (1999), *University Life in the Middle Ages*, London: UCL Press.

Cohen, A. M. et al. (2014), *The American Community College*, San Francisco: Jossey-Bass.

Collinge, A. (2009), *The Student Loan Scam: The Most Oppressive Debt in US History*, Boston: Beacon Press.

Collini, S. et al. (2000), *Economy, Polity, and Society: British Intellectual History, 1750–1950*, Cambridge: Cambridge University Press.

Collini, S. (2012), *What are Universities For?* London: Penguin.

Commission on the Future of Higher Education, see Spellings Report.

Committee of University Chairmen (CUC) (1995, and subsequent editions), *Guide for Members of Governing Bodies of Universities and Colleges*, Bristol: HEFCE.

Committee of Vice-Chancellors and Principals (1985), *Report of the Steering Committee for Efficiency Studies in Universities* (Jarratt Report), London: CVCP.

Committee on Higher Education (1963), *Report* (Robbins Report), London: HMSO.

Conrad, C. and Dunek, L. (2012) *Cultivating Inquiry-Driven Learners: A College Education for the 21st Century*, Baltimore: The Johns Hopkins University Press.

Cooper, A. (8 March 2012), 'Private Values and For-Profit Standards', *Times Higher Education*, 34.

Corbyn, Z. (11 February 2010), ' "Golden Triangle" to Win Funding Riches', *Times Higher Education*, 20.

Cornford, F. M. (1908), *Microcosmographia Academica: Being a Guide for the Young Academic Politician*, London: Bowes & Bowes.

Coventry University College (accessed 22 September 2012), <http://www.coventry.ac.uk/CUC/Pages/Coventry.university.college.aspx>.

Crequer, N. (1989), 'The Passing of the Education Reform Act', *Higher Education Quarterly*, 43 (1), 3–19.

Crouch, C. (2011), *The Strange Non-Death of Neo-Liberalism*, Cambridge: Polity Press.

CUA (1992), *Universities in the Marketplace*, Manchester: CUA.

Davies, A. (1986), *A Very Peculiar Practice*, London: Coronet.

Davies, A. (1988), *A Very Peculiar Practice: The New Frontier*, London: Methuen.

Davies, H. (2010), *The Financial Crisis: Who is to Blame?* Cambridge: Polity Press.

Davis, V. (2007), *William Wykeham: A Life*, London: Hambledon Continuum.

Deem, R., Hillyard, S., and Reed, M. (2007), *Knowledge, Higher Education and the New Managerialism: The Changing Management of UK Universities*, Oxford: Oxford University Press.

Delbanco, A. (2012), *College: What it Was, Is, and Should Be*, Princeton: Princeton University Press.

Department for Business, Innovation, and Skills (June 2011), *Higher Education: Students at the Heart of the System*, London: BIS.

Department for Business, Innovation, and Skills (August 2011), *A New, Fit-For-Purpose Regulatory Framework for the Higher Education Sector*, London: BIS.

Department for Business, Innovation, and Skills (2013), *Massive Open Online Courses and Online Distant Learning*, Research Paper 130, London: BIS.

Department for Education and Skills (2003), *The Future of Higher Education*, Norwich: HMSO.

Department for Education and Skills (2003a), *Higher Education Funding and Delivery to 2005–06*, London, Department for Education and Skills.

Department of Education and Science (1987), *Review of the University Grants Committee* (Croham Review), London: HMSO.

Diggle, P. and Chetwynd, A. (18 April 2013), 'Correlation limitations', *Times Higher Education*, 39.

Docherty, T. (2011), *For the University: Democracy and the Future of the Institution*, London: Bloomsbury Academic.

Dolan, S. (2010), *How to Make Millions Without a Degree, and How to Get by Even if You Have One*, Kibworth Beauchamp: Matador.

Dougill, J. (1998), *Oxford in English Literature: The Making and Undoing of the 'English Athens'*, Ann Arbor: University of Michigan Press.

Douglas, G. H. (1992), *Education without Impact: How our Universities Fail the Young*, New York: Birch Lane & Carol Publishing.

Duryea, E. D. (2000), *The Academic Corporation: A History of College and University Governing Boards*, London: Falmer Press.

Ecclestone, K. and Hayes, D. (2009), *The Dangerous Rise of Therapeutic Education*, London: Routledge.

Education Reform Act (1988), *Public General Acts and Measures*, London: HMSO.

Ehrenberg, R. G. (2000), *Tuition Rising: Why College Costs so Much*, Cambridge: Harvard University Press.

Ehrenberg, R. G. (2007), *What's Happening to Public Higher Education: The Shifting Financial Burden*, Baltimore: The Johns Hopkins University Press.

Eliot, C. W. (1909), *University Administration*, Cambridge: Harvard University Press.

Engel, A. J. (1983), *From Clergyman to Don: The Rise of the Academic Profession in Nineteenth-Century Oxford*, Oxford: Oxford University Press.

Engell, J. and Dangerfield, A. (2005), *Saving Higher Education in the Age of Money*, Charlottesville: University of Virginia Press.

Fallis, G. (2014), *Rethinking Higher Education: Participation, Research, and Differentiation*, Montreal: McGill-Queen's University Press.

Farrington, D. and Palfreyman, D. (2012), *The Law of Higher Education*, Oxford: Oxford University Press.

Fazackerley, A. (28 April 2006), 'Rifts Threaten Unified Voice', *Times Higher Education*, 2.

Flexner, A. (1930), *Universities: American, English, German*, New York: Oxford University Press.

Florida, R. (2005), *The Flight of the Creative Class*, New York: Harper Business.

Florida, R. (2008), *The Rise of the Creative Class*, New York: Basic Books.

Friedman, M. (1962), *Capitalism and Freedom*, Chicago: University of Chicago Press.

Furedi, F. (16 June 2011), 'Grayling cries freedom', *Times Higher Education*, 28.

Further and Higher Education Act (1992), *Public General Acts and Measures*, London: HMSO.

Gaston, P. L. (2013), *Higher Education Accreditation: How It's Changing, Why it Must*, Sterling: Stylus Publishing.

Geiger, R. L. (2004), *Knowledge and Money: Universities and the Paradox of the Marketplace*, Stanford: Stanford University Press.

Gibney, E. (1 November 2012), 'Reach for the Stars', *Times Higher Education*, 37–41.

Gingrich, J. R. (2011), *Making Markets in the Welfare State: The Politics of Varying Market Reforms*, Cambridge: Cambridge University Press.

Ginsberg, B. (2011), *The Fall of the Faculty: The Rise of the All-Administrative University and Why It Matters*, New York: Oxford University Press.

Golden, D. (2006), *The Price of Admission*, New York: Crown.

Goodman, R. et al. (2013), *Higher Education and the State: Changing Relationships in Europe and East Asia*, Oxford: Symposium Books.

Gordon, G. and Whitchurch, C. (eds.) (2010), *Academic and Professional Identities in Higher Education: The Challenges of a Diversifying Workforce*, Abingdon: Routledge.

Gornitzka, A. et al. (2005), *Reform and Change in Higher Education: Analysing Policy Implementation*, Dordrecht: Springer.

Green, V. H. H. (1969), *British Institutions: The Universities*, London: Penguin.

Greenaway, D. and Haynes, M. (2000), *Funding Universities to Meet National and International Challenges*, London: The Russell Group.

Gross, N. (2013), *Why are Professors Liberal and Why do Conservatives Lose?*, Cambridge: Harvard University Press.

Grove, J. (16 May 2013), 'Southampton Shows Teeth and Watchdog Backs Down', *Times Higher Education*, 6–7.

Guardian (1 May 2013), 'RAE 2008: results for UK universities', <http://www.guardian.co.uk/education/table,2008/dec/18/rae-2008-results-uk-universiti...>.

GuildHE (accessed 23 January 2013), <http://www.guildhe.ac.uk/en/about_guildHE/index.cfm>.

GuildHE (accessed 23 January 2013), <http://www.guildhe.ac.uk/en/members-list/index.cfm>.

GuildHE (accessed 16 November 2013), 'GuildHE Members Recommended for University Title', <http://www.guildhe.ac.uk>.

Hacker, A. and Dreifus, C. (2010), *Higher Education? How Colleges Are Wasting Our Money and Failing Our Kids—and What We Can Do About It*, New York: Times Books.

Halsey, A. H. (1961), 'Pyramid of Prestige', *Universities Quarterly*, 15 (4), 341–344.

Halsey, A. H. (1992), *Decline of Donnish Dominion: The British Academic Professions in the Twentieth Century*, Oxford: Oxford University Press.

Halvorson, G. C. (2009), *Health Care Will Not Reform Itself: A Critic's Guide to Refocusing and Reforming American Health Care*, New York: Productivity Press.

Hammond, M. (2013), *Ungovernable Skills Britain: A National Disaster Since 1851*, London: Lambert Academic Publishing.

Harrison, B. (ed.) (1994), *The History of the University of Oxford: Volume VII, The Twentieth Century*, Oxford: Oxford University Press.

Harrison, B. (2009), *Seeking a Role: The United Kingdom, 1951–1970*, Oxford: Oxford University Press.

Harrison, B. (2010), *Finding a Role?—The United Kingdom, 1970–1990*, Oxford: Oxford University Press.

Harrop, S. (1994), *Decade of change: The University of Liverpool, 1981–1991*, Liverpool: Liverpool University Press.

Hazelkorn, E. (2011), *Rankings and the Reshaping of Higher Education: The Battle for World-Class Excellence*, Basingstoke: Palgrave Macmillan.

Hazelkorn, E. (2013), 'The Reshaping of Higher Education: How Rankings are Influencing Higher Education Decision-Making and Stakeholder Opinion', *The Europa World of Learning 2013*, London: Routledge, Vol. 1, 3–8.

Heller, D. E. (2011), *The States and Public Higher Education Policy: Affordability, Access, and Accountability*, Baltimore: The Johns Hopkins Press.

Heller, D. E. and Callender, C. (eds.) (2013), *Student Financing of Higher Education: A Comparative Perspective*, Abingdon: Routledge.

Helpman, E. (2004), *The Mystery of Economic Growth*, Cambridge: Harvard University Press.

Hentschke, G. C. et al. (2010), *For-Profit Colleges and Universities: Their Markets, Regulation, Performance and Place in Higher Education*, Sterling: Stylus Publishing.

Hersh, R. H. and Merrow, J. (2005), *Declining by Degrees: Higher Education at Risk*, New York: Palgrave Macmillan.

Higher Education Commission (2013), *Regulating Higher Education: Protecting Students, Encouraging Innovation, Enhancing Excellence*, London: Higher Education Commission.

Higher Education Funding Council for England (2000), *Diversity in Higher Education: HEFCE Policy Statement*, Bristol: HEFCE.

Higher Education Funding Council for England (2003), *Guide to Performance Indicators in Higher Education*, Bristol: HEFCE.

Higher Education Funding for England (2003a), *HEFCE Strategic Plan 2003–08*, Bristol: HEFCE.

Higher Education Funding Council for England (October 2012), A Risk-Based Approach to Quality Assurance: Outcomes of Consultation and Next Steps, Bristol: HEFCE.

Higher Education Funding Council for England (2012), *National Scholarship Programme 2013–14: Provisional Allocations and Guidance for Institutions*, HEFCE: Bristol.

Higher Education Funding Council for England (accessed 8 June 2013), <http://www.hefce.ac.uk/whatwedo/currentworktowidenparticipation/nationalscholarshipprogramme>.

Higher Education Policy Institute (May 2011), 'Private Providers in UK Higher Education: Some Policy Options', (HEPI Report 53) Oxford: HEPI (<http://www.hepi.ac.uk>).

Higher Education Policy Institute (May 2012), 'The Academic Experience of Students at English Universities—2012 Report', (HEPI Report 57), Oxford: HEPI (<http://www.hepi.ac.uk>).

Higher Education Policy Institute/Which? (May 2013), 'The Academic Experience of Students at English Universities–2013 Report', (HEPI Report 61) Oxford: HEPI (<http://www.hepi.ac.uk>).

Hill, P. and Fazackerley, A. (9 December 2005), 'V-C Body Told to Accept Division', *Times Higher Education*, 2.

Hilton, B. (2006), *A Mad, Bad, and Dangerous People?* Oxford: Oxford University Press.

Holmwood, J. (2011), *A Manifesto for the Public University*, London: Bloomsbury Academic.

Hoppen, K. T. (1998), *The Mid-Victorian Generation, 1846–1886*, Oxford: Oxford University Press.

Howker, E. and Malik, S. (2010), *Jilted Generation: How Britain has Bankrupted its Youth*, London: Icon Books.

Huisman, J. (ed.) (2009), *International Perspectives on the Governance of Higher Education*, Abingdon: Routledge.

Huisman, J., de Boer, H., and Botas, P. C. P. (2012), 'Where Do We Go From Here? The Future of English Higher Education', *Higher Education Quarterly*, 66 (4), 341–362.

Hussey, T. and Smith, P. (2010), *The Trouble with Higher Education: A Critical Examination of our Universities*, London: Routledge.

Ibbetson, D. J. (1999), *A Historical Introduction to the Law of Obligations*, Oxford: Oxford University Press.

Ives, E. et al. (2000), *The First Civic University: Birmingham, 1880–1980*, Birmingham: University of Birmingham Press.

Jencks, C. and Riesman, D. (1968), *The Academic Revolution*, New York: Doubleday.

Jenkins, S. (1995), *Accountable to None*, London: Hamish Hamilton.

Johnstone, D. B. and Marcucci, P. N. (2010), *Financing Higher Education Worldwide: Who Pays? Who Should Pay?* Baltimore: The Johns Hopkins University Press.

Joint Funding Councils (2003), *Review of Research Assessment* (Roberts Review), Bristol: Joint Funding Councils.

Joint Funding Councils (June 2005), *Guidance on Submissions*, Bristol: Joint Funding Councils.

Jump, P. (29 March 2012), 'Elite Powers of Concentration', *Times Higher Education*, 7.

Kahlenberg, R. D. (2010), *Affirmative Action for the Rich: Legacy Preferences in College Admissions*, New York: Century Foundation.

Kahneman, D. (2011), *Thinking, Fast and Slow*, London: Penguin.

Kamenetz, A (2010), *DIY U: Edupunks, Edupreneurs, and the Coming Transformation of Higher Education*, Vermont: Chelsea Green Publishing.

Kandiko, C. B. and Weyers, M. (eds.) (2013), *The Global Student Experience: An International and Comparative Analysis*, Abingdon: Routledge.

Kaplin, W. A and Lee, B. A. (2013), *The Law of Higher Education*, San Francisco: Jossey-Bass.

Karabel, J. (2005), *The Chosen: The Hidden History of Admission and Exclusion at Harvard, Yale, and Princeton*, Boston: Houghton Mifflin Company.

Kay, J. (2003), *The Truth About Markets*, London: Penguin.

Kelly, A. P. and Carey, K. (2013), *Stretching the Higher Education Dollar: How Innovation Can Improve Access, Equity and Affordability*, Cambridge: Harvard Education Press.

Kelly, T. (1981), *For Advancement of Learning: The University of Liverpool, 1881–1991*, Liverpool: Liverpool University Press.

Kimball, R. (1990), *Tenured Radicals: How Politics has Corrupted our Higher Education*, New York: HarperCollins

King, A. and Crewe, I. (2013), *The Blunders of our Governments*, London: Oneworld Publications.

King, R. (2009), *Governing Universities Globally: Organizations, Regulation and Rankings*, Cheltenham: Edward Elgar.

King, R. et al. (2011), *Handbook on Globalization and Higher Education*, Cheltenham: Edward Elgar.

King, R. et al. (2013), *The Globalization of Higher Education*, Cheltenham: Edward Elgar.

Kinser, K. (2013), 'Paying for For-Profit Higher Education: Implications of the United States Case', in Heller, D. and Callender, C. (eds.) *Student Financing of Higher Education: A Comparative Perspective*, Abingdon: Routledge, 98–114.

Kirp, D. L. (2003), *Shakespeare, Einstein and the Bottom Line: The Marketing of Higher Education*, Cambridge: Harvard University Press.

Kogan, M. and Kogan, D. (1983), *The Attack on Higher Education*, London: Kogan Page.

Kogan, M. and Hanney, S. (2000), *Reforming Higher Education*, London: Jessica Kingsley.

Labaree, D. (1997), *How to Succeed in School Without Really Trying: The Credentials Race in American Education*, New Haven: Yale University Press.

Land, R. and Gordon, G. (eds.) (2013), *Enhancing Quality in Higher Education*, Abingdon: Routledge.

Lane, J. E. and Johnstone, D. B. (2012), *Universities and Colleges as Economic Drivers*, Albany: State University of New York Press.

Lane, J. E. and Johnstone, D. B. (2013), *Higher Education Systems 3.0: Harnessing Systemness, Delivering Performance*, Albany: State University of New York Press.

Lewis, H. R. (2006), *Excellence Without a Soul: How a Great University Forgot Education*, New York: PublicAffairs/Perseus.

Lindblom, C. E. (2001), *The Market System: What It Is, How It Works, and What To Make of It*, New Haven: Yale University Press.

Lleras, M. P. (2007), *Investing in Human Capital: A Capital Markets Approach to Student Funding*, Cambridge: Cambridge University Press.

Lodge, D. (1978), *Changing Places*, London: Penguin.

Lodge, D. (1985), *Small World*, London: Penguin.

Lodge, D. (1989), *Nice Work*, London: Penguin.

Lucas, C. J. (1994), *American Higher Education: A History*, New York: St Martin's Griffin.

Lucas, C. J. (1996), *Crisis in the Academy: Rethinking Higher Education in America*, Basingstoke: Macmillan.

Macleod, R. and Moseley, R., (1980), 'The "Naturals" and Victorian Cambridge: Reflections on the Autonomy of an Elite', *Oxford Review of Education*, 6 (2), 177–195.

Magalhaes, A. and A. Amaral (2009), 'Mapping Out Discourses on Higher Education Governance', in Huisman, J. (ed.), *International Perspectives on the Governance of Higher Education: Alternative Frameworks for Coordination*, New York, Routledge, 182–197.

Magnus, G. (2012), *The Age of Aging*, New York: Wiley.

Marginson, S. and Considine, M. (2000), *The Enterprise University*, Cambridge: Cambridge University Press.

Martin, R. E. (2011), *The College Cost Disease: Higher Cost and Lower Quality*, Cheltenham: Edward Elgar.

Marwick, A. (1998), *The Sixties: Cultural Revolution in Britain, France, Italy, and the United States, c.1958–c.1974*, Oxford: Oxford University Press.

Massy, W. F. (2003), *Honoring the Trust: Quality and Cost Containment in Higher Education*, Boston: Anker.

Mayer, C. (2013), *Firm Commitment: Why the Corporation is Failing Us and How To Restore Trust in It*, Oxford: Oxford University Press.

Mazzucato, M. (2013), *The Entrepreneurial State: Debunking Public v Private Sector Myths*, London: Anthem Press.

McBurnie, G. and Ziguras, C. (2007), *Transnational Education: Issues and Trends in Offshore Higher Education*, Abingdon: Routledge.

McClaran, A. (2 May 2013), 'Developing the New Higher Education Review', in HEPI, *New Arrangements for Quality Assurance in Higher Education*, Occasional Reports, No. 6.

McGettigan, A. (2013), *The Great University Gamble: Money, Markets and the Future of Higher Education*, London: Pluto Press.

McMahon, W. W. (2009), *Higher Learning, Greater Good: The Private and Social Benefits of Higher Education*, Baltimore: The Johns Hopkins University Press.

McMurrin, S. M. (ed.) (1976), *On the Meaning of the University: Essays on the Occasion of the Inauguration of David Pierpoint Gardner as Tenth President of the University of Utah*, Salt Lake City: The University of Utah Press.

Meltzer, A. H. (2012), *Why Capitalism?* New York: Oxford University Press.

Middlehurst, R. (2013), *The Growth of Private and For-Profit Higher Education Providers in the UK: Implications for Policy and Practice*, London: Higher Education Policy Network, SRHE.

Miller, G. E. et al. (2013), *Leading the E-Learning Transformation of Higher Education: Meeting the Challenges of Techology and Distance Education*, Sterling: Stylus Press.

Million+ (13 September 2010), A Graduate Tax: Would it Work? <http://www.millionplus.ac.uk>.

Million+ (17 May 2011), Research that Matters <http://www.millionplus.ac.uk>.

Million+ (19 September 2011), Universities Driving Social Mobility—Beyond the Oxbridge Obsession <http://www.millionplus.ac.uk>.

Million+ (accessed 24 January 2013) <http://www.millionplus.ac.uk/who-we-are/our-affiliates/>.

Million+ (accessed 24 January 2013a) <http://www.millionplus.ac.uk/who-we-are/our-role>.

Million+ and London Economics (30 November 2010), Fair Progressive and Good Value? <http://www.millionplus.ac.uk>.

Ministry of Education (1960), *Grants to Students*, (Anderson Committee Report), Cmnd 1051, London: HMSO.

Mirowski, P. (2013), *Never Let a Serious Crisis Go to Waste: How Neoliberalism Survived the Financial Meltdown*, London: Verso.

Moberly, W. (1949), *The Crisis in the University*, London, SCM Press.

Molesworth, M. et al. (2012), *The Marketisation of Higher Education and the Student as Consumer*, New York: Routledge.

Moodie, G. (1983), 'Buffer, Coupling and Broker: Reflections on 60 Years of the UGC', *Higher Education*, 12 (3), 331–347.

Moodie, G. C. and Eustace, R. (1974), *Power and Authority in British Universities*, London: Allen & Unwin.

Moore, C. (2013), *Margaret Thatcher: The Authorised Biography—Volume One: Not for Turning*, London: Allen Lane.

Morgan, J. (1 March 2012), 'Enigma Variations', *Times Higher Education,* 37–41.

Morgan, J. (26 July 2012), 'Exception Becomes the Rule as Three in Four Charge £9k Fees', *Times Higher Education*, 6–7.

Morgan, J. (16 August 2012), 'Are Inspectors Due to Call? *Times Higher Education*, 9.

Morgan, J. (16 August 2012), 'Non-Teaching Bodies Will be Players, Pearson Boss Says', *Times Higher Education*, 12.

Morgan, J. (1 November 2012), 'Elite Embittered as HEFCE Decides Not to Risk Calling Time on Audits', *Times Higher Education*, 9.

Morgan, J. (12 December 2013), 'What's Not to Like? Elite Reply to Dropped Cap Shocks Willetts', *Times Higher Education*, 6–7.

Morgan, K. O. (1999), *The People's Peace: Britain, 1945–1990*, Oxford: Oxford University Press.

Morris, M. and Hjort, M. (2012), *Creativity and Academic Activism: Instituting Cultural Studies*, Durham: Duke University Press.

National Committee of Inquiry into Higher Education (accessed 10 December 2012) *Higher Education in the Learning Society* (Dearing Report), <http://www.leeds.ac.uk/educol/ncihe/>.

National Committee of Inquiry into Higher Education (NCIHE) (1997), *Higher Education in the Learning Society: Summary Report*, (Dearing Report), Norwich, HMSO.

Naylor, R. (2007), *Whose Degree is it Anyway?—Why, How and Where Universities are Failing Our Students*, Petersfield: Pencil-Sharp.

Neave, G. (1998), 'Growing Pains: The Dearing Report from a European Perspective', *Higher Education Quarterly*, Volume 52, No.1, 118–136.

Neild, R. (2012), *The Financial History of Cambridge University*, London: Thames River Press.

New College of the Humanities (accessed 22 September 2012), <http://www.nchum.org>.

Newfield, C. (2008), *Unmaking the Public University: The Forty Years Assault on the Middle Classes*, Cambridge: Harvard University Press.

Newman, J. H. (1959), *The Idea of a University*, New York: Image Books.

Newman, M. (4 December 2008), 'UUK Polls: Inclusivity Call Belies Rival Groupings', *Times Higher Education*, 10.

Newman, M. (19 November 2009), 'Do You Want to be in My Gang?' *Times Higher Education*, 33–37.

1994 Group (December 2010), *Widening Participation through Targeted Outreach Programmes*, <http://www.1994group.ac.uk/publications>.

1994 Group (September 2011), Mapping Research Excellence: Exploring the Links between Research Excellence and Research Funding Policy (a Research Report by Professor Paul Wellings and Rachel Winzer) <http://www.1994Group.ac.uk/MappingResearchExcellence>.

1994 Group (accessed 24 January 2013), <http://www.1994Group.ac.uk/aboutus>.

OFFA (accessed 5 June 2013), <http://www.offa.org.uk/press-releases/offa-announces-decisions-on-revised-2012-13-access-agreements>.

OFFA (accessed 9 June 2013), <http://www.offa.org.uk/agreements/london-metropolitan-university>.

OFFA (accessed 9 June 2013a), <http://www.offa.org.uk/agreements/university-west-of-england>.

OFFA (accessed 9 June 2013b), <http://www.offa.org.uk/agreements/university-college-london>.

OFFA (accessed 9 June 2013c), <http://www.offa.org.uk/agreements/university-of-warwick>.

OFFA (accessed 9 June 2013d), <http://www.offa.org.uk/agreements/university-of-manchester>.

OFFA (accessed 9 June 2013e), <http://www.offa.org.uk/agreements/university>.

OFFA (accessed 12 June 2013), <http://www.offa.org.uk/press-releases/commitment-to-widening-participation-continues>.

OFFA (accessed 12 June 2013a), <http://www.offa.org.uk/agreements/university>.

Ogilvie, R. M. (1962), in Niblett, W. R. (ed.), *The Expanding University*, London: Faber.

Owen, T. (1980), 'The University Grants Committee', *Oxford Review of Education*, 6 (3), 225–278.

Palfreyman, D. (1989), 'The Warwick Way: A Case Study of Innovation and Entrepreneurship Within a University Context', *Journal of Entrepreneurship and Regional Development*, 1(2) 207–219.

Palfreyman, D. (ed.) (2008), *The Oxford Tutorial*, Oxford: OxCHEPS (Oxford Centre for Higher Education Policy Studies).

Palfreyman, D. (2010), *London's Livery Companies*, Olney: Oracle Publishing.

Palfreyman, D. (2011), *London's Inns of Court*, Olney: Oracle Publishing.

Palfreyman, D. and Tapper, T. (eds.) (2009), *Structuring Mass Higher Education: The Role of Elite Institutions*, Abingdon: Routledge.

Paolucci, R. (2013), *Learning with MOOCs: Massive Open Online Courses*, The Interlearning Company: The Open e-Learning Research Project.

Parkin, F. (1986), *The Mind and Body Shop*, London: Fontana.

Parry, G. (4 November 2012), 'Policy Failure in English Higher Education: The Case of Colleges', paper presented to The Centre for Higher Education Studies, Institute of Education, University of London.

Paxman, J. (1990), *Friends in High Places: Who Runs Britain?* London: Penguin.

Perlman, B. (1988), *The Academic Intrapreneur*, New York: Praeger.

Perkin, H. (1969), *New Universities in the United Kingdom,* Paris: OECD.

Perkin, H. (1989), *The Rise of Professional Society: England since 1880*, London: Routledge.

Persily, N. et al. (2013), *The Health Care Case: The Supreme Court's Decision and Its Implications*, New York: Oxford University Press.

Phillimore, A. J. (1989), 'University Research University Grants Committee's Evaluation of British Universities, 1985–86', *Research Policy*, 18 (5), 255–271.

Pinheiro, R. et al. (2012), *Universities and Regional Development: A Critical Assessment of Tensions and Contradictions*, Abingdon: Routledge.

Pinheiro, R. and Stensaker, B. (forthcoming), 'Designing the Entrepreneurial University: The Interpretation of a Global Idea, Aarhus University from 2005', *Public Organization Review*.

Pollitt, C. and Bouckaert, G. (2004), *Public Management Reform: A Comparative Analysis*, Oxford: Oxford University Press.

Posner, R. A. (2009), *A Failure of Capitalism: The Crisis of '08 and the Descent Into Depression*, Cambridge: Harvard University Press.

Power, M. (1997), *The Audit Society: Rituals of Verification*, Oxford: Oxford University Press.

Prasad, M. (2012), *The Land of Too Much: American Abundance and the Paradox of Poverty*, Cambridge: Harvard University Press.

Pratt, J. (1997), *The Polytechnic Experiment, 1965–1992*, Buckingham: SRHE/Open University Press.

Priest, D. M. and St John, E. P. (eds.) (2006), *Privatization and Public Universities*, Bloomington: Indiana University Press.

Prosser, T. (2013), *The Regulatory Enterprise: Government, Regulation, and Legitimacy*, Oxford: Oxford University Press.

Pullan, B. (2004), *A History of the University of Manchester, 1973–1990*, Manchester: Manchester University Press.

Pusser, B. et al. (2012), *Universities and the Public Sphere: Knowledge Creation and State Building in the Era of Globalization*, Abingdon: Routledge.

Quality Assurance Agency (accessed 12 December 2012), *Quality Code for Higher Education*, Gloucester: QAA (http://www.qaa.ac.uk/assuringstandardsandquality/quality-code).

Quality Assurance Agency (28 January 2013), *Higher Education Review: A more risk-based approach to the quality assurance of higher education*, Circular letter 03/13, Bristol: QAA.

Quality Assurance Agency (accessed 26 June 2013), <http://www.qaa.ac.uk/assuringstandardsandquality/quality-code>.

Quality Assurance Agency (accessed 26 June 2013a), <http://www.qaa.ac.uk/InstitutionReports/Pages>.

Quality Assurance Agency (accessed 26 June 2013b), <http://www.qaa.ac.uk/InstitutionReports/Pages/University-of-Warwick.aspx>.

Quality Assurance Agency (accessed 26 June 2013c), <http://www.qaa.ac.uk/InstiutionReports/Pages/London-Metropolitan.aspx>.

Quality Assurance Agency (accessed 26 June 2013d), <http://www.qaa.ac.uk/InstitutionReports/Pages/UWE-Bristol.aspx>.

Radford, A. W. (2013), *Top Student, Top School? How Social Class Shapes Where Valedictorians Go To College*, Chicago: University of Chicago Press.

RAE1996 (accessed 15 April 2013), 'The Outcome', <http://www.rae.ac.uk/1996/c1_96.html>.

RAE2001 (accessed 15 April 2013), 'The Outcome', <http://www.rae.ac.uk/2001/Pubs4_01/section3.asp>.

RAE2008, (accessed 23 April 2013), 'Quality Profiles: Introduction', <http://www.rae.ac.uk/results/intro.aspx>.

RAE2008a (accessed 23 April 2013), 'Panels', <http://www.rae.ac.uk/panels/>.

RAE2008b (accessed 23 April 2013), 'Quality Profiles by Institution (HEI)', <http://www.rae.ac.uk/results/selectHEI.aspx>.

RAE2008 (accessed 18 June 2013), <http://www.rae.ac.uk/aboutus/subs.asp>.

RAE2008 (accessed 20 June 2013), <http://www.rae.ac.uk/submissions/selectHEI.aspx>.

Rait, R. S. (1918), *Life in the Medieval University*, Cambridge: Cambridge University Press.

Rashdall, H. (1895 and 1936), *The Universities of Europe in the Middle Ages*, Oxford: Oxford University Press.

Readings, B. (1996), *The University in Ruins*, Cambridge: Harvard University Press.

Regini, M. (2011), *European Universities and the Challenge of the Market: A Comparative Analysis*, Cheltenham: Edward Elgar.

Research Councils UK (accessed 18 April 2013), 'Excellent with Impact: Peer Review', <http://www.rcuk.ac.uk/research/Pages/PeerReview.aspx>.

Reynolds, G. H. (2012), *The Higher Education Bubble*, New York: Encounter Books.

Rhoads, R. A. and Torres, C. A. (2006), *The University, State, and Market: The Political Economy of Globalisation in the Americas*, Stanford: Stanford University Press.

Rhodes, R. (1997), *Understanding Governance: Policy Networks, Governance, Reflexivity, and Accountability*, Buckingham: Open University Press.

Rhodes, R. (ed.) (2000), *Transforming British Government, Volume 1: Changing Institutions*, London: Macmillan.

Rhodes, R. (ed.) (2000a), *Transforming British Government, Volume 2: Changing Roles and Relationships*, London: Macmillan.

Riesman, D. (1958), *Constraint and Variety in American Education*, New York: Doubleday.

Riesman, D. (1980), *On Higher Education: The Academic Enterprise in an Era of Rising Student Consumerism*, San Francisco: Jossey-Bass.

Riesman, D. (1998), *On Higher Education: The Academic Enterprise in an Era of Rising Student Consumerism*, New York: Doubleday.

Riley, N. M. (2011), *The Faculty Lounges—and Other Reasons Why You Won't Get the College Education You Paid For*, Chicago: Ivan R. Dee.

Robbins, the Robbins Report (1963), see *Committee on Higher Education.*

Robbins, Lord (1980), *Higher Education Revisited*, London: Macmillan.

Roberts, G., (May 2003), *Review of Research Assessment: Report by Sir Gareth Roberts to the UK Funding Bodies*, Bristol: Joint Funding Councils.

Robertson, D. (1998), 'Who Won the War of Dearing's Ear', *Higher Education Review*, 30 (2), 7–24.

Robertson, D. (1999) 'The Dearing Inquiry as process—delegated thinking and the limits of expert advice', *Higher Education Quarterly*, 53 (2), 116–140.

Robinson, E. (1968), *The New Polytechnics: The People's Universities*, London: Penguin.

Rolfe, G. (2013), *The University in Dissent: Scholarship in the Corporate University*, London: Routledge.

Rothblatt, S. (1968), *The Revolution of the Dons: Cambridge and Society in Victorian England*, London: Faber & Faber.

Ruch, R. S. (2001), *Higher Education Inc.: The Rise of the For-Profit University*, Baltimore: The Johns Hopkins University Press.

Rudolph, F. (1990), *The American College and University: A History*, Athens: University of Georgia Press.

Russell Group (12 October 2010), Response to the Browne Review of University Funding, <http://www.russellgroup.ac.uk>.

Russell Group (2012), 'Jewels in the Crown: The Importance and Characteristics of the UK's World-Class Universities', Russell Group Papers, Issue No. 4.

Russell Group (2 February 2013), The Concentration of Research Funding in the UK: Driving Excellence and Competing Globally, <http://www.russellgroup.ac.uk>.

Russell Group (2013), Offa Access Agreements for 2014/15, <http://www.russellgroup.ac.uk/russell-group-latest-news/154-2013/5426-offa-access-a>.

Ryan, A. (1998), *Liberal Anxieties and Liberal Education*, New York: Hill & Wang.

Ryan, A. (2012), *On Politics*, New York: Liveright.

Sakamoto, R. and Chapman, D. W. (eds.) (2011), *Cross-border Partnerships in Higher Education: Strategies and Issues*, Abingdon: Routledge.

Salmi, J. (2009), *The Challenge of Establishing World-Class Universities*, Washington DC: The World Bank.

Salter, B. and Tapper, T. (1994), *The State and Higher Education*, Ilford: Woburn Press.

Sandbrook, D. (2010), *State of Emergency—The Way We Were: Britain, 1970–1974*, London: Penguin.

Sandbrook, D. (2012), *Seasons in the Sun: The Battle for Britain, 1974–1979*, London: Penguin.

Sandel, M. (2012), *What Money Can't Buy: The Moral Limits of Markets*, London: Penguin.

Sanderson, M. (1972), *The Universities and British Industry, 1850–1970*, London: Routledge & Kegan Paul.

Sanderson, M. (1975), *The Universities in the Nineteenth Century*, London: Routledge & Kegan Paul.

Sanderson, M. (2002), *The History of the University of East Anglia, Norwich*, London: Hambledon and London.

Schaefer, W. D. (1990), *Education Without Compromise: From Chaos to Coherence in Higher Education*, San Francisco: Jossey-Bass.

Schrecker, E. (2010), *The Lost Soul of Higher Education: Corporatization, the Assault on Academic Freedom, and the End of the American University*, New York: The New Press.

Scott, P. (1984), *The Crisis of the University*, London: Croom Helm.

Scott, P. (2001), 'Conclusion: Triumph and Retreat', in Warner, D. and Palfreyman, D. (eds.), *The State of UK Higher Education: Managing Change and Diversity*, Buckingham: Open University Press/SRHE, 186–204.

Searle, G. R. (2004), *A New England?—Peace and War, 1886–1918*, Oxford: Oxford University Press.

Searle, J. (1969), *The Campus War*, London: Penguin.

Secretary of State for Education (31 October 1988), *Letter to Lord Chilver, Chairman of the Universities Funding Council*, London: Department for Education.

Selingo, J. J. (2013), *College (Un)Bound: The Future of Higher Education and What It Means for Students*, Las Vegas: Amazon Publishing.

Sharp, P. (1987), *The Creation of the Local Authority Sector of Higher Education*, Barcombe: Falmer Press.

Sharpe, T. (1976), *Porterhouse Blue*, London: Arrow Books.

Sharpe, T. (1996), *Grantchester Grind*, London: Pan Books.

Shattock, M. (1994), *The UGC and the Management of British Universities*, Buckingham: Open University Press/SRHE.

Shattock, M. (1998), 'Dearing on Governance: The Wrong Prescription', *Higher Education Quarterly*, 52 (1), 35–47.

Shattock, M. (2006), *Managing Good Governance in Higher Education*, Maidenhead: Open University Press.

Shattock, M. (2009), *Entrepreneurialism in Universities and the Knowledge Economy: Diversification and Organisational Change in European Higher Education*, Maidenhead: Open University Press/SRHE

Shattock, M. (2012), *Making Policy in British Higher Education, 1945–2011*, Maidenhead: McGraw Hill Education/Open University Press.

Shattock, M. (30 May 2013), 'The Best Board I Ever Sat On', *Times Higher Education*, 39–41.

Shattock, M. (ed.) (forthcoming), *International Trends in University Governance: Autonomy, Self-Government and the Distribution of Authority*, Abingdon: Routledge, Taylor and Francis.

Shattock, M. and Berdahl, R. (1984), 'The British University Grants Committee, 1919–83: Changing Relationship with Government and the Universities', *Higher Education*, 13 (5), 471–499.

Shattuck, K. (2013), *Assuring Quality in Online Education*, Sterling, Stylus Publishing.

Shin, J. C. et al. (2011), *University Rankings: Theoretical Basis, Methodology and Impacts on Global Higher Education*, Dordrecht: Springer.

Shinn, C. (1986), *Paying the Piper: the Development of the University Grants Committee, 1919–1946*, Lewes: Falmer Press.

Slaughter, S. and Cantwell, B. (2012), 'Transatlantic Moves to the Market: The United States and the European Union', *Higher Education*, 63 (5), 583–606.

Slaughter, S. and Leslie, L. L. (1997), *Academic Capitalism: Politics, Policies, and the Entrepreneurial University*, Baltimore: The Johns Hopkins University Press.

Slaughter, S. and Rhoades, G. (2004), *Academic Capitalism and the New Economy: Markets, States and Higher Education*, Baltimore: The Johns Hopkins University Press.

Smith, P. (1990), *Killing the Spirit: Higher Education in America*, New York: Viking Penguin.

Smith, T. (1987), 'The UGC's Research Rankings Exercise', *Higher Education Quarterly*, 41 (4), 303–316.

Soley, L. (1995), *Leaving the Ivory Tower: The Corporate Takeover of Academia*, Boston: South End Press.

Sommer, J. W. (ed.) (1995), *The Academy in Crisis: The Political Economy of Higher Education*, New Brunswick: Transaction Publishers.

Sowell, T. (2011), *Economic Facts and Fallacies*, New York: Basic Books.

Sparrow, J. (1967), *Mark Pattison and the Idea of a University*, Cambridge: Cambridge University Press.

Spellings Report (2006), *A Test of Leadership: Charting the Future of US Higher Education: Report of the Spellings Commission*, Washington: US Department of Education.

Stanfield, J. (2009), *The Broken University*, London: Adam Smith Institute.

Stankiewicz, R. (1986), *Academics and Entrepreneurs*, London: Pinter.

Steger, M. B. and Roy, K. K. (2010), *Neoliberalism: A Very Short Introduction*, Oxford: Oxford University Press.

Stensaker, B. and Harvey, L. (eds.) (2011), *Accountability in Higher Education: Global Perspectives on Trust and Power*, Abingdon: Routledge.

Stevens, R. (2003), *From University to Uni: The Politics of Higher Education in England since 1944*, London: Politico's Publishing.

Stiglitz, J. E. (2013), *The Price of Inequality*, London: Penguin.

Strathern, M. (2000), *Audit Cultures: Anthropological Studies in Accountability, Ethics and the Academy*, Abingdon: Routledge.

Sullivan, T. A. et al. (2012), *Improving Measurement of Productivity in Higher Education*, Washington: The National Academies Press.

Sykes, C. J. (1988), *ProfScam: Professors and the Demise of Higher Education*, New York: St Martin's Griffin.

Tamanaha, B. Z. (2012), *Failing Law Schools*, Chicago: University of Chicago Press.

Tapper, T. (2007), *The Governance of British Higher Education: The Struggle for Policy Control*, Dordrecht: Springer.

Tapper, T. and Palfreyman, D. (eds.) (2005) *Understanding Mass Higher Education: Comparative Perspectives on Access*, Abingdon: Routledge.

Tapper, T. and Palfreyman, D. (2010), *The Collegial Tradition in the Age of Mass Higher Education*, Dordrecht: Springer.

Tapper, T. and Palfreyman, D. (2011), *Oxford, the Collegiate University: Conflict, Consensus and Continuity*, Dordrecht: Springer.

Tapper, T. and Salter, B. (1998), 'The Dearing Report and the Maintenance of Academic Standards: Towards a New Academic Corporatism', *Higher Education Quarterly*, 52 (1), 22–34.

Taylor, M. C. (2010), *Crisis on Campus: A Bold Plan for Reforming Our Colleges and Universities*, New York: Alfred A. Kopf.

Teixeira, P. (2011), 'Eppure si Muove—Marketisation and Privatisation Trends in the EHEA', *Journal of the European Higher Education Area*, 4, 57–72.

Teixeira, P. et al. (2004), *Markets in Higher Education: Rhetoric or Reality?* Dordrecht: Kluwer.

Teixeira, P. and Dill, D. D. (2011), *Public Vices, Public Virtues? Assessing the Effects of Marketization in Higher Education*, Rotterdam: Sense Publishers.

Temple, P. (ed.) (2012), *Universities in the Knowledge Economy: Higher Education Organisation and Global Change*, Abingdon: Routledge.

Thatcher, M. (1993), *The Downing Street Years*, London: HarperCollins.

Thelin, J. R. (2011), *A History of American Higher Education*, Baltimore: The Johns Hopkins University Press.

Thompson, E. P. (1971), *Warwick University Limited: Industry, Management and Universities*, Harmondsworth: Penguin.

Tierney, W. G. and Hentschke, G. C. (2007), *New Players, Different Game: Understanding the Rise of For-Profit Colleges and Universities*, Baltimore: The Johns Hopkins University Press.

Tight, M. (2009), *Higher Education in the UK since 1945*, Buckingham: Open University Press.

Times Higher Education (17 March 2011), 'Losses of Concentration: Post-92s Hit Hardest by Quality Related Shake-Up', *Times Higher Education*, 6–7.

Timmins, N. (2001), *The Five Giants: A Biography of the Welfare State*, London: HarperCollins.

Treasury (2003), *Lambert Review of University-Business Collaboration: Final Report*, London: HM Treasury.

Trow, M. (1973), *Problems in the Transition from Elite to Mass Higher Education*, (Carnegie Commission on Higher Education), Paris: OECD.

Trow, M. (1998), 'The Dearing Report: A Transatlantic View', *Higher Education Quarterly*, 52 (1), 93–117.

Trowler, P. et al. (2012), *Tribes and Territories in the 21st Century: Rethinking the significance of disciplines in higher education*, Abingdon: Routledge.

Truscot, B. (1943), *Redbrick University*, London: Faber.

Truscot, B. (1945), *Redbrick and These Vital Days*, London: Faber.

Tuchman, G. (2009), *Wannabe U: Inside the Corporate University*, Chicago: University of Chicago Press.

Tucker, M. S. (2011), *Surpassing Shanghai: An Agenda for American Education Built on the World's Leading Systems*, Cambridge: Harvard Educational Publishing Group.

Turnbull, G. (1742), *Observations upon Liberal Education*, Liberty Fund, Indianapolis, 2003.

Tysome, T. (6 March 1998), 'Old Boys' Club Needs Reform', *Times Higher Education*, 5.

Tysome, T. (22 September 2006), 'SCOP Revamp Sharpens Focus', *Times Higher Education*, 6.

Universities Funding Council (accessed 15 April 2013), Research Assessment Exercise 1992: The Outcome, <http://www.rae.ac.uk/1992/c26_92html>.

Universities UK (March 2010), *The Growth of Private and For-Profit Higher Education Providers in the United Kingdom*, London: Universities UK.

Universities UK (2011), *Patterns and Trends in UK Higher Education*, 2011, London: Universities UK.

Universities UK (accessed 22 January 2013), <http://www.universitiesuk.ac.uk/AboutUs/WhoWeAre/Pages/Our-History.aspx>.

Universities UK (accessed 22 January 2013a), <http://www.universitiesuk.ac.uk/AboutUs/OrganisationalStructure/Pages/default.aspx>.

University Alliance (accessed 24 January 2013), <http://www.unialliance.ac.uk/about/>.

University Alliance (12 July 2011), Funding Research Excellence: Research Group Size, Critical Mass and Performance, <http://www.unialliance.ac.uk/site/2011/07/12/funding-research-excellence-research-gr>.

University Grants Committee (1962), *University Development, 1957–1964*, House of Commons: Cmnd 2267.

University Grants Committees (1979), *Report on Russian and Russian Studies in British Universities*, London: HMSO.

Vanston, P. J. (2010), *Crump*, Leicester: Matador.

Veblen, T. (1918), *The Higher Learning in America: A Memorandum on the Conduct of Universities by Business Men*, New York: B. W. Huebsch.

Vedder, R. (2004), *Going Broke by Degree: Why College Costs Too Much*, Washington: The AEI Press.

Vernon, K. (2004), *Universities and the State in England, 1850–1939*, London: RoutledgeFalmer.

Vught, F. A. von and Ziegele, F. (2012), *Multidimensional Ranking: The Design and Development of U-Multirank*, Dordrecht: Springer.

Wagner, L. (1998), 'Dearing is Dead—Blunkett is Born? The Future Funding of Higher Education', *Higher Education Quarterly*, 52 (1), 64–76.

Wagner, L. (2004), *Foundation Degree: Task Force Report to Ministers*, Nottingham: Department for Education and Skills Publications.

Walsh, T. (2011), *Unlocking the Gates: How and Why Leading Universities are Opening Up Access to Their Courses*, Princeton: Princeton University Press.

Ward, S. C. (2012), *Neoliberalism and the Global Restructuring of Knowledge and Education*, New York: Routledge.

Ward-Perkins, B. (2005), *The Fall of Rome and the End of Civilisation*, Oxford: Oxford University Press.

Warner, D. and Palfreyman, D. (eds.) (2001), *The State of UK Higher Education: Managing Change and Diversity*, Buckingham: Open University Press.

Warner, D. and Palfreyman, D. (eds.) (2003), *Managing Crisis*, Maidenhead: Open University Press.

Washburn, J. (2005), *University Inc: The Corporate Corruption of Higher Education*, New York: Basic Books.

Watson, D. (1998), 'The Limits to Diversity', in Jarry, D. and Parker, M. (eds.), *The New Higher Education: Issues and Directions for the Post-Dearing University*, Stoke-on-Trent: Staffordshire University Press, 65–81.

Watson, D. (2007), *Managing Civic and Community Engagement*, Maidenhead: Open University Press.

Watson, D. (2009), *The Question of Morale: Managing Happiness and Unhappiness in University Life*, Maidenhead: Open University Press.

Watson, D. (2013), *The Question of Conscience: Higher Education and Personal Responsibility*, London: Institute of Education Press.

Watson, D. and Bowden, R. (2007), 'The Fate of the Dearing Recommendations: Policy and Performance in UK HE, 1997–2007', in Watson, D. and Amoah, M. (eds.) *The Dearing Report Ten Years On*, Bedford Way Papers, Institute of Education, University of London, 6–50.

Watson, D. et al. (eds.) (2011), *The Engaged University: International Perspectives on Civic Engagement*, Abingdon: Routledge.

Whitchurch, C. (2013), *Reconstructing Identities in Higher Education: The Rise of Third Space Professionals*, Abingdon: Routledge/SRHE.

Wildavsky, B. et al. (2011), *Reinventing Higher Education: The Promise of Innovation*, Cambridge: Harvard Education Press.

Willetts, D. (2010), *The Pinch: How the Baby Boomers Took Their Children's Future— and How They Can Give It Back*, London: Atlantic Books.

Willetts, D. (2013), *Robbins Revisited: Bigger and Better Higher Education*, London: Social Market Foundation.

Williams, J. (2013), *Consuming Higher Education: Why Learning Can't be Bought*, London: Bloomsbury.

Wolf, A. (2002), *Does Education Matter? Myths About Education and Economic Growth*, London: Penguin.

Wolf, A. (21 January 2005), 'Many agonise over the development of organised "sub-groups" of universities—Russell, Mainstream, 1994 and so on. I think they signal salvation', *Times Higher Education*, 13.

Wolf, A. and McNally, S. (2011), *Education and Economic Performance*, Cheltenham: Edward Elgar.

Wolf, C. (1993), *Markets or Governments: Choosing Between Imperfect Alternatives*, Cambridge: MIT Press.

Young, H. (1991), *One of Us: A Biography of Margaret Thatcher*, London: Macmillan.

Zemsky, R. (2009), *Making Reform Work: The Case for Transforming American Higher Education*, New Brunswick: Rutgers University Press.

Zemsky, R. (2013), *Checklist for Change: Making American Higher Education a Sustainable Enterprise*, New Brunswick: Rutgers University Press.

Zemsky, R. et al. (2005), *Remaking the American University: Market-smart and Mission-centered*, New Brunswick: Rutgers University Press.

Zumeta, W. et al. (2012), *Financing American Higher Education in the Era of Globalization*, Cambridge: Harvard University Press.

Index